Authors of Their Lives

still not read 4-2 — 223

Aug 16 10
got to about / 187 — 200

aug 14 — 10 — A
have more reading all
now, and am
putting this book aside

Authors of Their Lives

The Personal Correspondence of British Immigrants to North America in the Nineteenth Century

David A. Gerber

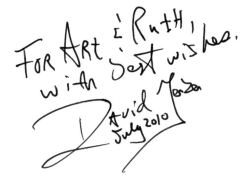

For Art i Ruth,
with best wishes.
David Morton
July 2010

NEW YORK UNIVERSITY PRESS

New York and London

NEW YORK UNIVERSITY PRESS
New York and London
www.nyupress.org

First published in paperback in 2008

Library of Congress Cataloging-in-Publication Data
Gerber, David A., 1944–
Authors of their lives : the personal correspondence of British
immigrants to North America in the nineteenth century /
David A. Gerber.
p.   cm.
Includes bibliographical references and index.
ISBN-13: 978-0-8147-3200-7 (pbk. : alk. paper)
ISBN-10: 0-8147-3200-3 (pbk. : alk. paper)
ISBN-13: 978-0-8147-3171-0 (cloth : alk. paper)
ISBN-10: 0-8147-3171-6 (cloth : alk. paper)
   1. British Americans—Correspondence. 2. British—Canada—
Correspondence. 3. Immigrants—United States—Correspondence.
4. Immigrants—Canada—Correspondence. 5. Letter writing—
History—19th century. 6. Trans-nationalism—History—19th
century—Sources. 7. United States—Emigration and immigration—
History—19th century—Sources. 8. Canada—Emigration and
immigration—History—19th century—Sources. 9. Great Britain—
Emigration and immigration—History—19th century—Sources.
   10. Immigrants' writings, American.   I. Title.
E184.B7G47 2005
973.5'092'241—dc22   2005015602

New York University Press books are printed on acid-free paper,
and their binding materials are chosen for strength and durability.

Manufactured in the United States of America

c 10 9 8 7 6 5 4 3 2 1
p 10 9 8 7 6 5 4 3 2 1

In Memory of My Grandparents,
Miasha and Sam Gerber and
Matty and Bill Hellman

Contents

All illustrations appear as a group following p. 166.

Acknowledgments

Many individuals and institutions, too numerous to mention, facilitated this study. Special mention needs to be made of the generosity of the Baldy Center for Law and Social Policy at the University at Buffalo (SUNY), which has provided me with funds to sustain my research and a forum for the presentation of my ideas before extraordinarily intelligent and helpful colleagues, and of the help of Jane Morris, who skillfully and patiently edited the manuscript. I also acknowledge the assistance of the Publication Subvention Fund of the College of Arts and Sciences at the University of Buffalo (SUNY).

I would also like to thank Professor Charlotte Erickson, a much valued friend from whom I have learned more than I ever can explain about immigrants and their letters and, through our own correspondence, about letter-writing itself. The original inspiration for this study came with my first reading of Erickson's fine collection and analysis of British immigrant letters, *Invisible Immigrants: The Adaptation of English and Scottish Immigrants in Nineteenth-Century America.* Erickson succeeded in making these immigrants anything but invisible. She revealed the worlds within worlds that could be found in their letters, and suggested the world-making functions of correspondence.

Finally, I note the assistance of the Deputy Keeper of the Records, Public Record Office of Northern Ireland in granting permission to use letters in the collections of that repository.

Portions of this book were previously published as:

"The Immigrant Letter between Positivism and Populism: The Uses of Immigrant Personal Correspondence in Twentieth-Century American Scholarship," *Journal of American Ethnic History* 16 (Summer 1997): 3–34.

"Ethnic Identification and the Project of Individual Identity: The Life of Mary Ann Wodrow Archbald (1768–1840) of Little Cumbrae Island,

Scotland and Auriesville, New York," *Immigrants and Minorities* 17 (July 1998): 1–22. Courtesy of Taylor and Francis, http://tandf.co.uk/journals.

"Epistolary Ethics: Personal Correspondence and the Culture of Emigration in the Nineteenth Century," *Journal of American Ethnic History* 19 (Summer 2000): 3–23.

"Theories and Lives: Transnationalism and the Conceptualization of International Migrations to the United States," *IMIS-Beiträge* 15 (2000): 31–53. Institute for Migration Research and Intercultural Studies, University of Osnabrück, Germany.

Introduction
Letters and Immigrants

The Abiding Significance of Personal Letters

Immigrants before the era of instant electronic communication were compelled to write letters to family and friends in their homelands.[1] The great age of European mass international migrations in the nineteenth and early twentieth centuries was also an era of rapidly proliferating formal primary education and rising popular literacy. Across the lines of social class and region, growing numbers of European immigrants, like those leaving Britain for Canada and the United States who form the basis for this work, possessed some literacy skills. Some wrote with considerable technical facility, but most had to strain against significant limitations in their use of written language. Among the many challenges to individual improvement posed by immigration, distance and separation proved a powerful stimulus to the improvement of self-expression. Complementing that challenge was the mastery of the rules of postal systems—the first impersonal, modern bureaucracy that most nineteenth-century immigrants would encounter in their lifetimes.

Even today, when immigrants have available to them a number of forms of convenient, instantaneous electronic communication—video phones, international long distance telephone service, fax, and e-mail—many prefer to write personal letters in the old-fashioned way when communicating to family and friends.[2] One reason, of course, is that the mails continue to be inexpensive. One does not have to own a computer or a fax machine, or buy time on-line at an Internet café to write a letter and to post it for a nominal cost. The technology of the personal letter remains inexpensive and easily accessible, even more so now than in the past, when pen nibs, paper, and ink were sometimes scarce, and were luxuries for people with limited means.

But it is not solely the low costs, reliability, and convenience of the mails that explain the abiding popularity of personal letters among immigrants. The letter asserts its claims on its own emotional terms. The material object of the personal letter is an intimate artifact of the letter-writer. The handwriting of absent loved ones that the recipients of letters in the nineteenth century, like those recipients more recently, have claimed to be thrilled to see on newly received envelopes, inscribes the writer's unique self; and one can return to the material object of the letter again and again to evoke that presence. The personal letter is simultaneously a poor substitute for and an important embodiment of those from whom we are separated. Its existence marks an absence, but it assists the correspondents in bonding relationships rendered vulnerable by separation. It is the closest approximation that both parties involved in a correspondence may come to that which they most desire, but cannot obtain—an intimate conversation. It is significant that those immigrants, such as the Englishmen John Langton, a settler in the Canadian bush in 1833, and Richard Flower, a settler on the Illinois prairie in 1819, who kept diaries of their ocean passage and resettlement in North America, eventually put their diaries into letter form when conveying them to their families.[3] The diaries could certainly be shared, but they lacked the ability to speak to the intimate bonds both men had with those with whom they wished to correspond.

The importance of the easily passed-over, conventionalized apparatus of personal address—those endearments, salutations, inquiries about health and happiness, and assurances that the writer is safe and secure —that so distinguish the personal letter cannot be understood if it is simply written off as habit or a way of filling the page. Rather, these touches are what make personal letters unique, and fulfill the emotional expectations of the correspondents. A diary may be a dialogue with oneself; a personal letter is an intimate, if long-distance, conversation with another.[4]

Why Did They Correspond?

Why should immigrant correspondents care so profoundly if they have produced, or they have received, direct and tangible evidence that they continue to share an intimacy with those whom they love, but from whom they are separated? Why is the sight of handwriting somehow reassuring? Why is the word-of-mouth of a mutual acquaintance who is in a position to deliver oral messages to or from those far away, any less laden with meaning? A personal letter from one about whom we are concerned may alleviate our anxieties by assuring us in that person's own words that someone far away we care about, with whom we have been out of contact, is indeed alive, safe and well.

There is yet another reason, one that is especially relevant to understanding the less immediately accessible psychological depths of the consciousness of immigrants. What we know most about immigrants from a variety of literatures, in a number of academic disciplines, is that they embark on a project of remaking their lives, traversing vast physical and cultural spaces in the service of improving their opportunities for material security (and perhaps even prosperity) and hence for greater personal independence and, on whatever terms they defined it, social respectability. These largely material goals typically are the immigrant's first project, for they are the source of what motivates the life-transforming decision to uproot oneself. Just as is the case today, in the nineteenth century many of these projects were a success by the material criteria of those who have undertaken migration.

What we know less about is what has been jeopardized or lost in pursuit of the fulfillment of this project. Immigrants have always risked a radical rupture of the self, a break in their understandings of who they are. We strive for continuity in our lives; personal identity depends on continuity. We need to know that we are the same person now that we were before, even as we continue to develop through experience and reflection throughout the course of our lives. It is impossible to imagine that we can be ourselves without such knowledge, and without being able constantly to be creating, through memory and retrospection, the personal narrative—an identity narrative—of relations to places and people upon which such knowledge depends.[5]

An important source of personal identity is our relationships to those with whom we share the oldest of such relationships. The significant individuals in such relationships hold in common with us both memories of a long shared past and an experience of a place that we have thought of as a *homeplace,* both a physical location and a center of security, intimacy, and community. They share, too, continuous participation in various discourses of daily life that endow these relationships with significant and sustaining emotions. Memories may not always be pleasant ones, nor conversations always amicable, nor home always associated with security, let alone affection, for these memories to have a powerful hold on our consciousness of who we are. At some level of our being, they are indeed who we are. When such relationships are rendered vulnerable by separation, what is threatened is not only a bond between two people, but also the personal continuity that is the ultimate measure of who we are. But relationships are not merely *maintained* in personal letters; they continue to grow, with the conventions, restraints, and opportunities presented by the letter forming a new context for their ongoing development. As Bruce Redford has observed in a study of relationships developed in correspondence, personal letters do not simply mirror worlds, they are world-making.[6]

To be sure, new bonds are formed and old ones reestablished in the places where immigrants resettle. Through the study of family, social networks, neighborhood, and ethnic groups, historians of international migration have intensively analyzed these dynamic new or newly reconstituted bonds, the formation of which for immigrants has been an important goal, at times parallel to and at other times intersecting with the search for opportunity.[7] At best, these efforts were likely at some level and for some period of time to be frustrated; at worst, they might fail completely. Not all immigrants succeeded in bringing their closest family members, let alone more distant relations and friends, to resettle alongside them; and for others, that second project, however large or small a net was cast, took years of patient and painful planning and saving, in the process of which they led a more or less difficult life of toil and privation. Many left behind and would never see again, parents too elderly to travel or unwilling to do so, and brothers and sisters who were already well-established in their own lives and who took care of those parents in their old age.

We need not romanticize these relationships among separated individuals to appreciate their significance. After all, some left family because they could not be sustained within the material framework of the domestic economy. In effect, they lived with the knowledge that through no fault of their own, or anyone else's for that matter, they were superfluous. Moreover, a little-acknowledged dimension of immigration decisions, which the evidence of personal letters will reveal to us, was tensions and strains within the interpersonal relations of families that made continuing to live together a source of difficulty and pain, and made immigration far away an attractive proposition. If, however, immigrants had experienced ambivalent relationships and had complex psychologies that developed out of complicated lives, there is no reason for us to think that those relationships were any less significant in determining their personal identities. The difficulties prompted by separation were no less painful for such ambivalence, and, in fact, regret over the past might make separation more painful.

The well-studied public face of the second project—ethnic identification, residence in ethnic neighborhoods, and participation in ethnic social networks and formal associations helped considerably to appease this hunger for continuity. Ethnicity provides a fictive kinship, an alternative genealogy to one's actual family and community history of intimate relations. In the ethnic group, immigrants might find new friends and neighbors and a spouse, and begin the reconstruction of personal bonds. At the least, immigrants found people who were experiencing the same history of gain and loss, who shared the same general memories of places and leave-takings, and who interpreted many of the larger meanings of phenomena and life experiences in the same way. But if we are to understand the significance of immigrant personal correspondence, it is necessary to understand the limitations of the concept of ethnicity for understanding individual selves. The concept *ethnicity* is often asked to bear too many explanatory burdens, and thus crowds out other ways of understanding the consciousness and behavior of individuals labeled "ethnic."[8]

Even surrounded by the ethnic worlds of their creation, immigrants could never completely reproduce the familiar world of the significant primary relationships that formed the core of the personal identities they took out of their homelands. To sustain those relationships, rich in powerful memories and emotions that fed the immigrant's existential hunger for continuity, nineteenth-century immigrants depended on the intimacy of personal correspondence.[9] About the world of the immigrant's long-distance personal relationships we know much less than of the public world of ethnic group life.

The Immigrant Letter: Interpretive Challenges and Opportunities

Immigrant letters are probably the largest single body of the writings of ordinary people to which historians have access. Not all immigrants participated in this international exchange of personal letters. Underrepresented or completely absent from the ranks of archived letters written by British immigrants to North America this study analyzes are illiterates (unless someone literate wrote in their behalf); those who sought completely to sever connections with family and friends; those with completed families; young children living with their parents; and women, who even when literate were, as immigrants when accompanied by males, often spoken for in correspondence by husbands, fathers, or brothers. Of the seventy-one collections of letters consulted for this study, only nine (12 percent) are composed of letters exclusively written by women; another five (7 percent) are collections in which a number of letters were signed at times by women (and hence, it is assumed, written by them) and a number signed at other times by men. We find the same imbalanced representation of significant categories of people on the homeland side of correspondence. Then, too, there are those un-countable others—letter-writers whose letters simply were never saved, collected, and preserved—who constitute one of the ultimate frustrations in accounting for the representativeness of any sample of immigrant letters.

The problem of who is and is not represented in immigrant letters is not the end of the fundamental analytical difficulties that the immigrant letters pose. The individual immigrant personal letter—in contrast to, for example, a business letter—is characterized by significant diversity of subject matter. Because there was so much in their lives that was new and, they believed, unimaginable to others at home, alongside many unanticipated sources of continuity, immigrants often seem to have been compelled to discuss a wide range of phenomena, events, and experiences in the same text. Also, they struggled to find interesting subject matter because they wished to write letters their correspondents would value, and they often roamed through their experiences in the hope of striking the right note. Sometimes, bored or distracted, they were simply anxious to fill the page, and a scroll-like recitation of themes, from politics and religion to health and commodity prices, presented itself as one way to do so. It is difficult to know how to conceptualize documents with such diversity of content. Core ideas are rarely presented. Linkages among themes are hard to find.

Themes and patterns often emerge only with the opportunity to read a relatively large number of letters between the same correspondents. But the continuities and commonalities always seem to remain tentative, and reliance on them often risks imposing order on materials that defy it. Thus, with its diversity and lack of a core purpose beyond the mostly unspoken recognition of the necessity of communicating for the sake of maintaining a bond, the typical immigrant letter defies the effort of some analysts to understand it with reference to grand emplotment schemes based on classical narrative devices, such as tragedy, comedy, and the epic.[10] Elizabeth J. MacArthur's understanding of imagined personal letters in epistolary fiction is just as relevant for conceiving the personal correspondence of historical subjects: what needs to be plotted is the relationship the correspondents seek to maintain through corresponding, not their often relatively formless letters, which maintain their position in an eternal present.[11]

These are the problems that ultimately arise from making sense of the explicit content of letters, but imposing problems also emerge from what one does not find in letters. Gaps, breaks, and absences pose difficulties for researchers everywhere they turn.

There are four principal sources of the vacuum in which letters must somehow be decoded. First, in many instances it is difficult to learn anything beyond the most basic biographical information about either letter-writers or those to whom they wrote, so contextualizing either party in ways, whether social, economic, or even interpersonal, that assist in interpreting their correspondence, is difficult. Rarely, moreover, do we have access to the letters that were sent to immigrant letter-writers, so we are tuned in on a one-way conversation. It is not only for the sake of convenience that this cycle of correspondence has widely come to be known among historians as "the immigrant letter," for the letters of the immigrants themselves represent the large majority of archived letters. We may at times hear the echoes of the voice of the absent correspondent speaking through the writer, for example, offering instructions on what to write and what not to write, or criticizing the content, form, or style of previous letters, to which the writer explicitly responds. But such double-voicing is relatively rare, perhaps especially to the extent that it requires a technical facility with language that eluded many writers.

The embedding of the absent correspondent's voice in the letters of the other writer points to a larger circumstance in immigrant correspondence that the concept *immigrant letter* cannot adequately capture. All immigrant letters, like personal letters in general, are a mutual creation of two correspondents. In truth, immigrant letters are a transnational phenomenon, a unique cultural location in which correspondents may form a relationship that uses state postal systems to transcend national boundaries. The relationship they maintain is neither here nor there, but in both the homeland and the land of resettlement simultaneously. Still, again and again, readers have to seek out the voice of the absent other, decoding what remains on the surface a one-way conversation, and this necessitates a good deal of guesswork on the reader's part.

The problem of the one-way conversation deepens another, inescapable issue, which is a second significant concern in interpreting letters: the problem of what letter-writers choose *not* to write. We expect that writers will have opinions, and explicitly slant their testimonies to make a point. But what is not said, to the extent that it is not even obviously implied, is more elusive. We cannot know what it is, or whether it is not there as a consequence of intention, or neglect, or a judgment about its irrelevance to or the harm it might do the reader or the writer. Complete candor, for example, about the difficulties of emigration and resettlement, such as the rigors or terrors of the ocean voyage, or the difficulties of finding work might be deemed undesirable by the immigrant writer, if it were likely to evoke anxiety and worry in the recipient, or if it presented evidence of insurmountable difficulties that discouraged others from emigrating and joining an immigrant. Judging what is not addressed would be easier if more could be known of the recipients and about the quality of the relationships that the writer and the reader shared.

A third difficulty in interpreting immigrant letters is that we cannot really account for why some individuals' letters survive, but doubtless a larger number, written by untold others, have not. The key to the problem of the letter as an artifact of a process of retention and collection ultimately may lie in solving the elusive problem of why some people value the past and the people who inhabit it, when so many people in modern Western societies seem not to do so. It involves explaining the consciousness of latter generations of the original letter-writer's or recipient's homeland relatives, about whom we usually know even less than we do about the letter-writers themselves. When confronted with the necessity of cleaning house, these descendants elected not to throw away boxes of old paper in the unrecognizable handwriting of long departed (in both senses of the word) kinfolk.

This study has depended on letters archived within collections in libraries and other repositories, or in published anthologies of archived letters that have been edited by historians, rather than on letters to be found in private hands, so there is yet another step in the process of retention that is especially relevant here: eventually, one of these survivors chose to place this now private, family collection in a public repository, where its preservation and care would be assured, and where researchers could one day have access to it.

Yet before grateful latter-day researchers become too enamored of these farsighted generations who saved these precious documents for posterity, it is necessary to ask whether prior to donation they destroyed letters deemed embarrassing to family and inappropriate for the eyes of strangers. The letter-writers themselves, moreover, sometimes destroyed letters in anger or fear of scandal, though this is rarely addressed in their correspondence, so later generations might well have been innocent of previous, deliberate destruction of letters.

Unfortunately, no researcher has yet undertaken an extended exploration of the contingencies that help to explain the immigrant letter as artifact, though these contingencies significantly serve to limit the interpretive claims based on immigrant letters. Nor has any study sought to explain either the valorizing and preservation or the dismissal and destruction of immigrant letters.[12] But there is a relevant implication of these issues which we need to acknowledge: whether we approach the matter on the level of the individual collection or of the entire universe of immigrant personal correspondence, as fundamental a question for systematic analysis as the representativeness of the archived collections open to researchers must remain virtually unresolvable. Meanwhile, the consciousness dawns that what might separate immigrant letter-writers represented in archived collections from other immigrants who are not represented may have nothing to do with such longtime analytical preoccupations of historians as the problem of the growth and incidence of literacy. Instead, it might be an artifact of a highly personal and individualized process of retention, collection, and preservation.

A fourth difficulty are the problems posed in testing most letters for accuracy and authorial authenticity. Some letters that appear to be personal documents were consciously composed as propaganda, usually for or against emigration. They were intended for publication in newspapers or pamphlets. Or they might be circulated informally, in their original form or through conversation—a sort of vernacular publication for the less educated ordinary folk in the manner of the letter-writing Enlightenment intellectual's Republic of Letters. In all these forms, such letters all too often served to misinform, for emigration was a passionately debated political issue throughout Europe and North America, and letters might be useful evidence in making one's point, pro or con, in the public arena.[13]

It is not difficult most of the time to detect mischievous editing for political or ideological purposes, but it does require the experience that comes with reading significant numbers of immigrant letters. Nineteenth-century letter compilations, such as the *Emigrant's Guide in Ten Letters Addressed to the Taxpayers of England* (1829), edited by the English radical democrat William Cobbett, fairly give the game away.[14] Contemporaries knew that Cobbett himself, in his habitual outspoken manner, favored immigration to the United States. But in this publication he was supposed to be separating facts from his opinions. The tone and content, however, hardly convince readers that Cobbett tried to do so. His reprinted letters by British immigrants to friends and family rarely strike a negative note. All goes so well for these people in the United States that their testimony is ultimately not credible. In reality, most immigrants in their letters were skilled at making close and careful distinctions about both the gains and losses in which their decision to leave their homelands eventuated. Even when their appraisal of their decision was explicitly positive, few failed to acknowledge that emigration was not without its costs. Accuracy aside, they wished that those who might follow them and might end up having a negative experience would not blame the writer for misleading them. A flat, impersonal tone and the single-minded development of only one theme—emigration, good or bad—is also suggestive of tendentiousness and heavy editing, if not outright fabrication. In contemporary publications, such as *The Emigrant to North America from Memoranda of a Settler in Canada* (1843), the point of which for the anonymous author ("an immigrant farmer" and loyal British subject) is to argue for the superiority of Canada as a destination over the United States, the excerpted, undated letters all sound the same, are devoid of discussions of family except when they demonstrate why Canada is a suitable place to settle, and contain both grammatically formed direct quotes and narrations of complex events, the sort of technical writing that eluded many immigrant stylists.[15] Even those capable of such writing were too preoccupied with ordinary subject matter out of the daily life to write narrative, and they were most often too pressed for time to write well-crafted propaganda. The impression is not simply that the author had an axe to grind, which he freely and explicitly admitted, but rather that he radically trimmed his evidence—or worse, made it up—in order to make his point.

Characteristics of the Letters Consulted

This study uses no letters that were published in the nineteenth century in popular print media or in published compilations, in which the editor was a third party not originally involved in the correspondence. The problem of authentication would not only be imposing and time-consuming, but also be a diversion from the effort to understand how personal relationships are maintained through personal correspondence. With few exceptions, the letter-series that are the basis of this study are found in archival collections in public repositories in Australia, Canada, the Republic of Ireland, the United Kingdom and Northern Ireland, and the United States, or in two published collections of twenty-five and three letter-series respectively, Charlotte Erickson's *Invisible Immigrants* (1972) and Ronald Wells's *Ulster Migration to America* (1991), which have set high standards for excellence in the tasks of editing and contextualizing immigrant letters.[16]

In addition to the efforts to remove bogus letters from the research for this study and to come as close as possible to exclusive dependence on original materials, the study is guided by a number of understandings and self-imposed standards:

This is a study of the letters of English, Scottish, and Irish Protestant immigrants to both Canada and the United States. Of the seventy-one letter-series consulted, forty-three (58 percent) have been produced by English immigrants, twenty-three (31 percent) by Irish Protestants, and eight (11 percent) by Scots. Sixty-one (86 percent) of these collections represent letter-writers who immigrated to the United States and ten (14 percent) to Canada. Interesting in their own right among European immigrant groups in numerous ways, a particular virtue of these peoples for this study is that they wrote in English, the only language which the author is able to read in the depth required for analysis of texts that require close and careful attention.

Because this is a study of the maintenance of personal relationships that letters facilitate and the ways immigrants used letters to achieve that goal, the letters here are restricted to those that passed among family and friends. In consequence, the connection between writer and recipient is relatively easily authenticated and investigated through the letters themselves and occasionally, when they prove useful to finding relatively obscure individuals, through other types of sources, such as genealogical records, censuses, and published local histories.

The collections depended upon most heavily for the principal analytical directions of the study are characterized by a series of letters written over the course of at least two years. This extended duration facilitates knowledge of those involved in the exchange and creates a basis for confidence in the integrity of the collections used. Collections with letters written over a briefer duration, and those in which there are only a small number of letters no matter how many years' duration are represented, are used here and there for documentation, but they will not be relied upon to establish major directions in interpretation.

In the case of one of the letter-series published by Erickson that has figured prominently in this book, the letters of the English Kansas farm wife Catherine (Kate) Grayston Bond, and a smaller number of letters from her brother James Grayston, the archived originals were consulted as well as Erickson's edited versions. (This was also done with several other letter-series found in Erickson's collection, but these are for the most part—with the exception of the letters of the skilled craftsman David Laing—letters of lesser importance to the direction of the interpretation.) In addition to ensuring accuracy, this proved an exercise in analyzing editorial decisions, for as interested as we both have been in quite different ways of understanding letters and in greatly different questions about them, Erickson deleted some content that I would not have, had I edited the collection for publication.[17] Whenever possible, I sought to find original letters rather than depend upon transcriptions in the case of letter-series of particular importance. I hoped that in doing so, even if the transcriptions were easier to read and hence became "working drafts," I could check on the accuracy of transcription. However, this was seldom possible, as the originals had either been lost or retained in private hands.

British Immigrants in Nineteenth-Century North America

Readers searching for a conventional history of British immigrants to North America might be disappointed with this study. The usual demographic, social, political, and economic themes by which immigrants are studied at the group level, and their emigration, resettlement, occupations, property holding, and ethnicization are analyzed, are not the subjects of this book, which is exclusively concerned with personal correspondence between individuals. Based on seventy-one collections of immigrant letters, the study can make no claim to representing an immigrant population in America that probably (exclusive of Catholic Ireland) totaled over two million individuals in the nineteenth century.

The individuals studied here were chosen not on the basis of national, geographic, or socioeconomic representativeness, by the usual criteria such as occupation, wealth, and region of origin, within either the British population or the immigrant population of Scots, English, and Irish Protestants. Instead they were chosen because of the availability of the letters they authored and the conformity of those letter-series in most cases to the criteria adopted for what sort of texts were useful to sustain the analysis offered in this study. Moreover, individuals are the unit of study, not immigrant groups or various types of cohorts such as occupational groupings, and the social contexts in which these individuals are viewed are those of the primary relationships which compose the networks they participate in through correspondence. This is not to say that the individuals studied here are atypical. They do share many socioeconomic characteristics with large numbers of British immigrants, though not precisely in the ratios of the general British immigrant population. It is only to say that such characteristics were not the point in choosing to study them.

Nonetheless, there are two key contexts in which the general history of British immigration to North America in the nineteenth century is especially relevant in guiding us through the problems confronted in examining the letters of these immigrants. The first is found at the conjuncture of the relationship between who these immigrants were in social and economic terms, why they emigrated from Britain, and what their aspirations were in resettling in North America. Reviewing these issues helps to establish that many of these immigrants came to North America with permanent resettlement in mind, or, if they held out the possibility of returning to England, Scotland, or Ireland, as many did, they soon came to realize they could not do so and live as well as they were living in North America. In consequence, these immigrants had a considerable emotional stake in their letters. They came eventually to understand that their letters must embody permanently their relationships with those who would not follow them to North America.

The second context concerns the study's focus on personal identities and primary relationships. Much that has been written about the easy assimilation of these British Protestant immigrants in Canada and the United States suggests their close cultural similarity to the core Anglo-

American people they settled among. In consequence, it could be argued that they might well have not had much group consciousness at all, and it might follow from this that they would be more concerned with personal relationships and personal identity issues. The immigrants' second project would be singularly their concern, and this study would have no implications, beyond these British, for thinking about other immigrant groups.

It would be a misreading of the consciousness and the behavior of these English, Scottish, and Irish Protestant immigrants, however, to find them without group consciousness. For variously among each people, and variously, too, in the contexts of both the United States and Canada, these immigrants certainly possessed a good deal of ethnicity. Though they did not develop ethnic institutions on the same scale as did more culturally distinctive European immigrant peoples such as the Germans, Irish, Jews, or Poles, these British immigrants possessed what has come to be called *ethnicity*.

The British are thus offered here as an example of a general, neglected phenomenon in immigration studies, for it is the author's contention that "the immigrants' second project" was and remains characteristic of the striving of all individuals caught up in the life-transforming processes of history. Whether one conceives of immigrants as violently *uprooted* or as strategically *transplanted,* the popular metaphors for American immigration history developed by Oscar Handlin and John Bodnar respectively, international migration put in sharp relief for all immigrants such questions as, "Who am I?" and "What is the relationship between the person I was in my homeland, and the person I am now in North America?"[18] It is doubtful that these questions were posed directly or consciously, let alone in this particular language, which may rightly strike the reader as having distinctly therapeutic resonances of contemporary Western culture. By their letter-writing, however, they proved that these issues were very much on their minds.

The primary letter-writers represented in this study are a distinctly middling group of people. Neither rich nor poor, they came to North America in most cases between the 1820s and 1860s with skills and in some cases with savings, or they were able to get support in their resettlement with resources provided by family in the British Isles. Although Canada attracted many of the poorer British immigrants, who were often assisted by landlords and parish officials to emigrate, the letter-writers in eight of the ten Canadian cases were farmers with relatively significant personal resources. All eight of them were able to afford both down payments on parcels of land, whether improved or unimproved, and some of the early costs of farm-making, though the means they brought for doing so varied significantly. A number of these immigrants in both the United States and in Canada were able to take advantage of existing family, friendship, occupational, or village networks that cushioned their resettlement. In some cases, these networks dated back to eighteenth-century migrations to British North America.

Of the seventy-one primary letter-writers, both men (62) and women (9), thirty-three (46 percent) were involved in farming, twelve (17 percent) in traditional skilled crafts (building trades, stone quarrying, mining); eight (11 percent), industrializing trades (textiles, cutlery); fifteen (21 percent) in the professions and commerce (commercial agents and clerks, shopkeepers, schoolteachers, engineers, medical doctors, etc.); and two (3 percent) in domestic service (governess, gardener). Among them, we find no unskilled laborers in either industry or agriculture, or dispossessed estate tenant farmers of the sort who were swelling the ranks of the British poor, and later in the century would also characterize a significant segment of the eastern and southern European immigration to North America. The unusually high figure for those in the professions and commerce attests to the middle-rung socioeconomic status of some of these immigrants.

We are accustomed by much immigration history to think of immigration as having exclusively economic motivation. This study offers the view that the emigration of a number of these individual immigrant letter-writers was motivated substantially by highly individualized difficulties—for example, the inability to get along with siblings or parents, deteriorating marriages, the embarrassment of debt in intimate village trading communities, and restlessness with dependence on family for opportunity and material security—and not solely by the structural push and pull forces we usually associate with the emigration decisions of large occupational cohorts. On the other hand, the forbidding prospect of various modernizing economic transformations in agriculture and industry in the British Isles and of being able to take advantage of opportunity in North America ultimately made emigration a plausible decision within the framework of their individualized discontents. After all, they might well have relocated within the British Isles to deal with their individual circumstances. North America offered simultaneously both relief from those personal difficulties and the prospect of security and even prosperity. Others of these immigrants, however, conform to our picture of the traditional economic migrant in search of opportunity. These are individuals who seem to have plotted a course across the ocean based on a knowledge of job markets and wage scales, and had highly targeted material goals, and whose letters reveal none of these individualized difficulties in their personal relations.

The economic incentives to leave Britain were provided by a variety of well-known short- and long-term considerations, including, in agriculture, poor crops and crop blights, rising rents, and falling prices of agricultural commodities, and in industry, technological displacement and the destruction of old skilled crafts, especially in the textile trades. But what bound most of these economic immigrants together was, in the largest sense, a desire to escape from the clutches of modernizing agricultural and industrial rationalization that was commercializing farming and reducing craftsmen to wage labor.[19] To that extent, they were venturesome conservatives, who hoped to reestablish themselves in North America in a familiar way of life that could be led according to the virtues of a traditional moral economy being destroyed in Britain's transformation to modern capitalism.

There were certainly those wishing only to escape temporarily an immediate material difficulty, such as a bad wage scale or a farm rent increase; and a few, such as the Scottish textile craftsman John Ronaldson, the English coal miner John Thomas, and the English housepainter Ernest Lister, whose intentions from the beginning were to stay several years and return with as large a pot of money as they could secure in the hope of maximizing their own choices within the emerging British economy. But inspiring many, including artisans, skilled factory workers, and professionals alike, was belief in the libertarian, yeomen mythology of rural self-sufficiency by which they aspired to independence on inexpensive, fertile acreage in the North American interior.[20] This vision united the agricultural majority among the letter-writers with people from quite different backgrounds in Britain, such as the skilled textile craftsmen of the related Morris families, who used work in Pennsylvania textile mills to buy farmland in southern Ohio; or William Julius Mickle, a well-educated young man from London who bought farmland in Canada for his father, Charles Julius, a librarian at East India Company House who dreamed of rustic simplicity in the Canadian backcountry; or Thomas Steel, the medical doctor who took up farming on the Wisconsin prairies; or Thomas Spencer Niblock, the ne'er-do-well son of an English schoolmaster who failed at farming in Canada.

As Erickson has pointed out, British migrants such as these emigrated not because of extremely low living standards, or even of the prospect of an imminent decline in living standards, but because of a desire to avoid unwelcome change. Settling on American or Canadian frontiers, or dreaming of doing so while working for wages in a mill, they accepted lower per capita incomes, poorer housing, more expensive manufactured goods, and a less developed public and commercial infrastructure in exchange for the prospect of avoiding the modernizing transformations then being experienced in Britain. Moreover, seeking to avoid the transformations associated with modernization, they soon learned, as did Steel, Niblock, and countless others whose letters record their false starts and difficulties, that North American agriculture required endless adaptability.[21] In seeking to avoid proletarianization, skilled craftsmen shared a similar vision of greater independence from the factory system, reinforced by the prospect of higher wages, though it was understood that prices of many finished goods were higher in North America. These craftsmen, too, like Andrew Greenlees, who left County Antrim in the north of Ireland in the early 1850s to settle first in upstate New York and worked for over two decades at a trade before taking advantage of the Homestead Act and buying a farm in Kansas, might also share the yeoman vision.[22]

What these immigrants were seeking in emigrating was not simply a new job or occupation, but ultimately a different way of life from the modern social order that they feared was about to engulf them at home. Some who held this vision accepted at the time they left that their emigration was permanent, but for others such goals were not necessarily incompatible with the hope that a return to Britain was eventually possible. Most understood that it might take years to return with enough savings from their New World venture to ensure material independence in Britain, which was the only condition on which they contemplated return. Few could ever realistically fulfill that dream of independence in Britain based on wealth made in North America. Return migration was rare among these immigrants.

In the case of other immigrant groups, permanent settlement yielded a strong public ethnic group life, with durable institutions, organizations, political mobilizations, and proximate settlement patterns that endured over many decades. While the American and Canadian situations are quite different, and while there are diverse patterns among Scots, Irish Protestants, and English in both societies, in neither Canada nor in the United States do we find strong evidence of this type of ethnicity among British immigrants. In the United States in the nineteenth century, we do find evidence of the organization among them of charitable endeavors, lodges, and commemorative activities. Outside major urban areas, however, these peoples did not maintain their own public group life, as opposed to informal social circles, in spite of large numbers that might provide a critical mass for doing so. They were integrated into American churches, fraternal organizations, military companies, and neighborhoods. Because they had no language of their own to defend and could be adequately served for general news by American newspapers, they maintained a relatively feeble presence in ethnic journalism. They did not form a voting bloc to advance an ethnic agenda, an absence strongly reinforced by the fact that their less formal, more interpersonal formulation of ethnicity was rarely given to ideological expressions of ethnic issues they could take into politics. Their characteristic anti-Irish Catholic feeling was easily assimilated into American nativism, which readily found a home in the existing political party system on the strength of American prejudices, without requiring a British vote to push it forward.[23]

In Canada, the situation was different, because of the imperial connection and a contrasting time frame for provincial social and political development. The Scots, Irish Protestants, and English immigrants in the nineteenth century became the charter groups for the founding of a new society, one emanating from what would become known as Ontario and lacking a long colonial past of the sort present in the United States or in Quebec and the Canadian Maritimes. Though here and there they organized ethnic commemorations and benevolent societies, and engaged in symbolic assertions of ethnicity, their separate public identities were significantly submerged in emerging national and regional institutions of which they were the founders. Arriving early in significant numbers, they set the standards for what came to be thought of as *Canadian*. Their only rivals for that distinction were the Anglo-American Loyalists, who were refugees from the American Revolution, but this population was soon eclipsed by the tide of British immigration. All three British immigrant peoples variously contributed to the formative populations of the major churches—the Church of England, the Methodists, and the Presbyterians. The identity of such institutions was ultimately less ethnic than Canadian. Yet the Irish Protestants, who were the largest immigrant group in Ontario at the time of Confederation, did organize Orange Society lodges throughout Canada, and these became an active, conservative force in politics easily mobilized after 1830 against Roman Catholics, as the Irish Catholic population grew and a Catholic hierarchy and Catholic institutions emerged.[24]

In contrast to the Irish Protestant Orangemen, little resembling ethnic politics can be found among the English or Scots in Canada. Their politics reflected various ideological formulations of an agenda defined by Canadian nation-building and maintenance of the imperial connection, which led them less to ethnic organization than to identification with British and colonial institutions and with anti-Americanism. Such was the case, for example, with Ralph Wade, whose articulate and often opinionated letters to kinfolk in England from Canada are discussed throughout this study. Wade, a progressive farmer who emigrated in 1845 and joined a branch of his family established by an older brother, settled on a farm in the Port Hope area. He soon became a Canadian patriot within the context of the Empire. He wrote of the desirability of "our beloved Queen Victoria" visiting Canada, because, as he said on a number of occasions, the people of England thought "too meanly" of Canada, as backward, wild, and remote, and needed another source of information that pointed to the province's rapid progress after 1840. Wade had to acknowledge, however, that the United States had made significantly greater strides than Canada and that Canadians, whom he reluctantly admitted copied American ways, had come to "represent a halfway point between John Bull and Brother Jonathan." He sought to dispel incorrect impressions about Canada not only so that it could take its rightful place within the Empire, but also so that it was not tempted on the path to Americanization and political union with the United States.[25]

From such an uneven pattern of ethnic group development, one might reach the conclusion that, especially in the United States, these English, Scots, and Irish Protestants lacked ethnic consciousness and identity. Certainly their letters are not preoccupied with questions of ethnic identity, and most of the letter-writers, over the course of years, infrequently, if ever, reflect on possessing a sense of group identification. Moreover, in spite of the cultural diversity around them, they do not reflect much on the meanings of this pluralism or on their place within it. But in bringing them into contact with people unlike themselves and, especially in the American context, a public culture much different than the one they had left, immigration impelled them toward reflection on public identities and peoplehood. Though often explicitly expressed more in terms of difference from others (and strong disapproval of those differences), rather than in terms of affirmations of affiliation or peoplehood, the latter nonetheless remained implicit in these judgments. To work at discovering who one is not suggests at some level a simultaneous effort to define an identification for oneself. In this sense, their ethnicity was less an encompassing way of life as it was for latecomers, such as Poles or Italians, who were significantly culturally distinctive from the founding British-Canadian and Anglo-American populations, than a subtle process of perceptions of difference among peoples and an appreciation of what was one's own.

To a significant extent, comparisons with Irish Catholics, and to a somewhat lesser extent with French Canadian Catholics, were a basis for these judgments in both Canada and the United States. But judgments were also made based on the gathering understanding of those who on the surface seemed very similar in cultural terms: in the United States, the British compared themselves to white Americans, and in Canada, they compared themselves, whether Scots, Irish Protestants, or English, to one another and to the descendants of the American Loyalists. Similarity worked to sharpen the recognition of differences on at least two levels. Expecting similarity, one is led to take special notice when confronted by difference. Moreover, the sharing of a common language among these British immigrants, and in the American context between them and the Anglo-American majority, worked to expose them directly to insults, slights, and misunderstandings. They could not walk away from verbal encounters with other English speakers with the shoulder shrugging and perhaps benign resignation that comes with not having any idea what is being said.[26]

Probably the most emotionally laden source of recognition of difference was encounters with Irish Catholics, which called up to consciousness a rich heritage of British prejudices. Linda Colley's understanding of the origins of modern British national identity in, among other sources, Protestant chauvinism and anti-Catholicism (against both the Catholic powers of Europe and Irish Catholics), is certainly confirmed in these letter-writers' comments on their encounters with Irish Catholics, though it is difficult to sort out where religious bigotry begins and national prejudices end in such evaluations. Much, including intra-

Protestant conflicts, divided Scots, English, and Irish Protestants among themselves and from one another, but anti-Catholicism, particularly its specifically Irish variant, was a source of unity among them in the diaspora, as it was in Europe. This commentary appears occasionally, for not every letter-writer is placed in a position by circumstance to mark Irish Catholics. But it makes up in intensity of its characteristically negative expression and its implied or often explicit preference for Britishness what it lacks in frequency, and it is rare indeed for positive evaluations of Irish Catholics to provide balance for the much more insistently negative ones.[27] Emigrating largely from villages, small towns, and rural areas in England and Scotland, these immigrant letter-writers probably had experienced little contact with the Irish Catholic population resident in Britain, which was urban, so these were first encounters mediated only by folkish prejudices. But the Irish Protestants, too, found these encounters just as jarring. An absence of intimate, as opposed to impersonal and formal, contacts in Ireland is attributable both to segregated living patterns in neighborhoods of some cities in the North, but even more extensively, whether spatially separated or not, to a social distance bred of class and religious differences and low rates of intermarriage. Irish Protestants often closely encountered their own Catholic countrymen as if for the first time.[28] The Irish diaspora might well have been for them an incubator of bigotry toward the Catholic Irish.

Irish Catholics were viewed as lazy, filthy, vice-ridden, improvident, superstitious, ineffectual, and ignorant, and their religion was thought to bear significant responsibility for keeping them that way.[29] First encounters that thrust these Protestant immigrants into contact with Catholicism and Irish Catholics during the process of emigration and resettlement often induced these declarations. John Fisher, who emigrated from England and settled on a farm in Lenawee County, Michigan, in 1831 took the occasion presented when his trans-Atlantic ship finally docked at Quebec City to visit the Catholic cathedral, "the most splendid edifice I ever beheld," where nonetheless the "superstition and ignorance is beyond description."[30] Fisher, a devout Christian, sought out this opportunity, but it instructed him only by confirming the superiority of his Protestant faith. Fisher had not shared a shipboard passage with Irish Catholics. Had he done so, he might well have developed an aversion like that of Henry Johnson, an Irish Protestant shopkeeper who had left Ireland to escape debt and briefly settled in Canada before succumbing to cholera. Johnson's Liverpool to New York City passage was aboard a ship, he carefully noted, that had four hundred to five hundred Irish Catholics but only forty Protestants. "A more Cowardly set of hounds than the same papists I have never seen," Johnson wrote in his first letter to his wife from Canada, "In time of danger they do nothing but sprinkle holy water, cry, pray, cross themselves and all sorts of Tomfoolery instead of giving a hand to pump the ship and then when the danger was over they could carry on all sorts of wickedness and they are just the same Any place you meet them at home or abroad."[31]

John Kerr, another Irish Protestant emigrant who worked at times as a schoolteacher and was then employed in Arkansas as a bookkeeper in a mercantile house, would have agreed. A methodical man, given to taking infinite pains with details, he had gone to New Orleans to meet the ship that had carried his younger brother, Sam, across the Atlantic, and observed the festivities of the passengers on their last night before debarking. In matters of principle and conscience, Kerr was quite capable, in the abstract, of expressing sympathy for Daniel O'Connell and Irish nationalist politics, and denouncing Irish Protestant bigotry, but again, a close encounter, like Johnson's, brought out strong feelings of aversion. What he observed was especially likely to ignite his prejudices. Though he does not identify these Irish as Catholics, his use of "they" and the distance he sets between himself and them strongly suggests about whom he was speaking. "I could not help thinking that the Irish character presented a feature different from any other nation," he said. That night he saw them drinking,

> running around the vessel, staggering, swearing, boasting of how they could fight, etc. There they were in all their native filth, unwashed and unshorn, swallowing drafts of their countries curse and as careless of what was to come of them as if they were to take possession of a farm each and be independent tomorrow. Just at a time when they required all the forethought and prudence they possessed, they drowned all in drink. Did ever the lunatic display greater folly than this?[32]

Comments of this sort are typical of the harshly negative evaluation of Irish Catholics that appears in British immigrant letters. Indeed only one of these letter-writers takes the opposite viewpoint when brought into intimate contact with Irish Catholics, and praises their character as a people. An emigrant from Scotland who settled in the Mohawk Valley

she could learn she could
act generously on what she had learned

of New York State in 1807, Mary Ann Archbald, as she herself admitted, was not predisposed to be sympathetic to the Irish Catholics, but she nonetheless learned to respect the Irish immigrant laborers who worked on the construction of a section of the Erie Canal at the edge of her farm, near the banks of the Mohawk River. The work was superintended by her son, and twenty of the Irish laborers boarded at her home. She came to value their warm-hearted kindness, devoutness, work ethic, and sobriety enough to invite all of them to her daughter's wedding. When they were falsely accused of a crime, and sentenced locally in a highly prejudiced court, on the basis of perjured testimony, to five years in jail, she petitioned Governor DeWitt Clinton in their behalf, and helped to win their freedom. Her letter to Clinton is interesting, for it suggests the distance she had to traverse to reach a favorable conclusion. "My early prejudices were all against the Irish but (as national prejudices are all more or less unjust) I have lately seen instances of generosity and attachment of Irish to each other that would cover a multitude of faults."[33] Not exactly a ringing endorsement, but at that, it followed a path that none of the other letter-writers were able to take.

Though Archbald may be a noteworthy counterpoint, there is nonetheless something extraordinary about the tremendous imbalances in these evaluations. No people encountered by British immigrants, including American and Canadian native peoples and African Americans, who usually inspire sympathetic commentary, evoke this type of bigoted writing. The British hated slavery and denounced it strongly; few settled in the South (only four of seventy-one primary letter-writers) in consequence of its existence and the limits it set on the non-slaveholding white man's opportunity.[34] But they expressed little sympathy for the impoverished Catholic Irish. At once condemnatory, debasing, truculent, and yet articulate, their remarks about Catholics, especially the Catholic Irish, offered reinforcement for the feelings of national identification that were part of their British birthright.

In the American context, such anti-Catholic and anti-Irish feeling might have been the source of an ideological and emotional connection between native white Americans and British Protestants. To some extent this was true, as Kate Bond, whose letters demonstrated these prejudices abundantly over the course of decades, noted approvingly and probably humorously in 1870 in her first archived letter to her brother, "The Yankes tell us if there would be more English they could send some Irish back." But distance and a degree of tension characterized the relations between British immigrants and Americans. Later that same year, Kate herself gave testimony to this. She wrote that she was not sure what sort of Christmas celebration she and Jim would have, because they had not been able to make any friends in Connecticut. "The Yankes are very distant peopel. They don't thinck much of John Bulls, but we have lots of mutton and the master said he was to kill a pig for Christmas. So we don't care much about them."[35]

Bond's simple formulation of her relationship to Americans and to American society summarizes neatly the way many British in the United States came to feel about the land they resettled in and its people in the early years after their immigration. Active hostility toward the British, in the form of legal or customary discrimination, or violence certainly did not exist; nor has any historian who has investigated British immigration found evidence of the onslaught of popular prejudices and debilitating stereotypes which Irish Catholics experienced daily in encounters with Americans.

Yet British immigrants were trenchant critics of Americans (all of whom they often lumped into the single category, *Yankee*), and they maintained a certain distance from them. At the same time they acknowledged, as did Bond herself in relishing a plentitude of mutton and pork, that American social arrangements and political institutions were suitable, if at times problematic, vehicles for the fulfillment of their material needs and ambitions. Alongside their hatred of slavery, this was their route toward the increasingly warm feelings toward their adopted country that led to warm professions of northern patriotism and military service during the Civil War. If they could not love the country's people, they could see the value in the country's institutions and aspirations.

From across the northern border, the British settling in Canada took on identity by making similar calculations about Americans. If Canada were, as Ralph Wade said, part John Bull and part Brother Jonathan, English immigrants settling there who shared Wade's views definitely preferred the former to the latter. His nephew, John, summed up his evaluation in 1835 in comparisons of the American Old Northwest and Canada as a destination for English immigration. Soil, infrastructure, climate, and apparently everything else in the Old Northwest were very good, but he added, attempting vaguely to address certain intangible preferences, "I should give preference to Canada for English people as the land and other things are more congenial to their feelings."[36] Henry

Johnson came somewhat closer after traveling through both New York State and the Niagara Peninsula of Canada. The latter, he said in a letter from Hamilton, Upper Canada, was "quite different—all Scotch and North of Ireland people," and hence "homely and civil."[37]

Contact with Americans routinely moved British immigrants to these expressions of preference, which were also statements of self-understanding. They encountered Americans as a foreign and very different people, and they never evoked a common, if distant, ancestry. While in general British immigrants had many criticisms of Americans, these varied with the political, social, and religious orientations of individuals to the point at which they might actually be contradictory from one individual to another. They were divided, for example, in the nature of their frequent criticisms of the quality of American religiosity. Those such as Archbald and Thomas Steel, who were inclined toward liberal Protestantism, disliked what they took to be a strain of insistent intolerance, if not fanaticism, in American evangelical Protestantism, while an Orthodox Calvinist like Henry Johnson felt that American indifference to the Sabbath demonstrated a complete lack of regard for religion. Some individuals strove to be fair and balanced in their evaluations, and made room in their critical testimonies for exceptions or admitted their lack of familiarity with a broad enough spectrum of Americans over a significant enough period of time to make their evaluations meaningful.

But at the core of most of these criticisms lay one theme, consistently expressed in a variety of ways: Americans were guided more than anything else by self-interested material calculation, and hence prone to sharp trading practices, indifference to community and sociability, distrust in all dealings with others, lack of compassion for strangers and the needy, and blindness to such instances of searing injustice in their society as slavery.[38] In contrast, that hypermasculine personification of Englishness (and in some formulations of Britishness itself favored in immigrant expression), John Bull was the opposite in every way. John Bull was bluff, open, warm-hearted, convivial, actuated by the spirit of fair play, and generous. He may have sought to improve his lot, and enjoyed the prospect of living well, but he did not seek gain for its own sake, at least in these idealized constructions of him, and he did not seek it at another's expense.[39] "If you were dying they would Scarcely give you a cup of water without paying," said Henry Johnson of his experience of "the Country the people their Manners and Customs" during his passage across New York State on the Erie Canal, "and for everything you do get they charge very high although the first cost price is very low."[40] Johnson preferred Canada, but the vast majority remained in the United States, which also was a magnet for large numbers of British immigrants who left Canada, discontented with the relative lack of opportunity there.[41] Nonetheless, in spite of their frequent criticisms and the difficulties they experienced in having close relations with Americans, they had to acknowledge that with its limitless, fertile, and cheap land, free markets, rapidly developing infrastructure, and low taxes and light-handed government, the United States was the place where British immigrants had the best chance of fulfilling their aspirations.

Their criticisms of Americans were, in fact, another side of those same aspirations. The unacceptable behaviors they thought typical of Americans are those associated with modern economic individualism, and hence with the emerging capitalist order from which they had fled Europe. When they harkened back in a moment of nostalgic reverie or of disgust with the people among whom they had settled to the romanticized village of their youth, and then idealized its people ("How different the people at home." said Archbald, summing up her usual response over the decades to her difficulties with Americans), it was to a world that was rapidly disappearing.[42] The United States briefly gave them an opening to escape those transformations, though the trajectory of its development was, of course, the same. The very economic, political, and social forces that briefly created that opening ultimately ensured the triumph of modern capitalism.

But to the extent that large numbers of British immigrants remained alienated from those forces, they would retain an understanding of themselves as different from Americans, who seemed to personify them. In consequence, while they did not build a public ethnic associational or institutional life to reinforce those differences, in private relations the immigrant generation often preferred one another's company. "Acquaintance has not raised the Americans much in my opinion—there is I am sorry to say a total want of principle amongst them particularly in political matters," Steel wrote his father after three years in Wisconsin. He was on that occasion specifically referring to a plan of the local highway commissioner to put a road, which he deemed unneeded but for which he was to be assessed, across his property. He had made the same point from time to time based on his experience in other matters. Under the circumstances, it is not surprising to find Steel declaring,

"The English and Scotch continue my steady friends but the Yankees are fond of change and have not quite so high a standard of morals as the others." He further explained in a letter three years later, "The Americans are so different from us in their habits and modes of thinking and etc., that little community of sentiment can exist in the English settlers." Though these suspicions of Americans grew rather than contracted the longer Steel lived in Wisconsin, he did make overtures of friendship toward particular American neighbors, generally without success. Meanwhile, he rode considerable distances, even in the depths of winter at the time of Robert Burns Day, to socialize with fellow Scots and other British, who seemed to have felt the same way as Steel about where they might best seek friends. He noted, for example, that the Welsh in his area preferred the services of a British doctor to those of American practitioners.[43]

Trust was usually the irreducible element in these British testimonies about preference for their own people over Americans. Americans seemed too self-interested to be trustworthy. In his initial encounters with Americans, John Kerr came to believe that a "trait in the character of Americans which is easily noticed is an entire want of disinterest in friendship." He spelled this out explicitly in explaining how fortunate he was to have been befriended by an Irish Presbyterian minister. "You may be assured that a faithful friend is valuable in this country, where the people are so selfish and avaricious," he wrote his uncle, "There is scarcely one in ten who would not take advantage of any person who will place confidence in them. Everything honorable seems to be seared up or rooted out by that reigning passion, the lure of money, which pervades all classes from the priest to the infidel."[44] Widely shared, such views of Americans caused a degree of wariness in social interactions, and were powerful incentives to limit one's most significant interactions to the circle of fellow ethnics. These judgments certainly mock commonsense notions of the ease with which cultural similarities may have led the British to interact effortlessly with Americans.

Though such testimonies of ethnic fellow feeling and disappointment with Americans were heartfelt, it is important to place them in context in thinking about the immigrant letter. Immigrant personal correspondence did not exist for the purpose of analyzing the American social order, evaluating the relative merits and flaws of the peoples the immigrants encountered, or charting the rise of ethnic consciousness. While it may occasionally have cast reflections on social identities, the immigrant letter was concerned more with personal identities and private relationships.

The Organization of This Study

Part I of this book is concerned with the analysis of the elements of immigrant epistolarity: how it is understood by previous interpreters; and how our understandings might be broadened and deepened. To understand the immigrant letter on its own terms and not as the servant of other projects, the analysis in chapters 1 and 2 contends, it is necessary first to understand the difficulties its interpreters in the past have had conceptualizing the meanings and purposes of immigrant personal correspondence, and then to proceed to an understanding of the crucial links between the self in relationship under circumstances of long-distance separation and the exercise of literacy. The remaining four chapters of Part I lay out a framework for understanding how letters were crafted and conveyed by British correspondents in North America in the nineteenth century, and how their letters worked to achieve their varied and often illusive meanings.

Part II then proposes to shift the discussion from the letter itself as an object of study to an intensive investigation of personal correspondence in the lives of four immigrants—Thomas Spencer Niblock, Catherine Bond, Mary Ann Archbald, and Thomas Steel—to Canada and the United States and the relationships embodied in their correspondence. These four chapters may be a departure in tone to the extent that they are written as a type of biographical narrative rather than analytical expositions, but they are intended to serve as case-studies that develop the analysis established in Part I. In framing immigrant letter-writing through case studies, the study returns to an understanding central to its larger understandings: if we are to understand immigrant letters, we must begin with individuals and the significant others with whom they corresponded.

Immigrant Epistolarity

Introduction

Currently, immigrant letters are used mostly to provide color and drama in historical narratives, or to document societal-level and group-level generalizations based on other primary sources, social science theory, or manipulation of aggregate data taken from published, mostly official, sources, such as census records. A number of excellent books employ immigrant letters in this way, but nonetheless when they use them as documentation, authors seldom confront the necessity of understanding the personal letter as a type of text, or the corresponding parties as a relationship. Instead they cull quotes, facts, and opinions in line with what they already believe they know. For many years, immigrant letters have also been a basis for edited collections.[1] While the collection is not a new way to present immigrant letters, recent collections, beginning with Erickson's *Invisible Immigrants* (1972), have set high editorial standards in their respect for the integrity of the letters they publish, and provide expert general socioeconomic contextualization.[2] But like the collections of the more distant past, and to some extent like the interpretive scholarship that uses letters as evidence, these collections do not analyze letters as texts nor the relationships which letters sustain.[3] That is not their purpose. Rather, the point of such collections has always been not to understand the complex sources of the author's voice, but to let the letter-writers speak for themselves, while providing some background information that enables readers to place the writer in the general societal framework of a certain time and place. The centrality of the collection format for the development of immigrant letters, which is unmatched in the case of any other primary source used by historians, deserves analysis of its own, and will be addressed in the next chapter.

Throughout much of the twentieth century and into the new millennium, historians and other social scientists have found in these letters great opportunities and singular frustrations. The analysis in Part I of this study contends that the intellectual and creative problems that interpreters have encountered lie deeper, in the practice of their scholarly work, than in the problems inherent in immigrant letters themselves. The artifactual and textual natures of the historian's primary sources or the social scientist's data make all sources problematic at some level. Instead, our difficulties with immigrant letters lie more in the lack of an approach for analyzing personal correspondence, which is also a problem of comprehending the self-understandings and modes of self-expression of ordinary people, who are neither literary nor intellectual, and who produce often crude and hurried texts for practical purposes. Yet the apparent creative simplicity and matter-of-fact purposes of immigrant letters are deceptive. How can we penetrate these elusive surfaces?

The principal historians of the experience of immigration and resettlement have been social historians. There are two, related sources of the understandings which social historians take to conceptualizing immigrant letters. First, social historians of immigration have been heirs to warring interpretive traditions, one populist and the other empiricist, regarding immigrant letters. It is necessary to understand those traditions, both of which failed to achieve much analytically in studying immigrant letters, to see how contemporary analysts have been taught to make sense of letters. Second, there is the influence of the historiographical revolution that came to be known as the New Social History, by which the conditions and experiences of daily life for ordinary people have been opened up, frequently with great creativity and power, for historical inquiry. In the last three or four decades, social historians have been especially skilled in understanding large categorical social groups—social classes, ethnic groups, religious denominations, and men and women. But they have often seemed to assume that to know the group is somehow to know the individuals within it. While the group and the larger social structure of which it is an integral part set the shifting boundaries with which individual selves have negotiated their existence, they have never completely defined the individual. It is this tentative space, within which individuals emerge, with their perplexing and seemingly infinite variations of the general themes present in society and culture, that social historians are less prone to understand. Yet it is this understanding that is most needed in interpreting immigrant personal correspondence. In order to attain this understanding, however, analysis must not only be directed inward toward the individual from an understanding of social processes, structures, institutions, groups, and communities, but also outward from the individual self, in relation to other individual selves, to the world.[4]

1

Traditions of Inquiry

In the last decade, the immigrant letter has enjoyed a resurgence of attention among researchers, especially among social historians and scholars interested in popular literature. This has not always been the case. The marginality of the immigrant letter, especially within social history, until very recently stands in sharp contrast to its central position in both History and Sociology throughout the first half of the twentieth century. The immigrant letter was then generally regarded as the document that could provide the basis for reconstruction of both the sociological and the historical disciplines. In a foundational work of American sociology, *The Polish Peasant in Europe and America (1918–1920)*, William I. Thomas and Florian Znaniecki utilized letters to and from immigrants in the United States at the center of a work that was intended to move American sociology toward more scientific theorizing rooted in empirical research.[1] Voted by social scientists in 1938 the most influential work in American sociology in the years since World War I, *The Polish Peasant* is now recognized as providing intellectual foundations for most of the central nonbehaviorist, phenomenological trends in the discipline—life history, symbolic interactionism, ethnomethodology, and personality theory.[2]

Less influential in the formation of disciplines, but ultimately more influential in thinking about the immigrant letter, were those works of early- and mid-twentieth-century American social history that saw the immigrant letter as the basis for a new American history. As early as the 1920s, the immigration historians George Stephenson, Marcus Lee Hansen, and Theodore Blegen were proposing that the immigrant letter be used to create a more inclusive, democratic history of the United States that might replace the traditional master narrative created by scholars, journalists, educators, and politicians, with its elite, Anglo-Saxon, male perspective.[3] From Norway, where he had gone to collect immigrant letters, Theodore Blegen announced in 1929 the intention to create, as he said, an American history conceived from "the bottom up."[4] (Stephenson and Hansen made similar research trips in search of immigrant letters.) With its egalitarian, pluralist aims, the narrative these historians proposed became a project of the New Social History, which emerged in the 1960s and quickly gained prominence in the United States, Canada, Western Europe, and Australia. The desire to give voice to ordinary people of the past also had considerable influence on the development of the collection format as the leading approach to understanding and presenting immigrant letters.

Neither populist nor social scientific orientations were successful in creating a tradition of systematic inquiry that might guide analysts to realize the full potential of immigrant personal correspondence as a documentary resource. Both traditions of inquiry made the immigrant letter a servant of other disciplinary and ideological projects that failed to realize the potential of the immigrant letter to assist us in understanding the lives of immigrants. But the methodological and conceptual issues that arise out of the examination of both traditions of inquiry are instructive in efforts to come to terms with interpretive dilemmas that seem inherent in any effort to use personal letters for analytical purposes.

The Polish Peasant is rich with first-person sources. These include a full-length immigrant autobiography and a number of letter-series written over a significant length of time to and from Poland, which allow us a degree of familiarity with the letter-writers that we cannot attain from isolated, individual letters. But, as several generations of sociologists have come to agree, the potential of these materials to assist us in un-derstanding the lives and mental worlds of immigrants is never realized. Indeed, a vast gap exists between the interesting, casual insights on individual letter-series and the highly schematized renderings of their significance in the concluding "Methodological Note," which the authors conceived as the work's principal contribution to the development of sociology.[5] Thomas and Znaniecki had warned their readers that, the specificity of its title aside, *The Polish Peasant* is not a study of the Polish emigration and diaspora, but instead "an exemplification of a standpoint and method."[6] The study was intended to provide directions for sociology, as it embarked on a systematic analysis of America's emergent urban-industrial social order.

To understand the aspirations, failures, and contributions of this massive work, it is first necessary to be aware of the competing and conflicting claims that worked on Thomas, the senior researcher, as he planned and executed the study. In the process, we may come to understand how, in its pursuit of a positivist social science, *The Polish Peasant* came to be an imperfect guide in developing the immigrant letter as a source for understanding.

Thomas had no particular scholarly interest in Polish immigrants. The decision to study the Poles involved a considerable degree of coincidence and opportunism. He had access to a grant of $50,000 from the Helen Culver Fund for Race Psychology to analyze the resettlement difficulties of the southern and eastern European immigrants then streaming into the United States, and he sought to use this problem as the basis of research that would allow him to test disciplinary concepts and methods he had been formulating for many years.[7] The Polish peasantry seemed the perfect test-case—and not simply because there were so many Poles in Chicago. Thomas, and no less Florian Znaniecki, a genteel Polish academic, saw it as backward and stupid. They characterized the Polish peasantry's cultural level as primitive in seeking to explain what they took to be the ritualized, static nature of peasant social interactions. The Poles' experience with modernization was likely to be jarring, raw, and immediate, and hence to place important analytical problems, such as urbanization and proletarianization, in vivid focus.[8]

The questions Thomas brought to the study were on the cutting edge of sociological inquiry in the early years of the twentieth century. Thomas was not alone in his understanding that a new, positivist intellectual framework was needed for the discipline in order to move it away from the Western philosophical assumption of a universal human nature, from value-based social work ethnography, and from mechanistic, biologically based schema, such as instinct theory. Thomas's response proceeded from a rejection of both social determinism that denied individual agency and from conceptions of social change as ceaseless, inchoate, normless movement.

Thomas's interest in conceiving social change from the position of the individual led him to advance the centrality of social psychology. In the concept of *attitude*, he found a basis for establishing the mechanism of consciousness by which individuals subjectively oriented themselves to their world. The attitude guided the individual in social interaction by defining, on the individual's own terms, the situation being experienced. How was the researcher to find and examine attitudes? Thomas correctly reasoned that consciousness could not be directly inferred from behavior. He sought ways of understanding the immigrants through analysis not of their actions, but rather of their own words. He rejected quantifiable survey research as likely to make attitudes appear fixed and formal. He instead offered the dynamic, fluid possibilities to be found in individual case studies, based on life-histories, personal letters, and other writings of individuals. He stated that these must not be treated as repositories of fact, but rather as interpretable texts, open to competing and contrasting analyses. He also looked to folkloric materials from oral tradition, which gave insight into group cultural influences on the individual.[9]

As he developed these far-reaching goals, Thomas was also developing a schema for analyzing the moral and organizational consequences of modern social change. He conceived of modernization as the movement from: (1) an orderly, premodern state, characterized by effective mechanisms of what he called "social control" of the individual through tradition, community, and above all else family solidarity; to (2) a disordered and demoralized state, characterized by individualism and rational calculation that arose as a consequence of one's involvement in capitalist market relations; and then to (3) a reorganized state, characterized by new communal and institutional forms that serve to remoralize and regulate the individual.[10]

Thomas and Znaniecki's conception of the Polish peasant as immigrant, and hence of the purposes and functions of immigrant letters, grew out of this schema of modern social change. While they recognized that Poland was experiencing the transition to an urban-industrial society, it was immigration to the more dynamic United States that prompted the rapid breakdown of the mechanisms of social control in the peasantry.[11] At the individual level, proof was found in attitudes revealed in letters to and from the immigrants, which gave evidence of a desire to maintain family solidarity (and to sustain family-like relations with certain close nonfamily members) and of the threats increasingly imperiling that solidarity.

The authors were impressed by the volume of letters to and from the diaspora generated by the Poles and also by the length of the letters they wrote. On the technical level alone, writing and reading were difficult for most peasants, and also involved, the authors believed, "a rather painful effort of reflection and sacrifice of time." These extraordinary exercises in literacy were to be explained by the desire to preserve continuity for the individual through the unity of the family: "to manifest the persistence of familial solidarity in spite of separation." The peasant letter, Thomas and Znaniecki rightly suggested, was essentially a social document, encoded within which, in form and language, were the rituals of family solidarity. Yet the letters also revealed, they believed, strains in family life over money, property, the choice of marriage partners, and the persistence of separation itself. These were seen by the authors as evidence of the breakdown of traditional social controls located within the family, the consequences of which were demoralization, deviance, and disorganization.[12]

Did the personal letters and other first-person materials on which Thomas and Znaniecki depended successfully document their central contentions about social change and social control? Students of the work have pointed out problems at three levels. First, the materials seem constantly to strain against the narrow conceptual boundaries of the interpretation, largely because the letters reveal so much diversity of theme and variation of expression among the writers. To maintain that all the concerns addressed in a typical immigrant letter—work, raising children, schooling, property, loneliness, and relationships with relatives, friends, and neighbors, and the like—may be neatly packaged to prove declining solidarity and increasing disorganization is both reductionist and a misreading of the family dynamics. In effect, it was to maintain that all the difficulties and conflicts within the Polish immigrant family were exclusively the product of a specific sociohistorical epoch rather than a part of normal family functioning among individuals, with different subjectivity, who attempt to get along with one another, often under close and constrained circumstances. Second, the narrowness of the range within which the letters were interpreted was a consequence of the authors' disciplinary goals, which ultimately were a product of their aspiration to establish general laws of social change and of individual social behavior. The schema of modern social development and of individual responses to change was essentially a hypothetical formulation of one such law. To wrest *laws*, in contrast to the less mechanical notion of *patterns*, from the diversity, confusion, contradiction, and general unpredictability of social life requires advancing propositions so general that they lose the capacity to explain anything about human social phenomena.

It is, in fact, to confuse human history with natural history, a confusion that may account for the third level of difficulty: the impoverished historical and anthropological contextualization of the work's interpretation of immigrant letters and other first-person materials. The Polish peasantry, especially in its American diaspora, is conceived in ways that work to render it without historical memory, culture, or community, which, in turn, has the effect of undermining our ability to understand the Poles on their own terms and the terms of their experience. Yet again, the authors' formal disciplinary logic becomes the only standard we have for understanding the letter-writers and their letters. Though the Polish context is developed at length, the American is underanalyzed and comes to represent an archetype of liberal, capitalist modernity.[13]

Such a vision leaves no place for understanding the relevance of alternative perspectives on the sources of meaning and belonging, such as community, religion, ethnicity, gender, and social class. The authors recognized the significance of ethnicity (in their view, as a defensive and transitory group, not individual reaction to disorganization), but devoted little analysis to the role of Polonia—the communal networks, institutions, and neighborhoods of the Polish diaspora—in establishing a culture of daily life that might provide a viable pattern of meanings for individuals to explain their experience. The immigrants emerge atomized, cultureless, and normless. They do not so much shape a narrative of their lives, achieving meaningful continuities along with their family, friends, and kin, out of their culture and experience, but rather face, as Dorothy Ross observes, an unending series of *situations*, which must be responded to according to their own inexorable logic.[14]

In spite of Thomas's insistence on individual agency, the Poles in his rendering are inert to the point at which they seem often pathological. They react, mostly to forces in the world rather than seek to shape them, though in the case of the women, they are seen as occasionally proactive in attempting to revitalize family bonds. But they are not creative in the face of forces that are overwhelming them and seem to render them powerless. Evidence of other frameworks defining their circumstances for them is dismissed as, in effect, incorrect or self-deceptive before the facts of an objective world.[15] One role of personal correspondence in the lives of individual letter-writers, as will be evident throughout this study, was to provide a setting for creating precisely these frameworks for achieving meaning.

While *The Polish Peasant* would have enormous influence on the development of qualitative research in sociology, its legacy for social historians and others interested in first-person documents and in particular the immigrant letter is certainly ambiguous. Having demonstrated, if simply by publishing edited versions of them, the enormous richness of immigrant self-expression, the work did directly inspire some historians' interest in developing these sources. Oscar Handlin used immigrant letters, among other first-person sources, to advance a similar disorganization argument in *The Uprooted*, one of the twentieth century's most significant works in American history.[16] Charlotte Erickson's *Invisible Immigrants* sought, within the collection format, to revive the rigorous analytical evaluation of letters of immigrant letters, and though mostly advancing a very different interpretive schema based on the socioeconomic and occupational origins of emigration, begins with praise for the high standard of scholarship in *The Polish Peasant*.[17] For the purposes of this study, the authors certainly pointed us in the right direction in seeking to conceptualize the immigrant letter as an extension of personal relationships that developed specific goals within the framework of such relationships.

But Thomas and Znaniecki were unable to realize the potential of the materials with which they worked. They lacked a way of understanding the range of problems that their first-person sources, and especially the personal letters, presented as interpretable texts. They attempted to impose one key to interpretation upon texts that demand multiple frames and need to be understood from within the experience and consciousness of their authors, both as individuals and, in the case of letters, as parties involved in the mutual creation of a correspondence. From his own social scientific position, Thomas grew disappointed with the results of his encounter with first-person sources, and came to believe that such texts were useless unless they could be rendered in quantifiable terms.[18] He emerges, therefore, as an inspiration for content analysis, a method for determining by means of quantification the pattern of general themes in texts, which has been used in the historical analysis of first-person writing, though only infrequently in the case of the immigrant letter.[19]

If we are able to agree on the categories operationalizing it, content analysis is a useful method for quantitatively establishing regularities of themes and modes of expression. Its utility for immigrant letters, however, is limited. As Donald Harman Akenson has noted, each immigrant letter is a subset of a body of writing, the boundaries of which are often completely unknowable. The researcher frequently does not know, and indeed can never know, how many immigrant letters, even within the individual letter-series written by the same correspondents, have been lost or destroyed relative to the number that have survived and are now open for investigation. Failing that knowledge, a truly scientific test of those regularities eludes us.[20] But that is really not the ultimate problem of content analysis. Having brought us far enough under the best of circumstances to understand those patterns, it cannot address a much more difficult task—establishing what those patterns mean.

While the publication of *The Polish Peasant* doubtless had an influence on those immigration historians of the 1920s who were interested in using immigrant letters in their own work, other sources of inspiration were probably more powerful. Theodore Blegen, George Stephenson, and Marcus Lee Hansen were each children of Swedish, Danish, or Norwegian immigrant parents.[21] They entered the American historical profession to find it overwhelmingly Anglo-American in identity and culture. They encountered an American historiography that, with the exception of broad suggestions found in the work of Frederick Jackson Turner (the mentor of both Hansen and Stephenson), left little space for the study of the immigrant world out of which each of them had come.[22] That world possessed its own historical consciousness, which prior to the 1920s had been institutionalized mostly in local lodges and churches. The 1920s and 1930s saw an intensification and professionalization of this activity at the national level in a number of initiatives. The Norwegian-American Historical Association was founded in 1925, the year of the Norse-American Centennial, commemorating the beginnings of mass migration of Norwegians to the United States. In 1926, with the three hundredth anniversary of the establishment of New Sweden in the colony of Delaware twelve years away, the American Swedish Historical Foundation was founded. Four years later, the Augustana Historical Society, affiliated with the Lutheran Church, was formed to encourage research on Swedish Americans.[23]

These Scandinavian American historians created a powerful language, capturing a democratic sensibility, to justify their interest. We find this language asserting itself here and there with varying degrees of intensity throughout the remainder of the twentieth century. It appears in the writings of a number of social and literary historians, especially in the work of those who have edited collections of immigrant letters and stake their claims to attention, in part, on giving a voice to ordinary people.[24] It is a *populist* language, rich in emotional and ideological resonances in North American experience, that defends the claim of ordi-

Ams wanted new breakthrough

nary people to dignity, to the right to speak and be heard about their experience as immigrants, workers, parents, and citizens, and to inclusion in the American historical narrative. The New Social History and more recently Multiculturalism have endowed these claims with unprecedented disciplinary legitimacy. In fact, they have been so legitimized by the New Social History that they long ago lost their original character as dissent. Though it has never completely disappeared, one now sees the populist language that was the vehicle for its assertion used less explicitly than in the past, because the study of ordinary men and women no longer requires an ideological defense.[25]

Blegen, Stephenson, and Hansen brought two competing goals to their careers, one disciplinary and the other political, in the broad sense of the term, and the immigrant letter was at the center of each of them. First, the letter was part of a disciplinary project. They wished to place immigration history on a solid scholarly footing, so that studies of the immigrant were no longer bound either to biased social welfare ethnography and policy studies, a goal they shared with Thomas and other sociologists, or to the ethnic's own compensatory, defensive, and non-scholarly fileopietistic history, with its nostalgia, resentment and, as Blegen said caustically, "alleged glories."[26] Each of these three historians saw the immigrant letter as the ideal source for research to facilitate this shift, for it could be argued plausibly that, far from being merely a quaint artifact, it had helped to change the fundamental course of history. The immigrant letter, especially when published and widely circulated, was said to have been a great spur to mass emigration, which certainly transformed both Europe and North America, and linked their histories inseparably.[27] The creation of an intellectually rigorous immigration history itself was part of a broader goal: to transform the then hegemonic, master narrative of American history by moving it away from what Blegen called the "inverted provincialism" of contemporary political and constitutional history, with their regional, class, gender, and ethnic biases favoring the study of male, Anglo-American elites.[28] This goal took its inspiration from the democratic aspirations of the work of Frederick Jackson Turner, but its interpretive purposes lacked precision, just as had Turner's.

At times, Blegen (and Hansen, less aggressively) both seemed to call for a new national synthesis rooted not in political, but in social, history, which Blegen would also call "folk-cultural history." This was to be history done, as Blegen said long before the term became fashionable, "from the bottom-up," the history of ordinary men and, as he insisted, long before Second Wave feminism, women. At other times, however, he suggested that his goal was not a new national history ("the big picture"), but instead a series of "small pictures" that might better illuminate the master narrative for the lay reader, because the people populating these sketches were quite ordinary people. But he begged the question of how these pictures, large and small, were to fit together. How might a master narrative be conceived that would combine the story of the Founding Fathers with those of the Norwegian immigrant farmer in rural Minnesota, the Slovak steel worker in the Pittsburgh steel district, the Scottish textile worker in New England, and the Irish woman domestic servant in Chicago? One notes finally the racial limits of inclusiveness, for just as is true of the work of the inspirational Turner, who vastly underplayed the importance of slavery and race, these theoreticians of early-twentieth-century social history were not ready to integrate the African American narrative into American historiography.[29]

As the politically charged language of "inverted provincialism" suggests, disciplinary goals mixed with a populist sensibility that occasionally asserted itself in a defense of immigrant letters as a source that was partisan, not in a narrow sectarian or electoral sense, but in an ideological one. The second set of goals was asserting this ideological populism in order to put forward the claims of those whom Alan Conway, the editor of a collection of Welsh immigrant letters, called "the forgotten men and women," who were left out of history, not simply to inclusion, but to the dignity of being given a voice and being understood on their own cultural terms.[30] For some writers interested in the immigrant letter, this has involved the assertion of the claims of individuals and of individuality, and has been accompanied by a criticism of historical scholarship and of modern society in general for the massification of the individual.[31] The deflation of the significance of the individual might seem especially problematic in the case of immigration history, because even mass migration ultimately must be conceived logically, as Blegen and Hansen each insisted, as the product of an individual or family decision, and hence made in the context of individualized as well as general circumstances.[32]

Other analysts of immigrant letters have taken a contrary position, and have been less interested in the individual as such, and instead caught up in the romance of "the people" or of "Everyman," and occasionally, too, "Everywoman." They conceive of the immigrant letter as a specific instance of general emotions and a common folk psychology, and hence assert its claims as the authentic voice of folk consciousness.[33]

Whichever claim is asserted, the collection format, which has thrived under the influence of populist sensibility and discourse well beyond the long-passed period of the prominence of the Scandinavian American social historians, has proven the perfect medium for giving voice to the people, in all their diversity of self-expression and experience. Indeed, with no other documentary source available to historians has the collection format been as frequently employed. This is perhaps as much testimony to these powerful motivations as to the difficulty of creating a methodology for systematic inquiry into immigrant personal correspondence. If we cannot easily find a way to conceive of immigrant letters as texts and find meanings in them on that basis, we can reprint them, and allow them in their original form to speak to us, and to edify and move us.

In combining powerful emotions and strong beliefs with admirable editorial ambitions, populist discourse has much more deeply penetrated the consciousness of social historians than have positivist methods and goals. There is little trace today of Thomas and Znaniecki's aspirations and methods for examining personal letters. Structuralism and positivism, for which the two sociologists were important advocates and exemplars, have been under attack in the humanities and social sciences for decades, and have lost the captivating hold on research that they held particularly in the first decades after World War II. But a good deal of the democratic feeling about the subjects and purposes of history that moved Stephenson, Hansen, and Blegen is still very much with us.

At times in advancing this goal of recognition, it seems as if populist discourse, despite the rigorous and objective standards of the professional historians who initiated it, would succeed in introducing fileopietism through the backdoor. Even so academic an historian as Hansen might be moved at the inception of an important essay summarizing the state of the field, to say of the mass migrations from Europe to North America, "If an epic is the tale of a heroic soul struggling valiantly against hostile forces, then fifty million epics were lived between those years."[34] But possession of this sensibility did not require conceiving of the immigrant in heroic terms. (Certainly Hansen would not preoccupy himself with the task in his own writings.) Stephenson provided the more representative argument. Writing in 1929, Stephenson contended that since immigration history already possessed enough particularized monographs and statistical data bases, what was now required was for an imaginative scholar to "sound the depths of the human soul," and on the basis of the immigrants' own letters and other writings create "a masterpiece of historical synthesis." He cautioned that those depths yielded great complexity, as one would discover within them "the noblest as well as the basest motives that play on the human heart."[35]

From an analytical perspective, this complexity has been conceived as a source of potential strength for any serious analytical project. It is not merely that one finds plausible, three-dimensional human beings in immigrant letters. Instead, as historians from Stephenson to Kamphoefner, Helbich and Sommer have contended, the simplicity and lack of guile that they have assumed to be characteristic of ordinary people are said to account for the fact that what is bad as well as good in the immigrants appear right on the surface of the text. In immigrant letters, it is said, we find evidence of purity and authenticity of emotions, and indeed perhaps of insight too, that a more educated and sophisticated commentator was believed to be less likely to express, or perhaps even to possess.[36]

Such naiveté, moreover, is said to stimulate sympathy in readers. In doing so, it is supposed to enhance one of the benefits to the researcher and to the lay reader alike that has been advanced by many of the populist-inclined advocates of the immigrant letter as a documentary source: the letter does not allow us to distance ourselves in the way that more impersonal materials do. Instead the reader is forced emotionally to live in the writer's moment and on his or her own terms.[37] This experience, it is claimed, also has benefits for the discipline of History in general. For Lloyd Husvedt, writing in 1984, the immigrant letter represents an antidote to a pervasive structuralism that denies the "human dimension":

> Historical writing must by necessity be objective, concern itself with statistics, and find a fundamental frame of reference, be it political, economic, or social. Hence, much history is written with an emotional remoteness that fails to capture the deeply human aspects of some of the sources cited in the footnotes. . . . Diaries, journals, and letters are the human fires that smolder underneath the footnotes.[38]

In such an antistructuralist critique we hear echoes not only of Stephenson's dissent about the direction of immigration studies six decades earlier, but also of the contemporary indictment of academic scholarship for its inaccessibility to the general reader and its lack of engagement with the concerns of that reader's immediate, experiential world.[39] Close examination of immigrant personal correspondence does give us access to dimensions of the immigrants' lives—personal identities and personal relationships—that are indeed often neglected to the extent that historical studies have concentrated less on individual experiences than on analysis of large data sets and the behavior of massive cohorts of populations. But in contrast to Husvedt, whose interest is in recapturing the raw experiences and emotions of actors in the past, the present study offers a claim for analysis at the individual level as a way of testing our generalizations about people in large groups. Moreover, the claim serves to pose the question of what we learn about each set of inquiries, at the individual and at the cohort levels, by looking at the other. Analysis at the individual and cohort levels then becomes complementary rather than mutually exclusive or conflicting activities.

Even more significant for the present inquiry are the implications of the views of Husvedt and others about the presumed *authenticity* of immigrant letters. Whether they are good or bad people, the argument runs, the writers, because less educated, intellectual, and hence thoughtful, are said to be less able to mask their emotions and motives. They lack the intellect and sophistication to make themselves appear in any way other than the way they really are. Thus, the immigrant letter is a source that gives us direct access to the authentic, unmediated consciousness of the masses of ordinary immigrants, who are more or less conceived of in this formulation as more feeling than thinking people.

There is much that is problematic in these assertions. First is the failure to recognize the tremendous social and individual diversity of the immigrants, even within the same national groups, and to seek to understand the immigrants on their own terms, rather than simply to conceive of them as an antitype, representing what is not obnoxious—in this case, purity of motives and expression—to the analyst. Second is the cult of authenticity that has long centered around immigrant letters, and has become an especially limiting approach for the textual analysis of letters. Ultimately it proves as much a dead end for analysis as the positivism of Thomas and Znaniecki. Are immigrant letters a pure and unmediated expression of folk consciousness that somehow can speak for themselves, requiring no analysis to be understood? The answer is, "No," because not even privation, exile, and such intense experiences as peasants might endure during a four-month crossing of the ocean on a sailing ship render anyone solely *experiential*—that is, in possession of a consciousness shaped directly and only by experience, and hence somehow more authentic than one mediated, for example, by formal learning or by ordinary discourse with one's significant others.

There will be more to say on this problem in the next chapter, but for now it is enough to note that the claim of authenticity mistakes the nature of experience, not to mention the ways human beings develop in the world. As Joan Scott and others make clear, experience is not outside of individuals; it is not merely *lived through*. We become ourselves through experience. Consciousness is shaped by the multiple discourses and relationships of the past and present in which, creatively and reflexively, we participate, and out of which we continue to develop throughout the course of a lifetime. Language is the vehicle by which we formulate meanings for our experience in the world. If we do not conceive of immigrants in this way, the claim of authenticity tempts us to essentialize them, so that they become examples of a fixed menu of traits, usually virtues, rather than developing, thoughtful human beings, who are like us in struggling to create meanings by which to know themselves in their world. If we go to their letters looking for only those traits, we are closing ourselves off to the complexities, contradictions, and varieties of purposes, understandings, and emotions the immigrants brought to letter-writing.[40]

Such products of human thought and creativity as immigrant letters are mediated in complex ways. The nature and extent of the mediation that forms the consciousness of the letter-writing immigrant is apparent when we examine the ways in which the language of newspaper journalism, the Bible, and preaching, contemporary literature—fiction and nonfiction alike—political and civic oratory, and other people's letters enter into the writing of those composing letters.

We owe to the literary historians Stephen Fender and Orm Øverland what are perhaps the most complete, recent efforts to understand the rise and development of such mediation in immigrant writings. Both authors attempt to understand the immigrant letter as an instance of intertextuality. They ask how it is that discursive practices are developed that lead such texts as personal letters, sermons, and newspaper editorials to settle into similar patterns, and hence come to resemble one another. Øverland is interested in Norwegian immigrant letters, while Fender considers letters and other types of writings of British immigrants. While Øverland argues plausibly that Norwegian immigrant letters come to resemble one another mostly because Norwegians read one another's letters, and hence come to have common expectations about letters, Fender establishes a larger historical and cultural context for the discursive traditions of British emigration. He argues that, over the course of centuries, from the Puritans to the farmers and artisans of the nineteenth century, all British immigrants to what would eventually become the United States shared a common psychological need to justify leaving their homeland, with its powerful claims to cultural and political superiority. This need for self-justification grew after the American Revolution, when the choice of the American destination became, in effect, an assertion of ideological preference. Arising out of common impulses, he argues, all British immigrant writings, public and private alike, came to share a dependence on common tropes and themes that were constantly recycled to serve the larger purposes of self-justification. Fender may be vulnerable to the criticism that he has attempted to fit these complex and diverse materials into a Procrustean bed not dissimilar in conceptual terms to the effort of Thomas and Znaniecki. Øverland's situational analysis may be more plausible than the dependence on a transhistorical consciousness for understanding the practices of British correspondents. The source of what Fender takes to be self-justification for emigration may be less the product of national history than of personal history, existing within the framework of relationships within families and among friends. First and foremost, international migrants left families and loved ones, and they were conscious of the difficulties of departing from *homeplaces,* rich in personal associations and relationships, before they considered the implications of leaving *homelands,* in the sense of polities or nation-states.[41]

But Fender is admirably sensitive to the nuances and sources of the language of these quotidian texts. He offers us some stunning examples that prove that, among immigrant letter-writers, our greatest geniuses might be our most indebted producers of texts. He provides a particularly telling illustration of the point in his analysis of a passage found in a letter by John Fisher, the English farmer who settled in Michigan in

1831. Fisher provides a ringing defense of America and a condemnation of his homeland in an 1832 letter to his brothers:

> I have left England and its gloomy climes for one of brilliant sunshine and inspiring purity. I have left the country cowering with doubt and danger, where the rich man trembels and the poor man frowns, where all repine at the present and dread the future. I have left this country and am in a country where all is life and animation. . . . Is not this a community in which one may rejoice to live? Is not this a land in which one may be proud to be received as a citizen? Is not this a land in which one may be happy to fix his destiny and ambition? I answer for one; it is.

Among immigrants, Fisher was a highly literate individual. He wrote fairly well from a technical perspective, and expressed himself with ease and even flair. He was a reader, and claimed that the books, including a volume of Milton, he brought with him to America eased his loneliness during his first year of farming in Michigan. He claimed to read three newspapers regularly. Yet a flight into such bombastic civic rhetoric was hardly characteristic of his writing. Fender discovered that his inspiration was, in fact, a recent speech given by Washington Irving which had been reported widely in the press only two days before Fisher wrote a letter to his brothers, and which Fisher quoted verbatim. In failing to furnish either quotation marks or any attribution—an example of what we might think of as *vernacular plagiarism*—Fisher bettered his chances of impressing his family with the brilliance of his writing, and left no clues for later researchers who might have been interested in the sources of his thinking.[42] In fact, it would have been appropriate to believe, in lieu of evidence of the derivation of Fisher's rhetorical flight, that the reader had access to the unmediated voice of an immigrant patriot quickly won over to Americanism.

But one need not have the good fortune to locate such word-for-word congruencies to understand the extent to which immigrant letter-writers, and not only those especially at home with literacy like Fisher, participated in discourses that shaped their writing. Like so many British immigrant letter-writers, skillful writers and less skillful alike, Fisher's writing usually bears much more obviously the mark of a more general indebtedness to the language of preaching and of the Bible than it does to journalistic language or political speech. In 1837, he said hurriedly toward the end of a letter to his mother and brothers:

> Pray for me that the acquiring of the things of this life may not engage the whole of my attention but that I may seek first the kingdom of God and [?] I am afraid that business is gradually [turning my] thoughts from God and religion, But may God [grant] I may be aroused from my state of lethargy [before] it is late.[43]

Preaching and Bible reading were sources of continuing education for ordinary people. The frequency with which letter-writers, whether the more highly literate like John Fisher, or those with more tentative literacy skills, expressed aspirations to hearing preaching and spoke with enthusiasm of the fulfillment of those aspirations establishes a hunger not only for the spiritual, but also for intellectual stimulation, and provides the contemporary reader with a context for understanding what was perhaps the most significant mediation of their thought beyond reading the letters of those with whom they corresponded.[44]

Perhaps because until recent decades resistance was anticipated from within the historical profession to the study of ordinary people and daily life, populist-inspired interest in the immigrant letter has always discussed openly, and at some length, the general problems of authenticity, accuracy, and representativeness that are inevitably part of thinking about letters. These difficulties are recognized as not unlike the difficulties historians must variously confront with all the materials they use. They have been dealt with expertly in the case of such outstanding recent collections as those by Erickson; Kamphoefner, Helbich and Sommer; Cameron, Haines, and Maude; Miller, Schrier, Boling, and Doyle; and Fitzpatrick through elaborate acknowledgment of editorial issues, care in evaluation of authorship, consistent editing using explicit criteria, and general historical and biographical contextualization of population movement, employment, resettlement decisions, and ethnicity.[45]

Nor has the assertion of the claims on History of the common man and woman necessarily brought with it the belief that everything about them is of value to the historian. One might assert these claims of ordinary people, and still be embarrassed by or impatient with their commonness and their difficulties expressing themselves. The immigrant letter is especially problematic from this perspective, because it was often, though hardly invariably, composed by people who wrote poorly (by the standards of their time, not to mention our own), and because it routinely contains a great deal of mundane personal information regarding health, deaths, births, prices, wages, food, and the like, personal inquiries, and formulaic expression of endearments, blessings, congratulations, sympathy, and condolence. In consequence, a persistent tension in the defense of the immigrant letter has been the effort, on the one hand, to establish its value to the literary canon as a particular type of writing, and on the other hand, to formulate countercanonical arguments about the need to accept it on its own terms. To those like Erickson, who claims that of the hundreds of letters in her published collection, some show wit and many tell good stories, but "few . . . may be said to have literary merit,"[46] the Mormon literary historian William Mulder formulated a response that reveals these strains. At first, Mulder identified the immigrant letter as "a literature of the unlettered . . . the simple utterance of plain people." "If not literature itself," he continued, however, with an anxious nod to the authority of the literary canon, "it represents the beginnings of literature, the stuff out of which the *My Antonia's* are eventually made."[47]

Social historians have been equally perplexed by the status of the letter in the context of the canons of historical scholarship. The immigrant letter might be historical, yet paradoxically not be part of History. If by *History,* that is, one meant the standard grand narrative of Western historiography, with its mixture of political, legal, constitutional, and economic themes, then the commonplaces recorded in immigrant letters might seem outright trivial. Writing in 1975 in the Preface to his collection of Swedish letters, Arnold Barton acknowledged that:

> most immigrant letters have in fact little of interest to relate. They are often filled with cliches, concerned with mundane matters and local news from the old home parish. Many consist largely of religious platitudes, hearsay information, accounts culled from the newspapers, comments on the weather, reports on wages and the prices of commodities, news from family members, and greeting to long lists of relatives and friends at home.[48]

While Blegen insisted that the canon of History must itself be enlarged to find space for just such details of daily life, other historians were justifying the use of the immigrant letter by contending that it might shed light on History. The problem was usually resolved by establishing its link to the causes of mass international migration, but prior to the inception of the New Social History in the 1970s, there was still a tentativeness about the letter as History. In 1969, E. R. R. Green, the historian of Ulster Protestant immigration to North America, might spend pages describing convincingly what the immigrant letter could reveal about the ordinary individual's experience of emigration, but in his conclusion nonetheless draw back from accepting it as History. The immigrant letter, Green stated, was a source for "social analysis" mostly, but sometimes had value to History when it contained information about politics or the Civil War.[49]

Such views now seem transparently wrong-headed. For the last four decades most historians have accepted ordinary people and daily life as at, or very near, the center of historical investigation. They find uses in their efforts to study family, friendship, work, love, travel, religion, or consumer habits and aspirations for the detail found in personal letters that in the past Barton or Green might have dismissed as trivial or as not really History.

Moreover, that people who were mostly unaccustomed to formal and frequent writing were able to get all this detail into a letter in a form and in language that was comprehensible to their correspondents, and simultaneously often served such crucial practical purposes as instruction about the process of emigration and resettlement for those who would be the next link in the chain of serial migration was no small accomplishment. Simply writing about keeping in contact through the mails, which required negotiating the reciprocal exchange of letters and sharing information about postal reliability, rates, schedules, and regulations, was a complex assignment. This sheds light on the presumed lack of literary value in the immigrant letter. Commenting on Erickson's statement that her collection's immigrant letters have no literary merit, David Fitzpatrick, the historian of Irish Australian letters, argues that the letter's effectiveness is best judged more on utilitarian grounds than on aesthetic ones. "Within their own established forms," he contends, "many achieve 'merit' in the sense of communicating facts, thoughts, or desire in a controlled form." Hébard, a student of the letters of ordinary people in eighteenth-century France, agrees, but takes an even more utilitarian position. These letters must be judged not on form and language, but rather within the context of the social "space" in which they have been produced and received. Content is less important for analytical purposes, therefore, than the letter's social functions in the relationships of corresponding individuals.[50]

But as Fitzpatrick himself demonstrates in his own collection and the sensitive analysis of Irish Australian letters that accompanies it, immigrant letters sometimes give compelling evidence of depths of feelings and self-consciousness of mental states and emotions, such as longing, anxiety, grief, or anger, in a poetic language that may well be appreciated on just such aesthetic grounds as we are told to exclude from consideration. The title of Fitzpatrick's collection, *Oceans of Consolation*, is taken from an immigrant letter, in which the writer in Australia uses this striking trope to describe the impact of receiving a letter from his father in County Clare.[51]

This sort of writing is hardly a coincidental or unconscious by-product of practical expression. Immigrants and homeland correspondents did not write solely to convey information. They sought to express their emotions and to arouse the emotions of their readers, and to the extent they did so, they strained to find another, more aesthetic language to express themselves than the one they used to discuss mundane matters. They appear often to have succeeded, for their correspondents wrote in return of being moved to tears, and of tears staining and ink running down the page. They certainly succeeded at times, according to their own testimony, in moving themselves to tears as they wrote, as Nathan Haley, an Englishman who left an unhappy marriage, small children, and debts in 1820 to earn money in the United States, gave evidence in writing from Liverpool on the eve of his departure:

> I have very little time and much to say; but my heart is full, my eyes oreflows, my hand trembles, farewell. No I have not done yet. I see when I look over I have found too much fault in what is writen. But my children, my children, strikes me as much that it does unman me. I am weeping My feelings are softer than some mens and after weeping for you and my family a long time I go on.[52]

In such passages of letters, the reader senses the force of an extraordinary creativity that strains against its technical deficiencies. We see this even more frequently in the expression of religious faith, in which familiarity with the ever-present language of preaching and the Bible helps greatly to overcome technical limitations. Ann Whittaker, who came from England to Illinois with her husband in the 1840s to engage in subsistence farming, slid easily, if erratically and ungrammatically, in the first paragraph of a letter to her brother, from apologies for not having written for two years, to the more or less mundane topics of health, the neighborhood Baptist church, a recent wedding, and her general satisfaction with life in America, before suddenly exclaiming:

> I find for my own part that there is nothing like living to God for then we have the promise of this life and also of that which his to come. Godliness with contentment his great gain. My dear Brother, if you have not begun to serve the Lord it his high time to be and doing. The judgment of God are abroad in the land.[53]

It seems clear that Whittaker meant to "write well" here—that is, gravely and strikingly. The shift in tone and content, from mundane to profound, is hardly accidental, for she is mobilizing and crafting language to which she has frequently been exposed, to convey thoughts that cannot be expressed in ordinary writing and that require an aesthetic sense. When we open ourselves to understanding the rich vein of language and culture that has been tapped to feed the imagination of writers such as Whittaker, we begin to understand what complex productions these letters can be, and what aesthetic ambitions the authors themselves often had for them.

Yet doubts of the sort voiced by Green and others have had a profound impact on the way immigrant letters have been presented and analyzed. In the context of the collection format, the result has been heavy editing of language, and frequent and in some cases substantial deletions of content, and in further consequence, a sanitized, skeletal presentation that sows the seeds of underanalysis. Other editors have reacted by showing a preference for letters written for contemporary publication that were composed by relatively proficient writers. Or they have reprinted letters, as did Alan Conway in his collection of Welsh letters that was especially concerned only with those parts of texts that provided encouragement to emigrate and evaluated America from the immigrants' perspective, that were heavily edited by those who originally published them. In effect, Conway opted to let readers from the distant past make the difficult editorial decisions.[54]

As Fitzpatrick has noted, most collections begin by stating not what they include, but instead the sorts of systematic exclusions the editor has chosen to make.[55] Erickson, for example, deletes "references to letters, health, and messages from other immigrants and to other persons, once the network of friends and acquaintances of the immigrant has been established in early letters," and edits heavily "most accounts of ocean voyages, most lists of American prices and some other rather shallow descriptions."[56] Barton excludes "hearsay information, impersonal descriptions of places or events, and purely family matters."[57] Changes to form, language, and grammar are even more insistently regarded as responsible editorial work than changes to content. Even among those editors who wish most insistently to stand aside and let the letter-writers speak for themselves, without patronizing editorial interventions, collections begin with explanations of the editing required to make letters more easily readable. These might include paragraphization, punctuation, capitalization, and deletions of redundancies.[58]

In evaluating such editorial work, it is necessary at the outset to note that presenting letters for publication and analyzing them intensively to determine what content and style reveal about letter-writers and their correspondents are two quite different enterprises, though the latter projects may well depend on the former in whole, or, as is the case with the present study, in part as a basis for research. Editors of anthologies may experience practical difficulties achieving a balance between the strictures about the length of books laid down by their publishers, with their interest in commercially viable projects, and the preservation of the integrity of the materials with which they are working.[59] What seems clearly to be trivial is an easy target for deletion by a responsible editor. Surely, too, it is responsible to make letters comprehensible to the reader, so language and form need to be edited to achieve clarity and consistency. Translation compounds the difficulties of editorial obligation. Though a homogenized, deindividualized "representative" voice that belongs to no one in particular—except perhaps the editor—does come to overwhelm some collections, most editors of collections of immigrant letters are quite conscious of the burden they assume in changing historical documents. They know that to fail to preserve the integrity of the immigrant letters under their editorial control is to break the covenant historians enter into to represent fairly those who can no longer represent themselves.

Yet a competing point has a claim to our attention: the more we consider the language, form, and content of the immigrant letter as problems that we must correct, rather than an opportunity to extend and to deepen our understanding, the further we may drift from being able to have the letter instruct us on the mental worlds, experiences, and purposes of the letter-writers. To the extent that collections have been the dominant medium for advancing the immigrant letter in the past, in contrast to the analytical mode of Thomas and Znaniecki, editors' choices have ultimately been of crucial significance in determining how most of us have come to understand the immigrant letter. Those choices have been mostly to invite us to share the immediate experience of the writer and to let the letter-writers speak for themselves, without confronting the psychological or cognitive difficulties that lie in wait for us if we accept the invitation.

It is profitable to compare Thomas and Znaniecki's effort to make sense of "personal enquiries, condolences, salutations, and endearments" with the methods of most editors, who dismiss such content as trivial. It is true that Thomas and Znaniecki did delete much of that content for publication. But far from dismissing it as trivial, they regarded its predictable appearance in letter after letter as important evidence of what they came to believe was the purpose of the Polish immigrant letter: the maintenance of family solidarity. They saw the ritualized expression and the language of these sentiments, along with inquiries about the health and welfare of, and religious blessings invoked upon, particular named individuals, as "bows," symbolic gestures of bonding and respect intended to make secure relationships rendered vulnerable in consequence of separation under the circumstances of modern social change.[60] One may dismiss their interpretation as too limited or as simply wrong. (I myself believe their general view of the role of immigrant letters in maintaining relationships of such significance that it is a foundation of this study.) But the goal of going beyond both the reprinting of immigrant letters or of using them as the basis for studies of targeted, limited issues in order to find ways to explore their purposes and the mechanisms through which those purposes are pursued is worthwhile.

Indeed, ample subjects for investigation often may be found in the lists of deletions that accompany the Introductions of most collections. The New Social History prepared us to see the analytical potential of many of the usual deletions. For example, much of what was once discussed as trivial, such as health, family gossip, friendship, personal inquiries, and so on, historians today might see as useful to thinking about how immigration networks are formed and chain migrations organized, and hence in documenting the workings of the processes of international migration. But immigrant personal correspondence is not about the process of international migration as such. It does not exist solely to perpetuate the movement of populations, though that was certainly one of its purposes. It is a social practice, which, within predictable rules and mutual understandings, inscribes personal relationships in letters in order to maintain these relationships and provide continuity for the correspondents. The next assignment is to develop ways of conceiving British immigrant personal correspondence that allows us to understand letters in these terms.

2

Forming Selves in Letters

The cycle of immigrant personal correspondence grew directly out of the existential circumstances shared by both the immigrants and those who remained in the homeland. Letters were the mobilization through language of an intense self-awareness of needs generated by those circumstances. Relationships that had once been experienced in the intimate setting of household and community were now vulnerable because of the prospect of permanent separation. Because personal identities are dependent on the individual's sense of continuity in relation to people and place, the migrant and the homeland correspondent were both placed in the position of having disrupted the personal narratives by which they knew themselves. Intimate conversation, the ordinary, world-making discourse of individuals, would no longer suffice to provide anchors for the individual, so writing—an even less accustomed practice for many than reading—had to suffice to accomplish the goal of achieving continuity. Though the circumstances varied considerably from individual to individual, all immigrant correspondence lies conceptually at this conjuncture of the self-in-relationship, personal identity, the narrative construction of the self, discourse, and acts of literacy.

David Laing, a Scottish skilled railroad worker living at Logansport, Indiana, provides an example of this conjuncture. He had been in the United States for at least twenty-three years when he resumed a correspondence with his sister "Johan" (perhaps, Johanna) in 1873. Laing had attempted to correspond with his sisters in the past, but at some point, for reasons we cannot know, years passed without any answer to his letters, and at last he gave up and stopped writing. Then, long after he had lost hope of ever hearing from either his sister or any member of his Scottish family again, he received a letter that reintroduced him to people long absent from his life. At least several of his siblings were born after he emigrated, so he did not even know what they looked like.

By this time, too, he did not know the surnames of the sisters, for they had married and taken their husbands' names. He rarely received any letters at this point in his life, yet occasionally he stopped hopefully at the post office to inquire after his mail. Because it was Valentine's Day, at first he took the letter the clerk was about to hand him to be a prank perpetrated by his workmates, who had been teasing him about his prospects for receiving a romantic card from an admirer.[1]

As Laing explained in his reply three weeks later, the receipt of this letter filled him with both elation and acute frustration. On the one hand, there was the anticipation of renewing his relationship with his Scottish family and kin and overcoming the disruption in their connection that had left him feeling isolated. As he said, with evident emotion, "I am so hungry to hear from you all I am starving. I have read your letter at least twenty times since I receved it."[2] On the other hand, it was difficult for him to know what to write to his sister, added to the discomfort of which was that, though Laing was a skillful writer from a technical perspective, he was unaccustomed to writing letters, and he did not feel equal to the task.

In his reply to his sister's letter, he proceeded tentatively, skipping from subject to subject without developing any of them for more than a sentence or two. He described his workplace, and mentioned his success in his craft, and that his shop was a congenial place, filled with British immigrants like him. He wrote about his children—two deceased and five living sons, and especially his favorite child, his only daughter, Isabella, who had recently married. But he did not know what his sister might want to hear from him, and feared that he could never be as effective on paper as he could in a conversation: "Now here I am writing my thoughts to you in maters that perhaps you care nothing about. Oh how I wish I could see you & tell you my thoughts."[3] Indeed, on the strength of one letter after many years of silence, he had already, in the last three weeks, allowed himself to daydream about being reunited with his sister, though he knew this was unlikely. He would encourage her to come visit him or even to emigrate, but he said, echoing a familiar source of immigrant anxiety, "I would not ask you to come as you might not like the country & I would be to blame."[4]

Over the course of the next three years, before their archived correspondence suddenly ends, Laing and his sister did succeed, though not without some difficulties, in settling into a pattern of exchanging letters. It suited their desire to continue to communicate, but yielded, too, to the limits of their time and energy for doing so, and the various difficulties each of them experienced in writing. For her part, which we know only through Laing's replies to her letters, she had a skilled trade and, it seems, an upholstery business of her own, so she may have lacked the time, and perhaps the inclination, to write as frequently as her brother would have liked. At the inception of their correspondence, she may have had an ulterior motive in writing to him, for she soon introduced into their correspondence how he felt about the possibility of their sister Isabella coming to America. Perhaps, then, when she learned how profound David's emotional needs and inconvenient his practical requests were, she felt especially surprised by them, and unequal to the task of dealing with them. Maybe it was not accidental that a long silence on her part followed his request that she buy him a black suit and send it to Indiana.[5]

For his part, he faced a number of impediments to maintaining regular correspondence. For all his desire to reestablish contact with his sister, he had to confess that writing was often a trial for him. He was tired at the end of the workday when he had the time to write, a condition exacerbated by the fact that he had felt weak since his service in the Union army. He occasionally tried to write on Sunday evenings after a day of rest to compensate for this. His rooms at the boarding houses where he resided were uncomfortable, either too cold in winter, or too hot and filled with mosquitoes in summer, and his fingers cramped from the unusual exertions of holding the pen.[6] Yet he persevered, driven by a yearning for companionship and a sense of discontinuity and of homelessness, about which he more than once complained, that spurred him on to overcome his reticence and his fears about the inadequacy of the subject matter he introduced in his writing.

What were the origins of the state of mind in which Johan found her brother at the time she resumed writing to him? His marriage had recently collapsed; he had left home two years before, and his wife lived in their house twenty miles away in the town of Monticello. Several of his children were cold to him as a result of the breakup and his leave-taking. His mother, who had been living with him and his estranged wife for some years, and who at some level, perhaps connected with her hatred of American life, was the source of difficulty for his marriage, had died, probably within the last decade. He remained bitter about his wife's treatment of his aged mother. A boarding arrangement in the home of a woman, for whom he had a special fondness, ended when her son and provider got married and brought his bride home. Finally, the most crushing blow: his daughter Isabella never recovered from the effects of childbirth, eighteen months after which she died. Her husband quickly remarried a woman who made it increasingly difficult for Laing to see his beloved grandson. Though surrounded by his countrymen at work and in the community, and successful at gaining promotions and increases in pay, Laing wrote of his emotional devastation. "I am prospering in life," he wrote, "but I am so *lonely*."[7] Ethnicity and occupational mobility could not provide the continuity for which he hungered when he spoke of "starving" for want of connection with his own family. That he had been out of touch with his Scottish family for so long had evidently deepened his feelings of isolation and loneliness.

In order for Laing and his sister to create a mutually satisfactory exchange of letters that maintained their tentative, newly restored relationship, they had to negotiate, both implicitly and explicitly depending on the particular problems their correspondence presented, a number of issues. It was not sufficient that either of them simply describe the life they led and how they spent the day in their letters, though that had to be part of their writing. Knowledge of what could no longer be directly observed as a consequence of physical proximity certainly had to be supplied through written description. It was also necessary for them to craft a type of conversation through their letters in order that each might seek deeper levels of understanding of the other's life, and a level of intimacy could be achieved with which each was comfortable.

This could only be done if they attained a type of writing that reflected sensitivity to the other's desires about the content, form, and frequency of their correspondence. If their letters were intended to maintain their newly reformed relationship, they had to conceive of their correspondence with this purpose in mind. This necessitated writing about the correspondence itself in order to facilitate communication. They had to resolve the problem of how often they would exchange letters, and whether they would maintain a strict reciprocity regarding the frequency and length of their letters. In this, Laing was destined to be disappointed, because his sister proved to be a less diligent correspondent than he required at this difficult point in his life. Like many homeland correspondents, she tried to fill the void between her letters by sending him homeland newspapers, but he craved the emotional satisfactions of correspondence. Once, breaking with the usual convention of one-for-one reciprocity, he wrote a terse note to remind her that she

Letters could never really do it

for the deeper needs of expression

had not answered his last letter, though many months had passed since
he had sent it.[8]

They also had to confront a desire for particular details about the
other's life that may have created some discomfort. He asked questions
about the other sisters' lives, and about her line of work, which for
some reason she appeared reluctant for a time to provide. She inquired
into the sources of the domestic unhappiness to which he often alluded,
but he failed in several letters to go into any detail. Finally, he attempted
to answer her questions, but he faltered and abruptly changed the subject, before eventually returning to her questions. After four sentences
on his marriage, he excused himself and could say only that, if they
were somehow to have the chance to talk, he could tell her more. Writing of his losses in the solitary setting of a room in a stranger's home,
where he was alone with his memories and grief, proved emotionally
unbearable, and, as was the case with many immigrants unaccustomed
to writing, a most severe test of his ability to control language.[9] In matters of ultimate importance, letters usually proved for correspondents a
poor alternative to the intimate conversation the parties most desired.
At this point, David Laing's life and letters are unfortunately lost to us,
for the archived collection of his correspondence ends.

On the face of it, there are two ways in which David Laing's situation may strain our notions of what is representative in the lives of immigrants, and thus seems not to yield much in the way of grounds for
generalizing about other immigrants. First, there is the extremity of the
difficulties in his family life that he faced at the time we are able to enter
his life through his exchange of letters with his sister. Though such circumstances as the death of a child, continuing grief over the death of a
parent, the collapse of a marriage, a degree of estrangement from one's
children, and the loss of contact with one's homeland family are hardly
unknown among the immigrants in the collections that are the basis
of this study, to suffer all of them at once was certainly not common.
We are only privileged to know Laing at a time when all these disasters
seem to pile atop one another to drag him down. Ten years later, we
might find him in a less tragic situation—restored to his marriage and
home, enjoying good relations with all his sons, surrounded by grandchildren, and in regular communication with Johan and his other Scottish siblings.

But before dismissing Laing, it is necessary to understand the larger
problem his life suggests. Examination of the quest for continuity in the

service of personal identity, the immigrant's second project, has rarely been as intensely explored as the immigrant's public world, which is conceived as the creation of a stable social order built upon ethnic identification and affiliation, the domestic economy of the individual household, and socioeconomic aspirations. This narrative has mostly served to tell the story of assimilation and integration or ethnicization and pluralism. By such criteria, Laing was a success. He was promoted eventually to foreman, earned good money, had supported a large family and continued to support his wife and youngest children after leaving his home, and owned and paid taxes on the house at Monticello. (Indeed, if we had used only property tax records—a common historian's source for tracking obscure individuals—to learn about Laing's life, and neglected his correspondence, we might still believe that he was residing contentedly at home.) He lived surrounded by his fellow Britons, and had ample opportunity to be sustained by the memories and experiences they shared. Yet we know from his own testimony that these attainments were insufficient to fulfill his aspirations for a good life. Only when we grant the significance of this second project will we be able to understand the need for a more multidimensional perspective on lives such as Laing's that admits his personal circumstances, however complex and apparently singular, into our analysis.

Second, Laing's letters raise the problem of the representativeness of the suspension of correspondence with one's homeland family and the lapse of years before regular contact is restored. If our model for the typical immigrant correspondence conceives of the flow of letters beginning upon emigration and resettlement and continuing uninterrupted for years thereafter, perhaps until the death of one of the parties, then Laing's epistolary history does not seem to be a useful ground for thinking about the letters of immigrants. That model has a certain narrative tidiness to recommend it, for it may be neatly conceived in terms of a beginning, middle, and end. It does speak to many immigrant letter-series. But there are also numerous examples of suspended and restored or suddenly terminated correspondences that speak to estrangements from family, or to individual circumstances, such as illness or inability to establish a long-term residential stability, that disrupt maintaining regular letter contact. Such examples, however, may also ultimately be artifacts of a process of collecting and archiving letters, and have nothing to do with the interpersonal processes among correspondents at all.

With immigrant letters, there seems a compelling and instructive exception to every rule, so what appears to be unrepresentative cannot be easily dismissed, at the least because it warns us about the tentativeness of our rules.

An even more significant point for our inquiry may be derived from the example of the hiatus in David Laing's correspondence with his sister. The precise history of their epistolary relationship aside, there was nothing unique at all about the issues faced by Laing and his sister in establishing their correspondence and maintaining a relationship, epistolary and personal, through the post. In fact, the gap in time in their correspondence dramatizes the importance of letters in the immigrant's second project, for David Laing is just as insistent about his longing to maintain a relationship with his Scottish family as more recent immigrants who have only just begun to awaken to the full dimensions of the personal discontinuities in their new lives. Moreover, Laing's situation as a correspondent was similar to that of all other correspondents, because in order for Laing and his sister to create a mutually satisfactory exchange of letters, they had to negotiate a number of issues with which writing to remain in contact presented. The rhythms and rules of the sort of conversation for which Laing continued to yearn, even as he wrote his sister, are based on a synchronous and unstated, implicit ethics, partly a product of practice and culture, and partly of the situation and interaction of the particular participants.[10] Those that govern a correspondence must often be more deliberately negotiated, for in contrast to ordinary speech in a conversation, writing cannot utilize the unspoken signs and cues and body language that instruct face-to-face conversational encounters.

David Laing's letters suggest our need to develop an understanding of how correspondence developed out of such negotiations, became instrumental in the maintenance and development of personal relationships, and soon became constitutive of those relationships. In contrast to Laing and his sister, even correspondents who had been writing for years had to engage in these same negotiations. Such negotiations were ongoing and never finalized, in the same way that relationships are an ongoing and changing work of individuals. Perhaps they had never been put in the position of having to *think about* conversing, and in their letters now were forced to do so for the first time. Perhaps the formality of the letter proved daunting. Perhaps norms of reciprocity

What "discourse" means here

governing the cycle of sending and receiving required attention, because of changes accompanying aging, sickness or disability, or practical circumstances, such as moving far from a convenient post office.

The entire process of crafting and exchanging immigrant personal letters, therefore, was a long-distance and formalized instance of the processes of interpersonal relations. More than simply writing, letters are discourse, because their creation involves not simply a creative *I*, but also a *you*. Correspondents must play both roles simultaneously and with one constantly in the thoughts of the other, if they are going to achieve a correspondence.[11] This chapter will now focus on the psychological, social, and cultural foundations of the epistolary relationship in order to understand how an interpersonal relationship may take form in letters, and how letters work to fulfill, or, as was sometimes the case fail to fulfill, the aspirations and needs of the correspondents.

One important reason why the immigrant's second project has been neglected by social historians of immigration is that much of the literature they have produced has generally, though with distinct variations, totalized and privileged ethnicity at the expense of understanding issues of personal identity. In these writings, ethnicity has become the single most significant basis of the immigrant's self-understanding. When paired with the concept of assimilation, which has been the most prominent tool in North American immigration studies for almost a century and with which it has long been allied, the emphasis of ethnicity has denied us access to a realistic psychology of the international migrant. To be sure, assimilation and ethnicity have been powerful analytical tools for opening discussions of both the organization of immigrant communities and the long-term pattern of cultural and social change within the generations descended from immigration. But the limitations of both in helping us to understand the individual immigrant's life and consciousness are not often acknowledged. Assimilation has served to efface the relevance of the migrant's past, which must be at the center of any effort to understand immigrant personal correspondence, for the exchange of letters was based on the desire to maintain connection with that past. Ethnicity has served to substitute analysis of the group for knowledge of the individual. The frequency with which the word *identity* appears in this literature in connection with ethnicity suggests this understanding of the salience of ethnicity. Though it is often prominent among the many points of *identification* available to the individual, rarely does ethnicity assume the totality of an individual's personal identity.[12]

The necessary distinction between identity and identification, as Philip Gleason has demonstrated, emerges from a number of philosophical, psychological, and sociological texts, most of which are not involved principally, or at all, in examining ethnicity, but have much to say that may help us to understand ethnicity's conceptual powers and limitations. Among the sociologists and social psychologists who developed role and reference group theory, *identification* is understood to signify subject-positionings that are voluntary and particularistic, and are episodically experienced and episodically brought to consciousness. They involve the internalization of the role system of a group and consideration of oneself as a group member, and they reflect ultimately a need for belonging and conversely the need for boundaries between ourselves and others whom we perceive to be different.[13]

If we understand identification in these terms, *identity* is freed to take on equally central, but much more broadly encompassing, meanings. Identity may then be understood, as Erik Erickson conceived it in writings that were to attract the attention particularly of historians of childhood, as the lifelong, existential project through which we compose self-understandings that provide us, through the medium of a personal, autobiographical identity narrative linking past and present, with the knowledge of continuity over time. Erickson was perhaps the most eminent theorist of identity in the United States in the mid-twentieth century. He was successful in creating a widespread understanding that personal identity is not frozen into a stable, unchanging core in early childhood, as in early Freudian formulations, but is a process in perpetual development through the life-course. It evolves on three interrelated levels: the somatic, in which we are aware that we live within a body that is separate, singular, and ours to attempt to control and to use as an instrument for projecting ourselves; the interpersonal, in which by way of multileveled, mostly semiconscious comparisons and contrasts made in our interactions with others, we develop the sense of being simultaneously apart from and connected to others; and the societal, in which through group, community, and national identifications, we find a sense of belonging to more abstract entities and learn their norms, rules, and conventions. At the heart of identity is memory, which provides us with ways of understanding that we are the same person today that we were minutes, years, or decades ago.[14]

Ethnicity has the potential to provide us with an awareness of personal continuity: it establishes an understanding of origin that may provide us with a location from which we are able to begin our personal narratives that establish continuity over the life-course. Even in societies as culturally diverse as the United States or Canada, in which ethnicity has attained significant public legitimacy, family, friendship, and residential community have played an even greater role in these narratives of continuity. In contrast to ethnicity, which is in Benedict Anderson's terms "an imagined community" that involves the presumption of kinship with mostly distant others, past and present, whom we do not actually know in any but an abstract way, these sources of human connection involve face-to-face human relationships that often can be dated from the earliest point in our conscious awareness of ourselves in the world.[15] Our understanding of these bonds necessarily changes and develops as we move through life, but they provide vital sources for continuous dialogue, external and internal, that is constitutive of personal identity.

Ethnic *group identifications*, which are the products of ideology and of cultural representations (for example, stereotypes, both positive and negative), may certainly inform individual narratives of continuity. But ethnic group identifications are mostly the conscious creation and re-creation of ethnic leaders—organization agents, intellectuals, and artists, who take on ethnicity, and urge it on others, as a type of ideal model of the self that makes a public statement of pride and solidarity. The relevance of ethnic identity to the daily lives of ordinary people seems at best episodic, especially to the significant extent that they are shaped by the need to give form and meaning to an imagined, abstract loyalty.[16]

Thus, the sources and salience of ethnic group identification may vary greatly from group to group, circumstance to circumstance, and person to person, and hence it may be more or less a factor in personal identity. By its nature, therefore, ethnicity may explain little about any given individual. Certainly ethnicity does not provide us with much assistance in understanding the British immigrants whose letters are the foundations for our analysis of immigrant epistolarity. Though the extent of ethnic identification and organization varied among these English, Scottish, and Irish Protestant immigrants, in general, as we have seen, they manifested an ethnicity that was optional, shallow, and episodic at the public and group level. Ethnicity was certainly not mean-

Self as basis

ingless for them, but it lacked the salience it has possessed for those more culturally distinctive groups whose distance from the American majority, in such significant matters as language or religion, was much greater.

While ethnicity may explain little about any given individual, it is difficult to imagine an individual who is not engaged in the continuous project of composing a personal identity throughout the course of a lifetime. To be sure, in the context of North America, the British are an example of relatively low ethnicity in contrast, for example, to such peoples as Irish Catholics or Italians or Jews. But, as British examples of manifestations of ethnicity make clear—in such matters, in the first generation, as one's choice of friends and those with whom one informally socialized—ethnicity had as much, if not more to do with a hunger for continuity than with an ideological commitment to group membership or national affiliation. Such a desire for personal continuity was hardly the sole possession of the British emigrants to North America in the nineteenth century. To be a self, bearing a personal identity that situates us in space and time and within a framework of human relationships, is not the province of one people. It represents instead a basic element in the nature of being a human being. It is not exclusively a Western invention, for to believe that is to mistake the ideology of individualism, which is Western, for individuality or selfhood, which, to the extent that all individuals possess an evolving understanding of themselves as both physically and psychologically separate from as well as related to others, is human.[17] SPIRO

Emigration puts a singular strain on personal identity, because it is a radical challenge to continuity. It may set individuals adrift by sundering their relationships to places, things, and people. Not only does it remove, if only for a time, practical, material, and psychological sources of support, but it also disrupts the emigrant's own self-awareness, for it is through this continuous relationship to places, things, and above all, to other people, that we know ourselves.

Anthony Giddens has suggested that to be a self is to possess "the capacity *to keep a particular narrative going*"—that is, an autobiographical narrative emplotment of the individual life that, through reflection and recollection, establishes continuity over time and seeks to integrate the diverse elements of experience. If so, emigration is a profound challenge to the self-defining narrative of identity. The stakes involved for the emigrant, are, in fact, enormous. They ultimately involve alienation

what a masterful

from one's self and hence psychological chaos that few people could accept. As we shall see, even some emigrant men who appear to embrace a formless and chaotic existence, uprooting constantly and deserting their wives and children, and living as if there were nothing to their lives but the eternal experience of the present, end up writing letters, sometimes after decades, that seek to reestablish contact with family and friends. As Mark Freeman has written, "To live without narrative . . . is to live in an essentially meaningless perpetual present, devoid of form and coherence; it is to experience the world as disconnected and fragmented, an endless series of things that happen." If this formless perpetual present cannot link us to the past, it fails utterly as a route into the future, for without recollection and reflection, individuals lack a guide in plotting the course of their lives. Individual ways of narrative telling and the ways of mentally organizing experience that prove conducive to them, Jerome Bruner explains, "become so habitual that they finally become recipes for structuring experience itself." As such, they lay down routes into and from memory, which work at "not only guiding the life narrative up to the present but directing it into the future."[18]

Recent developments in a number of emerging bodies of knowledge —especially discourse theory and varieties of antibehaviorist psychology (both discursive and social constructionist psychologies)—assist us in understanding the foundations of the immigrant's second project and clarify the relation of the processes of selfhood to society and culture, and hence to history. What relevance might these schools of thought, conceived largely to understand people in twentieth-century modernity and postmodernity, have for understanding the lives of nineteenth-century British immigrants going to postfrontier societies in North America? The answer is, "A great deal." But it is necessary to open ourselves to the modernity of the experience of the international migrants of that historical epoch. Their lives were framed within boundaries set by the processes of modernization—emergent global capitalism and the international exchange of labor within the technologies and forms of organization of the time. They were buffeted by the instabilities and discontinuities, such as emigration and resettlement themselves, that necessitated adopting plural subject positionings appropriate to the shifting contexts of daily life common to modern individuals.

England (and, less evenly, its Welsh, Scottish, and Irish Celtic fringe) was the first society to undergo broad-scale modernization, and the United States was not far behind. Immigrants had a great deal of ambivalence about these world-transforming social processes, regarding them as holding out both material opportunity and insecurity. As they sorted out their choices, Europe represented insecurity and North America opportunity. But the cost of emigration—leaving all that was familiar—was only too well known to them. Personal correspondence under circumstances of international migration in the nineteenth century resulted from the related conditions of long-term separation among individuals, which was by no means a new phenomenon in history, and the opportunity made available by modernizing transportation and communication systems to continue routinely to maintain regular contact, which was a new phenomenon. This situation within emergent global modernity demanded that people develop the material, psychological, and cultural resources to read and write letters and to get and send them. In seeking to gather the resources to confront the immigrant's second project—to resolve the challenge posed to personal identity—immigrants experienced increasing self-awareness, for they took responsibility not only for the maintenance of their relationships, but also for accounting for themselves. To this extent, contemporary ideas about the nature of self actually are relevant for the understanding of David Laing and countless other immigrant letter-writers.

These connections suggest the need for a model of self at the outset of this inquiry. The view of self as the real or authentic person—a core or essence that may be summarized in a list of singular traits—lying buried deep within us has been replaced by a different conception. Self is now seen as a process, fluid and relational, that continuously works at integrating change and continuity to produce a coherence that is personal identity, and that individuals understand in narrative terms.[9] Two propositions advance the basic contentions that comprise this view. First, selves are never complete: they are active and volitional, redefining themselves, so that personal identity is not a given, but must be achieved dynamically. An extraordinary quality of human consciousness is reflexivity, which is the capacity to step back and reflect upon past and present experience, while simultaneously assimilating those reflections into our self-understanding, understanding of the world and understanding of the self in the world, and hence enabling them to guide our actions in the world. Reflexivity, Andrea Deciu Ritivoi says in a powerful study of immigrant self-understanding, unites the individual at different points in autobiographical time, and offers a means for making sense of the personal past and personal present. Immigrants, she writes, more than most people, are aware of this usually semiconscious mental work, for in leaving the original setting in which personal identity is formed, they are led to understand that the self is never a finished, integrated person, and that, in fact, another version of oneself exists who, through memory, "is always insidiously lurking into personal identity." The immigrants appearing in this book are especially unlikely to escape such knowledge, for their reflections on their own personal identity are often prompted by writing and the move from semiconscious mental activity to prose.[20]

Second, the self is not self-contained, a singular or unitary core, but multifaceted, so that it spreads out and changes across a broad field of social and interpersonal relations. We seem different people in different settings, but we are not protean, since we must be consistent with a personal past. Human beings certainly possess a desire for coherence in understanding themselves and a related awareness of themselves in terms of continuity—that is, a self-awareness. It is useful in conceptualizing these facets of self to make a distinction between self-as-object and self-as-process. Self-as-object is our objectified awareness of continuity. This is the knowledge that we possess that we are the same across time and space. It provides an understanding of our location relative to other human beings and to the various environments in which we live. Self-as-process is the continuing work of self-making amidst the creative work of living, in which experience becomes constitutive of being.[21]

What are the experiential and cognitive mechanisms of self-awareness? Much of the preceding discussion may seem to suggest that the self is transhistorical and transcultural, which obviously cannot be true, because however similar human beings may be in their basic nature, they have managed to create very different worlds. At the boundaries, processes of self-awareness are societal and cultural, and hence specific in time and place.[22] They are societal, because social structure is a significant determinant of the behavioral patterns and possibilities available in daily life. They are cultural, because all efforts, such as secular ideology and religion, to create and evaluate meaning in life and to evaluate the nature of self, are attained through language.

Consciousness of self-awareness itself has a varied, contingent history, which is reflected in the evolution of language and provides the vocabulary through which we can think of self. The nineteenth-century British immigrants whose letters we study were heirs to a language that had long been in the process of becoming an excellent vehicle for speaking of self. In English, *self* and *individual* began to take on their modern, vernacular meanings in the seventeenth century, and may be viewed as artifacts of the earliest phases of the transition to modern society. According to the *Oxford English Dictionary,* usages such as *self* (1674), *self-knowledge* (1634), *self-examination* (1647), and *self-consciousness* (1687) then entered the language.[23] In early modern England, these linguistic evolutions, which moved English toward a facility in the expression of the nature and the conditions of individuation, were complemented by various social and cultural manifestations of individuation, such as increasing freedom from family criteria in the choice of a mate, increasing privacy in living arrangements, and the proliferation of family and individual portraits, of mirrors and of chairs rather than benches.[24] Language and social practice worked to establish the growing recognition of the separateness of the individual person from an objective world and the emerging belief that a real, authentic person lay, hidden and protected, inside human beings. These developments have been explained as consequences of complex social, economic, and political processes, such as urbanization, the growth of capitalist markets and the expansion of the scope and scale of trade, and political democratization, by which England gradually became a modern society.

Through a longer, but for centuries parallel process of evolution, the grammar of English had by the seventeenth century already begun to evolve toward dropping, to a greater extent than any other European language, the encoding of social relations in the language, so that the choice of pronouns, for example, was no longer motivated by occasion or social status. Thus, as *thou* had devolved by the eighteenth century into dialect, and even Quakers increasingly dropped it, English came to have only one form of the pronoun *you,* establishing a rough linguistic equality between selves. Moreover, as Peter Mühlhäusler and Rom Harré have noted, while all languages have the capacity to express one-dimensional first-person statements, the English language became especially rich in vocabulary and constructions that make for commentary about self, self-awareness, others as selves, and boundaries between self and other.[25] Though use of this language of self requires technical facility with the manipulation of English, the quickening pace of the democratization of literacy in the English-speaking world in the nineteenth century implies the availability of this language to vast numbers of people, including our letter-writers, as the vehicle of self-awareness.

At the center of the processes of self-awareness are interpersonal relationships, which are framed at once by society and culture and by dynamic interpersonal processes. A long tradition of social psychological analysis, from William James and George Herbert Mead to contemporary social constructionists, has sought to clarify the place of others, whether as a generalized impersonal body or as individual significant others in ordinary relationships, in the development of self and self-awareness.[26] All analysts have agreed with the proposition that the self is social, and that there is a relationship between interpersonal relationships and intrapersonal consciousness. The self is social, therefore, not in the sense of a self-contained being that enters into relations with other self-contained individuals, but rather because others occupy our consciousness. Through intersubjectivity, the constant assimilation of the other, we gain consciousness of ourselves. Our relation to others, within the context of societal and cultural processes, is the principal stimulus to reflexivity, and the more significant the others, the more intense and lasting is their entry into the forming of self.[27]

Self and *other* mutually craft a world of shared meanings through language, and in consequence are bonded, so that neither may be thought of as self-contained. Language, as the Russian discourse theorist Mikhail Bakhtin explained, is a social process, rooted in social structure and culture, through which people exercise agency, achieve solidarity, and develop self-awareness—and, in short, achieve selfhood. In daily life, discourse, the ordinary exchange of information, opinions, attitudes, and views within the context of established social forms or texts, is the mechanism of these activities, and conversation is its principal manifestation.[28] But Bakhtin's is a dynamic understanding of conversation. "Language, when it means," said Bakhtin, "is somebody talking to somebody else, even when that someone is one's inner addressee." Conversations run in our heads as well as between speakers who are physically present to address each other, so that the processes of discourse, while always intersubjective and interpersonal, may be anticipatory and fictive as well as actual. Certainly in personal letters the voice of the other is always present, for the letter-writer composes for a particular, known individual in a process that is an implicit conversation with, or a psychological probing of, the addressee. Conversation or correspondence, much of the creative activity in living, consists of anticipating responses to one's utterances and, in consequence, crafting one's responses in certain ways suited to the other, while attempting not to sacrifice one's own individuality.[29]

Understanding the centrality of ordinary conversation in human life moves us closer to conceiving the foundations of immigrant epistolarity. Immigrants were barred by their situation from the nourishing, self-sustaining, social activity of conversation with those who had been among their most significant others. It was not nostalgia or family loyalty or isolation and loneliness by themselves that led David Laing to say he was "starving" for letter contact with Johan and his other sisters. Nor was it confusion that led him to confess, even as he demanded more frequently written responses to his letters, that he could not put to words what he needed to say about his many disappointments and failures, and that what he required was a conversation. What accounted for these positions was a hunger to resume his part in a basic human process that in multiple ways confirmed his being.

Yet for Laing and others there was no practical substitute for writing, so they strove to express themselves as best they could, and to exercise what Bruce Redford fittingly calls "the converse of the pen."[30] In this often painful effort, their personal letters need to be seen more as a discursive practice than a fixed literary genre. Personal letters have genre-like features, such as endearments and salutations, but they are texts that are deeply embedded in time, space, and singular personal circumstance. Real and changing human relationships pervade their purposes and processes. As consciousness is intersubjective, personal letters are intertextual, because the positions articulated in the letters of the other, as the writer interprets them, are implicit in the writer's responses.

But though they resemble conversation in their fluidity and variability, personal letters had to be written and read. The preparation these correspondents brought to the task in terms of their technical skills and abilities to express themselves is hardly a side issue. We turn now, therefore, to investigate skills brought to the task of writing and reading.

While there are many uncertainties about the representativeness of archived immigrant letters as a body of evidence and hence about their creators, one certainty stands—within a broad range of competencies, their authors were literate. Like a growing number of people throughout Europe in the nineteenth century, they knew how to read and to write their native language. Probably many who did not write letters were also literate, and though no instances have been discovered in the collections of archived letters used for this study, there were also probably individuals who were illiterate who paid someone to write letters, which were sent in their names, for them, or got the services of a friend toward the same end. (On the other hand, illiterates frequently participated in the cooperative, communal work of creating letters composed by groups of family and friends.) But though literacy may not make these letter-writers unique, it was nonetheless the sine qua non of corresponding, and may well tell us something about the correspondents and nineteenth-century immigrants in general that aids in the understanding of the creation and purposes of their letters.

At the start, this presence of literacy suggests the need to abandon the "huddled masses" stereotype of European immigrants in the historical past that views them as objects of pathos, who were not only victimized by, but also essentially ignorant of the forces at work in the world around them, and merely reactive and herdlike in their responses to those forces. The widespread literacy we observe among immigrants in the nineteenth century—and most certainly *British* immigrants—suggests that immigrants possessed capacities for obtaining information and larger perspectives on their worlds that were powerful tools in the struggle for control of their lives. While it is tempting to say that the incidence of literacy among British immigrants was uniquely high, we should at least take note of the fact that research on immigrant letters has been or is being done for a vast swath of Europe's international migrants, including among them many peoples often categorized in the ranks of the tradition-bound, premodern peasantry: Danish, Dutch, Finnish, German, Irish Catholic, Italian, Jewish, Lithuanian, Norwegian, Poles, Portuguese, Russian, Slovenian, Swedish, Ukrainian, and Welsh. We should remember, too, that while William I. Thomas might speak of the primitive culture level of the Polish peasantry, he depended on its letters and other writings in conceiving of the first great academic work of North American immigration studies. The "huddled masses" may have known a great deal more than they are usually given credit for knowing, and literacy might be more relevant to understanding them than we have previously conceived.

Historians and other analysts interested in the general role of literacy in society and culture have approached the matter in two distinct ways. One line of inquiry, associated with anthropologists, developmental psychologists, and communications theorists such as Jack Goody, A. R. Luria, Marshall McLuhan, David R. Olson, and Walter Ong, is concerned with the larger psychological and cultural consequences of literacy for the history of civilizations and of human consciousness.[31] It advances the view that the acquisition of literacy has been consequential for the development of skills in abstract thinking that constitute a qualitative leap in the tools available to human consciousness over those of a strictly oral culture. This perspective cannot be investigated at length here, but several aspects of the claims made in its defense are relevant for thinking about David Laing and others. It seems entirely plausible that both reading and writing letters prompt a particular sort of reflexive activity that is abstract and imaginative, and increases self-awareness.

Lacking the sound cues, such as intonation and degree of loudness, and body language, such as facial expression, which are available in oral conversation, Olson maintains, writers and readers must engage in a distinct type of conceptual and imaginative thinking in interpreting the other's written language and in writing their own.[32] As we shall see, the necessity of filling the gap between writing and speech poses a most significant challenge to technically deficient writers. The thinking required by the exercise of literacy, furthermore, as both Luria and Ong contend, may lend itself to an intense self-awareness and inwardness lacking among illiterates and in oral cultures generally. For Ong, because they are solitary activities, reading and writing provide an excellent context for reflection. Involvement in personal correspondence certainly had the potential, for some correspondents, to prompt self-reflection. Though by their nature, personal letters are social, because deeply embedded in real relationships, for correspondents like Laing the process of composing them was solitary, prompting the potential for confrontation with a conflicted or confused self.[33] Though the exercise seems to have been painful for him, Laing probably did grow in self-awareness as a consequence of being placed in the position by his sister's questions of having to interrogate the history of his marriage and to try to lay out the reasons for its failure on paper, even if he was ultimately not very successful in doing so. He was not alone in his acute, and often troubling, self-awareness. There are other correspondents also who make explicit reference to being aware of themselves straining to think as they wrote, as if they could actually feel themselves struggling with self-consciousness.

However, at least two of the foundations of the larger argument often advanced for the uniqueness of literacy—that it constitutes a definite break with the culture of orality, and that, relatedly, its benefits arise partly out of the fact that it is practiced in isolation from others, in contrast to oral communication—cannot be sustained in generalizing about all nineteenth-century immigrant epistolarity. The lines between oral and literate cultures were constantly crossed in the nineteenth century.[34] This is especially the case in much of immigrant personal correspondence, for just as some letters, such as Laing's to his sister, are intensely private, others are just as intensely communal, or at least collaborative. From the perspective of either reading or writing, letters were frequently not a simple one-to-one exchange between individuals, and neither letter-reading nor letter-writing necessarily led to withdrawal from social interaction. In consequence, we must note that not only do different types of texts obviously spring from different strategies of creation, but that also the same kinds of texts, in this case personal letters, may themselves be created in a variety of ways.[35]

Historians have long been aware of the extent to which literacy was a skill that was shared. In many cases, whether at the writing or the reading stages, the immigrant letter was intensely communal, which also assisted correspondents in keeping down postal expenses. In Sweden and Norway, we have long known, immigrant letters were read in public, and widely circulated for that purpose (though it was not always the intention of the letter-writer that this be done) so that illiterates could gain access to them.[36] Though reading personal letters before strangers seems to have been much less common in Britain, letters most certainly were read aloud in the family circle, and seem authored by some correspondents with that end in view. Such letters reveal, as Wendy Cameron, Sheila Haines, and Mary McDougall Maude observe in their collection of English working-class immigrant letters sent from Canada, that the letters they reprinted were cowritten in various arrays of authorship. Sometimes they appeared in the handwriting of several writers, and other times in the handwriting of the writer with the best penmanship. As the letters consulted for this study suggest, such collaborations could be very extensive. For example, George Simons, who immigrated to North Royalton, Ohio, from England in about 1840, and five of the friends and kin who emigrated with him coauthored a joint letter to parents, friends, and relatives, in response to a joint letter they had received. Each of the six of them took turns addressing someone in England, and all of them together united to address one recently married young couple, whom they sought to persuade to join them in Ohio. It seems clear that the privacy of the communications to each addressee in this long, scroll-like letter could not be preserved, and that the letter might well have been meant to be read aloud in a group setting.[37]

More common was the cooperation of a married couple in jointly composing a letter. Joseph Hartley, a stonecutter who left Yorkshire in 1858 for work in the quarries outside Lockport, New York, and his wife Rebecca, a Cambridgeshire emigrant he met in Lockport, together composed a number of letters to his family after their marriage in 1861. Joseph wrote poorly and with difficulty, but was dedicated to corresponding, so Rebecca took charge of the writing. Yet Joseph's voice intrudes regularly to let us know he is assisting. On one occasion, for example, Rebecca records the discussion they are having simultaneously to composing the letter about whether to include information about what she is preparing for dinner in the letter. (Rebecca insisted on writing that they were having peas from their garden; Joseph argued that no one would be interested in such trivia; she prevailed through her control over the narration of their discussion!) It is difficult to know the incidence of these epistolary practices with any precision, for not only do they vary among all correspondents, but also from letter to letter within any single collection. In the case of the Hartleys, some of their letters are collaborative, while some seem written by Rebecca alone, especially as his health declined due to a lung disease common to stonecutters.[38]

Thus, whatever the exact circumstances of joint creation or reception, the immigrant letter often simultaneously had pronounced communal and oral aspects that make its interpretation a more complicated matter than can be accommodated by stark archetypes of literate versus oral cultures. There is an important sense, therefore, in which it often does not matter in the cycle of immigrant correspondence to whom these letters were addressed or, where we find composite authorship, who claimed to write them, for the mutual dependencies of oral and written cultures ensured that those of marginal literacy or no literacy might have their voices represented in letters sent and might be addressed in letters received. That a letter was composed by several people did not preclude all but one of them from being illiterate, while a letter addressed to all members of a family might only find but one of them capable of reading it.

But immigrant personal correspondence did not always have such intensely communal aspects, and to that extent, it sometimes did have effects that make the claims of Ong and others seem valid. Letters like

those exchanged between Laing and his sister have a confessional quality the thrust of which leads them to resemble the qualities and the consequences that Karen Lystra identified as present in love letters. The
context of intimacy and candor, repeated in continuous individual written acts of "self-examination and self-disclosure," present in love letters, Lystra claims, does lend itself to accepting the introspective notion
that there exists a singular, individuated, true self within us—one somehow better, more coherent and authentic, than that which we show to
most others.[39] While this is not true—for we are surely ourselves, for
better or worse, all the time—it is certainly the self we appreciate the
most. We must, however, keep in mind that like the love letter, the confessional generally is not representative of immigrant letters. Whether
this is an artifact of a collection process that culled the intensely private
letters from bodies of saved letters because of embarrassment or concerns about privacy, or of the fact that most immigrants had little to
confess and defined themselves mostly in the context of their deeply
communal familial relations, is difficult to know.

The second analytical perspective on literacy is associated with social
historians who have sought to understand, within various historical settings, the motivations of those who worked at becoming literate, the
institutional contexts and informal settings in which literacy might have
been acquired in the historical past, the differentials in the acquisition
of literacy among various social groups, the correlations between literacy and socioeconomic mobility, and the relationships between literate
and illiterate people within the same society. Because nineteenth-century
Britain witnessed a notably rapid democratization of literacy, much
has been written about these questions for that century, by the end of
which literacy was common throughout the population. The recognition exists, however, that the foundations of universal literacy were
laid in the previous two centuries with the development of mechanical
printing technology, the expansion of publishing, the expansion of state
employment, and the rise of publicly and especially privately funded
opportunities to acquire basic literacy. Well into the nineteenth century,
charity schools, Sunday schools, small, local "dame schools," and private instruction by literate parents accounted for more of the responsibility for literacy instruction than did state-funded activities.[40]

What emerges from this immense literature that is of interest to us
concerns both who became literate and why, and the process of becoming literate. The first set of findings establishes that there existed a great

popular desire for literacy that may not be explained as a product of socioeconomic aspirations. Literacy was no guarantee of better employment except at the highest end of the economy in the professions and in commerce. Nor was illiteracy a bar to improvement for the vast majority of male workers. Craftsmen depended on practical knowledge and skills learned through apprenticeship, and numeracy was probably more important to them than literacy. Industrial workers did not profit from the acquisition of literacy. Kinship ties continued to be responsible for job placement, not the roster of qualifications, education prominent among them, that would come more consequential in the twentieth century. Women workers also profited from literacy at the high ends of employment, probably to a greater extent than men in proportion to their total numbers. But the total effect of literacy on women's employment was probably not great, since fewer worked for wages and most were employed in domestic and personal service or in factories, where literacy was of less consequence.[41]

If the pursuit of socioeconomic opportunity does not appear to have been much enhanced by literacy, the strong desire for literacy we find among ordinary men and women may instead be explained by the desire to improve the quality of life through enhancing personal development. As David Vincent observes, "The exercise of the imagination was the greatest and most persistent incentive for gaining a command of the tools of literacy, and their first and most satisfying application." The great expansion in the publication of Bibles, popular literature (from the race track gazette to the small political magazine), guidebooks for prospective emigrants, and cheap editions of significant works of history, natural science, poetry, and fiction in the late eighteenth and particularly in the nineteenth century, was evidence of these aspirations for cultivation, self-improvement, and respectability. Even the estates of the working poor in Britain increasingly contained books. Such aspirations for self-improvement existed as family traditions too. Literate parents were 20 percent more likely than illiterate ones to have children who were literate.[42]

Some of our letter-writers make reference from time to time to their own reading, which covers a wide variety of genre, and in doing so, suggest not only what their tastes were, but also the ways in which literacy was shared within families and among friends. Titus Crawshaw, a textile artisan who left Huddersfield for Philadelphia in 1853, wrote his father to alert him to consult Titus's "favorite work, the *Botanic*

Guide," which he knew to be in his parents' house, in seeking cold remedies. John Fisher, who called the books he had brought to the United States from his parents' home his "greatest treasure," claimed to spend his lonely, bachelor evenings on his Michigan farm "with . . . Milton, . . . Young, and many more excelent writers who adorn my libery."[43] In general, however, within communities and families, complex patterns of literacy and degrees of proficiency existed. Neither the literate nor the illiterate were isolated from one another. Literates married illiterates; siblings might be literate in the case of one and illiterate in the case of another. Oral and literate cultures intermingled in complex patterns. Reading aloud within families frequently gave illiterates access to literate culture.[44]

The increasing desire for literacy in the middling and lower reaches of the social structure was satisfied by the massive growth of top-down initiatives at privately and publicly funded education that spread out unevenly throughout British society. In England, literacy was greater in the Midlands and the South, and in the cities and market and commercial towns than in rural areas, and the industrial population lagged somewhat behind the rest of society. Scotland witnessed what was probably the first national literacy campaign in the world in the century and a half before 1800, and near-universal literacy was reached by the mid-nineteenth century, a generation before England. In Scotland, urban areas and the Lowlands manifested greater literacy than the rural areas and the Highlands, where English-language instruction might be increasingly available, but was nonetheless instruction in a foreign language. In Ireland, similar differentials between the incidence of rural and urban literacy existed, but were complicated by differences between the greater literacy of Protestants and of Ulster relative to Catholics and the rest of the island. Important differentials in male and female access to literacy existed, especially in England, as a consequence of institutional provision, employment patterns, and parental desires. In 1855, 87 percent of both men and women could sign their names in Scotland, but a comparable figure did not exist in England until about 1885, when the gap between men and women was finally closed. Schooling for girls was less common in England during 1800–1870 than for boys except in rural areas, where the relative lack of employment opportunities led girls to go to school in relatively larger numbers than boys.[45]

These patterns have been established in research that traces the growth of a particular sort of literacy—*signature literacy*. The ability

Scotland lead the way? Why?

how girls got more schooling than boys.

to sign one's name has been established by consulting the ubiquitous parish marriage registers, because brides and grooms and their witnesses were asked to provide their signatures, or mark an "X," to attest to their identities. Since the ability to sign one's name was thought to be a less useful skill for most people than the ability to read, it was taught after reading, so evidence of writing ability, it is assumed, also establishes the incidence of the ability to read. Extensive writing, beyond signature literacy itself, was the last literacy skill taught.[46]

The implications of these stages in the process of acquiring the tools of literacy that separated instruction in reading and writing for our understanding of immigrant epistolarity is significant, because we are able to clarify with greater precision the relative position of our letter-writers in terms of their literacy skills. British immigrants, in general, seem to have been a highly literate cohort. In a study of literacy in the Canadian cities of Hamilton, London, and Kingston in the mid-nineteen century, which used signature literacy as its standard, Harvey Graff discovered that British Protestant immigrants, among the most literate groups in these cities, were more literate than the societies that they had left in England, Ireland, and Scotland; that their relatively high literacy crossed class lines; and that they came from the regions in Britain which we have already identified as possessing relatively high literacy.[47] Basic skills of the type needed for epistolary communication would appear to have been widely proliferated within the immigrant population, independent of the degree of formal education, craft skill, or occupation. But within this accomplished population, immigrant letter-writers would appear to be at the top of the pyramid of literates, because they possessed the ability to do extensive writing.

Women, however, form the exception. Not only was schooling less available to the majority of nonelite young women, but so, too, was education in literacy beyond reading, which helps to explain the lag until the late nineteenth century in England between women's and men's ability both to read and to write. Women did not require the ability to write by virtue of employment or civil status. They were less frequently formally schooled in writing, though the possibility certainly existed for informal instruction from parents, siblings, and friends.[48] One way to account for the fact that the overwhelming majority of archived collections of nineteenth-century British immigrant letters are written by men, and that even when cosigned by husband and wife, the man's voice nonetheless predominates, is that writing was a skill less proliferated

among women than among men. Women might have been readers, and
they might have learned to sign their names, but they may have lacked
access to learning the skills for doing extensive writing, and thus, unlike
Rebecca Hartley, been unable to compose a letter.

Large generalizations about cohorts which possessed and did not
possess the various skills that comprise literacy mask a wide spectrum
of technical abilities to manipulate language. The qualitative dimension
of literacy, however, is difficult to write about with precision, if only because there is an important sense in which men and women who could
make themselves understood in their letters have all the ability they
require. But technical ability does set limits on what can and cannot be
written, and hence understood by readers, so it seems worthwhile to
open a discussion of just what it is that might be meant by "technical
ability."

We might dismiss at the outset a narrow definition of technical competence that focuses exclusively on what for the present-day reader
appear the most glaring, visible aspects of writing defects. This would
include poor spelling, poor spatialization (paragraphization and punctuation), poor grammar (in the traditional sense of rules governing the
coordination of elements of language), and "incorrect" (which is to say
vulgar, colloquial, or dialectic) usage. It is possible to err in all such
matters and still produce a text that readers can understand, which, in
fact, is often the case in immigrant letters. But we also need to note that
written English had gone a long way toward standardization in such
matters by the mid-nineteenth century. Spreading outward from London
and elite social classes from the late sixteenth and early seventeenth
centuries to rural areas, the provinces, the Celtic periphery, and ple-
beian and working classes in the nineteenth century, the process of standardization was speeded by the proliferation of published dictionaries,
grammars, handbooks, and less directly by literature and the King
James Bible, and by persistent propaganda in behalf of the Queen's (or
King's) English, especially in speech but also in writing. This is not to
say that the language remained frozen in some elite model of proper
English, which was then forced on people. But there was a widespread
consciousness of a linguistic movement toward standardization at every
level of society and in many institutional settings. This was characterized by the decline of regional dialects; the increasing unity of models
of respectable written and spoken English; and a growing uniformity
of spelling, which was perhaps the best regulated aspect of English in

terms of the imposition of models of uniformity. Punctuation was less well-regulated, in part because nineteenth-century sentences were longer than sentences would be in the twentieth. Hence, they seemed to encourage more devices, and in direct proportion more idiosyncratically placed ones, for setting off their parts from one another. Grammar was not fixed in the way that spelling had become by 1800, though the considerable degree of individual variation observed in published work did come increasingly to be remarked on critically thereafter.[49]

What this variable evolution amounts to is a language moving toward standardization, but in the midst of considerable transition, such that at the least it is not easy to define technical ability precisely. Withal, therefore, it is interesting to note the considerable uniformity in these technical aspects of English in the archived letters. To be sure, not everyone spells well, punctuates consistently, or always writes grammatically. But what is interesting is the degree to which, on balance, throughout all the collections, there is evidence of writers straining to meet the requirements of a standardized language. The error detected in Ann Whittaker's letter in the last chapter, for example, of adding an "h" to the verb form "is" ("My dear brother, if you have not begin to serve the Lord it his high time to be up and doing."),[50] is one of the relatively common and consistent impositions that we detect of dialect on the standard written language. What is noteworthy is how conscious the contemporary reader of a large number of these letters becomes of such usages, because, though *individual* errors abound, there are so few examples of *consistent* nonstandard English of the type that Whittaker employs. Under any circumstance, errors might as easily be ascribed in many cases to hurried writing done under poor conditions, without opportunities for revision, as to ignorance of or indifference to standard English.

Though they may well make efforts at reading quite difficult for the present-day reader, such technical deficiencies do not reveal much about immigrant letter-writing. Though they sometimes apologize for poor technical competence as well as poor handwriting or smeared ink, the writers never threaten to stop writing letters because they have done it so poorly. They vow instead to persevere and to improve. Such deficiencies, including even the lack of punctuation, do not often greatly intrude on conveying meaning.

In contrast, a poor grasp of skills of a higher, conceptual order did set limits on writing. Spoken language has its conventions, but they are more or less exercised synchronously and spontaneously, and hence mostly not admitted to the conscious mind during conversation. In contrast, written language requires, within the specific context of a particular genre, at least three interwoven, conscious processes: planning to achieve goals that are both appropriate and sustainable; the generation of related sentences that convey meaning; and revision to correct errors, inconsistencies, and unclear formulations, whether done simultaneously with the writing of a "first draft," or in the composition of a "second draft" on a clean sheet of paper.[51] Within the framework of these more demanding competencies, immigrant British letter-writers demonstrated an extraordinary range of expertise in thematic coherence, internal integration, and control of language.

At the high end of the literacy continuum, we might imagine the Scottish immigrant Mary Ann Archbald. Archbald, who settled on a farm in central New York State in 1807 with her husband and four children, worked at cultivating her mind and perfecting her writing throughout her life. She read fiction, poetry, and newspapers, and kept copybooks in which she entered quotations from her readings and her own fugitive thoughts. While her method of composition is not precisely known, it seems likely that she usually wrote a draft of all or parts of each letter before perfecting a final text. She kept exact transcriptions of some of her letters in a copybook in order to preserve a record of her writing, and to work further to improve upon it. Her letters are almost always technically correct in regard to spelling, spatialization, and grammar, and they are written in a fine, steady hand that is practiced with a pen. But that is not the mark of their expertise, so much as the fact that they frequently display explicit self-analysis and complex analysis of the character of others; explicit and implicit voicing of those with whom she exchanged letters (especially her friend since childhood and constant correspondent, Margaret Wodrow); narration of complex circumstances; and critical views of her own perspectives. In contrast to Carolyn Heilbrun's view of the writing of nonelite women as not only lacking narrative complexity, but also "a clear sense of self" based on anything but their immediate personal relationships, Archbald's letters reveal a strong sense of self rooted in the narratives of not only her place in women's accustomed sphere, the family, but also in her participation in the community and in history. In short, she delivers the sort of writing most readers of this book would find laudable in execution and rewarding to read both in style and content.[52]

Toward the opposite end of the continuum, there is John Barker, a blacksmith and farmer who emigrated from Scotten in Lincolnshire with his family and settled near Connersville, Indiana, in 1853. Both in the literal and interpretive senses, Barker's letters are, to say the least, difficult to read, until one becomes practiced in decoding them. His handwriting is certainly legible, but his spelling is poor, if consistent in its errors, so that the reader eventually figures out that, for example, "whe" is "we" and "noe won" is "no one" or "none," though "noe" may also serve for "now."[53] Beyond that, however, there are many more profound impediments, the most basic and obvious of which grow out of a common problem in the writing of those unpracticed writers who never learned more than the rudiments of written language. Barker appears to be attempting in his letters to realize the cadences of the spoken word and of human conversation. It is not that he consciously wants to achieve a chatty tone of informality in order to deflate the pomposity of written language. Nor is it that he is unpracticed and anxious about whether the writing is effective, and therefore awkwardly falls back occasionally on some speech conventions, such as direct address (i.e., frequently calling out the addressee by name), in fear that without them points will not be registered on the reader.[54] Instead he fails to understand that he cannot do on paper what he does in speech. He helps prove by his failure that, as Peter Burke has observed, written language is not so much a transcription of speech, as a translation of it.[55] Without the assistance of body language, intonation, and other illocutionary cues, he needs to fill the void with written cues, but he does not know how to do that. The result is a scroll-like recitation, without clear sentence or paragraph boundaries, that resembles what we might expect if, after a long absence, we had met an enthusiastic, but scatterbrained friend, and asked the question, "So, what's new?"

His six-page letter of December 21, 1856, which is not addressed to anyone in particular at its inception, provides an example. There are no introductory endearments or formalities. Formal spatial boundaries are virtually nonexistent; there are no paragraphs in Barker's letter. There are no punctuation marks or capital letters to set off the beginning and ending of sentences, and there is no punctuation to provide internal division within the discrete thoughts that appear to be sentences. Thoughts and themes intrude unpredictably in the middle of other thoughts and themes, but none of them seems to achieve completion. The net effect is chaos. When relating, for example, that his daughter Fanny had the opportunity to go into service at a good wage,

Barker broke into the recitation of the compensation she was offered with, "but ower girls did not com to america to be in sarvis I want faney for to wate on mee but I be leeve it wheant be long for she is all ways as a Charmeh."[56] In other words, he wants Fanny to wait on him; and anyway, paid service should be considered beneath her in America, unlike in Britain; and besides, she is so charming, she will probably be married shortly. (Fanny was, in fact, soon married.)

Barker's inability to create narrative priorities and to separate large and small themes at times had peculiar results for our comprehension. In his next letter, which is written in the same run-on fashion with the same multilevel difficulties, Barker relates a trip to Cincinnati, which somehow also has to do with problems in getting along with Barton, one of his sons, but then suddenly breaks in with the narrative of the near-drowning of another son, William.

> I thought I would tell you one thing with tears in my eyes wen I was rit-ing this the day after I came from the sittey it was Sunday william & Edward & Barton went to waid in the River wich is not deep generely but william was go en a bout the midel of his Boddey when he droped in a ole rite over is head not having time to Call out william Canot swim.[57]

The relation ends with Edward's observation of his brother's difficulty, and his quick actions to save him from drowning, but it slips in the midst of this relation into a brief discussion of Barker's mistake in hiring Edward out to work for too little money. We might have easily missed the near-tragedy for being stuck on exactly what happened in Cincinnati. If ever there were a writer who might have profited from beginning his composition with an outline, or revising his first draft, it was Barker, for with enough practice he might have eventually come to understand that writing was not conversation and that he had to fill the gaps that resulted from the vast differences between the two forms of discourse. But there is no evidence that he recognized the need to do so. When confronted by the suggestion that he might plan his writing and become more effective in consequence, he would probably have an-swered that he did not have the time, and that he was hardly going to let horses go unshod and lose business to his competitors, while he perfected skills that seemed unnecessary. Besides, paper was often in short supply, and it was expensive, so why waste it with exercises in writing practice?

But to say that the present-day reader has problems reading Barker is not necessarily to say that his contemporaries did. While some letter-writers of all degrees of competency frequently apologize for the difficulties they experience in writing, it is significant to note how seldom they acknowledge that they have been corrected or upbraided for technical incompetence by those on the other end of their correspondence. (There is certainly no evidence that Barker's kinfolk objected to his chaotic writing, which was also rich in anecdotes and full of astute judgments and strong opinions, and thus interesting reading—once one figures out how to read it.) Correspondents do negotiate the issue of what it is to be written about, but seldom how it is written from the technical perspective. They wanted different content, not better grammar. Margaret Wodrow wanted more descriptions of and stories out of daily life from Mary Ann Archbald.[58] The father and sister of Dr. Thomas Steel desired vicarious tourism in the form of descriptions of the United States. Moreover, because they had a tentative understanding with Thomas that eventually they would join him in Wisconsin, they wished to know more about the area in which he lived.[59] But this is different than protesting against poor workmanship. We have few examples of that, and when they appear, they may tell us more about the relationship between parties than about writing and reading as such. In one persistent case, for example, charges of inadequacy were the product of the habitual tutelage by John Kerr, the Irish Protestant bookkeeper and sometime schoolteacher, of his younger siblings in a family of four long-orphaned brothers. These examples, we need to note, are among correspondents who practiced to one extent or another high-end literacy, and were probably much more attuned to errors, even small ones, than the more marginally literate, who either did not know the difference between poor and excellent writing or did not care.[60]

On balance, then, most immigrant letter-writers usually succeeded in conveying their meanings sufficiently that such protests were not necessary. One could write poorly from a technical standpoint, and somehow still project a distinctive voice, show considerable imagination, and tweak the curiosity, stir the feelings, and inspire the concern of one's readers. Of course, readers may well have been too polite to criticize. They may have wondered, too, if their own letters were any more competent, and hence settled for a correspondence in which all parties tried to do the best they could, and hoped to improve with time. Many immigrants did improve their letter-writing skills over time, especially when they began corresponding when young and inexperienced in writing. For example, the archived letters of James Horner, an Irish Protestant who went to Philadelphia in 1801 from the Londonderry area as a young man, encompass ten years, during which there is a gradual, ultimately dramatic improvement in the quality of the writing. In that decade, Horner was exposed to and purposely cultivated opportunities that would improve his comfort with written language and ultimately his own writing. He worked as a typemaker; learned a number of intellectual skills, such as navigation; taught school and served as a private tutor in the homes of prominent families; and maintained a general store. His first letters had no common threads tying them together, and jumped from topic to topic, while committing many technical errors. His final letters show much greater control of language; spin out metaphors about time and experience; and generalize convincingly about the United States and local society in Maryland, where he was residing.[61]

Horner's path to improvement—cultivating his mind over time through practical activities and practicing his writing through writing letters and reading other people's letters to him—seems a more common route than the quick fixes that were then available: books of instruction that provided instant models of appropriate letters for different occasions, or the visit to an amanuensis, who promised for a fee to spin out one's thoughts into correct, coherent, and integrated prose. While the contention that they were not in common use is unprovable, books of instruction do not seem to have been employed among immigrant letter-writers. There is no reference to their use, let alone their existence, in the letters read for this study. What the immigrant and homeland writers had to report to their families and friends was probably too varied and complex to be fit into the framework of models that specialized—even when they sought, as British manuals did, to focus their attention on the instruction of ordinary men and women—in such particularized purposes as expressing romantic love in the midst of an infatuation, thanking a hostess for dinner, and making an application for an apprenticeship or employment.[62] Furthermore, such manuals were not always consumed for the explicit purposes for which their authors intended them. In eighteenth-century England, Ruth Perry discovered, they instructed readers more in how to think and feel in diverse social settings than in specific elements of epistolary style.[63] In nineteenth-century France and

Italy, these books, which presented extended series of letters between, say, lovers, are known to have often been read for their fantasy value, as if they were epistolary novels, and not as instructional manuals.[64]

Perhaps the real influence of these manuals was that their existence alone, apart from the question of whether they were actually consulted and who consulted them, created an aura around letter-writing that suggested it required special manners and eloquence. Even in the nineteenth century, when the continental manuals came to espouse a natural, conversational tone, it was probably nonetheless a tone unlike that of any conversation in which most nonelite people had ever taken part.[65] The echoes of such beliefs, which were ultimately founded in the longtime association of epistolarity with cultural and political elites, may be seen occasionally when a quite ordinary writer begins a letter with the formal, "I now take up my pen," and engages in numerous, often misspelled and awkward expressions of *politesse*.[66] Very few, however, bothered to make such gestures. Perhaps, they sensed, there was a contradiction at the very heart of the message of these guides. On the one hand, the guides increasingly placed a considerable emphasis on the authenticity of the feelings and ideas presented in the letter; on the other hand, they sought to teach what to think and feel. Perhaps useful for such common formal tasks immigrants faced as writing attorneys about inherited property in the homeland, guidebook instruction must have seemed, for those tempted to depend on it, especially inappropriate in addressing parents and siblings with whom one had been interacting and conversing all one's life.

Getting practical assistance for a price from a professional was an alternative, though a costly one. Here and there, we do find traces of just such a strategy for instant improvement. Robert Smyth, an Irish Protestant, immigrated to Philadelphia from a village in Antrim in 1837 to join a recently emigrated brother and a long-resident uncle, who owned a distillery. He provides an example of someone who appears to have sought professional assistance, and in doing so, demonstrates the limitations of such dependence. Robert did not write poorly, though his letters tended to be composed of one long paragraph, largely unbroken by punctuation and filled with erratic capitalization. But he easily made himself understood. Yet prompted by the freedom from parental and village controls and stimulated by the excitement of Philadelphia, which he praised in an early letter to his parents, Smyth seems to have enjoyed experimenting with his identity, and played various games in his letters testing the credulity of the people at home.[67] In his letters, he created an aura of mystery, independence, and masculine toughness around himself, especially relative to his brothers. His letters in the first years after arrival do not say where he is living or what employment he has, and only hint at the relations he has with his relatives in Philadelphia. They suggest various indulgences, including sexual adventures,[68] a true rarity in men's letters. If they ever broach the subject of sexuality at all, they do so indirectly, and only for the sake of assuring the wife or girlfriend left behind of uninterrupted constancy. Eventually he would contend that he owed a position he claimed to have at the Philadelphia customs house to the fact that President Tyler "is a particular friend of mine." He explained that while on a trip in a western state to buy stock, he had whipped a man who had besmirched the president's honor.[69]

Why not in the midst of these experimentations, also attempt to write a vastly improved letter, one with pretensions to cultural sophistication? His fourth letter to his parents, in 1839, marked a sudden departure from his ordinary adequacy as a writer. The handwriting is different, and there are several stock, polite introductory and transitional phrases he had previously not used before: "I cannot let slip such a favorable opportunity of writing to you . . . ; I will endeavor to fill up these few lines with the true sentiments of my mind . . . ; I will now leave of this and let you know a little about the state of this Country at present."[70] Yet in general the syntax remained as twisted and unpredictable as ever. Whomever he was depending on probably was not much more skillful than Smyth himself, which might well have led him to his eventual decision to save himself the trouble and expense, and return to writing his own letters. His competencies would also improve over time. Others, too, might have learned to trust their own abilities, and not those of strangers whom they had to pay.

There is a larger point to be made about trusting one's own abilities, perhaps assisted in some cases by those within the intimate circle of one's friends or family in writing letters, and not those of paid strangers or of published authorities. Much has been written in recent decades, owing to the seminal work of Foucault and Barthes, about the tenuousness of the concept of authorship in light of certain qualities of texts, especially the variety of modes for creating them and their multiple purposes. The private letters of ordinary writers, Foucault argues, have signers not authors, because they are not the expressions of

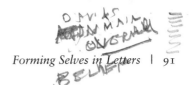

a creative and self-conscious mind, but social documents intended to spread information.[71] Immigrant letter-writers would have disagreed, and not merely because their letters were aimed at doing much more than spreading information. In insisting upon writing their own letters —whether as individuals in the case of David Laing, or as a couple in the case of Rebecca and Joseph Hartley, or as a group in the case of George Simons and his four cowriters—and signing them in order to establish their authorship, the overwhelming majority of them took responsibility for what they wrote, and stated, in effect, that their letters were an authentic representation of themselves at the time they wrote. Their frequent apologies for a lack of mastery of technicalities, for poor treatment of subject-matter, or for hurried execution, and for sloppy presentation underscore the extent to which they felt the need to take such responsibility. But whether they took pride in meeting their own goals, or felt ashamed for failing to do so, it was not because they felt the artist's responsibility for the integrity or beauty of the language, though a few of them, such as Mary Ann Archbald, certainly were not indifferent to that consideration. Instead, the depth of their respect and affection for those with whom they corresponded was being tested in their writing, and through this connection, so too was the integrity of the writer's personal identity. This was the source of their exercise of creativity in authoring their letters, and it encouraged them to improve their writing and to aim at making it interesting and readable. In this sense, their acts of authorship were acts of self-building, at once individual, but also deeply social to the extent that in personal letters as in conversation, selves are authored in answering another.[72]

To speak of this sort of authenticity—the faithful execution of an obligation to maintain a bond—is hardly to imply that everything written in these letters was true, that every word was actually the writer's own, or that letters somehow reveal the true, core self of the writer. Letters were less objective, factual reports, though they do contain substantial factual information, than devices for sustaining relationships and in doing so, confirming identities. What is true or authentic about these identities is that they sustained the individual letter-writer's desire to maintain a bond with the reader that achieves continuity. Faithfulness lay in the commitment to continue the correspondence. That letters might show evidence of self-deception or the deception of others is only to say that letters bore all the cumbersome baggage that relationships assume, and all the complexity of the people who wrote them.

3

Writing with a Purpose
Immigrant Epistolarity and the
Culture of Emigration

Immigrant personal correspondence became necessary because of the separation that resulted from emigration in an age before
instantaneous electronic communications and rapid means of transportation made it likely that intercontinental migrations need not be lifelong or eventuate in long silences. The desire for continuity necessitated
that personal relationships sundered in time and space be reformulated
and renegotiated. The letter served as the medium for doing so, but for
correspondents the letter soon passed from a medium for a relationship
to, in a practical sense, the relationship itself, for relationships became
constituted through words on paper.

Immigrants and those they left behind in their homelands formed a
transnational culture of emigration, which, though defined ultimately
by relationships that had existed in the homeland, united new and old
worlds in the singular transnational space of the letter. The concept of
culture is used in this context to suggest the mutually and continuously
constructed ideas, attitudes, and feelings that united emigrants and
those with whom they kept in contact in Britain. These aspects of culture were not fixed and formalized, but instead operated in a wide conceptual space where meanings that assist in making sense of the world
were sought and formed, and served to guide behavior.[1] At the heart
of this culture in the nineteenth century was personal correspondence,
which was neither in the homeland nor the new world, but rather on
paper and "in the mail," and overcame temporal and physical boundaries. International migrants began to participate in this culture before
leaving for their destinations. To the extent that they had read or heard
the letters of other international migrants read, and been party to the
excitement that surrounded the arrival of letters from distant places,

they had already entered into thinking about the meanings of the exchange of international mail with those who were thousands of miles away and likely never to be seen again, and who were only known year after year through their writings.

Even before the twentieth century, significant numbers of international migrants conceived of their emigrations and separations from family and friends as temporary. Their intentions were to return to their homelands, permanently or at least for a visit, or to send for their families. It was very common for the emigrants whose letters were read for this study to announce in their early letters that they were planning to come home for a visit within a few years. Was the imperative to renegotiate significant relationships in personal correspondence weaker when many possessed these goals? The letters in these archived collections and published work on international migrations would seem to indicate it was not.

The time frames suggested for even these putatively temporary separations tended to be indeterminate to the extent that a strong element of wishful thinking, as opposed to deliberate planning, seemed to have been at work. If reunion took place at all, it took considerably longer than originally anticipated to achieve it. A variety of unanticipated contingencies, such as illness, injury, unemployment, war, and the loss of savings, played havoc with individual plans. But at least as often, minds changed in their resolve to return when it became clear in toting up the positives and negatives of remaining in lands of resettlement that one had already made a considerable investment in a new life and needed to put all one's energies and savings into making it successful. These same contingencies and calculations worked in the other direction as well, for people changed their minds about emigrating to join those who had previously left. Thus, correspondents whose initial letters discuss facilitating and scheduling a speedy return or reunion or acceleration of the chain of migration to a new world, with the passage of time often slip over into another type of writing that is focused on sustaining epistolary bonds among those confronting long-term or permanent separation.[2] Under any circumstance, any given immigrant's network was rarely completed in the land of resettlement. There were usually people of significance to the immigrant who remained in the homeland. They were people whose age, or poor health, or relative security, or personal or material obligations made it unnecessary or impossible to consider emigration. Thus, there seemed always someone left behind to write to, perhaps if only to maintain a connection to an increasingly distant past. Eventually these correspondents would become infirm with age or die, or simply grow too emotionally distant to have much to say to those to whom they had been writing. But we are nonetheless left needing to understand that it was not only the "pioneers" of an emigration cohort that participated in this culture of emigration, but also the later waves of migrants, and in a few cases, even their North American-bred children.

The culture of emigration, about which historians have just begun to ask significant questions as they open up transnational space for analytical exploration, united the experiences in migration of millions of immigrants, whatever their national origins. Writing home and reading replies was common to the great diversity of peoples whose migrations spanned the globe in the nineteenth century. What this meant in making these immigrants—British, Chinese, Sikhs, Polish, Irish, Mexican, Japanese, Jews, Italians, Serbs, Greeks, Norwegians, Turks, and dozens of other groups—knowable to one another, and in defining the measure of their experience of uprooting and resettlement, across all the lines that otherwise divided them and even as their separate ethnic identifications were forming, may be one of the great unexplored themes in international social history.

In this chapter, the negotiations that surrounded writing letters back and forth across the ocean are examined. *Negotiation* is used in two senses of the word: first, to connote a process for bringing about a mutually satisfactory exchange of letters; and second, the disposition of the parties to participate in the process. Both senses of the concept operate simultaneously, but the former may be thought of as more or less *negotiation,* as it is traditionally conceived in terms of bargaining between individuals, while the latter is an internalized discussion within the consciousness of the individual correspondent.

In laying out an understanding of the negotiations that are part of the epistolary process, it is necessary to understand at the outset that these negotiations were as often unstated as they were explicit. As in conversation, correspondents did not frequently make reference, when responding to others, to direct questions they had been asked, or to requests for specific information solicited by the other party, or to mutual understandings already reached on what is to be discussed henceforth throughout the body of the correspondence. Similarly, an explicit and protracted negotiation of ground rules of correspondence, while present here and there, did not characterize the majority of exchanges, and when present did not take place across the entire spectrum of areas of concern developed in letters that will be outlined in this chapter. When explicit, such negotiation was mostly limited to a variety of individual issues, touching upon content and especially upon exchange and conveyance, that were raised episodically.

Yet letters do somehow settle into patterns. These patterns are based on understandings of general models of writing, especially of the generic personal letter with its ritualized endearments, salutations, and expressions of respect and concern, and on what writers feel comfortable reporting. But they are based principally on the fact that the addressee is always in the consciousness of the writer, so that when correspondence is not explicitly negotiated, it is implicitly negotiated in the minds of the parties, presuming on their knowledge of one another to achieve mutually satisfactory exchanges of letters. The writer is the first reader of a letter, and reads not only as "I," but also inevitably as "you." In maintaining a correspondence, as Janet Gurkin Altman has observed, the letter cannot be born "out of a desire to merely express oneself without regard to the eventual reader." Instead, on some level, a correspondence must be "the result of a union of writer and reader."[3]

Letters, therefore, not only sustained a dialogue between individuals, but were themselves also a mutual creation conceived in dialogue. However fixed the outer boundaries of the form of the personal letter, each set of correspondents was faced with the choice of conceiving together the organization and content of their correspondence. While creating the basis for continuing bonds, these negotiations served specifically to narrow the gap between writers and readers. In personal correspondence, writers take a formal responsibility for what they have written when they sign their name to the letter. This, of course, becomes literally evident when a salutation such as "sincerely yours," or "yours truly" precedes their signature. But, as in any type of writing, readers may derive their own meanings from texts, regardless of the writer's claim to ultimate responsibility for them, and so transform them in unintended ways. Yet immigrant letters seldom were open texts, subject to widely diverse interpretations. The possibility of a common reading emerged, because reader and writer not only share personal history from before the inception of their correspondence and mutual respect, but because they have also come to share common assumptions about their correspondence. It is this ethical discourse about purposes and obligations, in other words, that narrows the gap between writer and reader.[4]

But the gap is never completely closed, and the negotiations never cease, though in the press of other responsibilities and needs, they may be suspended for a time and correspondence might then settle into routine, or even stop. Events such as childbirth, sickness, and the death of parents or siblings, or the onset of material hardship due to injury or unemployment, or the making of plans to be reunited, or the rise of disputes about the distribution of inherited legacies, or the sudden rekindling of hostilities dating from the distant past may all serve to revitalize these negotiations, whether they are explicit or implicit. What remains constant is the commitment to remain in communication. Letters, it has already been noted, are not narratives, but a collaborative process that, unlike conventional narrative, resists closure. What may be narrated about personal correspondence is the history of the relationship that forms a correspondence.[5]

To say that the gap between writer and reader is never completely closed is to raise a number of problems that are difficult to conceptualize, but cannot be evaded. Circumstances will inevitably arise in which writers misapprehend what readers desire and readers cannot make sense of the letters their correspondents send them. A process of clarification, however, may ensue that serves to provide correction. But there are more complex interpersonal circumstances that also need to be addressed in connection with the durability of this gap between writer and reader. The most important of these involves the elusive subject of truth-telling. To speak in terms of negotiations and ethical discourse might seem, on the face of it, to imply openness, honesty, and forthright dealing. Yet not everything that appears in letters is truthful, and not everything that might be said is committed to paper.

This self-evident proposition should certainly come as no surprise, but it raises an important point in the interpretation of the epistolary relationship that needs to be made explicit at the start. In a thought-provoking work on the premodern European family, which is heavily based on research on collections of family letters, Steven Ozment has justified his dependence on letters to document family dynamics by stating, "Particularly in correspondence between family members, colleagues, friends, and lovers, where clarity and truth have a premium and can be matters of life and death, 'live' personal reactions to people, experiences, and events have been preserved as reliably as can be done in historical sources."[6] Immigrant letters reveal a very different perspective. Precisely because the psychological and practical stakes are highest of all in dealing with such significant others, it may well be the case that the costs of "clarity and truth" are sometimes deemed much too high. Most of us strive to be honest and forthright, but the consequences of being so, both for ourselves and for those who are dearest to us, often exact anguish and pain. This seems to have been the situation of many of our letter-writers. Excluding the occasional pathological liar or self-interested manipulator we will find among these correspondents, most of them certainly seemed disposed not to wish to deceive others, but a number of them did so routinely, mostly in petty ways. We must, therefore, contemplate the ethical problems posed by the problem of openness and concealment in the epistolary relationship.

One of these problems, the telling of untruths, has already been briefly considered in establishing that the commitment to maintain correspondence, rather than truth telling as such, is the mark of faithfulness between correspondents. There are all sorts of obvious reasons, some of them quite compelling, why correspondents might not want to tell the truth. Sickness, unemployment, poverty, marital discord, drunkenness, or abject failure might prompt worry and concern in one's readers. Hence the temptation to engage in the often noted (and parodied) "I am well and doing well" formulation, or go beyond it to claim accomplishments or security that did not exist, might be great. Moreover, emigrants took risks in leaving their homes, and were often discouraged by their families, who warned of disastrous consequences if old ways and homeplaces were abandoned. The tendency to exaggerate the gains derived from their steadfast resolve to emigrate is easily explained under such circumstances, though it is difficult to prove the precise motivation for exaggeration, let alone the material gains themselves. What we may observe with confidence, as Jerome Bruner has said, is that narrative truth, which assists in establishing continuity and stability for the individual, is often more important than literal truth when it comes to the formation of personal identities.[7] A good, coherent story, consistent with regard to the individual's self-understanding (even if not completely or even partially true), in the midst of the inevitable inconsistencies of life, may serve a variety of psychologically functional purposes, not to mention its benefits for sparing the feelings of others.

One senses how great a temptation this might be for someone like Robert Bowles, who left England for the United States at the age of thirty in 1823, and settled on a farm outside Cincinnati. He had inherited an estate in England that he was not able to maintain, and certainly was bitter about the problems this had caused him, all of which he seems to have attributed to the inequities of the social system in England. From the first letter Bowles wrote to his younger brothers shortly after arriving, he engages in unrelenting and outspoken defense of everything American and criticism of everything English—soil, climate, taxes, fruits, vegetables, church, state, health, local society, and the like. Within the first year of arrival, he soon brags about his crop yield and the quality and neatness of his fields, and the ease with which his credit has become established in his neighborhood. While Bowles wanted to encourage his brothers to come and join him, and this may have been a motive for his almost propagandistic writing, this one-dimensional discourse is so pervasive, repetitive, and heavy-handed that it ultimately comes to seem defensive. The reader begins to suspect that it is overdetermined by some past conflict, unspoken but lurking in the background, about his abandoning his obligations in England and emigrating as much as by a desire for family unity and the compensatory benefits of venting his anger.

We cannot know the truth of Bowles's situation during that first year in Ohio, and the correspondence includes only letters from that year. There are suggestions in his letters that his wife was quite miserable in America, to the extent that she began to have fears about being left alone, and this must have qualified somewhat his positive frame of mind about his immigration. He may, on the other hand, have experienced instant prosperity that compensated for his family difficulties. Perhaps, but if so, he was relatively unusual. Yet if Bowles had been successful in inducing his brothers to emigrate and join him, and they had found him to have greatly exaggerated, if not simply lied, about his good fortune, the game would have been over. If, on the other hand, he had said he was not doing well and they had come anyway, only to find him prospering, they would have reached other conclusions. It was a situation that lent itself to truth-telling, and most immigrants probably understood how vulnerable exaggerated claims and rank falsehoods were to detection.[8]

One did not need to achieve family reunion to be discovered to be telling lies in one's letters. With so many British emigrants coming to America and settling amongst one another and writing to their homelands frequently, their gossip was being internationalized. It circulated in the mails with alarming rapidity, and served to raise suspicions about the claims made by letter-writers to an extent that might prove quite embarrassing. William Darnley, an immigrant carpenter who left Stockport near Manchester to come to New York City in 1857 in search of work, discovered the force of gossip. It was Darnley's declared intention either to return home, or, more frequently articulated, to send for his wife and five children. When weeks turned to months and then to years and Darnley had still not sent for his wife and children, gossip based on letters from other immigrants began circulating in Stockport that Darnley was living with another woman in New York City, and had been heard to declare that his family was too expensive to support. If Darnley were attempting to keep a liaison secret, he had obviously failed as a consequence of gossip transmitted through the international mails. As the village in Britain reached out to extend its moral control of its former residents across the ocean, such gossip might be a powerful tool that inspired truth-telling.[9]

Of course, the circumstances in which a Bowles or a Darnley might be trapped in a lie also lent themselves to a strategy of silence, which, by its very nature, is a particularly complex problem for the conceptualization of the negotiations that comprised immigrant epistolarity. This is strategic silence, not the silence that eventuated from laziness or neglect about keeping up one's obligation to write. One need not lie but simply refuse to address certain matters, while at the same time maintaining the commitment to correspond and to write about everything else, including much that pleased one's unknowing correspondent. In understanding silence we need to approach it not as something to be overcome, as if it were our task to fill in the blanks—though admittedly it is difficult to escape the temptation to guess at what is not being said, just as today's readers may find it difficult to escape the strong temptation to imagine whether William Darnley was lying or telling the truth about his life in New York City. Darnley exposed, after all, is a more compelling story than Darnley indeterminate. The assumption in seeking to fill in these blank spots, however, is that the contemporary analyst is omniscient, and knows what belongs in the letter. If it is not there, then it should be there—a way of thinking that leads to a guessing game that is a plausible, but ultimately limited, analytical strategy. It is more availing of understanding not to overcome silence by filling in the blanks, but rather to explain how it is that intentional, strategic silence, where we are fortunate to find strong traces of it, may have been integrated into the negotiations that comprise epistolarity. Paradoxically, we must seek to understand silence, as Altman has rightly understood it in such circumstances, as a type of communication.[10]

Silence of this sort in letters was a powerful tool that simultaneously preserved one's ethical position—for silence, after all, is not the same as dishonesty—while protecting oneself against the full force of self-revelation and in most examples one's reader against the painful understanding that all was not well with the writer. It might also be a powerful equalizer in relationships, allowing an emigrant son or daughter greater authority in dealing with parents. Not only did the exchange of letters allow relationships that had been parental monologues before emigration to be equalized, but through silence the emigrant child had greater power to shape the agenda of correspondence, while continuing to display familial loyalty and respect for parents. One could, for example, simply temporarily delay answering a letter until one had something positive to report, a tactic confessed to his parents on several occasions by Titus Crawshaw, the emigrant cloth finisher from Huddersfield in England, who settled in Philadelphia in 1853. Crawshaw revealed in his letters a suspicion that his father held a low opinion of him, and thus seemed to find giving bad reports about himself especially difficult.[11]

Adult children were not the only ones who might utilize silence. Hattie Reid, an immigrant from Ipswich who lived in New York City in the 1870s and 1880s with her husband and young adult children, dropped hints for some time in her letters to her sister that all was not right in her marriage, but in such guarded ways that they were subject to a number of interpretations, and might well have seemed simply to be general observations on the need for abstinence or the wisdom of young girls deferring marriage until they were more mature. Then in July 1882, she began her letter with an extraordinary confession, "I am in great trouble. My life has been one long series of misfortunes since I have been a wife. I hid them from you as well as I could; knowing that it would only make you miserable without benefitting me; but now the climax has come and I have left him for ever." She went on to describe years of a hellish existence with a violent husband who had episodes of binge drinking which required police intervention, and which had recently led to a dramatic incident that was written up in the newspapers. It was perhaps the prospect of that publicity finding its way back to England that forced Hattie Reid to admit these profound difficulties.[12]

Neither falsehood nor silence is evidence of faithlessness so much as of the qualities, limitations, and points of danger and sensitivity in relationships, and hence of the tensions experienced in sustaining personal identities. For them, faithlessness would have been the failure to write and hence the demonstration of disloyalty to family or friends. In fact, even if not as frequently in dramatic circumstances as the Darnley and Reid families experienced, many epistolary relationships found correspondents misleading one another through falsehood and silence. Meanwhile, even in such especially difficult circumstances, the parties continued to negotiate their correspondence, and to write, read, and exchange letters, leaving out only what was too painful to address truthfully or at all, and hoping that they would be able to carry off their mostly well-intentioned masquerade.

Immigrant epistolarity falls into three categories of negotiations about purposeful writing: regulative, expressive, and descriptive. Regulative writing aims at organizing and maintaining relationships, and is essentially contact about remaining in contact. It comprises for letter-writers discussions about reciprocity and neglect in the exchange of letters, the conveyance of letters through the post or by private couriers, the privacy and confidentiality of letters, and the formation and maintenance of networks and webs of relations. Expressive writing serves to represent lived experience, and comprises writing about emotional states (and especially emotions that surround separation and the getting and sending of letters, and the spatiotemporal organization of correspondents relative to one another. Descriptive writing serves to recount and delineate a state of affairs, and comprises writing about the processes and techniques of exposition regarding daily concerns, events, and routines. In each of these matters, the balance between explicit discussion and implicit understanding varies considerably. At times, what are called negotiations here seem merely no more than a logical or natural understanding between parties who need not have negotiated anything to achieve a mutually beneficial exchange of letters. But the common-sense approach, which would lead us to ask, "What else would they be writing about, anyway?" will not get us very far analytically, for if epistolarity is about anything at all, it is about self and other in conscious as well as semiconscious dialogue about what is to be addressed and how it is to be addressed.

Regulative Writing

Reciprocity and Neglect

Reciprocity and neglect comprehend explanations for delays in writing: the mutual decision to put correspondence on a routine basis through establishing a reciprocal one-for-one schedule of epistolary exchange; notification that letters have been received or not received, especially when money accompanied the letter; explanations for the continued silence of one party, especially a spouse, requests for explanations for not receiving answers in a timely manner to letters sent; and threats to cut off correspondence, if silence in response to letters sent is maintained. The importance of such matters is not difficult to understand. The fundamental ethical obligation in the epistolary relationship is the commitment to remain in contact, and toward that end most correspondents agree relatively effortlessly to a schedule of one-to-one exchanges of letters. They are, in fact, careful not to violate that schedule, because in doing so they would create confusion in the same manner that confusion is created in speaking out of turn. Questions would go unanswered; information could not be processed; plans could not be made.

The commitment to stay in contact is a measure of respect and affection for the other. Violating that commitment leaves one open both to feelings of guilt and to recrimination. Moreover, writing is a time-consuming, strenuous activity that may be accompanied by a good deal of anxiety for those who do not commonly use literacy for work and recreation, and who do physical work that leaves them exhausted at the end of the day. Writers are not altruistic in regard to the exchange of letters; they want a return for the investment of time, effort, and emotion they put into their own letters. They sometimes break the cycle of one-to-one exchange, as did David Laing, when many months had passed without a letter from his sister, and write concerned or, as in Laing's case, curt notes reminding their correspondent that, in effect, an understanding is being broken.[13]

Writers feel the need to explain long silences, which they fear may be taken for a lack of affection and for neglect. Explanations are sometimes demanded of them by their correspondents. Silences, as we have observed, are usually attributed to the claims of work, illness, exhaustion, relocation, and the time-consuming search for work, and ultimately when writers are candid, to the reluctance to send bad news. The problem of suspended correspondence is complicated for the writer when remittances have been promised to those back home, but the writer lacks, as did Titus Crawshaw on several occasions, the money to offer even a small "present," as he referred to the money he sent to his parents. Assurances ultimately may be given, as was the case in Crawshaw's letters, that silences do not imply a loss of affection or respect.[14]

Writers may also be in the position to invite explanations for why they fail to get answers to their letters. These explanations are not unlike the ones that they themselves have offered when they were criticized for not writing. The gap is sometimes filled by sending local newspapers to one's correspondent when one does not write. The newspaper sends a signal that one is, after all, alive and continuing to function, but it nonetheless raises questions, anxieties, and suspicions about why one fails to write. To be faithful to one's obligation, as Dr. Thomas Steel discovered in exchanging a letter every two weeks with his father and sister, one must write, even if there is nothing to say, and even if the letter is shallow and ultimately becomes a caricature of itself. Steel's predictable epistolary formula—weather–farmhouse–medical practice–children–mutual acquaintances—usually suffices to fill two pages, but there are times, usually in the depths of midwinter, when he states that, in fact, he has nothing much to say and that life is too boring on the Wisconsin prairie in February to commit to description.[15]

Lack of confidence in one's literacy, or one's near-illiteracy itself, posed a particular burden in the context of reciprocity and neglect. We cannot know, of course, how many correspondences failed to take place because one of the parties became anxious about the quality of his or her writing. But the problem does become explicit in the case of families in which there were a wide variety of literacy skills, ranging from those who could confidently write a letter to those who were subliterate and illiterate. The silent partner consequently tended to be continually absent from the conversation, which might become a source of both embarrassment and feelings of isolation.

This presents itself as a problem especially for women, who were illiterate, or, probably more often, whose educations had not included extensive writing. John Birket, who left the English village of Bare with his wife Marjory and children in 1819 and settled first in Vermont and then near Peoria, Illinois, gave evidence of this in an 1843 letter. He had been writing to family in England for years, and sometimes signed the letters "John and Marjory Birket," but there was never a trace of his wife's voice in those letters. In 1843, he placed an addendum at the end of a letter to his brother that offered some explanation for his wife's silence, "My Dear wife wishes to be remembered to you all but begs to be excused from writing for want of education."[16] It is not possible to know whether Marjory was completely illiterate or simply lacked the ability for extensive writing, as was true of many women. But it seems clear that her name at the close of some letters was probably more a mark of respect for John's parents than a testimony to authorship. Some women attempted to conquer these misgivings about their ability, and were lauded for doing so in language that revealed recognition of the psychological and intellectual difficulties that needed to be overcome. Twelve years after leaving County Tyrone for Philadelphia, Matthew Brooks, an Irish Protestant, received a letter from his sister, to which he responded, "when I perused your small letter dear Sister it was the double gratification to me to think that you had taken courage to rite and compose a few words yourself."[17] Illiterates and those with poor skills might not have been isolated or scorned in the community, but their inability both to speak and to participate directly in the reciprocal exchange of letters was enough of a burden to them that it had to be overcome by nothing less than an act of "courage."

When a breakdown in the exchange of letters took place, the threat from one side of the ocean to break off correspondence constitutes a reciprocity crisis that the correspondents must resolve if they are to continue their relationship. A number of such crises are present in the Barker family correspondence between Indiana and England. Correspondents seem often to assume that the lack of response to their letters is due to neglect and lack of affection or respect, when it might be attributable to a breakdown in the postal system, or to illness or death. But when, as was the case with the Barkers, it was discovered that others were receiving mail from the same correspondents who were not answering their letters, no interpretation seemed possible but that one was being snubbed. To be sure, there are instances in which not sending a letter was intended to convey a message, if of a passive-aggressive type. Emotional coldness might be a purposeful way of protesting against some behavior or opinion of one's correspondent, or carrying forward some long-standing grievance. John Barker's son, Thomas, suggested that he did not hear from English kin because his brother William "sent word to them about mee and my wife," regarding, it appears, neglect of their father when he was very ill. With the exception of one brother, family living in the United States also stopped writing to him. His defense of his conduct did not lead to the restoration of correspondence from the English kin, but he continued to write and to plead that they correspond with him.[18]

In the case of Samuel Buchanan, the only son of an affluent Dublin family, his family's neglect of him was the product of a deep ambivalence that fluctuated between wanting to read him out of their lives and feeling the need, for compassionate reasons, to acknowledge him as their own. At age twenty-eight, in 1865, Buchanan had grown deeply in debt and experienced legal trouble in consequence. His mother, who had helped him on past occasions, now refused to do so. He stole some securities, it appears, abandoned his wife, and fled, first to Canada, and then to the United States, where, after living in Alabama and Tennessee, he eventually worked as a railroad engineer in South Carolina. Over the course of four decades, in a series of remarkable letters to his mother and his three sisters, an increasingly lonely and self-pitying Buchanan tried simultaneously to distance himself from his own shameful past behavior and maintain an epistolary relationship with his family. Sometimes his letters were answered, and other times they were not, or a newspaper was sent him in place of a personal letter. Only one of his sisters wrote to him; the other two apparently refused to do so. Buchanan protested their neglect, never alluding to its context, but eventually toward the end of his life, when he was sixty-eight, and one sister was dead and one of the two others in the throes of her final illness, he did ask for forgiveness. It is not clear whether his dying sister ever saw his letter.[19]

Historians have access almost entirely to collections of correspondence in which such conflicts are resolved without a permanent cessation of letters, and the parties have saved the letters rather than torn them up in a fit of rage and injured feeling. In none of the archived collections analyzed for this study does the exchange of letters appear formally to end amidst a reciprocity crisis. Even those suffering long-term neglect, like Buchanan and Barker, continue writing their letters. Whether bad feeling (from the suspicion that one has been neglected) remains permanently, buried at some level by the resumption of the correspondence, is another matter. But whatever the precise circumstances, most immigrants were not capable of permanently breaking the epistolary connection once it was begun.

Conveyance of Letters

Living in an era of instantaneous electronic communications and rapid, predictable mail and parcel delivery, it is difficult for today's letter-writer to understand the concerns that were prompted in the past by the seemingly simple acts of receiving and sending letters. As William Merrill Decker has observed in his thoughtful study of popular letter-writing in the nineteenth century, anxiety over delivery problems was an ever-present feature of all letter-writing in the nineteenth century.[20] Service between Europe and North America certainly became increasingly predictable and efficient by the mid-nineteenth century, but it was never completely taken for granted by correspondents. We will focus on the use of mail systems in the next chapter, but for now we may briefly review the ways in which use of the mails entered routinely into correspondence itself.

Unpredictable service, which might lead to the misunderstandings about the neglect just noted, was only one, and perhaps the most obvious way, in which postal systems set boundaries within which correspondents had to function, and became matters of constant concern to those exchanging letters. The cost of the conveyance of letters prompted concerns for perpetually cash strapped working people on both sides of the ocean. One practical consequence was concern about the number of sheets used in writing the letter, which, rather than weight, was the basis for determining the cost for sending a letter for much of the period under analysis in this study. The desire to keep down these costs often led correspondents to write in the margins and also crosswise, and thus cover every available space on the page.[21] After completing the usual horizontal array of writing employed in Western texts, they turned the paper on its side and began to write what was, in effect, vertically. Even if it was practical and saved money, it strained eyesight and perhaps patience. Prudence Birkbeck, who left England with her father Morris, brothers, and sister for the southern Illinois prairie in 1817, ended a densely packed letter to her uncle, in which she had gossiped amiably but at some length and every which direction on the page, by adding, "You will rue the day you gave us license to write crossed to you I fear."[22]

Immigrants wrote about the conveyance of letters from a number of perspectives, including instructions on the use of the proper North American address, taking note of changing place names and post office locations; and explanations for breaks in correspondence related to disruption of the mails because of bad weather and war, or of disruption of the receipt of personal mail because of changes of individual residence and/or changes in the location of post offices. Still other topics included identifying mail-carrying commercial vessels and shipping schedules, introduction of personal couriers who in their own international travels might hand-deliver letters when it was necessary or convenient to bypass postal systems, recognition and acknowledgment that letters were not reaching their destinations, and discussion of postal rates before the institutionalization of mandatory prepayment.

Correspondents frequently spent a great deal of time explaining such matters, which had obvious practical significance for the steady and reciprocal flow of letters. By no means, however, are these merely practical concerns. Discussions of this type often are framed in ways that demonstrate a writer's initiative, earnestness, and sense of obligation in maintaining the epistolary relationship. An emphasis on the expense, time, and care taken in finding ways of conveying letters signals both practical and emotional reliability. These discussions also provided material for filling the page and for offering interesting anecdotes about daily life.

In writing about her use of the personal couriers on whom she often depended to take her letters from her farm in Auriesville to New York to be placed on ships sailing to Britain from New York City, Mary Ann Archbald was able to inform Margaret Wodrow about the visitors who stopped at their farm and the stories of their travels and family connections, and, in discussing their characters and histories, evaluate the likelihood that they would be reliable in securing the passage of her letters. Other personal couriers over the course of many years from among the visitors to her farm were her own New York City cousins, the Ruthvens. They also often appear to have received Margaret's letters from Scotland to Mary Ann and forwarded them to Auriesville. All this made for writing in elaborate detail about familiar and unfamiliar people and their movements, and is a reminder of the dense web of relationships formed by correspondence, which also might include those who were not even one's immediate correspondents.[23]

Privacy and Confidentiality

Personal letters written by immigrants were not necessarily private letters. Immigrants probably wrote love letters, the privacy of which was widely understood to be inviolable, but none of these survives in the archived collections on which this study is based, probably for the reason that they were never intended to be seen by anyone but the addressee. Instead, the typical archived immigrant letter was to parents, siblings, and friends. Whatever their wishes in the matter, immigrant letter-writers could never be sure that thoughts committed to paper in these letters would not ultimately become public. Literate and oral cultures overlapped in complex ways. From the time of St. Paul's Epistles, there was a tradition of circulating letters and reading letters aloud in various public or semipublic settings, from the congregation to the extended family circle to the village square, for their spiritual, entertainment, or informational value.[24] Moreover, the desire to keep down postal costs lent itself to the production of letters crafted by more than one writer for more than one reader. Above all else, there was the communal aspect of the relationships that immigrant epistolarity served further to bond. They were embedded in families and networks of kin, friends, and neighbors that did not lend themselves to privacy.

People at home wanted to know what had become of emigrants. Everyone recognized that it was not within the power of the emigrant to write to everyone left behind in the homeland. The only means for remaining in contact often came down to the vicarious pleasure of learning about others from their letters to those one knew, or to writing letters that were simply begun, "Dear Friends," and addressed simultaneously to a collective of family and/or friends. Under these circumstances, even when the letter was not shared in its entirety with others, its contents might become known to people beyond the addressee, and thus be the subject of gossip within communities. The situation lent itself not only to passive self-censorship, but also to writing shared between correspondents that explicitly explored the problem of whether the letter or letters in general were to be shared with other parties.

How did immigrants and their correspondents understand issues of epistolary privacy and confidentiality? British immigrant letter-writers and their correspondents give every indication of desiring a private space between, on the one hand, them and their intimate relations and, on the other, the rest of the world. Furthermore, they showed little evidence of being too naive to understand the consequences for themselves and those about whom they wrote of having their unguarded thoughts made public. Most had village and small-town backgrounds, and understood only too well from the experience of living in such communities how quickly gossip circulated and how vicious it might be. If they did not understand that before they emigrated, like William Darnley, they might quickly and painfully come to understand it afterward, and be startled in the process by gossip's international reach.

Not surprisingly, therefore, a desire to keep their letters private seems quite generalized in this population of British letter-writers. It seems always to have been the emigrant who explicitly requested privacy and confidentiality, not the writer in the homeland. Decisions on matters of privacy and confidentiality were ultimately made because of the realistic assumption of the emigrant writer that, though thousands of miles away, he or she was still deeply entangled in a web of relationships, and thus could suffer hurtful censure or embarrassment or harmful practical consequences on one side of the ocean or another. That web was now more complex because it was international. It was not only that emigrants participated in networks that were international; it was more specifically that the transoceanic mails had internationalized gossip. Rumors, exaggerations, lies, and hurtful truth-telling circulated constantly in both directions. When Robert Porter, an Irish Protestant recently settled in Illinois, urged that his letter be kept private so that others would not find out how deeply discontented he and especially his wife were about just about everything on the prairies, he was probably thinking not only about his reputation for good judgment in Mullaglass, in County Down, but also among his immigrant countrymen in Illinois and Iowa.[25] Andrew Greenlees, the Irish Protestant artisan from County Antrim who came to upstate New York, understood the situation almost immediately. In an early letter to his parents, he warned them not to share his letters, which actually had little to say that was critical of anyone. Anything immigrants shared with homeland correspondents about the behavior of others, Greenlees observed, ended up back in the United States in a month, and could cause a "great deal of anger."[26]

As Greenlees implied, a good deal of the desire for privacy was simply based on the wish to avoid the unpleasant consequences of having to interact with people who came to discover that you had spoken about them negatively behind their backs, and might be seen as encouraging others to do the same. Richard Hails, a tailor who emigrated from North Shields in Northumberland in 1842 and settled in Massachusetts, cautioned his brother, after answering his brother's questions about whether other emigrants had assisted him, that he did not want his bitter criticism of some fellow emigrants to get back to their friends in North Shields. He did not, he said, "tell to make truble among

friends but only to answer your inquires."[27] Others feared hurt feelings
if people discovered that the writer had not fully represented his intentions toward them. John Dixon, a British Quaker who went with a
friend to the Quaker settlement at Earlham, Iowa, in 1871 to work, was
explicit about this desire to avoid interpersonal unpleasantness. He cautioned his parents and other relatives to whom he wrote his first letter
home that they must not share the intentions they had for the future.
Dixon had been given £200 by an uncle to buy land elsewhere than
among the Iowa Quakers. He feared it would get back to those in Iowa
who had helped him and desired him to stay at Earlham that this was
not his purpose; perhaps, too, he had misled them about his purpose.
Under any circumstance, his instructions were explicit:

> It is my wish to caution you, not to name anything to the Foxes and
> Dixons or anyone else, of what I have stated in this letter . . . except
> that it was about their kindness to me and etc., but no family or busi-
> ness matters, as it could come back here and prove probably unpleasant
> to them, and to us. they would like us to settle down near to them.[28]

The demand for privacy could also take the form of an active revolt
against local opinion rather than a desire to assuage it. Henry Johnson,
who had been jailed as a debtor in Antrim, and whose money troubles
seem to have been exacerbated by problems with alcohol, fled to Canada in 1848 to escape having to repay his creditors. Bitter that he had
received little assistance in his time of need, he told his wife that no one
was to know what he had written. Few cared for him, he said, so he
wished to be forgotten by them. It is possible, too, though he said nothing about it, that Johnson did not wish to advertise his whereabouts to
his creditors.[29] This was the reason why Joseph Wright, an Irish Quaker
who fled debt in 1801, warned his wife not to share his letters or whereabouts with anyone, lest his creditors pursue him in the United States.[30]
William Darnley, too, owed money in Stockport, and thus cautioned his
wife not to share his letters with local people. He feared that if his
insurance society realized he was out of the country, they would cancel
his policy on the assumption he would soon stop paying into the fund.[31]

All these cautions depended on the cooperation and discretion of
one's correspondent, and in these cases the writer felt it necessary to
solicit them actively. In particularly close and long-standing relationships, it might not even be necessary to request them. It seems certain

that Mary Ann Archbald's youngest daughter, Helen Louisa, had a child when not married. Archbald probably had no reservations about writing about this to her friend Margaret, for she discussed all her problems with Margaret, and she had absolute confidence in Margaret's friendship. Margaret cooperated to the extent that she saved the Archbalds from both present and future embarrassments. The letter in which this news is conveyed was doubtless one of the type that Margaret, who burned letters with sensitive content, would eventually destroy. For her part, unlike many of her other letters, Mary Ann made no transcription of the letter in which she informed Margaret of the pregnancy. As a result of what may well have been an unspoken agreement to maintain confidentiality, the archived Archbald correspondence contains no reference to the matter.[32]

The widespread desire for privacy in personal correspondence apparently had many faces. The desire that letters be made public, which was much rarer, had fewer of them. Only two instances have been encountered in these collections in which writers specifically request that their letters be widely shared with others beyond the addressee, and elaborate upon their reasons. Other correspondents merely say as a seeming afterthought, as did David Whyte, a textile mill worker who left Scotland in 1854 and settled in Watertown, Wisconsin, that their letter may be shown to friends, relatives, and other family members.[33] They were not preoccupied by the question of privacy and confidentiality, if they had considered it at all.

But the two cases in which the writers make a point of the need for disclosure involved the obverse of those in which privacy was sought to avoid embarrassment. Robert Smyth did not mind causing embarrassment, and William Darnley felt an airing was needed of some hurtful and embarrassing charges made against him that had found their way back to England. In Darnley's case, the charges, which long predated the more serious gossip about sexual irregularities, were that he had encouraged his friends John and Tom Moore to emigrate with him, but had done none of the things he had promised to do to help them find employment. In spite of his fears about his creditors and his insurance fund learning of his whereabouts, Darnley cared enough about his reputation among his friends that he wanted his wife to have the Moore family in Stockport read his response to the gossip about him.[34]

Robert Smyth, the Irish Protestant who went to Philadelphia, had no objection to having his letters circulated, and, anticipating understanding of what Stephen Fender has termed vernacular publication, actually used the word "publish" in connection with their informal circulation. He took very strong exception to his family's refusal to have a letter made public in which he criticized his brother James, who came to join him in Philadelphia, but was overwhelmed by the city, and quickly returned to Ireland. Robert felt James's behavior had left "a stean on the family for sheepishness that will never wash out"; and claimed that his acquaintances still alluded sarcastically to his brother's conduct in conversation—"it is the salute I get in the street to this day the woirds are those, well and your Brother did not say long in the country." He thought his brother's conduct cowardly and self-defeating. He himself was doing well in America, so why, Robert reasoned, if he were patient and strong, could not James? He instructed another of his brothers that his letters were to be made public unless he said otherwise, because it was the only way to educate local people about the United States, and he threatened to suspend correspondence unless this was done. Clearly he did not mind embarrassing James, whom he called a "bog-trotter," in the service of informing the village public.[35]

Letters such as Smyth's reveal the tentative place of immigrant letters in the evolving nineteenth-century public square in Britain, in which, under circumstances strictly defined by correspondents, personal letters might serve not only to sustain interpersonal relations but also to inform the public, and in doing so to assist in forming a public market for information. To the extent that the need to request, or in Smyth's case, to demand, disclosure was unusual and the circumstances surrounding it were dramatic or idiosyncratic, we see that for most British immigrant correspondents the standing assumption was always that, to one extent or another, privacy and confidentiality were to be the norm. Letters might be shown to immediate family or read in the family circle, and permission might be given for sections to be, with careful editing, read or certainly orally related beyond it, but for the most part writers and readers shared a notion that the personal was also private.

The Formation and Maintenance of Networks: Webs of Relations

Recall the impatience with the endless personal detail found in immigrant personal correspondence that editors and historians have shown in the more distant past: the elaborate plans for visits across the oceans, or for emigrations and reunions in North America; the endless lists of obscure aunts, uncles, cousins, and former neighbors whose health and welfare were solicited and to whom a fond "hello" was offered; the new immigrants from the village or the next village who had successfully crossed the ocean and been seen on their way to their own destinations; the detailed efforts to ensure the security of small sums of money passed between continents in letters; and the continuous cycle of births and deaths on both sides of the ocean. All of it seemed to amount to very little of substance. If one approached these letters for documentation to add color to the old master narratives and found instead lists of former workmates, cousins, and elderly neighbors to hail, and recitations of winter illnesses and deathbed scenes, one was destined to be frustrated. Contemporary historians and social scientists who study immigration, however, see in such details the basis for analysis of the forging and maintenance of the networks by which chain migrations were planned and executed, resources exchanged, and families reunited. The network is now conceived as crucial to inspiring the practical behaviors that form the basis of the immigrant's first project—emigration, resettlement, and the realizing of material aspirations. It is the location for the creation of social capital, a moral resource by which, as Thomas Faist has said in his study of contemporary immigration, relationships are firmed up and the norms of reciprocity that facilitate practical social action are forged.[36]

From our perspective, these webs of relations were also of crucial significance for the immigrant's second project. For the immigrants and their correspondents, this web of relations secured in letters a basis for the ongoing connection that provided important continuities by which personal identities became comprehensible. There was perhaps nothing more important to write about than those who constituted to varying degrees one's most significant others; they were in one's memory and thus constant companions throughout life. When these connections were shared among correspondents they deepened the ties of individuals. Even when separation remained permanent, through the letter the web of relations was maintained. The two projects nowhere interfaced more dynamically than in the web of relations, for the desire for reunion was a natural counterpart of the hunger for continuity. From the standpoint of the immigrant's psychological well-being, the creation of social capital sprang as much from the individual's need for the preservation of relationships as it did from the immigrant's practical plans and material needs.

The web of relations is the most constant feature of immigrant personal correspondence, not always in terms of the space devoted to it but in terms of its predictable appearance in letter after letter in all archived collections. There are certainly ritual qualities to the recitations of personal information that often constitute the bulk of letters. But while the comforts of sustaining these rituals across space and time must have been great, neither the ties nor the comforts they brought could last forever. The web of relations was most easily sustained in the first generation, but as this cohort passed from the scene, correspondents found themselves with fewer and fewer people they continued to share in common. Grandparents, parents, and aunts and uncles as well as more distant kin and friends in one's peer group died. Correspondents might continue to write about their own children, who were only known to those across the ocean from letters, and the children of others of their generation, but as family lines expanded on both sides of the Atlantic it was difficult to make emotional contact with ever-expanding lists of relations such as nieces' children and grandchildren, who then married and formed their own families.

Part of the shrinking of horizons that came with aging for many immigrants, could be observed in their letters. For example, the letters of Archbald and Wodrow include discussions of ever-fewer family and friends. Mary Ann might write about her daughters and sons, but Margaret could only remember them as little children. All of Archbald's children eventually married and had new family relations of their own during the middle years of this three decade-long exchange of letters.[37] Wodrow might imagine these adult children, but she could hardly participate in their lives or know them intimately. This truncating of horizons was especially evident in the Archbald-Wodrow correspondence, however, both because Margaret did not marry and had no nuclear family of her own to discuss, and because the dialogue of the two women was so intensely focused on the ongoing development of their feelings toward each other and toward their common past, even as that past grew ever more distant.

In other letter-series, the discontinuities that came with aging are much less evident. An example is provided by the correspondence of the Wade family, which also illustrates at the same time how immense and complex a web of relations might become. Originating out of County

Durham in England, two branches of this large family of artisans and progressive, improving farmers established themselves on extensive, productive farms at two locations in Canada (Hamilton Township near the western end of Lake Ontario and outside Port Hope on Lake Ontario) before 1850. (Another branch of the family had been living in New Brunswick since the late eighteenth century.) These nineteenth-century Wades were descended from two brothers, Robert, who emigrated in 1819, and Ralph, who emigrated in 1845. Robert and Ralph had two other brothers who remained in England. Branches of the extended family were also to be found in Geneva, New York, and Philadelphia. Keeping track of their family, kin, and friends was difficult work for Wade correspondents. The families tended to be large, and like many English families, had a small pool of given names that were used in every generation. Robert Wade, whose letters constitute the early years of the archived collection, and his wife Mary had twelve children. While Mary was having the last of her own children in Canada, her older British-born children were marrying and having their own families. After Robert died, letters from Canada in the archived collection are represented by those sent to England by Ralph, who introduces the husband of his late daughter, Dr. Robert Clark, with whom Ralph remained close throughout his long life, to the English family in his letters. Among the Wades, the web of relationships was made firmer by the fact that the second generation and kin by marriage took up the correspondence with the English kin as the first generation grew old and passed from the scene. In the years before Robert's death, he did not feel up to the task of writing, so he dictated his letters to his son John. Dr. Clark, too, wrote to his deceased wife's aunts, uncles, and cousins. These ties were further firmed by visits to Canada by the English kin and to England by the Canadians, which introduced the old and new generations to each other. Friends from England also came to Canada to visit and on one occasion brought livestock to enrich Ralph Wade's herds; and their presence, too, was made known in the correspondence. Ralph Wade, as we shall see in a later chapter, was still writing to England at age seventy-nine in 1868. His own peers were by then probably all dead in England, and he doubtless had difficulty keeping track of all the nieces and nephews and their children and their children's children, who constituted a third generation, in either England or Canada, but he continued to take an interest in participating in a significantly sized network.[38]

Second- and later generation correspondence, representing the multi-generational extension of the epistolary relationship, is largely absent from the archived collections. It is this that makes the exchange of letters between Dr. Clark and the Wades' English kin or between Sarah J. Porter and her cousin Martha in the north of Ireland so rare. Porter, the daughter of Robert Porter, had left Mullaglass in the north of Ireland as a young child, probably in the early 1870s, and settled with her parents on a prairie farm near Chabanse, Illinois. But years after emigration, she continued to correspond with an Irish cousin and did so until her death in 1916. Her letters suggest that she is the last person in the United States from her own nuclear family writing to Ireland.[39] At some point, then, we may anticipate that without the Sarah Porters the web collapses, and oral tradition and anecdote on both sides of the ocean often came to take the place of regular communication.

Expressive Discourse

Emotional States

Writing about emotional states in immigrant letters takes form on two levels that may both overlap or remain separate from one another. The first is writing that comprises emotional states related directly to the getting and sending and the writing and reading of letters. This includes the endearments and salutations that, though a formal feature of almost all letters, may be individually tailored—for example, to particular individuals—to be expressive of feeling; descriptions of immediate feelings of gratification upon receiving a letter and of pleasure upon hearing that one's own letter has been received and was appreciated; descriptions of pleasure that result from getting a letter from a particular individual correspondent; expressions of relief from anxiety as a result of receipt of a letter long overdue; expressions of urgency of the need to write to relieve anxiety that the writer fears was caused as a consequence of his or her long silence; and expressions of the feeling, mostly of pleasure, that while writing a letter one has experienced sensations of the sort of intimacy associated with personal and private conversation. All such writing about the emotions that appear to come directly out of the experience of letters ultimately emerges out of the deeper mysteries and intimacies at the center of the epistolary exchange.

It has already been observed that letters inscribe the bodies of their writers in ways that heighten the expression of emotional intimacies, and at times make for writing that is sensuous and evokes body sensations in the correspondent.[40] The letter has been touched by the other writer, whose handwriting is a material mark of a physical presence. When we are told that letters have been kept under the pillow, or carried in the bosom and near the heart, we are being given explicit avowal of this physical presence and the evocation of intimacy. When such remarks about feelings appear, as they often do, at the start of letters, they set an emotional context, providing from early in the text the impression of the sharing of intimate bonds and of a desire to lift the spirits of both parties amidst the difficulties of separation.

To be sure, one is supposed to have such feelings: they are expected, and their expression is easily conventionalized and made routine, as it surely was by such generic forms of the letter itself as greetings and salutations. The very ubiquity of this sort of expression—for it is found to one extent or another in all immigrant correspondence—suggests ritual. George Martin, a carpenter from Chevening, Kent, who emigrated in 1834 and ultimately settled in Rochester, New York, ended his letters, even angry ones in which he gave vent at considerable length to suspicions of a conspiracy of siblings to disinherit him, with his usual salutation, "So no more for now from your affectionate brother."[41] The ritual quality of just such expression does not, however, necessarily make it insincere. Many types of emotions that have to do with our ordinary interactions with others are not physical sensations or natural reactions that overtake us, as the fear of a spider might, but instead, as George Mandler has said, complex phenomena that simultaneously "are constituted of people's states, values, and arousals."[42] That we know what we should feel, and are prepared to feel it by habit and with reference to cultural representations to which we are constantly exposed, does not necessarily make emotions inauthentic, for there is a larger sense in which the enactment of emotions, such as anger, grief, pleasure, love, or jealousy, is consistent with and serves the end of enhancing personal identities. We have many of the emotions we possess because of who we think we are.[43]

Today's analysts of these letters usually cannot know whether the writer's states-of-mind actually mirrored the language of the writer's letter. What is known is that these expressions of feeling further the work of bonding that the letter sets out to achieve, even when, as in Martin's case, the bond may be experiencing tension, and the feeling was, to say the least, strained. Readers may find that the larger context through which we are able better to know the relationship will reveal more of its qualities.

The second level of writing that contains emotional expression refers directly and explicitly to the relationship itself rather than to the letter as an instantiation of the relationship, and comprises the expression of professions of sincerity and authenticity of feeling about the other; of nostalgia for the Old World homeplaces, principally as the setting of remembered relationships; of feelings about long-term separation, especially feelings rooted in religion or expressed in religious terms; and, as we shall see later in this chapter, expressions of guilt or sorrow about past conduct, or of lingering anger over past conflicts or treatment.

These emotional expressions certainly had direct and indirect relationship to the letter itself. Nostalgia is often present in the letters produced by British immigrants, so its meanings are especially significant. Nostalgia was originally conceived in the late seventeenth century as a life-threatening illness, a deadly form of homesickness that produced a paralyzing form of apathy. In the twentieth century, however, it came to be understood as the principal aspect of a more benign form of longing which, when unaccompanied by melancholy, has important and positive implications for identity. Some analysts, such as David Lowenthal, stress nostalgia's essentially defensive, psychologically compensatory benefits in offering continuity amidst disruption and the difficulties of adjustment to new circumstances. Nostalgia, writes Lowenthal, "reaffirms identities bruised by recent turmoil and frightened by the unsureness of the future." Others, however, now go further in making claims for the sustaining benefits of the nostalgic frame of mind, and see its role as reflexive mental work that aids in the reformulation of personal identities. In assisting in the integration of past and present, nostalgia may be the servant of a healthy self-examination that offers past and present as reflections that assist in explaining one another. Thus, in an analysis of the functions of nostalgia in literature written by immigrants, Ritivoi writes, "Nostalgia encourages the immigrant to see the contingent nature of personal identity as a conclusion, rather than a premise, and the search for developing a sense of one's self as a constantly renewed and renewable process." Nostalgia thus serves to assist in confronting "the dialectics between the search for continuity and the threat of discontinuity[,] to cover the gap between then and now." The act of writing itself prompted immigrants to experience and make use of both Lowenthal's and Ritivoi's understandings of nostalgia, for writing impelled the immigrant correspondent's imagination back in time to the domestic scenes and peer group activities of youth. But far from being mere escapism, this nostalgic writing, and the imaginative homeland ties it further sealed, may well have had a psychologically restorative value not only in providing a basis for belief in one's ability to cope with separation and with adversity and to adjust to new social circumstances, but also in bringing past and present selves into alignment.[44]

For Joseph Hartley, for example, writing Christmas greetings evoked memories that produced descriptions of holiday dinners at home in England. Hartley also wrote at the same time of reconstituting the same scenes in the United States, if his English family were to come for a visit. Within a few years after he came to the United States, Hartley realized with considerable sorrow that the possibilities of his English family joining him permanently, and in effect, restoring this fondly remembered past were very unlikely, and that he himself would not return to England. Yet the fantasy of a Christmas reunion and memories of Christmas past, especially of the singing of Christmas songs and sitting down together at the dinner table on Christmas Day, probably enriched the expectations he brought to the experience of the holiday, as he sat, far away, in his own family circle in Lockport, New York, and established new Christmas rituals. In this way, it was nostalgia that assisted Hartley in forming a bridge between his former life and his new, American existence.[45]

Writing that seeks to express professions of sincerity and authenticity may be prompted by correspondents criticizing the writer for the lack of professions of emotions in previous letters, and especially for the absence of signs of affection that they attach to receiving and writing letters. Children like Robert Smyth are called to account for not writing more affectionately to their parents. Smyth protested in his next letter that he would not use "some faintsy language or hypocritical pretension," but went on to express "tender feelings" in his own less decorous way.[46] Husbands are called to account by wives for failing to demonstrate sufficient feeling in their writing. John Ronaldson, a skilled Scottish textile craftsman who came to New York and Massachusetts temporarily to take advantage of high wages in his trade, sometimes omitted the "dear" and simply addressed his wife "Elizabeth" or "Eliza," and he ended his letters with variations on "I am yours etc." His letters are largely about work and money, and never expressed any satisfaction at hearing from his wife, who soon accused him of "coldness." But this seemed a long-standing issue between husband and wife, as Ronaldson suggested in replying that personally he could "never see the consistency of people using terms in their letters they did not use on common conversation," and in stating flatly that he would not encourage "caprice" by indulging in sentimental "flattery."[47]

Wives such as Elizabeth Ronaldson reacted to the tone of their husbands' letters, while others took a preemptive stance and told their husbands exactly what they must write to set the proper emotional tone. The wife of John Thomas, an English coal miner from the Wigan area who came to Schuylkill County, Pennsylvania, in 1871 with the intention of eventually sending for his family, wrote him, it seems, immediately after he left England, and asked him for assurances that he had not broken his marriage vows and that nothing had changed in his feelings for her. He replied in the first sentence of his letter to her, in deeply emotional terms, that he felt toward her exactly as he had when he said goodbye the morning he left for the United States. He knew, he said, that he would be "worse than a murderer" to have promised to be faithful, and then gone back on his solemn word.[48] Here, too, we may observe the processes of bonds being deepened in and through letters—or at least, as in Ronaldson's case, understandings being reached about the nature of bonds.

The complex association of religion, separation, and the expression of emotions in immigrant personal correspondence also touches deeply on the understanding of the ways in which bonds were understood and mediated through writing. Many immigrants hoped for family reunion on one side of the ocean or another, even in the age of sailing when the trip was long and harrowing; and if not permanent reunion, then perhaps a visit. Where, as was often the case, it became clear that neither was likely to happen, or that under any circumstance, even when some relative came over for a visit, that others would never be seen again, many dealt with the situation through the promises of eternal life promised them by their Christian faith. Death would eventuate in reunion. As Decker has observed, the exchange of letters itself was a suggestion of the promise of reunion in eternity, for it was a communion between souls that did not require the presence of bodies.[49] While correspondents continued to write about worldly subjects and to keep up the web of relations, they often took time out in their letters to write of this faith in reunion, which was expressed as emotional feeling. Kate Bond regularly committed these thoughts to paper. In an 1892 letter to her brother and sister-in-law in England, for example, she stated:

> We have our troubles and there is a time for us all if we are only ready when the time comes. We are a great way apart from each other. Still I always feel the same affection for all of you though I know we shall never meet here on earth, yet I feel shure we shall in heaven.[50]

Dependably, one finds that the description of emotional states and immediate feelings recur in women's letters. This would seem to confirm the long history of association between women, emotions, and the letter. The epistolary form, in literature and in life, has been understood since the Middle Ages as especially conducive to the expression of women's feelings. Letters have been said to lend themselves to a natural, unaffected, and vernacular prose associated with women's temperament and relative lack of formal education. Letters served, too, as instruments of manipulation for those, such as women, who lacked formal power and were proscribed in their use of the public sphere, and thus might use personal and private expressions of feeling to gain authority in dealing with others.[51]

Yet there can be no easy generalizations about gender and the expression of emotions in immigrant epistolarity. In order to understand this, we need to address first how to define the problem more precisely. It is certainly the case that there is evidence of separate female and male spheres in immigrant correspondence, and that this has a relationship to gender and emotionality in letters. Letters written jointly by couples, or letters in which the voice of a husband or a wife sometimes makes an appearance regularly give evidence of the different, but often certainly —especially in the case of farm couples—overlapping, social roles of men and women. In letters in which, say, the voice of a husband predominates in a few paragraphs, and then the wife writes the remainder of the letter, or in letters in which the letter is signed by both, but different voices sometimes appear nonetheless, we see the usual gendered division of labor and family responsibilities at work.

Richard and Leila Locke were Irish Protestants who left Dublin in 1885 and immigrated with four children to Point Pinellas, Florida, where they kept a store. They regularly wrote separate notes within a common, composite letter to Richard's sister Jeanette. In most of their letters, Richard wrote only of business matters and their problems making money, while Leila wrote of the children's health and education.[52] Where couples wrote jointly, as did Joseph and Rebecca Hartley and Robert and Mary Ann Porter, the reader finds the voice fluctuating between moneymaking and employment on the one hand, and family and home on the other. Women thus wrote of children, their health, growth, education, and all the difficulties associated with their maturation. They had ample occasion to write expressing worries and fears as well as joys and pleasures, as they observed their children.[53]

But this is not the same as a gendered division of emotions. There is a great deal of emotional writing by men also—much of it the expression of loneliness, grief over separation (and often the particular circumstances of separation), and feelings of being neglected by family who do not write often enough. David Laing, we recall, said he was "starving" for letter contact with his English sisters.[54] Joseph Wright, the Irish Quaker who came to the United States in 1801 to escape debt and settled in frontier eastern Ohio, wrote his wife that he wept at the unanticipated appearance of a letter from her.[55] James McGarrett, a Scotsman who settled in Massachusetts in 1835 and left many debts behind for his wife ("my dear heart") to deal with, told her that he wept while writing, when contemplating that he had left her to deal with his angry creditors.[56] John Thomas wrote of his affection for his wife to soothe her anxieties about their separation.[57] William Barker's son, Thomas, was angered at the failure of his English kin to write him and protested in 1861, "I think it strange that none of my Aunts nor Cousins can write to mee but you can tell them that if they cannot write to me I shall not write to them." He was still attempting to solicit mail from them in 1865, and wrote plaintively:

> it were unkind of You all in not writing to me I have wrote to you and I have wrote to Barker [a cousin] and I have wrote to Aunt and Uncle Pratt and to Martha and Cousin William, and I have not heard from any of you. . . . I want you to tell All of the Peopel that I know that I want them to write to mee.[58]

Men who express such neglect and hurt might be regarded, in today's academic discourse, as feminized, but, in contrast to these examples, most of the emotionality found in men's letters comes directly out of anxieties centered in the male sphere—debt, unemployment and poor wages, and the consequences of these for the inability to save money that might pay for the emigration of a wife and children left behind at home. The continuous anxious fretting over saving money became a feature of the correspondence of men such as Thomas or Darnley. Darnley routinely claimed to be faced with the difficult choice of sending money home now to help with daily needs or, though it would cause him further privation in the already spare life he said he was living in New York City, saving it in order to be able to pay for ship's passage. But the difficulty of generalizing also works in the other direction. Farm women such as Kate Bond, Ann Whittaker, and Mary Ann Archbald were copartners in the daily running of what was in effect a business as well as a means of daily sustenance, and devoted ample labor to farm-making. The letters of farmwives occasionally contain details about farm-making, including the buying of equipment, livestock, and land, and the current status of markets.[59]

Similar problems appear with the conceptualization of nostalgia from the perspective of gender. Charles Zwingmann, who has studied nostalgia among contemporary immigrants, argues that women suffer more than men, who in resettlement reestablish themselves in their accustomed work and quickly lose themselves in its routines, while women are more often isolated at home and feel acutely being taken out of the web of relations they enjoyed in their old worlds. Fred Davis argues that amidst circumstances of change, men become more nostalgic than women because they experience sharper discontinuities of status and roles, while women face mostly familiar circumstances of home, family, and kin. Neither formulation seems applicable to these nineteenth-century letter-writers.[60] Though hardly self-indulgent in dwelling on the past, Catherine Bond's letters at times suggest a longing for "Old England" even in the middle of the pressing household and farm routines and the raising of her children that constituted her new American life.[61] Her husband, her letters imply, feels this less acutely, and seems completely absorbed in expanding his planted acreage and buying farm equipment.

The two letter-writers who create the most frequently used, evocative expressive symbols for nostalgia are both women: Mary Ann Archbald, who writes at times of the "little isle" in the Firth of Clyde on which she and her family lived prior to emigration; and Mary Craig Cumming, an Irish Protestant who married in 1811 an Irish immigrant tobacco merchant living in Petersburg, Virginia, and wrote of her "castlebuilding," by which she meant daydreams of reunion in Ireland that focused especially on her former homeplaces and the house in which she was raised, in her letters to Ireland.[62] Though deeply involved in their families and communities, both women, and Cumming especially, suffered intense bouts of homesickness. Yet contra Zwingmann, men also suffer from a gnawing nostalgia. They, too, express regret at their losses, especially the loss, as Titus Crawshaw wrote his father, of "all of the friendship of your youth." Richard Hails, the tailor from North Shields who settled in Massachusetts, was not sustained sufficiently by his work or his marriage to escape brooding about such lost friendships. He wrote his brother of his frustrated desire for news of his old friends, and in speaking evocatively of his hunger for the maintenance of the continuity of his old relationships, created his own expressive symbol ("the house of my childhood"):

> My dear brother, will you do a kind office of your brother in enquireing something in reference to some of my old companions in your next? It will interest me much as I often think of them. . . . You can not realy think how I feel sometimes as I look back on the past. It is a requst I have often made anciously looked for an answer but could never gain any intelegence of them . . . bare in mind that whatever news I receve from England does interest me much more than any I can send you as it is from the house of my childhood.[63]

In the case of Andrew Greenlees, nostalgia seems a symptom of deeper psychological difficulties that persisted for years, through marriage and a prolonged cycle of mobility and short-term employment, until finally he went out to Kansas to take advantage of the Homestead Act and attained some socioeconomic and personal stability. Greenlees settled among friends and relatives in his first years at various locations in the United States, and he had a well-paying trade. Yet he was afflicted by melancholy, which grew particularly severe in the evening, and two years after his arrival in the United States, he experienced an episode of "nervousness, my head being a little troubled, and my mind inclining to weakness." His thoughts dwelled on the past: "Home, what a word, what a sweet word to the homeless." Though surrounded by and in contact with family, he dwelled, too, on the sundering of his web of relations of which he had been a part and on the belief that he was being forgotten by his former comrades: "Remember me to all our friends if I have any."[64]

With his physical symptoms, Greenlees may be an unusual case, but feelings of loss, uprootedness, and discontinuity were common to many immigrants. In most, transient dark moods swept over them, even as they went about the business of making new lives for themselves, and as they increasingly reconciled themselves to permanent separation from the place they still continued to see as a homeplace. To that extent, the immigrant's second project was an unending emotional labor.

Spatiotemporal Orientation

Writing that aims to achieve spatiotemporal orientation seeks to chart the passage of time, whether conventionally measured or experiential, between significant points in the writer's life-passage, most important among them emigration, and the time of the current letter. It serves also to mark the distance, whether locational, measured, or experiential, between new and old worlds. It analyzes the differences perceived in the experience of time and space in new and old worlds, situates the writer at the moment of writing in time and space, and notes the relative positioning in time and space of writer and reader. Immigrants juxtaposed at least three time-space frameworks: the personal and autobiographical; the relative positioning of old and new worlds—as in the seasons or holidays—at the time they wrote their letters; and a general geographical and societal framework that was oriented toward connections afforded by transportation and communication. Anyone who has read immigrant letters knows that writing of this type frequently appears. In an early letter home, immigrants often described the ocean voyage, and worked at understanding the experience of the ocean as a new, wholly foreign sort of space and of the suspension of time at sea.[65]

The search for such orientation did not abate after resettlement. Immigrants like Dr. Thomas Steel often use their letters as the place for noting how many years had passed since their leave-taking, and hence since the last meeting between reader and writer. They noted that distances are shorter in the United States or in Canada and that people in North America think nothing of traveling a thousand miles, while people in the reader's village thought it a significant journey to travel thirty. Homeland correspondents, like William Julius Mickle's father, responded in kind. Charles Julius Mickle and others wrote of consulting maps to situate themselves relative to letter-writers, and requested information on distances, modes of transportation, and the quality of land. John Langton, the 1833 English immigrant to Canada, and Thomas Steel included maps that they themselves had drawn. Steel's were especially elaborate creations. In one 1844 letter (reprinted on the cover of this book), he included a map of his county, telescoping the location of his township and his property within the map.[66]

Immigrants spoke nostalgically about the Old World homeplace, with its many associations in the web of relations, at a point seemingly frozen in time, as if time and space were fused there. But when they evoked symbolic dates and occasions, particularly Christmas and the annual local fairs, feasts, and rent days in Britain, these points also served as an opportunity for relative positioning in time and space. John Barker made this association clear in a letter in which he informed his family in England that his daughter had been married that July 9, the same day as Show Day in Scotten, his old village; not coincidentally in the same letter, he noted that having recently moved from Ohio to Indiana, they were now 4,600 miles from Scotten. Nathan Haley noted simply in a postscript, "It has been your Horton Tide or Fair," and asked his family and friends to remember him fondly with a toast on such occasions.[67] Those who were technically equal to the task sometimes marked out the time and place in which they wrote—the time of day, the room, the conditions of light, the season as it is revealed by the scene out the window, as if they expected the reader to step through a veil of time-space, and share these sensations with them. All such writing seeks to provide writer and reader with a common plane on which to know themselves in relation to one another, and to evoke feelings of intimacy in those to whom they write.

Yet how precisely they do so is elusive, for time and space are such habitual aspects of human life that they are difficult to conceptualize. In the middle of life's routines, time and space seem to exist separately and merely to be filled, but other perspectives link them together and to the larger problem of personal identity. All movement through space is movement simultaneously through time, so what seem to be parallel dimensions actually converge in human experience. Immigrants, who crossed vast distances and witnessed the passage of vastly different landscapes in doing so, while experiencing vast changes in the circumstances of their lives within both short and long time frames, were well aware of this. Important dates in their lives were marked by and understood in the context of movement, which had in turn significant implications for personal identity. In the Kantian perspective, time and space are not something to be filled, but instead are important ordering devices for the mind. Seen in this way, we may conceive of time and space as essential frameworks for the narrative of identity by which we achieve continuity throughout the course of our lives. Places are important for this narrative, for they are endowed with special meanings by virtue of having been experienced at particular times in life. No place carries the significance attached to home, or to the various homes one possesses throughout life.[68]

Space and time have not always been lived in the same way. The specific circumstances of space and time for the nineteenth-century British immigrant were characterized by a rapid expansion, and an increasing routinization, of the scope and scale of intercontinental and transoceanic travel, trade, communication, and social relations. The general implications of those processes will be explained in the next chapter on the international mails, but for now it is necessary to remark on one contemporary spatiotemporal aspect. Many people in the nineteenth century in Europe and North America lived with the sense of a radical change in the nature of space and time. Marx and other commentators wrote of the death of space and time as the inevitable result of the new technologies of transportation and communication, which came increasingly to span the globe, and that eventuated from the worldwide expansion of capitalism. Of course, time and space were not obliterated, but rather an older, preindustrial time standard and parochial sense of space were being rapidly supplanted in the West by modern understandings of space and time. As Wolfgang Schivelbusch has observed regarding the impact of the railroad, space seemed to shrink by virtue of the speed and efficiency achieved in overcoming it, a point the immigrants themselves made in marveling about how *short* long distances seemed to North Americans in the midst of the transportation revolution of the mid-nineteenth century.[69]

The nineteenth-century European immigrant was not a pioneer in international migration, for Europeans had been immigrating to North America and other locations distant from Europe for centuries. But the nineteenth-century European immigrant was a pioneer in modern international migration, which took place amidst this sense of the compression of space and time. Immigrants took advantage of increasingly routinized and speedy international shipping, though the dangers of the voyage in the age of sailing technology never really ceased, and for most passengers the experience could hardly be thought of in terms of comfort. It was possible to imagine returning to Britain for a visit, or having family come to visit in North America, and in fact this did happen, as the history of the Wades of Canada and the Bonds of Kansas demonstrates. That the voyage could begin to be imagined, for those who could afford to travel well, in terms of what today we might think of as a vacation is testimony to a new sense of space and time.[70] By the 1840s, once resettled in the United States and Canada, their letters also reveal that most had the experience of riding on the railroads, for some beginning with their first journeys into the interior to places of resettlement. The increasing organization and efficiency of the international mails was another instance of this transformation. By the 1850s, letters were crossing the Atlantic in two weeks, while only a few years before the advent of regular steam-powered mail packet service across the Atlantic, it had often taken them at least six weeks to reach their destinations.[71]

Yet immigrants lived with another time-space perspective that was distinctly different, for it marked the existential distance between what they had become and where they now found themselves, and the places they had left behind and a younger self they associated with those places. This essentially autobiographical perspective could not be quite as easily conceived as the global transformation of movement through space, which could be represented conveniently in quantifiable terms. The two perspectives were part of the consciousness of everyone engaged by modernity, but their presence was particularly acute in the consciousness of immigrants, who also lived continually within the framework of immediate relative positioning between old and new worlds.

Dr. Thomas Steel, who had an especially acute consciousness of time, provides an example. Steel's correspondence routinely engaged in relative positioning about weather and the seasons and about cycles of planting on his farm and his sister's London flower garden. Steel marveled each year on the anniversary of his emigration at how much time had passed since he left London for the Wisconsin prairie, for it seemed to him that his removal from Britain was much more recent than the actual chronological dates of his emigration and resettlement. Yet at the same time, he complained of the slow passage of time he experienced on his farm, especially in midwinter, when life became routine and the weather conspired to keep him indoors, and in midsummer, when heat and humidity made him uncomfortable and lethargic for days on end. His more distant personal past was a blur that he worked consciously at clarifying, especially that past surrounding the death from whooping cough of a brother and memories of his long-departed mother, through participation in seances, which he described in his letters in terms that made them seem like voyages in search of the artifacts of a previous civilization.

At the same time, Steel was well aware of the shrinking of global time and space, especially so to the extent that he was a frequent letter-writer and saw the time of passage of his letters and of those written him by his father and sister greatly decline. He also sought to encourage his reluctant father James to come with his sister Lilias (Lilly) to Wisconsin for a visit or permanent settlement, and dealt with their reservations about travel by writing of the increasing speed and efficiency of the ocean passage and of travel by train and steamship in North America.[72] Such spatiotemporal discourse served complex functions: to bond relationships; to understand lived experience and integrate it within identity; and to mark changes in the self and in the world. Few had the technical expertise or the ruminative powers to write within all three frameworks, but time-space did gnaw to one extent or another at the consciousness of most immigrants, precisely because it was so bound up with personal identities.

Descriptive Discourse

Processes and Techniques of Writing

Linda Kaufman has observed that of all the various types of writing, letter-writing highlights for writer and reader alike the circumstances of writing, both those external to the reader and the writer and those internal to their correspondence. Letters are written and read in the midst of the demands of daily life, often under conditions in which writers and readers are distracted and uncomfortable. In a sense, they are written on demand, as part of a cycle of reciprocal exchange.

Depending on the sensitivity of the writer to the reader, they also must be written with some consideration to answering questions and taking up issues the reader has raised in previous correspondence with the writer. Hence, a personal correspondence, especially of the long-term sort that many immigrants entered into, is ever a work-in-progress and essentially a process. In the process of writing, personal correspondence may also be said to make writers especially self-conscious about the heart of this process—writing itself. A correspondence is a contract in which writers and readers promise not only to exchange letters, but also come to aspire to write letters as interesting and as technically skilled as they are capable of writing.[73]

Immigrant letters routinely address these aspects of personal correspondence. Writing about the processes and techniques of writing includes frequent complaints about the often difficult circumstances of writing (for example, the lack of a flat surface; extreme cold or heat; watery ink that freezes in the bottle; aching hands, often attributed to rheumatism; poor light; failing eyesight; bothersome insects; noisy children; and the need to hurry to take advantage of the next opportunity presented by postal schedules); explanation of and apologies for poor style, content, and/or technique, often combined with promises to improve; and criticisms of the same aspects of letters sent by one's correspondent. Whether they were educated and well-practiced writers or not, many immigrant writers were acutely aware of what they believed to be the inadequacy of their letters. Perhaps they were aware that their writing lacked the fluidity of their conversation, and were frustrated by that inadequacy, even though they lacked any notion of how they might improve. In writing to his wife's English kin, John Barker's son-in-law William Ridge, a laborer, was keen in his first letter to make sure that they understood that he had tried to the best of his ability. Apologizing awkwardly for both content and form, he said, "Excuse me for writing such Augly lette as this for I don't know anything about you."[74] He explained that he had promised his wife Fanney, who most likely could not write herself, that he would write in her behalf.

Excuses of this sort were much more common than criticisms of their correspondent's writing, doubtless because of a fear of giving offense. Explicit criticisms of others come under circumstances that suggest something of the relationship between the correspondents. One of the most persistent instances of such criticism was a product of the habitual tutelage of his siblings by a brother, as we have already observed in the case of John Kerr, who was the eldest of four orphaned brothers.[75] Titus Crawshaw, too, was intent on exacting improvements from his brother in England. He was especially keen to see his brother's spelling improve, and recommended that the boy memorize the spelling of useful words and have their father proofread his letters. "That," Crawshaw said with authority, "will learn you to spell and write." Crawshaw quickly learned the perils of playing tutor when his brother stopped writing to him. "Thomas has no occasion to quit writing because I told him to be carefull and spell his words better," Crawshaw explained, "I think he had better write oftener. He will do himself a great deal of good and I am sure e his not to old to learn."[76]

Lurking over the shoulder of those who are self-critical, the contemporary reader sometimes detects just below the surface of the text the voice of an authority figure such as John Kerr castigating the writer for not only the inadequacies of the letter, but also perhaps for larger character flaws. Of course, writers are their first readers, and may be in a position to anticipate the reception of letters of poor quality. Thomas Steel, who wrote well technically and in a strong and confident hand, was quite aware that some of his letters would be received as dull and rambling, and apologized in advance for them.[77] But there do seem examples in which self-criticism, not only of one's writing but also of other aspects of one's character at the same time, appears overdetermined by personal factors independent of the letter itself. Crawshaw himself continually apologized for not writing as often as he needed in order to keep up a reciprocal exchange, which he attributed to his embarrassment over his inability to send money home. He felt his letters were inadequate because he could not proudly say something like, "Enclosed you will find an American bank note." He continually abased himself for this and for other self-assumed defects of character, such as having to leave the army because of malaria, in his letters to his father, finally observing:

> You learned me how to write and I am to neglectful to send you a specimen of it. I hope you will forgive me. I can't forgive myself. I ought to be able to help you having nothing but myself to keep, but you see I am no good either to your or anybody else. I am a blank on the face of the earth.[78]

Letters like these provide evidence of relationships between correspondents that certainly appear to be neurotic. They may also be suggestive of the interpersonal context of a decision to emigrate to escape overbearing authority figures that haunt the life of the writer.

Concerns, Events, and Routines of Daily Life

There are many worthwhile things out of daily life that one may write about in a letter—among them, births, deaths, sickness, marriages, the growth and development of children, work, property acquisition, starting and maintaining a business, food, the cost of living, the place of residence, relocation and travel, friendships, community involvement, church and religious beliefs, politics and public life, legacies and inheritance, and politics and public affairs. On another level of abstraction, but intimately related to such matters, is a problem that immigrants in particular faced in choosing what to write: their level of satisfaction or dissatisfaction about their decision to emigrate. Immigrants often wished to justify their actions in leaving their homelands by doing a sort of calculus of satisfaction that proved, in effect, that their improved diet, housing, farmland, wages, and opportunities for leisure and recreation amounted to a better life. Some wrote about electoral politics, taxes, and the light hand of government in North America as part of this calculus, occasionally making their own perorations to North American freedoms and opportunity, but they did not do so often. Exposure to American public life for those in the homeland, as they sometimes observed, could as easily be obtained by sending out a newspaper, just as their correspondents abroad sent them newspapers. Sending newspapers cleared space in the letter for the familial and the personal. Only when public affairs and events, such as the Civil War, touched dramatically and directly on the lives of the correspondent were they usually addressed at length in the letter. Immigrants also wished to share the prospect of that better life with family, friends, and kin who might be inspired to emigrate by their example. Such a desire was balanced by their fear that they would be blamed if those they encouraged, however indirectly, emigrated and became discontent or failed in North America to adjust and to make a decent living.[79] For their part, both out of personal concern and their own considerations of emigration, those in the homeland were eager to know whether these social and material aspects of daily life added up for those who had left them behind. To the extent that they felt caught in the middle among all the conflicting desires, some immigrants, such as George Martin and John McBride, an Irish Protestant from Antrim who had settled near Watertown, New York in 1820, fretted explicitly, frequently, and at length in their letters about what was the right stance to take.[80]

When the parties are separated across vast distances and by a significant span of time from one another, the development of each topic in a letter takes on a special importance, because what cannot and probably never will be observed directly cannot be shared unless it is adequately described and explained. Moreover, when such topics as the prevalence of sickness, or wage scales, or the quality and availability of land touched ultimately upon the wisdom of emigration, they assumed added importance. But among all these daily concerns, events, and routines, how did the parties know which ones in particular to write about? How did they know how to please their readers or make clear their own satisfaction or dissatisfaction with the letters they received?

Writing in this category of discourse typically concerns this problem of what is being written about, or not written about, daily activities in public and private life. They made suggestions about what to include in letters. They complained about the inadequacy of what was being written to them. They expressed frustration about not knowing what to write about themselves. They discussed the problem of having to send bad news. They anxiously inquired about why certain matters seemed never to be opened in letters. Because daily life and emigration decisions were so intimately connected, they often addressed the ultimate question that arose in many epistolary relationships: whether to encourage, or to discourage, or to assume a neutral stance toward the emigration of one's correspondent in the homeland.

Often the questions of what to write about are not opened for negotiation at all or only episodically. After all, the parties have known one another for years prior to their separation, and have been a part of the same web of relations. They have a good notion from the start of what is of significance to the other, and how to address fulfilling the reader's expectations. Parents' anxieties about the welfare of their emigrant children may be allayed by discussing health, employment, residence, and the welfare of the emigrant's own family. The emigrant's anxieties about aging parents left behind in the homeland can never be allayed, but the brothers and sisters who lived with them can offer assurances that they are well-cared for. Such writing seems to come naturally, without the prompting of negotiations.

Negotiations do enter the picture from time to time in many exchanges of letters. Sometimes homeland readers, such as James and Lilly Steel, Margaret Wodrow, and Charles Julius and Charles Mickle want less description of daily life and more vicarious tourism—descriptions of the landscape and the manners and morals of North Americans and narratives of public interactions, and so on—so that their imaginations might be able to play alongside the writer's own related experience. Charles Julius, the father, and Charles, the brother, of William Julius Mickle, wrote the young man explicitly about the inadequacy of his letters from Canada, stating, "Be more particular in writing the particulars of all that is interesting to friends at a distance."[81] The writer of a letter may not like being corrected and told what to write, but these were small matters, and generally responded to positively in order to please people about whom one cared. At other times, however, the demands for certain type of content take on much weightier significance. One such source for negotiating content concerns legacies and inheritances that eventuate from the death of parents or siblings in the homeland. When months and then years go by without the subject of the immigrant's share of the property left by a deceased parent being raised—or if once raised, the disposition of the immigrant's share ever being settled —suspicions are raised, and clarification and action are demanded.

The archived collections of George Martin and Radcliffe Quine, a ship's carpenter who emigrated from the Isle of Man in 1844 and spent years wandering from job to job in Canada and the United States, both allude to bitter feeling and ugly charges eventuating out of concern that siblings in England had taken their own share of family legacies that had been left to them. "I consider this case," wrote Quine in 1879 of his belief that his brother John had cheated him of his inheritance, "the moost disgraseful perguered swindling case that evere was recourded in my native land." Quine's requests, demands, and pleas were still being sent to John in 1885 in his last archived letter from a Seattle hospital, where he had gone after suffering a severe epileptic seizure.[82] Alternately angered by their failure to write him and by the thought of having been disinherited by his mother and then on the instructions of his brother, George, from his sisters' wills, Sam Buchanan too raised the issue in his correspondence with his sisters.[83]

Other difficult negotiations over the content of letters were a consequence of gender. In a number of collections in which the sender is an immigrant male writing to a wife or sister, he does not quite know what to say, or he labors on with content that seems strained and shallow for want of being able to find a basis for common interests. John Ronaldson, the Scottish textile craftsman, found himself eventually in a letter to his wife "at a loss for something to fill this paper with." There was nothing in the village where he was working that was of interest, he explained, and added, "I might write about many things in this country but you have no interest in public topics of this country. I mean the most of women don't bother themselves about some subjects, I think tis as well." In short, Ronaldson was really not sure what his wife was interested in having him write about, and does not seem ever to have asked.[84]

Robert McElderry, an Irish Protestant bookkeeper who emigrated in 1850 and took a position in Lynchburg, Virginia, often began letters to his sister complaining that she did not write him about things that interested him, or that he did not know what to write her. He actually delayed writing her for an extended period of time because, he claimed, he had no idea what in his life might be of significance to her. He did not have any trouble, however, writing to his brothers, with whom he unselfconsciously discussed politics, commerce, and job markets.[85] It was, perhaps, this sort of quandary about what to write that would interest a woman that led Dr. Steel to increasingly surrender the task of writing to his sister, Lilly, to his wife, Catherine—at least, that is, until he discovered spiritualism, and began to converse with the soul of their long-dead mother. Steel continued to write his father with exceptional regularity.[86]

In such instances, the consequences of gendered spheres of activity served to inhibit communication, though by no means to make it impossible. It is important, once again, to keep in mind that even in these cases, in the midst of which the act of writing and, in McElderry's case, even reading, became such a tedious occupation for want of shared interests, there continued to exist a desire to correspond. The frustrated dialogue about what to write is awkward testimony to that desire. There is another context in which we need to take note of McElderry's and Ronaldson's remarks, which seem so stereotypically, and insensitively, male. Most men had no apparent difficulty knowing what to write to their mothers, sisters, and wives, and did not have to struggle to fill the page. The correspondence of men such as John Thomas or Joseph Wright fell easily into the role of household head and dominant partner in their letters to their wives, especially when it came to telling them how to spend the money they sent home, or instructing them on the many steps they needed to take to organize their own emigration, so that the family might be reunited. Like the range of men's emotional expression that we have already noted, the complexity of the range of these gendered negotiations over content points to the need to recognize the considerable variety of stances immigrant men adopted in writing.

Explicit negotiation of the immigrant letter asserts itself unevenly throughout the collections consulted for this study. By far the most common type of discourse is the regulative. Contact about remaining in contact, and in particular about the conveyance of letters, is present at one time or another in almost every collection, and not surprisingly too, when one considers the newness of the experience for many of using the international mails and the dubious reliability of postal systems, especially in the earlier decades of the nineteenth century. Reciprocity issues are almost as frequently addressed, usually in their commonest form— discussion of whether a letter has been received or not received, which took on special importance when money accompanied the letter. From the point of view of relationships between individuals, these are the most neutral of subjects, for they are less likely to be fraught with the potential for misunderstanding or a breakdown in relations, or to carry emotional baggage from the past that creates a context of bitterness and mistrust. As far as the other types of epistolary discourse are concerned, they assert themselves explicitly here and there in all collections, but are often a matter of implicit negotiation. Writers make semiconscious adjustments to their letters as they write, gearing what they say and how they say it to the reader. The reader is, after all, probably someone they have long known. If it is not someone they themselves personally know, it is someone known, for example, to their spouse, as in the case of Rebecca Hartley writing to Joseph's family. Conscious adjustments may be made in response to direct questions, which have the virtue of soliciting information, feelings, and perspectives without criticizing the writers for the fact that they were not there in the first place.

Explicit negotiations that are protracted, on the other hand, seem often to point to troubled, insecure, or tentative relationships, which were rendered even more vulnerable by separation, but in which at least one of the parties doggedly maintains a commitment to remain in contact. Take the example of Joseph Willcocks, an Irish Protestant who emigrated to Canada in 1800 and died fighting on the American side in the War of 1812. Willcocks appears to have lost the confidence of his older brother prior to emigrating, probably for some combination of personal irresponsibility and for the part he played in the failed Irish rebellion of 1798. He certainly seems to have been a man of poor judgment and mercurial temperament. Willcocks complained frequently, over the course of seven years, about neglect, and threatened to break off their correspondence. But these complaints did no good. His brother wrote him irregularly and, to add insult to injury, was reluctant to give him any assistance at all in obtaining a letter testifying to his good character, a recommendation that would have aided him in improving his employment. Willcocks did not carry out his threat to stop writing, however, perhaps in part because he continued to hope that ultimately his brother would assist him. But his letters also bear witness to strong family feeling, so self-interest was only one element prompting him to continue writing.[87]

The examples of Joseph Willcocks and certainly someone like the escaped felon Sam Buchanan appear to be so atypical that they do not merit becoming the basis for serious thinking about most epistolary relationships. But there are two compelling grounds on which to rethink the assumptions that lead to such a conclusion. First, while the specifics of Willcocks's and Buchanan's lives are certainly atypical, many of these immigrants seem to have come out of family backgrounds that were tense, troubled, or tentative, and that remained so even though an ocean separated the parties.

Such personal problems in the human relationships within families may be one of the undiscovered themes of the history of immigration that letters may assist us to retrieve. The general economic, social, and political forces that have been used to explain the origins of international migrations seem quite plausible when applied to masses of people, occupational groups, and regions, but markedly less so when we consider the individual, whose motivations are likely to be much more complicated than the sum total of large-scale, material push and pull forces. Letters frequently reveal family dynamics that may help to explain why some individuals within regions, social classes, and employment cohorts emigrate and others in the same socioeconomic cohort and region do not. In the context of family dynamics, to be sure, we have long understood the variable effects of inheritance traditions and laws on the emigration patterns of, for example, younger sons, who cannot hope to inherit a farm or a business where there is impartible inheritance, and do not want to work for their older siblings, which often amounted, under any circumstance, to an untenable agreement to share scarcity.

But there may be less tangible, more emotion-laden problems, without a direct structural linkage to law and custom that is present in inheritance, that lead certain individuals to emigrate: perceptions of parental favoritism among siblings; parental or sibling disapproval of marriage choices; parental strictness that limited personal freedom; laboring on family farms or in family enterprises without receiving expressions of gratitude, let alone adequate compensation from fathers or older brothers; and the like. These are matters of the emotional economy of families. They may be easily linked to the domestic, material economy in the familiar way in which love and money become intertwined in families. But they need not necessarily be driven by it. Emotional states and particularly the singular ways in which individuals relate to other individuals must be granted their own autonomous power in human history.[88]

Letters sometimes do give evidence of this much less recognized and less accessible dimension of immigration history that framed both the motivation to emigrate and the ongoing second project, which we have defined as the continuing postemigration formation of personal identity through reformulating relationships with those who remained at home in Britain. Early in the correspondence of some immigrants, we find apologies for past unspecified conduct and efforts made at reconciliation, as in the early letters of both brothers George Martin and William Petingale to their English family. In other collections, the past remains unspoken, but eats away at the immigrant writer.[89] Titus Crawshaw's letters reveal feelings of shame and inadequacy about his inability to make enough money to help his parents, but also eventually about his war record, though his employment reversals were certainly nothing out of the ordinary, and he left the Union Army, after seeing combat duty, because of malaria. Even his choice of spouse was an occasion for a spasm of masochism. Commenting on a photograph of his wife of eight months, he stated, "You will see she is not a regular beauty, but she is as good looking as me."[90]

In still other letter-series, memories of past episodes that have caused difficulties, misunderstandings, and continuing bitterness suddenly appear that remind us that these lives are every bit as complex and troubled as our own or those around us, if we open ourselves up to exploring them in the depth they require in order to be understood. Matthew Brooks, the Irish Protestant who settled in Philadelphia, is an especially striking example. Without warning of his anger in any of his five previous surviving letters to his sister, in 1872 Brooks wrote of his standing grievance against his brother James, whom he had not seen in almost four decades, since he left Ireland. He charged James, the oldest of the siblings, with "harshness" toward him when they were young men. James had treated him as a "hireling" on the family's farm and had denied him spending money.[91] Such anger over the shared past is certainly not a common, explicit feature of immigrant letters. The desire to maintain family peace, strongly enforced by feelings of deference and affection, may account for silences, even when grievances exist and linger. Beyond troubled relationships, there is the sense in which all relationships are tentative, because one's subjectivity is simply not the same as another's. From such a perspective, all relationships require dialogue and negotiation, explicit and implicit, if they are to be maintained.

Yet the continuing commitment to maintain these relationships and to negotiate and renegotiate their terms amidst changing circumstances characterizes immigrant letters. Its source—the aversion to the discontinuity that would have left the immigrant isolated and adrift, and no less, though perhaps not as dramatically, the homeland correspondent too—was at the heart of these epistolary ties.

4

Using Postal Systems
Transnational Networks on the
Edge of Modernity

The family of George Hollingsworth left the West Riding of Yorkshire in the 1820s in a series of progressive emigrations that over time led to resettlement in Leicester, Massachusetts, of George and his five sons (John, Jabez, Joseph, James, and Edwin) and their families. All the Hollingsworths were textile artisans. Originally George and his brothers hoped to be able to find work in American factories, but finding those factories every bit as exploitative as the ones in England from which they had fled, ultimately they chose to consider pooling their resources with those of yet a wider circle of extended family, including Joseph Haigh, who was married to George's sister, and a number of other uncles, aunts, and cousins still in England. Their plan was to buy their own small mill in Connecticut and run it on cooperative principles, while also engaging in cooperative agriculture. These ambitious plans did not succeed, in part because several of the five brothers, who had recently married and begun to have children, opted to go out on their own.[1]

In coordinating these far-reaching plans for family reunification, the Hollingsworths proved to be deft strategists at using their letters and the state postal systems of their day to maintain multiple international correspondences to effect the ends they believed for a time that they wished to accomplish. A volume of letters produced by George and his sons contains thirty-five letters, twenty-nine of which are exchanged directly among Hollingsworth family members. But a much more extensive range of correspondence is referred to than those that are reprinted in the published collection of Hollingsworth letters. It is far from easy to keep track of the scope and scale of all the correspondence suggested by this volume. George, Jabez, and especially Joseph, the principal correspondent in the published volume, all were writing letters for a decade to cousins, uncles and aunts, and friends, either in the United States or in England, whom they wanted to involve in their planning for cooperative industrial farming. They depended occasionally on personal couriers chosen from among family and friends, travelers and emigrants, but more often than not it seems on the state postal systems in England and the United States.[2]

This multiple correspondence was not inexpensive, as Joseph was made to remember when he broke the one-to-one cycle of exchange he was involved in with his uncle William Rawcliff, because he felt impelled to send various items of gossip, including his complaints about treatment by his family. Rawcliff was also receiving letters from other members of the Hollingsworth family in the United States. He could not keep up the pace of responding to all these letters, and he also appears to have found the costs of all this correspondence excessive. At the time, while prepayment of letters was possible, most correspondents let the recipient pay in anticipation of the possibility that the letter might never be successfully delivered. Joseph had to add these factors to his knowledge of how to sustain a correspondence with his uncle. It did not take Joseph long to realize his error. He had exchanged letters with his uncle before emigrating, and had always been answered reasonably promptly, so he was forced to consider what might account for the fact that he was being neglected.[3]

Other types of knowledge also seemed significant to George Hollingsworth in planning and sustaining his correspondence. Because George and his sons did not want their Connecticut neighbors to know of their plans to buy a local mill and distrusted the security of the local post office, they chose to send letters from a post office across the nearby state boundary in Massachusetts. While they trusted the postal system to use its vast bureaucratic machinery to get their letters to the destinations intended, they feared that the local clerks would read their letters, or that gossip might be started by those patrons observing their activities there.[4]

The Hollingsworth example tells us that we need to explore the getting and sending of letters and try to understand what it suggests about the immigrants' aspirations and their experience of using the post to obtain them. To do so, we need to shift our focus from reading and writing letters to receiving and sending them, and familiarize ourselves with the postal systems and other methods of conveying letters that were available in the nineteenth century. Consequently, we move at times from letters, the correspondence of individuals, to *mail,* the commodified product of postal systems.

Letter-writers, Janet Gurkin Altman observes, may choose to emphasize one of two perspectives in their correspondence. They may fix on the distance that separates the parties or on the bridge that spans that distance and makes possible their communication.[5] As we have seen, there is a great deal of emphasis in immigrant correspondence on separation and distance. But there was no less emphasis on the bridge, which frequently takes the form in writing about the problems and possibilities presented by the existence of postal systems organized for facilitating the exchange of letters. Nineteenth-century trans-Atlantic transportation assisted, alongside the growth in the scope and scale of markets, internal migrations of labor and the power and range of activities of states in modernizing societies, to give rise to the emergence of modern postal systems. International immigrants and their correspondents spanned two worlds in the history of both national and international postal exchange: the old order of unsystematized, slow, expensive, and erratic service, in which national systems were largely unintegrated by international agreements, and the slowly emerging, new order of routinized, predictable, inexpensive, and secure service, governed by international postal conventions, by which the modern post is known.[6]

Of necessity, they needed to become versed in both postal orders—well acquainted with the vagaries and inadequacies of the former as well as pioneers in taking advantage of the opportunities presented by the emerging modern postal system. They were not ready for the era when the words "letter" and "mail" were interchangeable, and in fact rarely used the word "mail." They were not yet able to understand that from one perspective each of their treasured letters, often crafted with so much difficulty and care, was ultimately destined to become part of a vast organized flood of written communications that was itself a global process overseen by massive, impersonal state bureaucracies and by international treaties.

One consequence of participating in the exchange of letters during this transitional period in the history of postal exchange was that nineteenth-century correspondents, especially international correspondents, had to take considerably more responsibility for the maintenance of the bridge of communication across the ocean than their counterparts would in later centuries.[7] They could not take for granted that a letter put in a postal mailbox down the street would predictably end up across the Atlantic Ocean in a relatively unvarying number of days, and that, if their correspondent answered them immediately, in a certain predictable number of days, they would soon find a letter in their private mailbox at home. For much of the period, except in the largest cities, there were no postal mailboxes, nor was there any home delivery. To send or receive mail one had to go to the post office, which might be miles away, and one had to master a puzzling array of changing rules, conventions, and schedules governing the form and the transit of the letter that enabled it to become *mail*—a commodity that might be shipped. Since postage was also considered expensive by most ordinary people who sent letters, the costs, as we have seen in Joseph Hollingsworth's case, bulked large in considering how often letters were to be sent and who was going to pay for them.

Even the tools for mastering the technology of the letter might be in short supply and mobilized with difficulty at individual initiative, especially among working-class people whose usual patterns for becoming literate and using literacy meant that they were more likely to possess reading than writing matter. Much that would be taken for granted in the twentieth century as the most basic of consumer goods for writing a letter could not be assumed in the nineteenth century. Paper was often in short supply and of poor quality, reflecting in turn the poor quality of the rags out of which cheap paper was made. Ink was mostly home-made, according to recipes passed down through oral tradition or appearing in cookbooks and published guides offering instruction in domestic skills. The cheaper the ingredients and the greater the use of water, the less staying power and water resistance ink possessed. Quills had to be fashioned into writing instruments by writers wielding pen knives, until reed pens became widely used in the early nineteenth century, and later when relatively cheap steel nibs became available in the mid-nineteenth century. Mechanical fountain pens were not introduced until the 1880s. Pencils began to be mass-produced in the nineteenth century, but were not preferred by letter-writers because the hard leads they often employed made very light impressions. Writers concerned with the appearance of their letters, but without time or the ability to do polished drafts, encountered a number of frustrations. They did not have rubber erasers to make changes, and had to scrape their paper with a pen knife or razor to remove text, a procedure that was only effective in the case of more expensive, thicker paper, but might destroy thinner, inferior paper. If intact, the scraped area could not be written over in ink unless a fine powder made of chalk and ground bone or fish scales was first spread on the paper. Yet thinner paper made for lighter weight, and hence, when weight rather than the number of sheets became the standard for determining postage, cheaper letters. Finally, before the use of gummed-flap envelopes after 1850, when the address of the recipient was written in a section of the folded letter itself, sealing wax had to be used to bind the letter into a small package for sending. The wax often damaged the paper around the seal, and hence might deface the letter and further limit the space for writing.[8]

To write a letter and then place it in a position to find its addressee, therefore, required gathering one's tools in a purposeful way and possessing specialized skill and knowledge. The surprising meanings of this mastery need to be explored at the same time as the specific skills it involved and the experience of using them are addressed.

The nineteenth-century British immigrant's experience looked two very different ways simultaneously. On the one hand, much about the immigrant's aspirations and behavior was deeply conservative. Resistance to facing the full force of the modernizing transformations that accompanied early industrial capitalism and which undermined their security was a principal context for their migration. British artisans who immigrated sought not only high wages, but also to avoid as much as possible being reduced to proletarianized factory hands. Across the lines of occupation and skill, a large number of British immigrants possessed traditional yeomen ideals, formulations of which may be traced back in Western culture into the Middle Ages. These immigrants viewed the rural, agrarian life as superior to the urban, industrial life, and aspired to achieve self-sufficiency, independence, and prosperity on a North American family farm, surrounded by family and perhaps one's kin or friends from the homeland. The desire to reconstruct as much as possible one's old situation in a new world certainly showed no craving for modernity. The desire to maintain the bonds of family, kinship, and friendship through the letter amidst circumstances of overwhelming change in one's personal situation was also a deeply conservative impulse. To solve the problems they encountered in realizing such goals in a rapidly modernizing world, however, immigrants had to embrace the mechanisms presented by modernization and to transform vital elements of their own cultures.[9]

This is apparent when we analyze immigrant epistolary. The purpose of the letter was to maintain existing bonds, but in order to maintain a correspondence under the circumstances of international migration in the nineteenth century the meanings of literacy and of the web of relations had to be transformed. The literature on the growth of literacy among ordinary people in Britain suggests that literacy was acquired more to improve the quality of life and expand personal knowledge of the world than for its material benefits.[10] The exchange of letters among immigrants and those significant others they corresponded with in their homelands certainly improved the quality of the lives of both parties, but literacy itself was transformed under circumstances in which it was fused to the project of sustaining migration chains. Not only did immigrants have to use a skill—writing—with which many were less than comfortable, but they also had to write about such complicated matters as prices, wages, job markets, the processes of international migration, and the availability and costs of arable land. They did so for complex purposes: to sort out the relative claims of both old and new worlds and to negotiate the complex moral and emotional problem of bringing about reunion, while not appearing to encourage immigration lest they end up being blamed for the unhappiness of those who could not adjust. The web of relations itself, which had always existed for mutual material and emotional support, became fused to the project of chain migration, and, as immigrants and homeland correspondents negotiated reunion over vast distances, they found the purposes and the skills they needed to possess transformed, as they sought to function effectively on an emergent global stage likewise transformed. Chain migration aside, ordinary family functioning in matters such as distributing legacies among individuals separated by oceans required the coordination of relationships by new means, especially when it involved courts and other state authorities as well as lawyers.

The international exchange of letters in the nineteenth century provides an excellent case study in the ways in which problem solving in pursuit of traditional goals required the development of new and transformed skills that allowed one to function effectively in a modernizing world. We might begin by observing how novel the exchange of mail probably was for many individuals among nineteenth-century British immigrants. The Welsh, Scots, and English, as Colin Pooley and Jean Turnbull have demonstrated in their study of internal migration within Britain, were mobile people in the late eighteenth and early nineteenth centuries. Many reestablished their locations with changes in residence, employment and personal circumstances, and though most of these moves were over quite short distances within Britain, sufficient numbers of people migrated far enough away to present the opportunity for the use of the government postal system to exchange letters with those they had left behind, and to the extent that they tended to go to larger, urban places, where postal systems were developed to a greater extent than in rural areas, they were exposed to the opportunity to use the posts.

As was the case elsewhere in Europe, such internal migrations, at least in the case of some individuals, may have predisposed them to international migration, the experience of which certainly set the stage for the need to use the post to communicate with those left behind.[11] Yet the experience of getting and sending letters via the official post remained rare for most individuals. Post offices, for all practical purposes the only places where mail could be deposited or received, were few and far between outside the major cities and towns. Postage, at an average of 6.25p per letter in the 1830s, was considered expensive.[12] As late as 1838, only four letters per capita were delivered annually in England.[13] The next year the Postal Reform Commission found that the working class rarely wrote letters, at least ones mailed through the state postal system, except during dire family emergencies and when postage was free, as it was when one could be sure that it would be paid by the addressee. The one routine exception was the exchange of letters and cards for pleasure at the time of special ceremonies and events, such as Valentine's Day. To that extent, use of the post was conceived as a pleasant indulgence.[14]

There is no way to know how many letters were sent outside the state postal system and delivered by personal couriers, such as traveling friends and willing passersby who were headed toward the right destination. Certainly immigrants made significant use of personal couriers, which may suggest that people had used them before emigration as an alternative to expensive, inconvenient postal services. But it is interesting to note how seldom homeland correspondents talk about getting and sending domestic mail, whether via the state postal system or personal sources. In this context, the correspondence within England, prior to emigration, between Joseph Hollingsworth and his uncle William Rawcliff, to which Joseph alludes in one of his letters from the United States, stands out.[15]

So too does the correspondence of the Hemsley family, English immigrants who settled in Belleville, Canada, in the 1840s. The Hemsleys were a large, multigenerational family composed of ten children from the marriage of Dinah and Richard Hemsley, who had died in 1830. Dinah remarried and emigrated with six of her children, three of whom settled with her in Belleville. They had many family and kin in England to whom they sent long, multivoiced letters. Dinah Hemsley-Bish, matriarch of the Canadian family, wanted their letters circulated among her four adult children in England, who complied by forwarding the letters she and her children wrote from Canada. We know this because with each forwarding of Dinah's letter, the English siblings and occasionally other recipients sometimes added a page of their own text.[16] Only in a few collections consulted for this study is there routine mention of sending and receiving domestic mail within Britain. Perhaps the practice of such forwarding was so common that it was not thought worthy of mention. Yet, given the care that these correspondents took to discuss the conveyance of mail, the space they took to add greetings to other parties than the addressee, and the concern they had with issues of privacy and disclosure, it is likely that they would have discussed forwarding, and there would be more evidence of the practice.

If experience with letter-writing and receiving within Britain does not seem to have been a routine feature of life for most people, so much as an occasional possibility, what may we say of an individual's experience of the international exchange of mail prior to emigration? About the same, though there is unfortunately even less direct evidence. Inferences may be drawn from two directions. First, governments in Canada, the United States, and Great Britain in the early nineteenth century recognized the growth of trans-Atlantic mail, and understood that this growth was driven by immigration as well as by commerce. Immigration generated a tremendous increase in letter-writing.[17]

Second, many of the immigrants whose letters have been read for this study had family, friends, and kin in North America prior to emigration with whom they were eventually permanently or temporarily reunited. Others, such as James and Kate Bond, had arranged their own employment in the United States before emigrating.[18] The implication is that there would have been exchanges of letters prior to the migrant's own leave-taking to plan these resettlements. Whether that exchange was with the migrant or with the migrant's parents, aunts and uncles, or older siblings, we cannot know. In other words, younger migrants may often have been third parties to exchanges involving older and more authoritative family members. Thus, personal responsibility for writing, sending, and reading letters for younger migrants especially may have been a novelty for them. They had observed the process, but had never superintended it until eventually placed in the position of having to do so. In this connection, it is interesting to note that in these archived collections, the first letter is not a planning letter, either to or from the North American correspondent, confirming the intention to emigrate and relating travel and resettlement options, but often instead a letter narrating the transoceanic journey or the first weeks in North America. The implication is that someone else may have done the planning for the migrant, especially the young migrant, including that planning done through the international post. Thereafter, the collections do often relate to chain migrations, in which the principal North American correspondent is an adviser and facilitator. Whether such scattered insights may add up to a generalization about the novelty of any sort of letter-writing for many immigrants, or ultimately simply represent, in the case of the evidence presented by first letters, an artifact of the letter collecting and archiving process, we cannot know for certain.

What does seem clear, if one approaches the matter from the standpoint of the psychology and experience of the immigrant correspondent, is that whether having responsibility for maintaining a correspondence, within Britain or across the ocean, was indeed a relatively novel experience or not, most were engaged in an activity for which they had experienced some preparation, but not enough to make it a routine matter. Immigrant correspondents give evidence of understanding the basic outlines of the epistolary process. They know that conventions, regulations, and rules provide boundaries for the activity; that a way must be found to convey them to the addressee; and that one has the right to anticipate an answer, to which, in turn, one is then obliged to respond. Beyond an understanding of the process in general, however, the specific aspects of fulfilling one's obligations correctly and promptly often seem daunting for individuals, suggesting that many might have been vicarious participants in personal correspondence, but not necessarily the principal, responsible party.

It may also be, however, that the seeming novelty of using the mails, especially the international mails, had as much to do with changing postal regimes as it did with the actual history of the individual as a correspondent. Whatever his or her past experiences with receiving, reading, writing, and sending letters, the individual immigrant now found that it was necessary to learn anew how to organize an epistolary exchange. Letters were becoming assimilated increasingly into the status of bureaucratically processed mail, and, in consequence, the rules were changing. For centuries, the imagery that surrounded the letter was that of intimacy, emotion, and privacy, but in the nineteenth century new and competing discourses intruded into the traditional association of epistolarity with the conversation of lovers or the advice of parents written to children resident at boarding schools or seminaries.

The letter now came to be contextualized within the world of the postal system and the post office, the institutional face of the postal system and one of the first modern state bureaucracies. Both were frequently represented in fiction, the press, and political discourses in terms of speed, hyperorganization, social control, impersonal power, and a peculiar combination of efficiency and unpredictability.[19] Within living memory, the process of conveying mail evolved from horseback to stagecoach and canal boat to railroad and steamship, which traversed space at speeds previously unimaginable. This fusing of speed and the delivery of precious personal goods, it has been argued, served for millions as both a mechanism for heightening time consciousness and as a symbol of progress and modernity. The sense of millennial expectancy associated with progress of the conveyance of mail is neatly summarized by a toast given in 1840 at a Boston banquet celebrating the inception of regularly scheduled (twice a month, but soon to be weekly) mail service by steamship among Britain, Halifax, and Boston: "To the memory of time and space, famous in their day and generation, but now annihilated by the steam engine."[20]

Time and space did come to be experienced differently. The conveyance of mail aboard steamships brought an end to the seasonality in trans-Atlantic postal exchange that had made winter exchanges of mail especially uncertain. The mail was also less a hostage of storms in any season than it had been in the age of sailing ships. Correspondents such as Thomas Steel, living in the settled interior regions of North America, now found that, with the assistance of the steamboats on rivers and lakes and railroads that were revolutionizing travel within the United States and eastern Canada, they could receive letters from Britain not in a month to two months, but every two weeks, and send them off as regularly.[21]

The increasing speed with which the mail was conveyed was only one aspect of the transformation of postal arrangements in Europe and North America. Between 1840 and 1870, related changes came with new practices that would bring down costs and rationalize procedures. Reforms in postal procedures continued until the end of the century. In addition, the final decades of the century saw the spread of earlier measures into less metropolitan regions. Exchanges of letters and letter-writing itself had always been technically complex and socially restricted activities.[22] To some extent, they would remain so. But the new practices associated with postal reforms in Britain, Canada, and the United States made letter-writing accessible to tens of millions of ordinary people to an unprecedented extent.

The old British postal system, which would be supplanted in the nineteenth century, had emerged in the seventeenth century and was widely admired in Europe. It was adequate and reliable for a light flow of mail in London and other large population centers. It was also characterized not only by seasonality in the availability of service and slowness in the conveyance of mail, but also by a number of cumbersome practices. There were relatively few places outside large cities and towns for sending and receiving mail, and since postal letter boxes and home delivery were not available to the large majority of potential postal users, the result was that those far from a post office found it difficult to take part in any exchange of letters. Rate structures for the conveyance of letters were determined by a complex formula that combined greatly variable distance calculations, weight, and the number of sheets that comprised the letter. Since the postal clerk who determined the cost of conveyance had to be able to count the number of sheets, letters could not be mailed in sealed envelopes. A package was created by folding the paper and leaving room for the address on a part of the external page. Then the letter was sealed with sealing wax. As a consequence, privacy could not be assured for at least a part of the letter on the back around the address. Thus, the amount of space for writing was further limited. It was this limitation of space and the costs of adding sheets to the letter that prompted crosswise writing. Furthermore, very little security was provided for sending money in the letter.[23]

Prepayment of postal costs was possible, but few people had sufficient trust that letters would reach their destinations that they were willing to pay at the time a letter was committed to the postal system.[24] The bookkeeping problems involved for postal authorities resulting from the absence of prepayment were enormous. This was especially true for international mail. A letter to Britain from the United States sent via the official postal systems had to pass through three different postal gateways, each with its own jurisdiction over costs: within the United States; the trans-Atlantic passage; and within Britain. Waybills had to be completed and forwarded for each of the three parts of the letter's transit.[25] When a correspondent like James Steel agreed to pay for his son's letters, he was taking on significant costs and trusting in the vagaries of a cumbersome accounting system on both sides of the Atlantic.[26]

But prepayment was not the only problem for international correspondents. The availability of official service was poor, especially for international mails. As late as 1830, the United States Post Office had no formal responsibility for collecting American mail that was to be sent on to foreign ports, though it did convey private letters when correspondents were fortunate enough to find it convenient to make the arrangements. This created significant problems for Canadians, because many depended on sending mail via New York over the long months in which winter weather virtually ended shipping on the St. Lawrence River. Year around, both American and Canadian correspondents often felt it necessary to find private carriers at American port cities if they expected to get their mail across the Atlantic. Those residing far from the Atlantic seaboard had to send their international mail to forwarding agents, friends, or relatives in New York City and other ports.[27] This was not too much of a burden if, like Mary Ann Archbald, one lived near major transportation arteries and had connections in New York City, Philadelphia, Baltimore, or elsewhere, but for others it imposed great obstacles.[28] The difficulties of getting letters posted from the United States because of both weather and the inadequacy of the roads that stagecoach lines traversed, virtually closed down Canadian correspondence during the long winter months, until the shipping season was reopened the next spring. British correspondents also depended on private shippers and personal couriers for the trans-Atlantic mail, but for different reasons. The state postal system was expensive and deemed unreliable.[29]

Postal authorities, government officials, and politicians in Canada, the United States, and Great Britain understood the need for reform from a variety of perspectives. There was a determination to monopolize postal services in order to earn revenue for the state and a desire to keep down administrative costs by rationing services and controlling the expansion of the number of postal workers. Also, the existing condition of mail service impeded commerce and, to the extent that the

undependability and the expense of the mails made it difficult for people to exchange personal letters, was thought to impede the mobility of
labor. In Britain, too, an argument in behalf of postal reform involved
social control of young mobile workers, and anticipated the anxieties
that the parents of many of our immigrant letter-writers would reveal
in their own correspondence to their children in North America.With
many young people migrating internally and abroad, reformers explained, the lack of adequate postal communications lessened parental
influence over potentially disruptive, rootless youth who were being set
adrift from traditional restraints. Also plentiful were humane arguments
that dwelled on familial affection and anxieties over the health and welfare of loved ones among separated individuals.[30]

The three decades after the reforms of 1840 created the modern
postal system in the United States and Britain, and in Canada, where
provincial authorities gradually assumed control of postal service from
British officials between 1851 and 1867. Each of the three governments
came to share a consensus on what the requirements of such a system
should be. British practice, too, served as a model to one extent or another for much needed reforms in Canada and the United States. More
post offices were opened, such that between 1838 and 1860 the number in the United States increased from 12,553 to 28,500. Letter boxes
came gradually to be installed on the streets of cities. Prepayment and
perforated stamps with adhesive backs were introduced, making possible the introduction, too, of sealable envelopes, which increased security
and made possible additional space for writing. Costs, which were significantly lowered, came to be determined by weight, not by the number
of sheets, with fewer and more predictable, additional costs for significant distances. Postal money orders were introduced in Britain in 1837
and in the United States in 1864. Sending newspapers had never been
costly, but the rates came down gradually in the mid-nineteenth century.
Home delivery was very gradually introduced, beginning in the major
cities. Speed and efficiency were markedly increased in internal mails by
the inception of railroad mail cars with sorting operations in Canada in
1854, and in the United States during the Civil War, which led to the
end of the cumbersome waybill system. The efficiency of the international mails was greatly improved in 1848, when Britain and the United
States signed a postal convention which allowed letters to pass through
both countries as if they were one postal market; two of the three gate-
keepers individual letters had once had to anticipate thus became irrel-

evant in the sender's calculations. The trans-Atlantic mails were simultaneously revolutionized, as we have noted, by the introduction of steamships carrying mail to Canada and the United States and back to Britain in 1840.[31]

These reforms were implemented gradually and unevenly, with significant variations lingering in the quality of service between city and country and between developed and less developed regions, and with some gaps in time-efficiency among the practices of the British, Canadian, and American postal systems. For decades, many people would live between the old and new postal regimes.[32] For example, prepayment did not immediately disappear, but was gradually absorbed into the new system. Titus Crawshaw and his English family were still negotiating whether to prepay their letters in the late 1850s. Crawshaw continued to take the view that because one never knew if letters were going to arrive, there was no sense paying in advance. What decided the matter for Crawshaw was that his family began to prepay in 1859, and fearing he would be considered stingy, he decided to do the same.[33]

Even with the introduction of stamps, most correspondents continued to go to the post office to price the exact costs of the letters they sent. Often this continued to involve going a considerable distance. Post offices in North America remained widely scattered; letter boxes were very unevenly distributed and virtually absent in rural areas. Reliable home delivery was not widespread in the United States, in contrast to Britain, until the twentieth century. Living in the 1880s in a village in South Carolina that lacked a post office, Samuel Buchanan could claim that walking the long distance to the nearest post office week after week and not receiving any letters from his sister was a double indignity.[34]

Envelopes were only gradually introduced, subject to availability and the willingness to surrender old ways. Titus Crawshaw had to send his father a package of preaddressed envelopes to help introduce him to the convenience of using them as well as to help ensure that his father's letters would be correctly addressed, since Crawshaw was living in a new location.[35] Weather and shipwrecks continued to disrupt service, as Andrew Greenlees discovered in 1860 in learning that a letter he had received from his father had been salvaged from the wreck of the *Hungarian*.[36] Postal service continued to be unpredictable—or believed to be unpredictable—and to that extent, immigrants and their correspondents continued to use personal couriers when it was convenient to do so.

Gradually, state postal systems came to bear more of the responsibility for personal mail, and ordinary correspondents felt increasingly compelled to master the emerging rules of postal exchange. This partly reflected a growth in the belief in the efficiency of these systems. If the decline in complaints and expressions of anxiety among letter-writers is any indication, confidence in the state postal systems did seem gradually to grow. The continual fears that letters were not arriving at their destination that were heard in early-nineteenth-century letters and were sometimes mixed with complaints about the inadequacy of forwarding arrangements for those who relocated, declined greatly after the 1830s. The immigrants and their correspondents also came to have less reluctance to send money along with their letters, as was evidenced in the Steel correspondence; James Steel routinely sent £5 notes to his son with his letters. There is little evidence that the money ever went astray, as it apparently had frequently enough in the 1830s and 1840s that a third Petingale brother, Thomas, an English immigrant from Norfolk then living in Albany, New York, might warn his sister that the post offices in the United States were "badly conducted" and unreliable, and hence nothing of value should ever be sent in letters. Personal couriers were still employed, but they were as much a money-saving convenience as a substitute for a system that no one found reliable.[37]

In learning routinely to use and to trust state postal systems, these correspondents became pioneers along the frontiers of global modernity, and they developed mental habits appropriate to functioning within the framework of modern institutions and systems. Though North America, especially the United States, has long been associated with rapid modernization, it was not residence in the New World as such that sealed these habits on international migrants, for once in the lands of resettlement, many sought to live as much as possible as they had aspired to live in Europe, and used new opportunities, such as the greater availability of arable land and higher wages, to realize old ambitions of independence, self-sufficiency, and freedom from the dictates of the wealthy and powerful. Ethnicity and the restoration of family ties in North America helped to insulate them from cultural influences that threatened such aspirations. Instead, we may conceive of the mechanisms that had to be grasped to solve the problems associated with realization of the immigrant's own goals as the more plausible candidates to explain how people with conservative goals came to be immersed in modernity.

For the moment, imagine the letters of immigrants and their correspondents not in the context of the bonds that correspondence was intended to maintain, but instead in the context of the principal engines of nineteenth-century global modernization—the rapid opening up of the world to capitalist development and the increasing shifting of labor forces over the face of the planet. Immigrant personal correspondence was ultimately a by-product of these forces and, by its very nature, it assisted them in breaking down conventional boundaries of time and space. From one perspective, immigrant personal correspondence was an early type of transnational social space. By this is meant not a physical place, but rather a social location for the staging of relationships, in which—in the case of the letter—through the medium of writing, immigrants and their correspondents surmounted conventional borders and organized their ongoing connections in order to solve the practical as well as existential problems associated with separation in a world of increasingly mobile people.

Among analysts of international migration, transnationality is thought of principally as a late-twentieth- and early-twenty-first-century phenomenon. Instantaneous electronic communications and rapid jet air travel now span the earth and enable international migrants to maintain active and frequent physical and communicative connections with their homelands in ways that, though certainly expensive, seem effortless, especially when compared with the older technologies of the age of sailing ships and postal communications. Today's immigrants, it is claimed, may live simultaneously in at least two worlds. But it is the way that these worlds are simultaneously configured that is a new phenomenon in the experience of international migration. Contemporary immigrants are immersed in global modernity, and are said to carve out for themselves unique ways of being that span and subvert conventional national boundaries, and are in effect neither here nor there, but supranational and cosmopolitan. Their experience is thus understood to represent something new in the long history of population movement, for, these analysts further claim, international immigrants of the past are best understood not in terms of their cosmopolitanism or connections to their homelands, but rather of assimilation and acculturation in the lands of resettlement. In effect, they had no choice but to accept permanent separation from their pasts, and give themselves over to integration in a new culture and society.[38]

There is much in these claims that requires correction and modification. Apart from the important issue of how many contemporary international migrants actually have the resources to take advantage of today's opportunities for a transnational life, the picture of the lives of past immigrants, especially those in the nineteenth century, needs to be adjusted in order to understand their participation in emerging global modernity. "Perhaps the greatest myth about globalization," the contemporary journalist Nicholas Kristof has written, "is that it is new." The nineteenth century, he rightly contends, was actually much more open to migrations of labor and capital and to free trade than was most of the twentieth century. Hence, the nineteenth century qualifies as the site where we might logically seek the origins of the contemporary world economy and the patterns of labor migration that form with it. Building on the extensive world trade that developed in the centuries of the voyages of European exploration, the nineteenth century saw unprecedented labor mobility facilitated by both the routinization of long-distance transportation and communication and the refusal of states to systematize visa and passport controls. It saw dramatic increases in capital movement, as groups of European capitalists began investing heavily in the United States, Canada, New Zealand, Australia, South Africa, and other areas of European colonial empires and spheres of economic influence.[39]

It is against the backdrop of this rapidly unfolding global market for labor that we need to see the outer boundaries of the lives of our nineteenth-century immigrants. In shifting our perspective in this way, we see not only what they have in common with today's international migrants, whose lives are also framed within the ongoing processes of global capitalism, but also the extent to which they were pioneers on the frontiers of global modernity. Much about their experience suggests this, and thus calls on us to modify some of the claims about the uniqueness of contemporary international migrants.

We begin by examining trans-Atlantic travel itself. Even in the age of sail and steam transportation, there were significant numbers of European migrants who, no matter how long they stayed in North America, never had the intention to spend their entire lives there, but rather to go to the place they continued to think of as home, with their savings. Among our British letter-writers, some like William Darnley, John Ronaldson, and John Thomas were labor immigrants, whose intention from the start was to work, earn a handsome pile of money, and return home to live better on their earnings. Others such as Kate and James Bond and Joseph Hartley were unclear at the inception of their emigration what their long-term plans were, and entertained the idea of reemigration before eventually deciding to stay in the United States. But whatever the precise goals and the ultimate course of their lives, international migrants such as these individuals spent a good part of their lives planning for that day, and in so doing, to varying degrees, coordinated, in a transnational way, their lives at both ends of their experience.[40] Consider, too, those international personal couriers who continue to appear and reappear in the lives of our nineteenth-century immigrant correspondents, and who as a friendly gesture took letters across the ocean and delivered them personally. The journey was not easy, but in qualitative terms, how different were these movements and the planning they required from the movement of contemporary international migrants?

Conceived in this way, we are able to make sense of aspects of immigrant correspondence that accrete on to the principal conservative goal of maintaining bonds that sustain personal identities, and that seem to embed our nineteenth-century letter-writers within modernizing systems and require them to adopt behaviors appropriate to mastering them.

One of the most common and significant functions of correspondence was orchestrating the exchange of resources across space and borders among correspondents. When the sums were small and could be sent as banknotes, remittances from the host society and subsidies from the homeland were routinely sent along with the letter itself. Coins were sometimes concealed in the sealing wax that closed the letter package. When money transfers were arranged through banks, forwarding agencies, and freight shippers, as was increasingly common, especially, as in the Steel and Mickle correspondence, on occasions in which especially large sums were needed to purchase land, it was in the letter that instructions were given about the process by which the recipient could retrieve the money.[41] The same might be said of sending gift packages— large, as in the boxes of medical equipment, books, and clothing that Lilly and James Steel regularly sent to Thomas and family, or small, as in the common exchanges of "likenesses" (photographs) that many correspondents, such as the Bonds or David Laing, traded with their British families.[42] These were sent through the state postal systems, or private shipping companies, or with personal couriers. But, however sent, the letter was always the place in which information was shared on what was needed or desirable, on the best means for its conveyance, and on when and where it could be expected to arrive.

The letter also served as the site in which arrangements were made for sending or bringing goods that might be sold to increase income. This mostly petty transnational commerce did not happen frequently, but it arose in unexpected places and among quite ordinary people, who sensed that shortages of consumer goods in postfrontier societies presented opportunities. The Wrights, Irish Quakers from Dublin who settled in eastern Ohio in 1801, used the sale of thread sent from Ireland by family members to assist in financing their resettlement in the United States, and looked to the revenue it might bring to finance a hoped for passage back to Ireland, which never was to take place. Thread was initially brought with them from Ireland. Though Joseph Wright hoped eventually to spin his own thread in America, he wished to have relatives, whom he sought to encourage to emigrate and join him, bring more Irish thread to sustain this petty but apparently somewhat lucrative trade.[43] Three decades later in Canada, William Julius Mickle and his brother were involved in making the same type of arrangements. Charles Mickle wrote to his brother from London inquiring about what items he could bring that could help them raise money for their own resettlement. William Julius recommended his brother bring out some pocket watches to sell.[44]

The discussion of commercial possibilities that accompanied the request for such resources is only one aspect of the ways in which the letter served as a medium for the exchange of social intelligence needed to negotiate the emerging markets and systems of a rapidly modernizing world. The discussion of commodity and consumer prices and of labor markets were ever-present in letters in both sides of the ocean. Correspondents also sent newspapers to one another, an exchange frequently given mention in letters and much appreciated (except when it became a substitute for personal communications), and this, too, furthered the transnational exchange of social intelligence. The exchange of social intelligence was framed within the context of the personal relations at the heart of immigrant epistolarity. Much of this exchange had to do with the ongoing discussion of the chain migration of those remaining behind in Britain. But simultaneously, it was an education in the emerging modern world. We may conceive not only the writing, but also the getting and sending of letters as offering similar opportunities for education in modernity. Negotiating international exchanges of letters implied meeting the requirements of an impersonal, bureaucratic system, perhaps the first large bureaucracy these correspondents encountered.

The anxious preoccupation of many with the procedures of that system suggests the novelty of the experience and the apprehensions it evoked.

Transnational social fields are sites of social relationships in which immigrants and the people they corresponded with in their homeland, in the past as in the twenty-first century, encountered and negotiated those aspects of modern society—disembedding and distanciation— that Anthony Giddens has identified as central to the daily experience of modernity. Distanciation is the spreading out of social relations across time and space, and disembedding is the lifting out of such relations from their local contexts, as social relations come to depend less on face-to-face encounters than on individuals acting in line with rules laid down in impersonal and centralized, bureaucratically organized "expert systems" and on "symbolic tokens," such as money or stamps. Both distanciation and disembedding are deterritorializing, for the relatively unique place, as a bounded locality, is rendered both less bounded and less unique, with a broadening range of connections to the world beyond it. The sense of security of individuals in modernity depends on being able to trust in expert systems that tie people to many of the impersonal forces that control much of their lives.

We are easily able to make sense of Giddens's argument when it comes to such early-twenty-first-century phenomena as credit cards, Internet shopping, electronic mail, and cash machines. But for an earlier time, especially the first three quarters of the nineteenth century, getting and sending letters may provide a parallel, transnational but liminal instance of the experience of modernity. The movements across the ocean of the immigrants of the period took place, and not of course coincidentally, at the same time as extensive, routinized European and North American postal systems were being established and linked together for the first time. A postal system is an expert system to which one trusts, in the case of a personal letter, a valued possession that is a part of oneself and a part of the recipient who is eventually to take possession of it.[45]

During much of the nineteenth century, when collection boxes and home delivery were rare, correspondents came directly in contact at the post office with the system's representatives, who mediated the relationship between an individual and a vast bureaucratic institution. A visit to the post office was thus a complex, and for many a novel, experience that while creating an unprecedented opportunity for efficient communication, also induced anxiety. It was a site for the interface of public and private, where personal matters might be exposed to public scrutiny. It was immersed simultaneously in local culture and face-to-face social relations *and* in a mostly distant, impersonal bureaucracy. One encountered one's neighbors for better—or worse, if one did not like them or felt, as did Thomas Steel and Thomas Spencer Niblock, that they took too much interest in the affairs of others and gossiped about the source of the letters other people were sent and its possible meanings for their financial and family affairs. Both Steel and Niblock changed their post offices at one time out of fears for their privacy and distaste for the local clientele.[46] The clerk was also a neighbor, and was certainly in a good position to generate gossip. He read postmarks, and thus could guess with reasonable accuracy when, for example, people with pressing debts were getting the letters from families that might hold the key to the debtor's ability to right his affairs.

The post office was also part of an imposing bureaucratic institution. There was no way to ensure that a letter ultimately reached its destination other than to trust, as people in modernity must, in the efficacy of rules laid down by unseen, distant, and impersonal authorities. Patrons of postal systems had to learn to negotiate their actions by rules that these authorities set. During the course of the nineteenth century, the international mails increasingly adopted regulations, such as costs tied to the size and weight of objects mailed, that correspondents needed to master in order to realize the mundane task of getting a letter to its destination. Methods of payment shifted, too, as we have seen, to prepayment and the use of stamps. If correspondents were to answer letters in a timely fashion, moreover, they needed to learn about collection times and inland and transoceanic transportation schedules.

Those maintaining correspondence with multiple parties in different locations had even more complex tasks. Radcliffe Quine wrote to a brother in New Zealand and his family on the Isle of Man, and coordinated these letters so that they could inform his correspondence with legal authorities on the Isle of Man, in his effort to make a claim to his share of his deceased parents' property.[47] William, Henry, and Thomas Petingale not only wrote one another from a number of different locations of residence in the United States, but also carried on a correspondence with their sisters and father in Norfolk in England. It appears that their sisters were in touch with a fourth brother, John George, who emigrated to Australia and from there to New Zealand, and communicated news about him to the brothers in the United States. Henry, too, conducted legal business surrounding their father's legacy through the international mails. Thomas and Henry and their English sisters carried on a delicate, triangulated discussion for years over Henry's drinking and his wife's charges, initially made to her sister-in-law in England, that he neglected his family.[48] For correspondents such as these, getting and sending letters was not as simple a task as it might now appear, at a time when using postal systems has become completely routine and requires little thought and planning. Yet ordinary people succeeded in sustaining a correspondence for many years.

The maintenance of personal relations, a deeply conservative impulse, through the use of the post, forced international migrants to become pioneers on the edge of transnational modernity. International migration prompted not only an expanding knowledge of a widening world, but also of the emerging systems that organized that world. We might consider Mary Ann Archbald's experience of getting and sending letters over the three decades she lived at Riverbank farm in Auriesville, New York, as representative of the enormous changes occurring within a short time in postal services. Within those decades, Archbald saw the local mail arrive and depart by, progressively, a postal rider on horseback, a canoe across the Mohawk River, stagecoach, canal boat on the Erie Canal, and, finally, railroad. The year she died, steamships began to carry letters across the Atlantic.[49]

These nineteenth-century international migrants were hardly self-conscious modernizers. Unwillingness to confront the full force of the modernizing transformations that accompanied early industrial capitalism and undermined their security was the principal context of their migration. But their experience, along the edge of modernity, in solving the practical problems that eventuated from international migration, enhances our understanding of nineteenth-century immigration to North America from Europe. While simultaneously looking backward and forward, these migrants fashioned in and through their letters a transnational field of action that confronted the changing circumstances of daily life and sustained their links with the past.

5

Establishing Voice, Theme, and Rhythm

Most immigrants and their homeland correspondents were familiar with the letter as a form of communication, but whether they had ever been responsible for organizing and sustaining a correspondence of their own, let alone a trans-Atlantic one, is another question. The obligations and knowledge involved in fulfilling these responsibilities were of a different order than writing the occasional letter to a friend or family member residing in the next town. This chapter examines the nature and execution of these responsibilities in the early period—up to five years, but as we shall soon see, subject to a number of qualifications—of correspondence.

The classic "first letter," as it came to be conceived by historians, is a dramatic narrative of adventure, danger, and redemption that conforms to the classic literary form, the romance. As the psychologist Dan P. McAdams has written, the message of the romance from Homer's *Odyssey* to such memorable movies as *Stand by Me* and *Raiders of the Lost Ark* is that "We embark on a long and difficult journey in life in which circumstances constantly change and new challenges continually arise. We must keep changing and moving if we are to win in the end. But we are confident that we will win."[1] In terms of the immigrant's experience, the elements of romantic drama that we expect to see articulated in the typical immigrant's first letter are departure amidst sadness; material deprivation or frustration over a lack of opportunity in one's homeland; apprehension about and hope for the future; danger at sea, and finally, safety in a land of promise and expectation for a new and better life.

A narrative of this sort might provide poetic, and for Americans and Canadians, patriotic, satisfactions, but one seldom encounters it in the immigrants' letters. There was no need to recapitulate the reasons for emigrating, for these were probably well known among the correspondents. Resettlement was a long and often confusing process, even for immigrants who migrated to join family and friends, and it rarely lent itself to neat summation in one letter, let alone in a letter sent early in one's experience as an immigrant. Perhaps more importantly, the emotions and memories that were left in the wake of departure, the ocean crossing, and the early period of resettlement were hardly easy to put into prose. Apart from the technical demands posed by the relation of complex events that were laden with emotional significance, there was resistance to calling up memories that were frequently the source of lasting pain.

No aspect of the narrative of emigration was more likely to be recalled with aversion than the ocean passage in the age of sailing craft, about which relatively few wrote positively, and some wrote little at all. The reason is not difficult to discern. They had experienced the ocean passage as terrifying and as a period of protracted suffering. Seasickness, often weeks of it, as in the cases of Mary Cumming, Joseph Hartley, and Titus Crawshaw, was a common experience that few wished to remember, let alone write about. Along with the lack of privacy, the unsteadiness of sailing craft, and the constant dampness, seasickness inhibited the writing of letters or keeping of a diary for later recall of details to put in a letter, and also canceled out other memories of the passage. So did storms and epidemics aboard ship. Like James Horner, who began his short description of his passage noting the death of thirty children from smallpox, what little Titus Crawshaw could relate in detail of his passage was a cholera epidemic that took some one hundred lives, and necessitated burial at sea. He witnessed the bodies being thrown into the sea "like dogs," and the ineffectual efforts to submerge them. "They tied a bag of coals to thear feet," he wrote, "but it was not heavy enough. They went just with their heads out. It was shocking to see them." This haunting image probably accompanied him throughout his life, as did, for others, a lasting fear of the sea itself. In this light, we may appreciate the fact that in spite of many letter-writers' promises to return home for visits periodically in the first years after emigrating, few who could afford it actually did so. Fear of the ocean voyage was often a factor in their unwillingness to return to Great Britain. For every Robert Smyth, who lived through a storm abroad ship by praying and singing hymns in anticipation of death but still went home to Ireland for a visit two years later, there were many more like Hartley, who, though deeply homesick, feared the prospect of another ocean voyage. After his emigration in 1858, his early letters note a desire to return for a visit, but he finally admitted he could not bring himself to do so. "I wood like to see you all that is alive," Hartley wrote his cousin three years after his arrival, "but I doant like the see."[2]

An uneventful passage could yield the same unwillingness to narrate the ocean passage. Without prolonged sickness, storms, or epidemic disease, the shipboard passage could present itself, as it did for Matthew Dinsdale, a Methodist preacher who emigrated in 1844 from Yorkshire and then settled in Illinois and Wisconsin before going off to the California Gold Rush, as too tedious for description. Anticipating danger or the sublime, for which his reading of contemporary fiction and poetry had prepared him, Dinsdale was disappointed instead to have been bored by the ocean passage and to have nothing to say. His future voyages, to and from California, where he made a substantial sum mining for gold, only contributed further to his dim view of ocean travel, for he experienced prolonged seasickness on both legs of that journey.[3]

Only a few writers could overcome their memories of sickness, boredom, or terror, and relate the ocean passage in detail and endow it with the feeling of drama. Richard Hails was one of these letter-writers, but his vivid description of the passage was written seven years after his emigration, less in the joy of narration than in response to the request of his brother, who was considering emigrating to join him. His narrative of "dull monotney" punctuated by seasickness, his vivid description of the behavior of passengers during rough weather, and the profound aversion he expressed toward the Irish Catholic passengers aboard ship, feelings shared with other English and Irish Protestant emigrants who expressed such hostility in recalling their own passages, might well have given his brother pause in forming his own plans to emigrate.[4]

The problems of authorship and of chronology in relation to the notion of the first letter provide us with two sets of other relevant analytical problems for understanding the inception of correspondence. Consider the nature of authorship. Joseph Hartley wrote home, but with great difficulty and with long lapses in his correspondence. "I have no reason for not writing to you," he said, trying to explain why he had failed to write in 1862, "only I don't like writing letters any I must owne it is my neglect." But at some time in 1862 or early in 1863 he married Rebecca, another English immigrant living in the quarry town of Lockport, New York. Rebecca's writing skills, though certainly uneven, were better than Joseph's, and eventually she took charge of writing letters to his family. Although a stranger to Joseph's family, she said in 1868 in one of the first letters she wrote in her husband's behalf, "[I] feel it is a dutay to take my pen to help my Joseph to hanswer your welcome letter." Thereafter, though the letters were sent to Joseph's family and kin, the couple's "we" replaces Joseph's "I," and when "I" now reenters the text, it is Rebecca's and not Joseph's. Rebecca's religious sentiments, descriptions of their children, and depictions of meals and domestic routines, such as canning fruit, enter the text, and she establishes her own voice, though Joseph's is never far in the background.[5] Where, then, do the Hartley letters begin, in 1858 or in 1863? It seems as if they have two beginnings, and that this might well have been perceived by both the Hartleys and their correspondents in Yorkshire.

A similar problem arises in an intergenerational guise in the Wright letters, when Joseph Wright Jr. began to author letters in his father's place to the same correspondents, and in an intrafamilial guise in the Steel and the Mickle letters, when Thomas Steel in the first case and William Julius Mickle in the second begin to write separate letters to their siblings, who lived in the same house with their parents, to whom they also wrote. They came, in effect, to sustain two sets of correspondence. In both these cases, it is relevant to think of two first letters.[6]

Consider, too, some of the problems of chronology and collection that are embedded in the notion of *first*. The first letters in archived collections need not necessarily be the actual first letters written by the immigrant, but rather a letter written considerably later, the presence of which is an artifact of a process of collection that can be revealed only by further research, outside the context of letters. Thus, for example, though Robert Smith, who left Norfolk in 1834 and settled on a farm in Lenawee County, Michigan, near his brother-in-law John Fisher, had been in the United States almost twenty years, the first of his three archived letters is dated 1851 and the two others, 1860. All three are written to another brother-in-law, Franklin Fisher. Nothing in these three letters suggests there were previous communications, but the matter is clearer when we note what Erickson discovered about this correspondence: while other Smith letters were probably discarded, these three letters were saved because they attained the status of legal documents. They provided acknowledgment of the receipt of monies from an estate.[7]

Other first letters we encounter in collections have a questionable status that cannot be so easily resolved by further research. We cannot know exactly what place they have in the chronological sequence of actual correspondence, though the way in which they are conceived and the language they employ seem to indicate that they may be what they present themselves as being, that is, first letters, in the archived collection. Assuming that there were not earlier letters that have been lost, what stands out about them is the relatively large number of years that pass between the writer's emigration and the date of the first archived letter.

Radcliffe Quine and Edward Phillips, an artisan who left a rural area near Shrewsbury as a boy in 1821 and resided in a number of American locations, both admitted to waiting seventeen years to write what appears to be their first letters to family. Quine, who frequently changed residences over the course of decades, while moving ever further westward toward British Columbia and Washington State, said he would make no "childish excuses" in addressing his family on the Isle of Man "for the first time," and attributed his long silence to "unaccountable negligence and foolish habit of procrastination."[8] For his part, Phillips did not think to offer excuses at all for his long silence, and began his first letter to his father with the extraordinarily understated, "After an absence of seventeen years I send you a few lines, which leave me and my family in good health, and I hope you enjoy the same." In his next letter, he did give a brief account of his life over the previous years, though he never explained his long silence. Phillips seems to have been no closer to the uncle whom he came to the United States to join, for he informed his father that he had only seen him once in the twelve years since he left his house to work for another man and then moved west.[9]

It is tempting to ascribe the long lapses seen in Quine's or Phillip's correspondence to weak family ties, but alongside that explanation it is necessary to consider the meanings of the fact that both Quine and Phillips did eventually write first letters to their British families—with no apparent ulterior motive, at least at the time, such as the desire to lay claim to an inheritance. Though negligent, such correspondents did want to reestablish contact. Their family relationships were important enough for their understandings of themselves that they eventually felt the need to write. Or they wrote again after a lapse of many years and thus, in a sense, they also produced two first letters. Perhaps, therefore, it is best to take Quine at his word and look for more practical reasons for the failure to sustain correspondence, before considering the sort of problems in the human relationships of family that could also provide explanations.

ABOVE: *London, Canada West* (1849) by Captain Edmund G. Hallewell (crayon and wash on paper, 18.4 × 27.9 cm). The post office Thomas Spencer Niblock elected to use for sending and receiving his letters was in the town of London, where he believed he was guaranteed the privacy not available in the little village of Delaware nearer his home. Walking into the center of London from the southwest in the first year of his short residence in Canada, Niblock might well have encountered this townscape as he moved toward crossing the Thames River. Collection of Museum London, London, Ontario, Canada, gift of Mrs. P. N. Stevens, England, 1958.

LEFT: *Gabo Island, Victoria* by F. A. Sleap (1884). In the same dangerous waters as nearby Tulleberga Island, the site of the shipwreck that took the lives of the Niblock family, Gabo Island is the location of a memorial to the Niblocks and other victims of the destruction of the steamboat *Monumental City.* The memorial is depicted to the left and in the middle of this engraving of various Gabo Island scenes. La Trobe Picture Collection, State Library of Victoria, Melbourne, Victoria, Australia.

ABOVE: *The Harbor at Little Cumbrae Island, Scotland* by Mary Ann Wodrow Archbald (n.d.). Taken from one of her own copybooks, in which she combined her drawings, poems, and random thoughts with quotations from favored books, this fondly depicted scene was accompanied by a poem to the left, lamenting the need to emigrate from Scotland and bidding Scotland "a last farewell." I gratefully acknowledge the permission of Robert W. Archbald for use of this illustration, which is found in his *The Archbald Family of Auriesville, New York* (Hastings-on-Hudson, NY: self-published, 1999).

LEFT: *Self-Portrait* by Mary Ann Wodrow Archbald, also taken from one of her copybooks (n.d.). I gratefully acknowledge the permission of Robert W. Archbald for use of this illustration, which is found in his *The Archbald Family of Auriesville, New York* (Hastings-on-Hudson, NY: self-published, 1999).

TOP: *Main Street East, Bunker Hill, Kansas* (postcard; ca. 1907). Though Catherine
Bond claimed that she liked "a western life," this scene of the village closest to Catherine
and James Bond's farm prompts our recognition of the tremendous change in visual
orientation which the Bonds underwent in their transition from the long settled and
manicured Lancashire countryside, in the vicinity of Liverpool, to the raw Kansas prairie.
Kansas Cities and Towns Photograph Collection, MS92-27, Department of Special
Collections, University Libraries, Wichita State University, Wichita, Kansas.

BOTTOM: *Catherine Steel and James Steel* (1847) by Thomas Steel. This drawing of his
wife and infant son accompanied one of Thomas Steel's letters to his father. In the
background are the Steels' homestead and some outbuildings, as well as a laborer
employed at some unspecified task. Thomas Steel to James Steel, Waukesha County,
Wisconsin, May 29, 1847, Thomas Steel Papers (1808–1896), Wisconsin Manuscripts,
51PB, Department of Archives and Libraries, Wisconsin State Historical Society. Image
number WHi-3836, Visual Materials Archive, Wisconsin Historical Society.

Cabin, Milwaukee County, Wisconsin (1844) by Thomas Steel. Dr. Thomas Steel spent his first winter on the Wisconsin prairies in this crowded cabin that he shared with the Smith family. In the letter to his father that contained this drawing he spoke of the crowded conditions surrounding him, huddled around the stove in the depths of winter, while two of the Smith's children read nearby. In other letters Steel occasionally incorporated maps, including the one that forms the cover illustration for this book. Thomas Steel to James Steel, Milwaukee County, Wisconsin, January 12, 1844, Thomas Steel Papers (1808–1896), Wisconsin Manuscripts, 51PB, Department of Archives and Libraries, Wisconsin Historical Society. Image number WHi-3832, Visual Materials Archive, Wisconsin Historical Society.

Some correspondence failed because of the difficulties of establishing reciprocity. David Laing simply gave up writing home to England because his sisters, who might have been too young at the time to take responsibility for a correspondence, never answered his letters. When after many years he finally received a letter from his sister, and they began to correspond, as if, in effect, for the first time, he did not know either her married name or her address, and had no idea how she had gotten hold of his own address.[10] Some immigrant correspondents seem not to have liked letter-writing and to have been guilty of chronic procrastination that lasted for years, but they either lacked Quine's candor or were unable to find the words to describe their state of mind, castigate themselves, and apologize. They, too, may be said to have written two or even more first letters.

An example is provided by John and Margaret Griffiths. English Mormons who emigrated from Shropshire in 1840 and settled in Hancock County, Illinois, alongside English and American coreligionists, near the Mormon center of Nauvoo, they do not appear to have written more than one letter after emigrating and arriving in Illinois. Their first archived letter, to Margaret's mother and father, is dated 1850, and was said to have been written "after a long silence." In fact, they appear to have sent no letter after the first one they wrote in December 1840. The reasons they stated for not writing are hardly convincing. She attributed their silence to the fact that other Mormons, including family and friends they had emigrated with, had gone to Utah in 1844, leaving them behind, after which, she said, "I had not the courage to rite." She meant perhaps that she was embarrassed by, or felt inadequate to explain, the breakup of the group that had left England together. Furthermore, since the letters the Griffiths and their relations had received from England had been addressed to a brother, Joseph Griffiths, who had gone to Utah, John did not feel it appropriate to answer them and hence to continue writing. The explanation might serve, if their behavior in the future did not suggest its lack of credibility. John attributed his failure to write to his brothers and sister between 1860 and 1865 to the Civil War. He said he had been too busy to write, because he was "engaged heart an soul against his wicked rebellion," though he gives no account of having served in the Union Army, and was probably too old to do so. He also attributed his silence to the fact that the last letter he had received, in 1860, had inquired about the prospects for immigrants, and because he could not recommend immigration to the United States during the war, he did not answer. But in these cases, too, the desire, however inadequately expressed, to maintain contact did not die. Even if it required the end of a war for him to find the inspiration to do so, John Griffiths did eventually answer the now long-standing request by providing information about immigration and offered to assist family members who emigrated. His letter was enthusiastic in tone and intent.[11] David Laing, too, approached renewing correspondence with his sisters positively. He stated, as we recall, that he was "starving" for contact with his sisters, and had read the letter from one of them "at least twenty times since I received it."[12] While the production of letters in these cases was not even or voluminous, the spirit behind it was unmistakably enthusiastic.

Another way to contextualize immigrants such as Quine, Phillips, the Griffiths, and Laing is to contrast them with those who never wrote home at all and whose postemigration existence is only known as it is obscurely reflected in the letters of others. This is true of the two emigrant daughters of the White family, Jane and Judith, Irish Protestants who emigrated separately from Sligo in 1804. Much to the sorrow of her mother, which was articulated in a number of letters over the course of a decade, Judith appears never to have written home after she left Ireland. But she did write Jane, though sometimes, it seems, it took her years to answer Jane's letters. Jane was to be the only source of information the Irish family had to reassure them that Judith was indeed alive. Certainly one detects here weak family ties and troubled relationships, but we cannot know the reasons for them. Years later, we find that Judith's American life had been a hard luck story: a sickly and elderly husband who had found it difficult to support his family; many children; no one to assist her with her household; frequent changes of residence; the failure of efforts to establish a private school for girls; and eventually, impoverishment and despair.[13] The relation between Judith's difficult life and her preemigration family history to her silence may never be known. Perhaps having nothing positive to write from the start of her life in the United States and being reluctant to lie, she found it difficult to write. On the other hand, it is hard to conceive of a life about which nothing positive can ever be said, even if what is said is only an expression of hope. In short, such relationships are a puzzle which, two centuries after the fact, it is very difficult to solve.

*

These problems in putting the first letter into focus suggest that the inception of immigrant correspondence begins far less dramatically and under far more complicated personal circumstances than any archetypical romance narrative of emigration and resettlement we might wish to conceive. Immigrant correspondence finds its rhythm, structure, themes, and voice through the efforts of individuals, each possessing an often complex history of family, kinship, and friendship relations, to realize the letter's larger purposes for the immigrant's identity narrative and to solve the practical problems of writing and of using the existing methods, both public and private, of postal exchange to convey their letters. From their early letters, immigrant letter-writers began to establish habits that governed the writing and the sending of their letters.

One practical problem that had to be confronted at the inception of correspondence was finding the space and time needed for writing, and thus for establishing habits conducive to the routine production of letters. This was an especially pressing problem to the extent that many immigrant letter-writers were not skillful stylists or technically competent, yet felt a desire to do the best that they could, particularly when writing to parents and siblings. Writing was difficult and laborious work for them. Those with more education and experience of letter-writing felt no less pained by the presumed inadequacy of their letters, and their high standards probably added to the burden they felt as they wrote. Even if they wrote reasonably well from a technical perspective, the work of gathering together pen and ink, and producing a clean copy that they deemed worthy of presenting to others, suggests problems that are difficult for us to imagine in the age of electronic word processing.

A lack of time and inadequate physical surroundings were frequently blamed for the inadequacies of letters. James Horner wrote from Philadelphia in 1801, at the end of his first letter to his parents in County Londonderry, that he hoped they would excuse his "bad writing," which he attributed to the fact that he had only an hour-and-a-half to write. Yet Horner's letter was only three-and-one-quarter sides of a folded sheet of standard-sized paper. Horner did not say how many drafts he had written to produce the relatively brief copy he sent, but there may well have been several, in light of the time he took to write his letter.[14] Moreover, the circumstances of daily life for farmers, artisans, industrial workers, and housewives, and for anyone living under frontier circumstances, did not lend themselves to having either the privacy or the time to write as well as they wished.

Like Horner, Dr. Thomas Steel, too, begged forgiveness for the quality of an early letter. From a small cabin in the woods that he shared with other English immigrants in Wisconsin, Steel wrote, "When you take into consideration this has been written in a log hut of the size I have described—in the evenings after a hard days work surrounded by ten companions all talking perhaps you will excuse its faults." Steel had no table, and placed the paper on which he wrote on his knee. As his companions walked by, they continually jerked his writing hand.[15] The typical disruptions of family life created similar distractions. Mary Ann Archbald did not ask her cousin Margaret Wodrow to excuse her writing, but she did complain over the course of many years of distractions caused by the demands of her children and eventually grandchildren, as she wrote her letters. After he was settled in his own house with a wife and small children, Dr. Steel, too, complained of the distractions that his children created for his ability to concentrate on his writing.[16]

Steel, Archbald, and to a lesser extent Horner, a young and less experienced writer, were all to varying degrees educated. We might expect them to have high standards for the letters they produced. Reading the letters of a Steel, Archbald, or Horner, in which such complaints are made and apologies offered, one is struck with the absence of the obvious technical imperfections. What these correspondents seem ultimately to believe, and what was lacking in the circumstances in which they were writing, was the time and space to think effectively enough to express the larger range of concerns that they were experiencing as they wrote. Less technically proficient writers, however, also complained about the effects of the circumstances in which they wrote on the copy they produced, though they focused less on what they were able to express than on the obvious deficiencies in their use of language.

William Barker, the Indiana blacksmith who shared with his father John a distinctly rudimentary writing style and a most uneven grasp of grammar, wrote to his uncle and aunt in his first letter about the difficulties he faced in composing his letter. In his case, however, it was the speed with which he felt forced to write:

> you seem like you wanted to her from me so bad so i thought i would write as quick as could but this is not much of a letter but you must exscuse my bad writing and bad spling but the next time will try to do better and i will have a letter ready to send to you as soon as i get yours.[17]

What Barker shared with much more proficient writers was the desire to find the time and space to write the best letter he was capable of writing by the criteria he brought to judging the quality. For immigrant letter-writers, time and space tended to collapse into one problem that needed to be solved—finding what was convenient in the context of a variety of practical and daily constraints. There were constraints imposed by work and personal obligation and others imposed by the problem of having their letters conveyed to Britain. Immigrants sought to control as much as possible the processes of writing and conveying letters and carve out space and time within these constraints for exerting that control.

One strategy that a number of correspondents developed early on in their epistolary careers was to write long diarylike letters over the course of weeks and months, and devote attention to them where and when they had the opportunity. Mary Ann Archbald would do this for years, but under particular circumstances: a ritualized New Year's letter, conceived as a substitute for the many New Year's Eve celebrations she shared with her cousin, Margaret. Archbald began the letter less with the goal of sending it immediately to keep her cousin informed of recent happenings than of conjuring up in prose her feelings about a valued relationship and her cherished memories of the past. If the letter were not posted until April, which the winter and early spring weather and condition of the roads and canals made likely, this posed no problem for Archbald, who augmented it in the interval between initial composition and posting.[18]

This, however, was not a typical pattern. Prompted by their desire to overcome separation, the majority of writers wrote letters to answer those letters they had received, and acted to keep alive the cycle of reciprocal exchange. They wrote with the idea that what they were composing was to be posted sooner rather than later, and they frequently felt they had taken too long to answer the letters they had received. They might start days in advance of intended posting, particularly if they knew themselves to be slow writers. More often, the reader has the impression of writers rushing, amidst competing responsibilities, to compose their letters in time to post them at the earliest available opportunity. This often meant the same day that they had begun their letter, or that they found themselves hurrying to complete a letter begun in previous days or weeks.

In a wide variety of settings, over a long period of time, from the beginning of the nineteenth century to its closing years, we find writers such as Richard and Leila Locke, William Smyth, Robert Smyth, Ann Whittaker, Robert Wade, Joseph Wright, Archbald, and Steel hurrying to close their letters, because the mail was about to leave from the local post office, or a neighbor, spouse, or child was about to go into town to run errands and was stopping at the post office. Occasionally, too, an acquaintance, who offered to hand-deliver a letter or place it in the British post, had stopped by to visit, and was just about to depart on a journey that would end in Britain itself. Even the postmaster might find himself having to rush a letter to get it sent out at the time desired. Richard Locke ran the postal station, which was inside his own general store, at Boniface, Florida. Locke still was barely able to finish a letter to his sister in Dublin, because the postal steamer was about to leave with the local mail. Time and again, the impression the reader of immigrant letters gets is of writing that was rushed.[19]

Closer inspection reveals that more than any other factor but the ethical norm of reciprocity, the rhythms of epistolary exchange were governed by the constraints imposed by the methods available for conveying mail. Samples of 137 letters posted by four correspondents before 1840 and 335 letters posted after 1840 by eight correspondents, from locations in both Canada and the United States, were drawn to look more closely at these rhythms. Eighteen hundred and forty was a significant year, because it marks the inception both of the transport of mail between North America and Britain by regularly scheduled steam packet, and of a period witnessing a wide variety of postal reforms (the introduction of stamps; the rise in the number of postal stations; and falling costs of postage) in Britain, the United States, and Canada.[20]

The samples establish for both periods of time no more than an 8 percent variance among letters dated for the individual weekdays.[21] The meaning of this relatively diffuse pattern of letters, dated rather evenly throughout the week, may well be that the schedule of writing corresponds more than anything else to the varying, localized collection cycles of the nearest post office. Similar conclusions are yielded when the samples are consulted to inquire about the seasons of the year in which writing is done. Prior to 1840 and the inception of the use of the steam packet to convey mail, winter conveyance on sailing ships was unpredictable. The growing use of steam transport after 1840, such that by 1852 there was weekly traffic between Liverpool and New York City and New York City and Liverpool throughout the year, routinized the winter exchange of letters. Prior to 1840, there was a variance of from 8 percent to 12 percent between letters dated in the winter months (January, February, March), and those dated in the other three seasons of the year. There was little difference between the volume of letters dated among the other seasons. After 1840, the variance between the winter months and the other seasons ranges from 3 percent to 5 percent, and there is even less variance among the other seasons than before 1840. Before 1840, 14 percent of the letters in the sample were dated in the winter months, while after 1840, 21 percent were.[22]

Inland transportation difficulties experienced in winter and in early spring when roads were flooded probably account for some of these differences, both before and after 1840, but those difficulties receded more unevenly and slowly than the rapid breakthrough that transoceanic steam shipping in winter constituted. They did have an effect, though it is difficult to measure with precision for the entire population of letter-writers, because of the problem of tracing the localized infrastructural improvements that facilitated the conveyance of their mail.

Mary Ann Archbald provides us with the clearest example of the effect of improvements in inland transportation on the rhythms of letter-writing, because she dates precisely in her correspondence the day, November 15, 1822, when the first canal boats passed her farm, which lay adjacent to the Erie Canal.[23] Two effects become apparent in tracing the rhythms of Archbald's correspondence from her first letters in 1807 to November 1822, and thereafter from December 1822 to her last letters prior to her death in 1840; and both suggest the importance of technology in providing the outer boundaries in which letter-writing was done. The first is a seasonal effect. While there could be no impact on sending letters in the winter, because the Erie Canal was closed in the winter, it is clear that the opportunity afforded to convey letters in the spring months was dramatically increased by the canal, which provided an alternative to flooded, muddy roads. Prior to November 1822, 15 percent of her letters were dated in the spring months, while thereafter, 34.5 percent of her letters were similarly dated. The other individual seasons of the year showed no such dramatic change.

Second, there is an effect on marking more precisely the time at which a letter was written. The extent to which Archbald's letters were dated by year alone, or year and month, and year and season, and not precisely dated by date, month, and year dramatically declined from

31 percent before November 1822 to 3 percent thereafter. The decline of imprecise dating may suggest the extent to which Archbald now had opportunities to post her letters reliably in periods of the year, especially the spring, when before she was not able to do so. An alternative hypothesis is derived from the views of some historians about the consequences for individuals of the use of postal systems. They argue that responsibility for the posting of mail, which linked people to a routinized, time-sensitive bureaucratic system, led to more acute time-consciousness in individuals.[24] If so, the matter cannot be proven with data of this sort, for letter-writers who were Archbald's contemporaries were much more likely, before and after 1822, than she was to date their letters precisely.[25] While some individual peculiarities may account for Archbald's dating of letters, as, for example, her ritualized New Year's letter, greater opportunities for the conveyance of mail in their own localities may account for the patterns of her contemporaries.

Writers learned quickly to accommodate themselves to the constraints imposed by postal systems, and sought to maximize the space they were afforded to write as well as they could and as often as they felt it necessary or obligated. Several patterns emerge that illustrate the appropriation of time-spaces for writing. In the general population of letter-writers, there is no particular bias in behalf of writing on Sunday, a day when leisure was more generally indulged than on weekdays. But among artisans and factory workers, whose employment had begun to conform to a modern industrial schedule, Sunday does emerge as the primary day on which their letters are dated to an extent far greater than we find among farmers and self-employed people who did not do manual work. The skilled craftsmen William Darnley (30 percent of whose letters were dated on Sunday), Joseph Hartley (23 percent), David Laing (71 percent), George Martin (56 percent), and John Ronaldson (66 percent) all favored Sundays for writing. (An equal distribution among the seven days of the week would be 14.3 percent of letters dated on each of the seven weekdays.)

Possessing time to write could be more than a matter of temporary freedom from working. It might also be the result of having nothing to compete for one's attention, especially in small towns, where there was little else to do, and where post offices often, conveniently, remained open on Sundays in spite of Sabbatarian objections. John Ronaldson explained to his wife that, while Sunday "is not as gloom here as in Scotland," there was little to do in the mill town of East Braintree, Massachusetts, where he worked as a flax dresser in the linen industry, but write to her.[26] David Laing spent his own Sundays visiting his adult children and grandchildren and socializing with his workmates, and wrote his letters on Sunday evenings. While few other writers showed a preference for writing on Sundays, it is nonetheless interesting that the occasional self-conscious Christian, possessing a pronounced progressive attitude or self-improvement ethos, as opposed to a pietistic Sabbatarian feeling, did favor writing on Sunday. The Canadian farmers Thomas Spencer Niblock (41 percent), who frequently expressed his Christian beliefs and had taken his personal library with him to the Canadian frontier, and Ralph Wade (33 percent), the churchgoing Methodist and progressive agriculturalist, both favored Sundays for writing. Among those like Niblock and Wade, letter-writing might well have been conceived as a type of exercise in self-cultivation and introspection appropriate to the Sabbath. In contrast, few others seemed desirous of using the Sabbath in this way, which is probably less a comment on the status of their Christian beliefs than the fact that writing was a difficult, laborious task that violated their desire for a day of rest or recreation.

One consequence of the usual pattern of writing with the schedule of postal collection in mind, and not concentrating letter-writing on the traditional day of rest, was that immigrant correspondents frequently faced the prospect of doing their writing in the midst of workaday responsibilities. Weekday evenings and early mornings, as well as singular times of the calendar, often afforded the opportunity to write during the week. Leila and Richard Locke had to accommodate their desire to regularly exchange letters with Richard's sister Jeanette, a loyal correspondent who regularly sent them letters, personal items, and money from Dublin, to the long hours they kept their grocery store open. The burden of writing fell most heavily on Leila, who was the principal correspondent, but she simultaneously kept house, cared for three young children, and helped in the store. Leila often wrote in the evening when exhausted, and bothered by the insects that swarmed around her lamp in their tropical Florida home. Richard might add a paragraph to her letter that night or in the early morning before opening the store.[27] While the Lockes did not write as a couple, Joseph and Rebecca Hartley chose to do so in the evenings, when Joseph returned from the stone quarries. These letters might be written in the kitchen, as Rebecca also worked at preparing dinner, or much later in the evening, when, like the Lockes, both of them were tired. On one occasion, Rebecca closed by stating, "You can excuse this bad writing, for it is 10 o'clock and we must go to bead."[28]

The unrelenting pressure to budget time in these work-filled lives led other correspondents to utilize the special times when they were left with relatively fewer responsibilities than usual to write. Kate Bond took the occasions afforded by her husband being out of the house or away overnight with their oldest son, helping with the harvest on neighboring farms, to sit down at her kitchen table and write to her sisters and brothers.[29] Steel, an especially disciplined correspondent who quickly arranged with his father and sister a schedule of reciprocal exchange from which he rarely deviated, also took advantage of singular opportunities. For Steel, it was not an empty house, but rather, as a physician, those healthier periods of the year, such as the drier times of summer, or just after the first frost, or in midwinter, when he was away less frequently making house calls.[30] Steel would have written regardless of his other responsibilities (and he would have complained in his letter about how exhausted he was), but the opportunity that he was afforded by the healthier times of the year was to write in a more relaxed situation, in which, at one sitting, he could compose a complete letter and develop thoughts more fully than when interrupted by professional obligations.

Efforts to control the process of correspondence by shaping both the time and the space in which it was accomplished were never completely successful. Unexpected crises occasioned by deaths, health and money problems on both sides of the ocean, and demands occasioned by legal matters, especially having to do with the disposition of estates by inheritors, required that letters be written immediately. Commemorative letter-writing also might shake the usual rhythms of writing, though it was possible to plan for it, as it was not for the crises or legal matters. Holiday letters, such as Christmas letters written by the Hartleys and by Kate Bond and the New Year's letters written by Archbald, served to provide immigrants with temporal orientation and an opportunity for satisfying emotions. So, too, did the letters composed by those, who like Hartley, John Barker, and Nathan Haley, wrote around the time of the annual local fair in the home village in England, as if to seize the occasion for crafting memories of village life. In so doing, they sought to augment their identity narratives, and bind themselves closer to their family and kinfolk. In marking the time of the annual local fair in his English village Haley formalized such purposes with a quote from Burns. "Hear what Burns says, 'A last request permit me then / When yearly your assembled a'i / One round ask it with a tear / To him your friend thats far awa.'"[31] In whatever form, the quest for continuity was the major task of all immigrant correspondence.

It is to be expected that the early period of correspondence would be preoccupied with reestablishing and reformulating relationships and giving shape to the larger network of which they were a part. Those who aspired to the regular exchange of letters craved the feelings of emotional intimacy and the warmth of private conversation that writing to loved ones and reading their letters from home inspired. Not all would express these emotions as explicitly, fluently, and frequently as did Mary Cumming, who wished to remain a living presence in her Irish family through her letters. She explained toward the close of an early letter, "I hope Mary Cumming is with you now." For Cumming, writing created a pleasant feeling of being in the bosom of her family. "Do you know it is like a second parting with you for me to quit writing?" she said as she closed one letter.[32] But the intimacy quickly assumed by others who dwelled less on exposing their feelings suggests very similar emotions. "I sit down with pleasure to write you because it resembles talking to you," said Thomas Morris, writing for himself and his wife, Jane, in his first letter to his father.[33] John Fisher's letters to his mother and to his siblings soon became full of jovial, self-mocking writing, and self-conscious wordplay, quotations from poetry, and surprising transitions. His letters are filled with direct address, by which he led his readers through his writing by referring here and there to "dear Mother" or "dear brother and sister," while making a point.[34] These strategies suggest a quality of fond relations and a desire to attain the intimacy of conversation.

Other correspondents were not able explicitly to create a mood of intimacy in words, but the larger context of their letters suggests a strong desire to reestablish themselves within the family circle. George Martin's very long first letter to his parents, signed also by his wife, combines a diarylike account of his passage, resettlement, and health problems with the plea for reconciliation over some unspecified difficulty that caused "bitterness of feeling" in the past, and the request that they send out his favorite books and periodicals. Martin's intent, it seems clear, is a long-term epistolary relationship.[35]

These desires suggested that an early task must be negotiating a cycle of reciprocal exchange. Prior to emigration, the parties doubtless agreed that letters would be exchanged. Some had already developed the habits of letter-writing. Before emigrating, Mary Ann Archbald had for decades been writing her cousin Margaret. Continuing to write was a matter of course, though Archbald recognized now that letters were to be the only source of contact and therefore of even greater importance than before. But their situation was atypical, since the women had lived in different, though nearby, places in Scotland and Mary Ann resided as well on a remote island.[36] The large majority of correspondents were leaving family and friends with whom they had lived in close proximity, and had not needed to correspond with in order to sustain relations. Agreements to initiate and sustain correspondence made before emigration were a mark of the anxiety that the prospect of long-term separation created for emigrants and homeland correspondents. Matthew Dinsdale set down the outlines of correspondence for the immediate future in a letter to his mother sent from Liverpool, while waiting for his ship to depart. He wanted, perhaps unrealistically, a letter waiting for him in New York City, informing him about the activities of his siblings and the status of the family farm, and promised he would post a letter home as soon as he arrived.[37]

Negotiations over reciprocal exchange involved a number of practical issues having to do with the conveyance of letters. One of these was providing new addresses, which also served as a context for establishing spatiotemporal orientation through discussions of distances and times of travel, principally from well-known points on the eastern seaboard that readers in Britain knew of or could easily find on a map. Exchanging addresses was often more than a matter of letting one's immediate correspondent know where one was, but rather of instructing a larger network with that information and also finding out where others, who were also in transit, were. This could be quite complicated in networks of mobile people.

The four Petingale brothers, Henry, John, Thomas, and William, not only wrote to their father and five sisters, but also to one another. They emigrated at different times over a period of years, and John went not to the United States but to Australia and then New Zealand. Henry returned to England after two years in the United States, and then again to North America. Each of them moved frequently. For them, exchanging addresses was a constant work of inquiry.[38] Addresses were not only exchanged among the correspondents in the archived collections. The network included others, too, related and unrelated, with whom there was a desire to exchange letters. They had first, however, to be located.

Henry Kimberly, a Lincolnshire farmer who settled on fifty acres in Wisconsin, had inquiries from his family in England about a mutual friend, another emigrant later to be found in New York, whom Kimberley's nephew, George Squier, wished to locate, but who had been temporarily lost to his friends. In his letters, Squier reported at length on the activities and whereabouts of migrating or already resettled individuals known to his uncle.[39]

Another practical issue surrounding conveyance was specifying the obligation to assume the costs of postage, a common matter for negotiation in immigrant correspondence. Few migrants could adopt the attitude assumed by John Fisher, who wrote that he did not care about the costs and wished everyone to write him who had the inclination, even if he were obligated at his end of the exchange to pay the costs. The matter posed a dilemma for others, for they had to strike a balance between assuming a material burden and safeguarding their emotional health, which depended on receiving and sending letters. But the same dilemma was faced on the other end of the exchange as well. Resolutions usually favored, as in Thomas Steel's case, the more affluent party, which was unlikely to be the recent emigrant. Because of their interest in maintaining a biweekly, and hence relatively costly exchange of letters, Steel's father and sister continued to pay the costs of correspondence even after he became self-sufficient.[40] But in other cases the negotiations over costs were ongoing, and resembled a tug-of-war. When Kimberly protested having to assume the costs of his cousin's last envelope, Squier replied that the problem was that there were two letters placed in one envelope, one from Squier and the other from a relative or friend. When he went to post the letter, Squier told the clerk he was only willing to pay for his letter. When told this could not be done, Squier refused to pay any costs and left it to his cousin in Wisconsin to do so.[41]

As in Kimberley's case, ongoing discussions over the costs of correspondence might occasionally take on a tone of irritation, but they did not lead to a crisis that resulted in a disruption of the flow of letters. The reason is not hard to discern. The correspondents felt a strong ethical obligation to the principle of reciprocity in the exchange of letters. For them, nothing was more important, including costs, than the exchange of letters. More frequently, what was a source of complaint was the violation of that principle—or seeming violations, for letters lost in transit could as easily account for the failure to receive mail as could neglect.

From the early years, some correspondence was wracked by tensions over reciprocity issues. Joseph Willcocks, William Kerr, and Robert Smyth each complained that their correspondents violated the principle of reciprocity and neglected them. Smyth also complained that the letters from his family lacked expressions of warmth for his new wife. Willcocks and Smyth actually threatened to stop writing over such issues, which neither would ultimately do. Smyth appears to have enjoyed the drama in the cycle of perceived slights and threats to suspend correspondence. His protests did inspire his family to write to him, but then they lapsed back into silence, and he would renew his criticisms and threats. Willcocks's brother was simply a poor correspondent and would never change in this regard, but his violations of reciprocity may have been motivated by more than procrastination. He never complied with Joseph's request that he write a letter of reference for him to help him attain a government position in Canada. Richard Willcocks did not trust his brother's judgment or approve of his behavior, which was perhaps attributable to Joseph's participation in the abortive Irish uprising of 1798, which had led to his migration. Joseph himself attributed his brother's silence to laziness.[42]

The ways in which the final, positive resolution of such issues might be experienced remind us of the emotional importance of correspondence in these lives. During his first year in Baltimore, when Joseph Wright finally received a letter from his wife Hannah after six months of worry and longing to hear from her, he wrote in response, "the sight of [it] almost overcame me, I did not open it till I went and sat down in the fields where I gave vent to my bosom and was glad to find my dear was in health with my children and friends and that even one of my letters had reached her."[43] Few others wrote of weeping, but most had a great many emotions invested in their correspondence, and the suspicion of neglect or the anxious realization that the fate of their letters was out of their control began to dawn early in the history of many exchanges of letters. But so, too, did the guilty feeling of not living up to one's own responsibilities. Just as Radcliffe Quine did not write for seventeen years and castigated himself in his first letter for his behavior, Joseph Hartley could say by way of apology at the start of a letter, after two years of silence, "I have no reason for not writing to you only I don't like writing letters any I must owne it is my neglect."[44]

Negotiations over content assumed a prominent part in early letters, as correspondents attempted to find themes and a tone that were mutually satisfactory to the writers and the recipients. Some were told what to write by their correspondents, who like James Steel or Charles Mickle in complaining about their son's letters, offered suggestions about what they wanted to find in the letters.[45] Because the correspondents were known to one another prior to their separation, however, it was not difficult for most of them to have ideas about what subjects were of interest to those they wrote.

Such intuitions were not only the possession of technically proficient writers. For all his resistance to writing, from the start of his correspondence Joseph Hartley wrote letters filled with interesting details of daily life, including not only his work and friendships with other migrants known to his correspondents, but also his participation in electoral parades and his excursions to nearby Niagara Falls. James Roberts, a Sheffield knifemaker who migrated to Connecticut with a son who shared his trade, a daughter-in-law, and another young woman and her child born out of wedlock, was also not an especially proficient writer, but showed enough enthusiasm for writing that he broke the reciprocal cycle of exchange on one early occasion. Writing to his principal correspondent, a son-in-law, he said, "I wrote to you in advance that is two letters to your one. It is because we have more news than you have, at least we think so," and explained that the young unwed mother, Mary Wilson, who had accompanied them from England and become discontented enough to threaten to return to England, had suddenly gotten married, and hence achieved instant respectability.[46]

Correspondents such as Hartley and Roberts gave evidence of learning to create in their writing a place to interpret, or at least record, their experience, for both themselves and others. In contrast were those more proficient writers, such as Robert McElderry, John Ronaldson, and Joseph Willcocks whose letters were punctuated by complaints that they had nothing to say because their life was without incident and nothing ever happened in the dull place where they lived. In the cases of McElderry and Ronaldson, the problem was a belief that what interested them, politics or business, would not be of concern to their female correspondents, a sister and a wife respectively.[47]

But such complaints about wanting for subject matter also masked two more profound difficulties that the immigrant correspondent commonly faced in the initial forays into letter-writing. The first was the tentativeness of both present and future during the early years after re-settlement, when plans were being formed and choices weighed, and disappointments were suffered that shed doubt on the project of emigration. Writing about choices and contingencies, especially when it involved linked events and processes and the prospective decisions of other people, could tax the ability of any writer, but it was a necessary element for many in reporting life as they were then living it. For the relatively recently settled immigrant, choice of residence, future employment, or the decision to leave wage work and buy a farm, and the chain migration of family and friends, might be linked to one another. The difficulty was describing this shifting complex of hopes and opportunities.

The noteworthy incidence of contingency constructions—"if" and "whether" usages—and deploying of the subjunctive tense in many early letters is testimony to this need to measure and to balance possibilities. As Kate Bond weighed the possibilities of one or the other of her brothers and possibly her sister joining her and her husband in Connecticut, her sentences needed to grow ever more complex in order to carry the analytical freight they were made to bear. This matter is analyzed more fully in the chapter devoted to Bond. For now, we might note one example. In a letter of September 1872, just into her second year in the United States, the second substantive paragraph has six contingency constructions linked to family emigration and chain migration in twenty-two sentences, and in the next paragraph two more in ten sentences.[48]

The early letters of Andrew and Jane Morris have the same mark in their writing, as they, too, examine and weigh the possibilities of being joined by family and friends. In an 1831 letter, written a year after their arrival in the United States from Lancashire when they were residing in Germantown, Pennsylvania, where Andrew worked in a mill, they evaluated the wisdom of the migration of parents and siblings and the implications of these migrations for their own plans, in this case to farm. In a paragraph of approximately eighteen lines there are six contingency constructions, as the Morrises anticipated the future from several points of view.[49] The writing involved is difficult and labored but, as in Bond's case, ultimately effective in charting a number of possibilities.

The problem of expressing plans and possibilities was a challenge to writing abilities. The problem of addressing disappointment and reversals of fortune was entirely another sort of challenge, posing not technical but emotional difficulties. Writers were anxious that in admitting failure and frustration, one might imply that the recent decision to emigrate had been wrong, and thus cast doubt on the quality of one's judgment. At the same time, one might cause worry among those who cared about one's happiness. A strategy for dealing with the problem that avoided the ethical problem of deception was to postpone writing until there was better news to deliver—or at least as long as one could without breaking off communication, or being completely insensitive to one's correspondent's needs.

Apologizing for his recent silence, John McBride said that he would have liked to write sooner, "but did not like till I could give some satisfaction." McBride went on to explain his difficulties finding work in a glutted labor market. When his father replied that he should come home, McBride responded indignantly that he would never do so if it meant accepting working for a wage, as he had experienced such work in the north of Ireland. He would not consent to such degradation again.[50] After three years in the United States, Titus Crawshaw appears to have stopped writing to his parents, only to resume when he found out through a third party that his mother was very sick. He explained, "I have had nothing but bad luck this two years," and described a protracted period of poverty and unemployment that made it impossible for him to send money home. He believed that his recent experience shed a doubtful light on his decision to emigrate: "I should not have wrote yet if I had not heard of Mother been so very bad and the reson is I am ashamed to write because I know I could have helped you a little if I had never come to this country."[51]

Detailed avowal of resettlement difficulties was less common, and rarer still was the discussion of more intimate aspects of their consequences, such as tension between spouses. An Irish writer (probably Robert Porter, though he failed to sign his name), recently resettled on the central Illinois prairies in the early 1870s, did just this in a letter to his "freands in Mullyglass [Mullaglass]." "It is my painful and unwilling task," he wrote, "to have to inform you that I am sorely disappointed in my chouse of Homes for we have found every thing so strange here that it would take more fortitude than eather of us is posessed withe to be happy." He went on to decry the flatness of the land, impassable roads, ferocious blizzards, and plagues of grasshoppers. But it was his wife's discontent that pained him the most, for she questioned his judgment in urging emigration. "The wife is very dissatisfied," he wrote, "and has comensed to refact [reflect?] on my night and day about me been so keen to come to this Country for She thinks we will come to want and that we cant Live here at all." It was her criticism of his decision specifically that led him to caution friends not to make his letter public.[52]

Why did this writer address these painful and embarrassing reflections on his situation? It was, he said, because of a sense of responsibility to those who might choose, without knowing all the facts, to emigrate in his recently laid down footsteps. "I do not like to say this," he said of the contents of his letter, "but it was allways my mota [motto?] to tell all the good and the bad and allway I mean to."[53] This concern for the ethics of their position as, in effect, role models and advisers for others was widely shared. Indeed the second difficulty having to do with the choice of subject matter related to the apprehensions about encouraging immigration. Nothing arose so quickly to impede the development of content in immigrant letters than the fear that in appearing to encourage emigration, they would eventually be blamed for the failed immigration and disappointed expectations of others.

Moreover, immigrant writers often possessed the plausible fear that those they encouraged to emigrate would come to believe that they could count on them for assistance and emigrate with resettlement around them in mind, and soon become dependent on them. Robert Craig's peculiar evasion in a letter—stating that everything he could think to say had already been said by others—takes on another dimension when we realize that Craig, an Irish Protestant friend of John McBride who had settled in Birmingham, Alabama, continued throughout his correspondence to worry about encouraging others to follow him. He found that too many discontented emigrants were like "the Israelites mourning after Egypt"—nostalgic for the oppression and difficulty they had left behind—and he refused to be criticized for encouraging those he believed did not know their own minds.[54] People expect, said McBride, agreeing, that they will come to the United States and instantly, "or at most in a few years," be turned into gentlemen, and when this fails to happen, they blamed letters sent home for wrongly influencing them and called the letter-writer a "liar" rather than crediting his luck or efforts in his own behalf. David Laing and John Fisher, to take other examples, voiced the same fears.[55] These fears placed such immigrants, of whom there seem to have been many more than those, like Steel, who never deviated from his belief that his father and sister would be better off joining him, in a profound state of inner tension. Both Laing and Fisher and numerous others relished the prospect of uniting their family and friends around them, but also came to fear the consequences of doing so.

It was in the early years that such dreams of unity were most active, so these tensions were apparent from the inception of correspondence. They form an important context for the negotiation of the emotions of separation. Such tensions frequently reveal themselves in restraint and balance and in a guarded tone in writing about the process of migration and about North American conditions and opportunities and, simultaneously, a hesitancy or delicacy in recommending a course of action for those who might be considering emigration. They might express themselves in convoluted formulations, such as Matthew Dinsdale used in addressing his mother. Dinsdale wanted his mother to join him in Wisconsin, but feared being too direct or insistent and projecting scenarios of the fine life he might make for her. Thus he wrote, "Now I want you to write me and tell me if I should wish you to come, if you will do so."[56] Or it might take the form of contradictory advice. Such was the case with the Morris brothers, Andrew and Thomas. Andrew advised against his parents' emigration because the sea voyage might be difficult at their age, while Thomas was unswerving in his optimism about the better life his father and mother would enjoy in the United States.[57]

The emigration of parents constituted a special problem precisely because of the uncertainties that age created, but such sensitivities were hardly restricted to cautions about how aging parents would fare. McBride and Laing felt the same cautions in addressing their siblings, relatives, or friends. The most common way to resolve these tensions was selectively to target one's counsel to individuals and pave the way for their resettlement. Kate Bond only encouraged her married brothers, especially those without large families, and her sister Sarah to emigrate after she had made productive inquiries locally in Connecticut about employment that they might obtain immediately upon arrival.[58] McBride attempted to do the same for his cousin John, the only person he encouraged to emigrate in his early years in the United States, but changing employment opportunities in the Watertown, New York, cotton mill where he was employed led him to doubt he could find John a job. Instead he offered to provide him with a home while he searched for his own employment.

But McBride was very selective in this choice of whom to assist. Apparently some of his reluctance to assist others was rooted in bitter personal experience. He cautioned his father, who may have been somewhat overly generous in offering his son's assistance to others, that he wanted no one showing up at his door with "letters of introduction to me for there are a great deal too many calls on me as it is; let them push their fortune as I have done."[59] John Wade adopted another strategy in writing to his uncle Ralph. When he wrote that he was considering emigration, Ralph surprised his Canadian kin, who thought he was "pretty snugly situated at home," and somewhat senior at age forty-seven to be starting over again. John offered practical advice on emigration, but he framed much of it in a way that subtly sought out unrealistic expectations in the hope that Ralph would reflect further. He did not discourage him, but he did review at length the reasons why some English immigrants had failed at farming in Canada, singling out, among a number of points, the fact that they were already comfortable in England, but thought they could make a quick fortune without reflecting on the rigors of postfrontier farming in Canada.[60]

Planning to return for a visit, a common element in the negotiation of the emotions of separation in early correspondence, offered the promise of reunion while simultaneously mooting the complex problem of initiating a chain of migrations. Return migration of the immigrant letter-writer tentatively folded at times into this promise of a visit, as if a visit might, perhaps, depending on savings from the North American venture and the larger context of opportunity, eventuate in permanent resettlement in Britain. Moreover, the promise of a visit, and/or the possibility of reemigration, also served as a way of making a definitive statement about the wisdom of the initial decision to emigrate, because it was often paired with a declaration of independence from conditions of work or farming in Britain. As McBride, who contemplated some sort of return until he was married to an American woman two years after settling in the United States, said in an early letter, "I trust in God I shall never have call to go home to stand like a Beggar at a Manufacturer's door[.]"[61]

Kate Bond made the same point eighteen months after arriving in Connecticut. After discussing the matter with her husband, she wrote to her sister-in-law, "You will see us coming some day, but not yet for we shall never come back to work for our living. But Jim tells me when we have been here five years I may go back and see you all. But I am quite settled here."[62] Hopes for a visit home most often receded as individuals became settled in their North American lives, married, and established families. For every Robert Smyth and Matthew Dinsdale, unmarried men who took their rapidly earned savings—in Dinsdale's case, with $4,000 from gold mining in California—and did indeed return for a visit, there were many married couples, like the Bonds or Hartleys, who ultimately gave up this vision, either because they feared the voyage or because they came to see returning to visit as time-consuming, costly, and a deviation from the principal purposes of their new lives.[63]

On the other hand, the incidence of return migration of those who had initially not been sure how long they would stay and contemplated permanent resettlement—in contrast to those artisans like John Ronaldson who came with the declared intention of working for a relatively brief period and returning—is difficult to know. One reason is that we cannot know in many cases why some archived collections of letters suddenly end. Lost letters, death, or estrangement are as plausible reasons as reemigration. One would expect to find evidence of intentions and planning in the letters of those intending to return, but this is often absent. It is significant to note that in all the twenty-five letter-series gathered by Charlotte Erickson, only one letter, written by Rebecca Butterworth, who left Lancashire with her husband, Jim, in approximately 1843 to farm in Arkansas, explicitly proposed the necessity of reemigration. Her letter is an intense narrative of sickness, death, and impoverishment, and a plea to her father for money for the passage. Her husband seemed completely unprepared for postfrontier farming. The couple were starving when Butterworth wrote her letter begging for help, and completely capitulating in the face of the failure of their American dream.[64] Whatever their situation, few were willing to declare a surrender and return.

The sensitivities about content apparent in the fears about encouraging the emigration of others alert us to the steps taken to control the information in letters, and ultimately to the issue of confidentiality, as it was negotiated from the inception of correspondence. While Robert Craig was reluctant to ask his correspondent, John McBride's father, not to share his letters with others, he tried to control exactly what message others took away from them: "Let my acquaintances know that this is a fine poor man's country and thats all the encouragement I give."[65] Some correspondents, however, sought control by requesting complete or near-complete confidentiality early in their letter-writing. Those who might speak ill of others, for example for failing to help them when they needed assistance during resettlement, knew how quickly gossip circulated and might get back via letters to North America. Their requests that such criticisms of third parties be kept private constituted the most common reasons for seeking confidentiality in the early years of correspondence.

There were material reasons, too, for desiring confidentiality. Debtors, such as Joseph Wright, worried that the long arm of British law would find them in North America and induce American authorities to force them to appease their creditors. Wright told his wife Hannah that she must not let anyone beyond the family circle know he was in Baltimore. His migration from the eastern seaboard to the backwoods of the eastern Ohio frontier, where he eventually settled with Hannah and their children, was an effort to flee further from creditors and their agents.[66] Henry Johnson, another debtor, sought to ensure the privacy of his letters to insulate himself against creditors in Ireland, but also out of narcissistic rage against those creditors who refused him any relief from debt and against others who refused to help him in his hour of need. He did not want his letter shared, he wrote his wife from Canada in his first letter: "It is only for yourself as there are few others care anything for me. So I wish to be forgotten by them."[67] The escape from debt was not the only source of a need for privacy that grew out of money matters. So, too, was the desire to avoid sharing one's plans and hopes. Thomas Pryterch was an orphan or illegitimate son of a wealthy man. He emigrated from Shrewsbury and used a small inheritance, in the form of a trust, to settle in the United States, first briefly in 1858 and then again in 1870. Pryterch learned not to trust the attorney to whom he wrote to retrieve his money. "It is too much talked about," he wrote to an older friend. He preferred to take loans from his friend than have to account for his needs with a lawyer who let others know how much he was spending and on what he spent it.[68] Pryterch thus signaled his friend that he depended on his discretion. He evidently felt the need to do so, but most correspondents did not, and depended on those with whom they had established relationships to act with discretion.

Thus far, most of these early negotiations were between the immigrant and the homeland correspondent. Because we have only one side of the correspondence in nearly all cases, we largely know them as they are reflected from the immigrant's position. Not all these early negotiations, however, were between correspondents at different ends of the exchange. There were also negotiations simultaneously at each end of the correspondence. At the inception, the most obvious examples are presented by immigrants' letters that appear, because they are jointly signed, to have been jointly composed by married couples, or those letters composed by one of the partners in a marriage in which there was the need to report on the couple's resettlement and plans for the future. Like marriage itself, such authorship, in all its varied guises, involved complex negotiations, whether explicit or implicit.

Like Kate Bond, many married immigrants took responsibility as individuals for writing letters to their families (including the families of their spouses) and friends. There are, however, many cases in which letters are jointly signed and thus appear to be jointly authored. One most obvious negotiation involved establishing the voice of letters that were crafted, at least formally, as dual constructions. To some extent, these joint collaborations were fictions, especially in cases in which the literacy of one of the parties was marginal.[69]

The illiterate or the technically less competent writer was present in coauthored letters in a variety of ways. They might simply nag a principal correspondent to sit down, write, and maintain the cycle of reciprocal exchange. Emily Tongate tried to explain to her aunt and uncle why they no longer received letters from her father, John Bishop, an English farm laborer who emigrated in 1857 and settled on an upstate New York farm, and mother, as they once had. It was not for want of her mother's efforts that her father failed to write to his family. "You must not blame mother because you have not had eny letters from father. It is not her falt. She have wanted him to write to you all times—and again but he did not and now he is so very sick and he is not able to do it."[70] John's wife apparently was unable to write herself, or perhaps she felt it inappropriate to address his family directly herself, though such a feeling would have been unusual. In other cases, the less literate or illiterate spouse was simply represented in the letter. Rebecca Hartley picked up the burden of writing to Joseph's family because he disliked writing, but his voice is at times in the background. She writes that Joseph is addressing her, while she herself is writing. The letters are thus appropriately cosigned, because Joseph at times tells Rebecca what to write and objects to some subjects that she wants to develop in the letter.[71]

Other early negotiations involving spouses ultimately concerned language usage itself. Because her husband was illiterate, Ann Whittaker, the English farmwife in Illinois, did all the writing in her family, which included letters to England and to her own children living in other American locations. The letters are not cosigned, but her writing shows traces of a type of negotiation over voice that is ever present in the letters of married couples, whether they are singly crafted or jointly authored. This is the "I-We" problem: the extent to which, in relating the activities of a couple, the letter speaks for the "I" of the immediate author, or the "we" that is the couple. In the background, of course, is the "he" that represents the husband.

The most delicate balances were achieved by couples who were engaged in genuine joint authorship, and by women, especially rural women in farm families. For such women, the complexity of their task in finding a voice ultimately reflected the complexity of the family farm as an enterprise sustained by separate but overlapping, gendered spheres of labor. With telling shifts in pronoun usage that are less frequently found in letters crafted by husbands writing about farming, these women wrote of their work, their husband's labors, and the shifting responsibilities that belonged to neither exclusively. There were several approaches to resolution of the problem of voice in these cases. Whittaker shifted easily between the authoritative "I" of a writer, with her own opinions and activities to report, and the "we" of a partner in a joint enterprise.[72] In her letters, however, Kate Bond revealed the extent of her husband's power over setting their priorities and establishing plans for their future as a couple. "I" and "we" appear in the same contexts as in Whittaker's letters, but frequently Bond ascribed to her husband Jim authority over establishing priorities and making the plans for their future.[73]

The brothers Andrew and Thomas Morris and their wives, both named Jane, had other approaches in their early letters to the problem of voice that contrasted with one another. Andrew and Jane cosigned a letter in which Andrew's "I" predominated throughout, but Jane appended a paragraph of her own, signed by her, at the end of it. In the case of Thomas and Jane, they, too, cosign a letter that is clearly in Thomas's voice, and there is no separate paragraph from Jane. Yet, in contrast to Andrew and Jane, who were then living in Germantown, Pennsylvania, where Andrew worked as a weaver, Thomas and Jane farmed in southern Ohio. When Thomas shifted his writing away from opinions about emigration and promises to help members of his British family if they were to emigrate, to the daily activities of farming, his "I" did turn to the collective "we." But not all men sought to achieve this collective voice when writing of the family farm. The same pattern does not occur when many years later Andrew and Jane left the city and bought land to farm near Thomas. The letters of Andrew and Jane are cosigned, but the collective "we" is almost wholly absent, and again there is no separate paragraph from Jane. Andrew does not write of farming in detail, and when he does, his "we" is an impersonal one, which is used, for example, to explain the cultivation of tobacco in a textbook-like fashion, or to represent him and his sons, who were old enough to farm with him.[74]

Such negotiations over voice were, of course, by no means restricted to the immigrants' letters. Evidence of them may also be found in the few homeland letters to which we have access. James Steel, Thomas's father, wrote letters in which we spoke for both him and his daughter, Lilly, whose voice inevitably was crowded out by the older man's insistent questions and opinions, which though phrased as if jointly conceived were not at all hers. Only when she wrote her own letters did she express her concerns, which were more directed at her personal unhappiness and feelings of being neglected by her brother, whose letters addressed only their father's questions.[75]

The parents and brother of William Julius Mickle divided their labors in writing to their son from the inception of their correspondence. Charles Julius, the father, and Charles, a brother, often sent separate letters in the same envelope. Charles Julius wrote about his desire to emigrate to Canada, his hope that his son could find a good plot of land for them to farm, and his effort to direct the details of land purchases from London. Charles wrote to underline these hopes, and to comment on their father's insecure tenure in his post at the East India Company Library in London and the dubious state of his health. Some of these letters contained brief writing in individual paragraphs from other, much younger siblings, who wrote about such things as pet rabbits, and occasionally from his mother, Sarah, who enjoined William Julius to go to church and live a moral life. Charles appears to have felt somewhat constrained by these circumstances, for when he wrote letters to William Julius that went out in their own envelope, he spoke more freely about his father's nervous, hypochondriacal state of mind. Both the Steel letters and the Mickle letters suggest that the practice of writing group letters, on either side of the ocean, might have inhibited candor, and required the search for an outlet in the initiation of another stream of letters in some correspondence. There are only a few examples, however, of the effort to start another correspondence in which the writer could be more frank than in a group letter. The Mickles themselves provide us with suggestions about the emotional context for explaining the relative rarity of this practice of separate streams of communication. The group letters that went out to William Julius, for all that they might have lacked in candor from Charles's perspective, were a fond act of family solidarity and a joint project that could involve everyone, from parents to the youngest siblings.[76]

The range and combination of voices and forms of address in the Mickle letters are particularly rich and complex, and provided William Julius not only with a good sampling of greetings and messages from his family of all ages, but also with a formidable task in responding to each of his correspondent's inquiries, endearments, expressions of concern, and current activities. The Mickles were a loving, educated, and articulate family. They relished writing for the intimacy it afforded and the practical goals it advanced. They were adept at sending letters and packages, and using the mails to arrange for the transfer of money through banking agents to William Julius, notwithstanding the disorganized circumstances of postal exchange in Canada in the early 1830s. These correspondents quickly and enthusiastically established rhythms and opened opportunities for a variety of voices. Other correspondents, however, encountered persistent problems, especially growing out of the prior relationships they shared, from the inception of their letter-writing, and it is to their correspondence that we now turn.

The occasionally tentative, but nonetheless enthusiastic, steps taken by most letter-writers to begin a correspondence set in sharp relief the examples of those who from the beginning of their efforts to correspond encountered significant psychological impediments in doing so. These were immigrants who wrote letters but took little pleasure in doing so, because writing put them back into the midst of difficult personal relationships and conjured up hurtful and oppressive memories.

One of the safest generalizations that an observer of immigrants may make is that they were invariably people with personal pasts rooted in family relationships. Yet this relational baggage, with its important implications for personal identity and primary relationships, has been much less the subject of inquiry by immigration historians than the reified notion of cultural baggage, which is founded on the untenable assumption of a list of more or less fixed cultural traits constant in massive populations of individuals.

The relational baggage that individual immigrants possessed was probably more fixed than any national or regional traits they might have possessed, and, though an emotional and practical asset for many, such as William Julius Mickle, a profoundly heavy burden for others. From the inception of some correspondence, readers are aware that there were difficulties from the preemigration past that continue to haunt relationships, even under the circumstances of separation. This should come as no surprise: human beings find it more difficult to change their families or to efface the memory of significant relationships than to change their language, place of residence, national allegiance, and occupation, which are by no means necessarily in themselves easy transitions. Most immigrants felt the need to reestablish primary relationships—even bad ones—through the exchange of letters. Correspondence sometimes reintroduced strained and even disastrous relationships to the immigrants' lives. Such relationships followed them across the ocean, and then evolved through correspondence, which was in some cases as troubled as one imagines the face-to-face encounters had once been. These difficulties are in evidence exactly where we expect to find them: in the relationships of husband and wife, of siblings, and of parents and children, especially fathers and sons.

Some relationships with family are haunted by transgressions that inspire lasting guilt and shame. The collection of the Irish immigrant Samuel Buchanan's letters was edited in order not to include direct evidence of his crimes, but it is clear that a shameful past of theft and abandonment of his wife and child colored his epistolary relationship with his birth family for years.[77]

Other collections also provide evidence of desertion. Nathan Haley emigrated in 1820, leaving a bad marriage and the burden of an expensive household. In his first letter, he requested that his parents pick up his few small debts and assist in providing for his small children. He acknowledged a history of heavy drinking. His early letters are filled with self-recrimination, but also with cloying self-pity. In 1823 he suggested he might return, as Erickson notes, like the prodigal son, after seven years, to resume his responsibilities, but his last archived letter in 1825 contained nothing of his plans and only a brief reference to his children. His letters spoke of making money in the United States, but said nothing about sending any of it home to contribute to their welfare. His parents do answer at least some of his letters, and in a cordial tone, it seems, they once requested more descriptions of the United States. But he also received letters from his sister's husband, who in an 1823 letter gave him "a good scoulding." The brother-in-law protested his own straightened circumstances, which perhaps grew out of the need to make some contribution to caring for Haley's children. The situation is obscure, but under any circumstance, the entire five years of the archived correspondence is haunted by broken relationships and the failure to meet obligations.[78]

In other correspondence, the nature of this oppressive past between parents and children is difficult to determine. Some collections of archived letters, such as the correspondence of George Martin and John McLees, begin their first letters with apologies, direct and indirect, to parents for past conduct. As McLees said in his letter, which was sent to his brother, he hoped someday to revisit Ireland "that I might embrace my father and ask forgiveness for all that is past." McLees wrote his father as well as his brother, but his father did not write him back, a fact which McLees claimed in another letter to the father hurt him deeply. Four years after resettling in the United States, his father died; it seems that McLees had never heard from him. Martin's case is similar. In his first letter home he asked his parents, somewhat indirectly and without admitting wrongdoing, for forgiveness for the past, stating, "if there is any bitterness of feeling on your side still existing pray let it be forgot in the dangers and troubles I have encountered since the morning we parted but let all this be forgot." It is clear that the breakdown in his relations with his parents was with his father. Though Martin did write to his father and may have gotten a reply, he noted in a letter to a brother ten years after his emigration that his father never wrote to him.[79] In each case, the root of the estrangement is never made explicit, but apologies coming so quickly on the heels of emigration might indicate the cause may have been emigration itself—or more precisely, a son's decision to emigrate in spite of his father's opposition. Flaunting parental authority and removing oneself from a father's moral direction might well have been the cause for permanent estrangement.

The estrangement between the Petingale brothers and their father, however, was certainly not over their decisions to emigrate. The elder Petingale, George, had a personal history of having clawed his way to affluence, and this caused permanent bitterness on his part toward those who might depend on him. He had five unmarried daughters to support. He seems to have desired his sons to go off on their own as soon as possible. Here, too, the archived collection begins with a letter of apology. A year before he left for the United States, William Petingale was writing to his father to apologize for unspecified "past conduct" that was "neither dutiful nor affectionate."[80] William is not the only one of the four brothers estranged from a father whom they usually address indirectly, through letters sent to one of their sisters. When it did take place, correspondence with their father seems to have been tortured, for it had to contend with what his son Henry called George's "aversion to repetitions and long-winded epistles"—anything, it seems, but short businesslike letters. There was also a tortured history of misunderstandings and failed interactions. Addressing George Petingale was similar to traversing a minefield. When Henry Petingale did eventually write to his father, his letter was misinterpreted as a request for money, and George wrote his son a curt note stating, Henry recalled, that he would not assist "any of [his] sons with another shilling." Henry disclaimed any interest in taking money from his father, thanked him for his past assistance, and launched into an extraordinary analysis of his father's emotional history and a declaration of the need of this son, seemingly wiser than his father, for his father's love:

> I was sorry to perceive in your letter a brevity, and absence of all feeling of interest, a sort of business like compliance with a disagreeable duty in writing to me. I hope such were not the feelings that actuated you. I know that you have a proud yet a feeling heart, though your early contact with an unfeeling world, unaided, unencouraged, by even parental solicitude, taught you a sad lesson of mistrust, and yet a cold proud feeling of self-reliance, the offspring of your position, which has paved your way to success through life. Father, you have always undervalued the influence of a few words of feeling or kind solicitude. I do not write this with a feeling of reproach but of regret.[81]

Though siblings were sometimes the bridge between parents and alienated children, relations among siblings may also have been haunted by past difficulties. The reader wonders what to make of the history shared between those like Radcliffe Quine and George Martin, who find they are being cheated out of an inheritance, and their siblings, whom they charge with cheating them. In both cases, the letters take a sudden, bitter turn following such charges. Martin may have been distant from his father, but he loyally wrote to his brothers and offered them assistance should they emigrate.[82] Perhaps the temptation to take advantage of one far away and unlikely ever to return was simply too great for those of weak character, even when the relationship was up to that point a fond one.

In the case of Matthew Brooks, however, there was a long-standing source of bitterness that went back to childhood, and was never forgotten by Brooks, who left the north of Ireland in 1827 and lived the rest of his life feeling that he had been pushed into exile by his family, principally his brother James. There are very few archived letters in his collection, and those that exist were almost always addressed to his one literate sister, Rebecca, rather than to his brother James, to whom he coaddressed but one letter. Against James, he possessed a lasting grievance. Without any apparent provocation, but with memories evoked in the act of writing, after nearly thirty years in the United States he wrote Rebecca that he felt "the same brotherly affection for you now that i had when you and i sat at the one tabel together in mornings," and that he thought of her more than he did his brother James, adding:

> i think that no ways strange for i remember his harshness to me and i remember your sympathie and good feeling equaly as well as when I was there James had the handeling of all the money that was made out of doors . . . and poor Matthew never could command a shilling of his own and doing the chief part of all hard work And my poor simpel father that is now in the grave never took those things into consideration i was sometimes under the necessity of begging a shilling or two from James in a fair or market and if i get it it was with a sour countenance and with the greatest reluctance for the last year or two that i was there i was no more though[t] of than as a hierling that is unecessary to mention.

Only in "a strange land," he concluded, had he "recvd. the benefit of my own industry."[83] This avowal of lasting bitterness was no doubt a true description of Brooks's feelings except in one particular area: it was probably false that he did not think often about his brother. It is likely that he thought of him quite a lot, and that the act of writing evoked memories that stoked the fire of his resentments against a brother whom he had been refusing to address directly since he emigrated.

The letters of some married couples also bear witness to being haunted by the past, but it is a living past that takes form in ongoing relationships, not one frozen, as for Brooks, in bitter memories of distant times. Most of the letter-series of couples separated by emigration are fond, and contain hopeful plans for reunion. They certainly give evidence of practical difficulties, some of them quite serious. For example there are debtors, such as Henry Johnson, Joseph Wright, and James McGarrett, who to varying degrees give evidence in their early letters of being conscious-stricken about leaving their wives behind to deal with creditors, while they resettled and made arrangements to bring their families to the United States. But in these cases the solidarity of each of the couples seemed strong.

In the examples of William Darnley, John Ronaldson, and John Thomas, though the marriages are untroubled by the pressing external problem of large debts, they do not seem nearly as resilient, and are strained to the breaking point by separation. What these three marriages have in common is conflict that emerges out of the circumstances of separation, but rests on a foundation of previous problems. In the case of the three debtors, their leave-taking was as much an escape, secretive and hasty, as it is a voluntary migration, and the solidarity of their marriages is increased by the threat imposed from external forces in the form of creditors and by the couple's plotting of the husband's escape.

The migrations of Darnley, Ronaldson, and Thomas, in contrast, were moneymaking schemes, and they believed that in making the trek across the Atlantic they were fulfilling their obligations to their families—"doing my duty to the utmost of my ability," as Ronaldson put it. The wives they left behind, in each case with children, had a variety of doubts about the enterprise. Eliza Ronaldson wished to accompany John, but he gave her a firm "No" that caused some enduring bitterness, which from his perspective seemed nothing less than a lack of gratitude for his willingness to accept loneliness as the price for making as much money as he could for his family in America. His businesslike letters to her never strike a note of affection, a fact she protested in her own letters. For his part, he protested her "complaints, abuse, and insinuations," but engaged in his own version of the same writing, combined with a marked tendency toward condescension. Ronaldson was unapologetic for the unaffectionate tone in his letters, explaining that he saw no point in speaking in letters as he would not do in speech, a practice he found pretentious. He did eventually send money home, and actually stepped briefly out of character and invited his wife to enjoy it.

"Take no excuses, and mind, spend the money. You must take more pleasure." But his frequent emphasis on the sacrifices he was making and the difficulties he faced probably did not make it easy for Eliza to heed his advice.[84]

In spite of their two years of transnational marital struggle before the archived collection suddenly ends (probably because Ronaldson returned to Scotland), the issue of fidelity never was introduced. The Ronaldsons' tug of war apparently did not need sexual jealousy to further enliven the emotional combat. In the cases of both Thomas and Darnley, their wives appear conscious that the temptation of other women, far from home and the censorious eyes of the village community, might well be the pretext for transforming temporary emigration into desertion, the nineteenth century's most prominent form of divorce for ordinary people in Western societies. Anxious and vulnerable, both women were left at home with a number of small children. Thomas expressed deep affection for his wife and children, and swore fidelity in a direct response to her fears in his first letter to her from the Pennsylvania mountain town where he went to mine coal. "Dear wife," Thomas wrote, offering reassurance,

> I should think that I was worse than a murderer to kiss your tear weted chicks when Parting telling you that Wich I did and depart from it. . . . I can Boast to day that my Parting words with you is whole and my vows at the alter is onbroken. It is easy to Bost Before Man But I can Boast Before the all seeing eye of God from whose Eye nothing can be hid and He knows that wich I have writen Hear is the truth the whole truth and nothing Elce.[85]

His conduct appears to have offered no basis at all for these fears. But the circumstances of his leave-taking, which involved an impulsive decision to accompany a friend, also a miner, to Pennsylvania, where they both had kin, does not seem to have inspired her confidence. He wrote of sending her money and, as his wife soon grew anxious about their separation as the months rolled by, of sending for his family. Because of subemployment and strikes, he was not able to save the sum he felt sufficient in the two years before he died as a consequence of burns sustained in a mine accident.

Darnley promised his wife just before he sailed, in a letter written from Liverpool, that "there is a better time coming for us," but he arrived in North America in the midst of the economic contraction of 1857, and first in Toronto and then in New York City, found it difficult to get well-paying, let alone full-time, employment as a building carpenter. Ill-health and unemployment soon overtook him, and disrupted his plans to send money home to his wife for the support of their children. Soon his wife was attempting to borrow money on one of his insurance policies in order to support the household, and when that source became exhausted, debt began to accumulate.

From the inception of his correspondence, Darnley expressed strong solidarity with his wife, sympathy for her in her loneliness and material needs, and affection for his children. He was lonely enough without them and frustrated enough in the pace of his saving, that in less than a year he began to speak of sending for them rather than waiting for a prolonged period to attain a sufficient sum to return home in triumph. But Darnley vacillated on the latter plan, and after fourteen months in North America, he began to write infrequently, because, he said on several occasions, "I had no good news to share." He also attributed his declining letter-writing to having no good place to write, and to having no money to send home. He continued to promise to send for her and told her to prepare herself to leave within months, but each promise was soon violated by complaints about a lack of money. After two years of this, Darnley's wife was suspicious. When she had not heard from him for four months, she grew sensitive to the plausibility of the local gossip in Stockport, which contended that he had left a family he could not maintain and had another woman in New York City, whom he was supporting and with whom he was living. Because he continued alternately to write that he was about to send for his family, and that he could afford to do so because the Civil War had disrupted the construction industry, Darnley's wife never accepted his vigorous protestations that he was innocent of infidelity, and continued her accusations for another three years. Darnley wrote bitterly that he had made a terrible mistake in emigrating, but was emphatic in stating that he would never return to Stockport, in effect, to declare defeat. The resolution to this increasingly bitter conflict, characterized by charges and protestations of innocence in letter after letter, cannot be known, because the correspondence between Darnley and his wife suddenly ends in 1863.[86]

If they were ever in a position to be reunited, it is not clear what future there would have been for the Darnleys' marriage. The situation reminds us that chain migrations were a more complicated matter than the accumulation of the resources for paying the costs of transportation and resettlement. In the context of our interest in immigrant epistolarity, it offers evidence that marital discord could be sustained for years through the post.

Epistolary harmony or epistolary conflict, immigrant correspondence usually achieved its structure, tone, and rhythms rapidly, within a relatively few years, as relationships continued to develop and grow out of their preemigration foundations. For all the uncertainties in knowing about the relationships that sustain them, it is clear that the parties were generally driven to sustain them. Discovering why correspondence dies, as does the Darnleys', and how the letters it produced are regarded long after they have been read, is much more difficult to conceptualize, and it is to these subjects that we now turn.

6

When Correspondence Wanes

While the subject of personal correspondence is pervaded by practical and theoretical difficulties, aspects of the exchange of letters that are especially difficult to conceptualize are the subjects of this chapter: the waning and termination of an exchange of letters between individuals and, relatedly, the fate of their letters thereafter. These are matters that have been almost wholly neglected in the near-century of scholarly attention, from Thomas and Znaniecki to the present, given to the correspondence of immigrants with their homelands. The problems involved are wide-ranging, from understanding who undertakes the writing of letters, and why they do so and then cease doing so, to analyzing how letters are saved and come to interface with both popular conceptions of the past and ultimately even the formal discourses of academic History. They frequently appear, as do so many other conceptual problems in the interpretation of correspondence, as puzzles in which gaps and absences have to be explained.

Three of the principal issues that must be considered make this clear. First, collections of archived letter-series are artifacts of an obscure and highly individualized process of saving, collection, and donation. We seldom know how or why these collections were brought together, and to this extent we cannot know how complete they are. Who brought the letter-series together for donation? What were their motives in doing so? What editorial prerogatives might they have exercised? Second, while in some cases it is clear why a correspondence ends—because, for example, of the death of one of the parties, or because families are reunited and no longer have to depend on letters for communication—in most cases the circumstances are obscure, and ultimately seem unknowable. Do the correspondents actually stop writing, or have later letters been lost, or perhaps purposely culled to destroy the embarrassing record of, for example, some conflict that alienated individuals and irreparably divided families and friends? Third, the end of a particular correspondence does not necessarily mark the end of letter-writing itself, for epistolary careers might well have continued with other correspondents. These letters might have become lost, been retained in private hands, or even archived in some location unknown to this researcher. Some correspondences may disappear, but obviously not so necessarily the individuals, as letter-writers, who had been engaged in them.

The gaps in our understandings of such matters heighten the emotional burdens of having to confront the close of a letter-series, when the reader has grown fond of, or at least interested in the fate of, the parties involved. For historians, the pathos of reading collections of letters that end suddenly and inconclusively is the realization of being cut off irretrievably from the possibility of knowing, and continuing to share, the relationship that forms the contextual narrative of a correspondence. Just as sad in such collections is the inexplicable loss of the individuals who often have assumed such vividness and vitality through their personal writings. Those collections that end because of death have their own pathos, but it is a sorrow that comes of being reminded once again that human life is ultimately finite and tragic.

The known and the unknown in the lives of the letter-writers themselves hardly exhaust the puzzle that is suggested by the waning and termination of a correspondence and the fate of the letters it generated. What of the relation of the next generation to the cycle of correspondence? One wonders why it is that there are so very few cases in which the children or related family of the next generation took over the obligations of and opportunities for letter-writing to aunts and uncles and others of their parents' generation. One wonders, too, why there are even fewer traces of letter exchanges among members of that next generation—among the immigrants' children and their cousins, across the ocean.

To pose these questions is ultimately to pose questions about the experiential and cultural limits of access, and about the personal desire to gain access, to their parents' worlds of the immigrants' children. Whether born in Europe and emigrated as infants or youngsters (the so-called "1.5 generation") or born in North America, they were simultaneously and progressively immersed in New World realities and alien to the world of the previous generation. It is also to pose questions about the consciousness of family history and of History as the formal, scholarly quest to create knowledge of the past, that was possessed by the immigrants' children, grandchildren, or great-grandchildren.

Whether these generations continued correspondence with the homeland or, as the weight of the evidence suggests, did not do so, it was
through the agency of these later generations that the first generation's
letters, when they actually survived their authors' removal from the
scene, would evolve into either artifacts or trash. It was also these generations that in North America and in Europe would ultimately lose
or gain the capacity to enhance their own identity narratives by virtue
of the fate of their parents' and ancestors' letters. Whether we find the
presence of collective amnesia or collective memory in later generations,
each of these orientations toward the family past seems as if it might
be contingent upon not only oral tradition, but also upon the practical
ability to gain access to the letters of the first generation after its departure from the stage of history.

How do collections of letters end? In the majority of collections consulted for this study, the answer, unfortunately, is they end inconclusively. For no apparent reason, after a certain point in time there are no
more letters. There are few, if any, suggestions in the previous letters
that an end is drawing near. Moreover, there is no particular pattern
represented by these collections that suddenly end. Some letter-series,
like the Titus Crawshaw letters to his parents and siblings, had gone on
for some years and become rather extensive in volume, but others, like
the David Laing letters, represent only a few years of correspondence
and include but a handful of letters.[1] Both collections end suddenly. A
wide variety of letter-series conform to this pattern; they are written by
individuals and couples, men and women, and writers who settle down
and those who continue to move after their initial resettlement. It seems
impossible to find an explanation that links these inconclusive bodies of
correspondence.

Readers think they may know enough to guess, at least within a certain range of probability, at what is happening, but ultimately the possibilities prove to be frustratingly extensive. Take the case of William
Darnley. Darnley and his wife and children may well have been reunited. She may have chosen to forgive him, or come to believe her suspicions of his infidelity in distant New York City were wrong and unjust
to him. Or, perhaps, she reasoned that whatever his sins, she needed
a breadwinner to help her raise their children. Or, perhaps, Darnley
elected to abandon his family in Stockport, cut off epistolary ties with
his wife, and go off with the woman he was indeed living with in New

York City.[2] Perhaps David Laing's sister, with whom he resumed correspondence after so many years of silence, decided against his advice to come to the United States to seek her own fortune, and showed up at his door in Logansport, Indiana, one day. Or, perhaps, with his marriage ended in all but name, his sons grown and gone their separate ways, his favorite child—daughter Isabella—dead, and his former son-in-law remarried to a woman whom Laing did not like, and who was unkind to him and made it difficult for him to visit his grandchild, the United States no longer held any promise for David Laing and he returned to England. Perhaps Titus Crawshaw, too, returned to England, tired of the cycle of employment and joblessness that he frequently experienced; or perhaps he simply tired of writing. The mind resists speculating that any of these three men might have suddenly died in an industrial accident, or of influenza. But that fate is equally plausible, if hardly satisfying to those who want closure within the framework of the relationships the letters establish for us.

The collections that do not end indeterminately provide us with much more analytical and emotional satisfaction. The range of situations is predictable, but much less so are the specific, individualized circumstances. The first of these is *alienation,* such as in the widely different instances of Rebecca Hartley, Joseph Willcocks, and James Horner. Hartley wished to continue to write to Joseph's family after he died of a lung disease common to stonecutters. "Please write to me," she said in the letter in which she reported Joseph's death, "for I am still your sister and will be glad to hear from you at any time." But she went a long way toward ensuring they would have no more to do with her. It was not only that she remarried within approximately six months of his death, but also the way she explained her conduct. Criticizing Joseph, she wrote to justify her remarriage: "You think i have forgotten Joseph no never can i forget him as long as i live i done every thing for him when he was living but he did not do as well for me as he ought to for i have worked hard ever since we was Marred."[3] In Willcocks's case, there is evidence of low-key estrangement between Joseph Willcocks and his brother Richard almost from the beginning of their correspondence, but Richard's continual violations of reciprocity and his failure to write a letter of reference in his brother's behalf after repeated requests may well have led Joseph to make good on his threat to cease writing. Willcocks's letters stop eight years before his death in 1814.[4] In contrast, Horner's letters end under circumstances in which there was no apparent conflict as there was with both Willcocks and Hartley. Horner emigrated as a youth, and this inexperience and lack of self-confidence were obvious from the inception of his correspondence with his family in Ireland. Yet over the course of a decade of letter-writing, he emerged as an articulate and self-possessed man. Under pressure to reemigrate from his parents, he refused. Meanwhile, his production of letters fell steadily, from six in the first year (1801) of his immigration to two in 1804, and one in both 1807 and 1810, until it then appears from the archived correspondence to have totally ceased.[5]

Boredom with or dislike of writing, as in the cases of Henry Squier and of the McElderry brothers, William and Robert, was another cause of termination. Squier began writing to his cousin Edwin Kimberley with great enthusiasm, shortly after Kimberley left England for Wisconsin in 1850. He wrote long newsy letters about the comings and goings of friends and family, postal problems, harvests, and weather in his early letters. But his zeal soon began to wane, perhaps because increasingly he found little to write about other than the relation of illnesses and deaths. He began to write less frequently, and his letters, which grew shorter, were quick to draw to their conclusion with comments such as, "My news bag is exhausted," and similar strategies for excusing brevity. In 1869, he was still writing, but was explicitly hostile to having to do so. He complained that he thought someone else should now be writing these letters, but was sorry "to find that I have it to do." He would make this complaint again, and write increasingly episodically until his letter-writing ceased completely.[6] Squier was at least enthusiastic about letter-writing in the beginning. Neither of the McElderrys, Robert and William, were, though they wrote dutifully to their brothers and sister in Ireland. Robert struggled to find something to write about that might interest his sister. The two brothers, both bachelors who might properly be characterized as fussy and opinionated—which was, in fact, how William characterized Robert—seem also frequently not to have been in contact with one another. Neither greatly enjoyed the company of others. After Robert died fighting for the Confederacy at Vicksburg, William showed little enthusiasm for keeping in contact with his Irish family. His last archived letter, which related the pleasure he took in going to his deserted New Orleans office on Christmas Day to be alone and read the newspaper, also announced that he disliked to write letters.[7]

Family conflict was another cause for termination. Active conflict, as opposed to passive alienation, manifested itself in two ways. One, as in the case of John McLees, was quarreling between the immigrant letter-writer and correspondents in the homeland. The other, as in the cases of the Barker and Birkbeck families, was quarreling within the family on one side of the ocean that had been contained while parents were alive, but became inflamed and greatly divisive soon after their death, and then seemed to spread out to involve those on the other side of the ocean. McLees complained that his brother wrote infrequently, but this common protest was transformed into part of a much more serious complaint when his brother was dilatory in writing him that their father had died, and failed thereafter to inform him about the disposition of their father's property. McLees's grievance was reinforced by the fact, of which he had made his brother aware, that he badly needed money to purchase some property.[8] In the case of the Barkers, John Barker's death in 1859, after three years of maintaining a correspondence with his family in England, found his six adult children engaged in an impossibly complex conflict, with a number of different roots. The older brothers were divided against one another; the younger brothers were in conflict with at last one of the older ones; one of the sisters, Fanny, denounced a brother; the wife of one of the brothers weighed in against her brother-in-law; and one of Fanny's brothers denounced her husband as a poor provider. We know this because, while squaring off against each other, some of the parties were seeking allies among their cousins, aunts, and uncles in England through the post, and winning them.[9] The network might well have imploded amidst these tensions, for the archived letters cease at a time when grievances were being explored and harsh accusations were being made. A similar conflict took place after Morris Birkbeck drowned in 1825 while fording the Fox River during a storm near the English settlement he had founded on the Illinois prairie. His son Richard had been quarreling with a brother-in-law, whom he disliked as an American, believing all Americans greedy, dishonest, and lacking in refinement, and whom he blamed for money problems that had for a time led him to drink and desert his family. His siblings rejected these charges, but Richard sought allies in England, and as a result perhaps the correspondence began to break down amidst mutual animosities.[10]

Conversely, *family reunification* could result in termination of correspondence. For John Langton, James McGarrett, William Julius Mickle, and Thomas Steel letter-writing ceased when parents, siblings, or spouses came to North America to join a family member who had emigrated earlier. John Langton continued to write to a brother in England, but the Langton letters that achieved fame as documents of life in the early Canadian bush are the archived, early ones to his father that were brought together for publication after Langton's death.[11]

Relatedly, family reunification in Europe in consequence of *return migration* was also a factor in causing letter-writing to cease. Rebecca Butterworth seems very likely to have returned to England with her husband after a disastrously unsuccessful effort at farming in Arkansas, while the industrial workers John Ronaldson and Ernest Lister had planned from the beginning of their emigration to America to return to England when they had made enough money.[12]

Finally, *death and mortal illness or disability prior to death* are by far the largest number of cases (15), in which there is explicit accounting for the waning and termination of a correspondence. Because almost all of the archived collections represent letters sent to Europe rather than those sent to North America, we are much more aware of the final illnesses and death of the immigrants than of their correspondents. In the one instance in which it is clear that correspondence terminated because of the death of the British letter-writer, we know with certainty that Samuel Buchanan's sister had passed away because the archived collection contains the correspondence between Buchanan and the estate attorneys, with whom he corresponded in a vain effort to claim his sister's assets.[13] The other cases all involve deaths in North America from natural causes, as many of them attendant upon sudden illness or accident in midlife as in old age. Hartley and John B. Thomas, the coal miner, died of work-related accidents or illness caused in midlife. Thomas Spencer Niblock died in a shipwreck off the coast of Australia, in the midst, it seems, of contemplating a return to Canada. We learn of most of these deaths in ways similar to our knowledge of the death of Buchanan's sister: there are additional letters in the archived collection, whether personal letters of condolence or letters relating to the disposition of property, that establish the circumstance of death, and in so doing ipso facto explain the termination of the correspondence.[14]

This brief review of the factors involved in the waning and termination of correspondence prepares us for what is perhaps an unexpected implication: there are actually relatively few collections in which it is clear that a correspondence of many years' duration ends with the death of one of the parties in old age. We are rarely privileged, therefore, to follow letter-writers through a significant stretch of the life-cycle, dating from immigration in youth or in early adulthood to old age and death, and reflect upon the development of themes, interests, and modes of expression in their letters at the different stages of life. In addition to the fact that we seldom have collections in which letters have been written evenly over the course of many years, there are relatively few collections that end with the natural close of life.

One consequence is that the lives of aging immigrants, a much underrepresented cohort in immigration studies, continue to remain obscure to us. Immigration studies have been focused on youth and young adults, because these are the age cohorts most likely to emigrate and form families, and they are the ones at the peak of their work lives. But as the years pass and these cohorts age, those within them seem to pass from history as agents in the lives of their families and communities. They become shadows at the fringes of the central arenas of social life rather than active participants within them. This passing is more an artifact of historians' interests than a reflection of the disappearance of the middle-aged and elderly from social relations. By way of correction, we might reflect on the place of the aging emigrant in both letter-writing and the networks formed through correspondence.

Ill-health and disability and attendant emotional turmoil did remove some aging immigrants from correspondence, and one imagines, too, to varying degrees, from active participation in the networks formed by it, but the picture is nonetheless an uneven one. These immigrants often wished to keep in letter contact but found it difficult to do so themselves, and sometimes required a surrogate to write in their behalf. In apologizing for her "bad writeing," Emily Tongate explained in an 1874 letter to her aunt and uncle why she had reluctantly taken the burden of corresponding on herself, and why her father, John Bishop, wrote so seldom now in spite of continual pressure to do so. Her mother had nagged at her father to write, but he had neglected the task, and now seemed too ill to be able to do so.[15] Yet on the very same day, perhaps shamed by the fact that his daughter felt the need to act in his behalf, John Bishop himself wrote a short, newsy, and good-natured letter which reported on the comings and goings of his adult children, to his sisters. He reported on his health and said he did not expect to live much longer, but nonetheless he expressed the "hope to here from you soon."[16]

Robert McCoy, an Irish Protestant farming in western Pennsylvania in the 1840s, presents a similar picture of a combination of the desire to communicate with his family in England and Ireland, and limitations we might associate with emotional and physical decline that kept him from actually doing so. His nephew, who lived eight miles from him, explained in a letter to his own brother why their uncle Robert no longer wrote. Robert suffered from rheumatism in his hands which made writing painful. Moreover, he had become "fretful" and lonely as a consequence of the recent loss of his wife and the removal of his two daughters from his household after their marriages. Yet depression and disability aside, McCoy thought maintaining correspondence was important enough that, though he himself would not write, he walked with a recent letter from Ireland he had received the eight miles to his nephew's house, so that it could be shared and answered. It was, in fact, the letter he had carried that his nephew was then answering.[17]

In contrast were those who maintained a regular exchange of letters almost to the very end of their lives and took it upon themselves, as long as it was in their power, never to violate the norms of reciprocal exchange. In doing so, they not only seemed to draw energies from the task of keeping in contact, even as their health declined and their mobility became restricted, but continued to assist in the vital work of holding networks together. In addition, through their writing at an advanced stage of life, they become significant sources of intergenerational memory and family oral tradition.

The outstanding examples in these archived collections are provided by Mary Ann Archbald and Ralph Wade, but the two of them contrast significantly in the precise nature of their commitment to maintaining their correspondences. Archbald's correspondence, as we shall see in a later chapter, was the expression of an intimate, lifelong friendship with her cousin Margaret Wodrow. As Archbald aged, the world of this lively and opinionated woman shrank considerably. Though after a long hiatus she again took up painting, and she continued to take great pleasure in reading, in the last decade of her life she was increasingly left housebound because of ill health and disability. The circle of her intimates contracted. Friends who had been occasional visitors, and other correspondents, both in Scotland and in the United States, died. Her husband and her daughter Margaret, her closest confidant other than Wodrow, were long dead. Her adult sons had established independent lives, one of them, Peter, in the same central New York village, but the other, James, in Pennsylvania, where he enjoyed a successful career as a mining engineer. She lived with her daughter Helen Louisa, a competent housekeeper who generously provided for all her mother's needs, but with whom, Archbald confided, she had little in common intellectually.

Archbald's correspondence with Wodrow contracted in volume and content alongside the shrinking circumstances of her life.[18] She produced fewer letters, and those she wrote were repetitious and less rich in observations of daily life. Yet this communion with her friend, though diminished in form, was soul-sustaining to the extent that it did not cease until the end of her life. Her last archived letter dates from six months before her death. Margaret's letters and her son James's letters, she said, in a representative comment two years before she died, had "now [become] my strongest ties to life."[19]

Somewhat like Robert McCoy was Ralph Wade's older brother Robert, who had arrived in Canada twenty-six years before Ralph. The two brothers sharply contrast in their letter-writing behavior as they aged. For over a decade, Robert maintained an active correspondence with Ralph and other kinfolk in England, but in Robert's fifties, his son John explained, his production of letters declined until finally he gave up trying to write, claiming that various effects of aging made it too difficult. John wrote at least two letters in his behalf and father and son wrote one letter jointly.[20]

By the time Ralph arrived in Canada in 1845, at age fifty-seven, Robert's letter-writing career seems, on the basis of the archived collection, to have ended, though he would live until 1849. Ralph began to write to his English family in the same year in which he resettled, and thus became the network's senior Canadian representative. Beginning in 1854, Ralph, too, would complain of the effects of aging and would continue to do so until his last archived letter fourteen months before his death. But his output of letters, in contrast to his older brother's, increased as he aged. Moreover, his letters grew more detailed and engagingly written, and they radiated benign feeling toward his family, near and far. A virtual compendium of the concerns of the emerging Anglo-Canadian middle class in Upper Canada, they combined family news and political, social, and economic reporting with Methodist piety, spirited declarations of loyalty to Queen, Empire, and country, and pointed evaluations of American and Irish Catholics.[21] He survived his generation in both North America and England, so that his letters were increasingly exchanged with his nephews and nieces, and contained not only reporting about their cohort in Canada, but also about that cohort's children, the third generation.

Ralph Wade has such a fine letters — But he is not ... interesting ones. — ... for one of his 4 ... on his last letter

Not only did Ralph serve to hold an increasingly vast kinship network together, but through his occasional relation of family history he
also became a principal source of intergenerational memory. Two years
before his death, in one of his last letters, for example, he wrote to his
kinfolk about one of their mothers, who as a girl had been his "guard-
ian" (by which he may have meant something akin to our contemporary "sitter") when he was a small boy. He went on to relate memories
of her, his childhood, the family and its various branches, and how long
various individuals had lived.[22] Later that year, this exceptionally vital
man gave evidence of how extensive his network of correspondents
was, and of those he had heard from through the letters of others, when
at the close of his letter he offered greetings to "friends at Darlington,
Epp, Auckland, Hartlepool and etc."[23] Perhaps he failed to single these
"friends" out as individuals because there were too many individuals to
be named, and he feared giving offense by excluding someone.

Whatever the forces in his own character that made Ralph Wade
successful in his role as a senior correspondent, he might have been
additionally inspired by the already recognized place of family letters in
assisting in the formation of the collective memory of the family network in which he participated. Ralph knew that his brother Robert's
letters had been saved by the family in England. He may have been
reminded of this when he returned to England in 1856 for a visit.[24] One
imagines Ralph and his kinfolk sitting in the parlor, reading Robert
Wade's 1819 narrative of the journey across the Atlantic and up the St.
Lawrence, and his early letters that told of the efforts to establish a
farm and of the growth of the family's holdings and of its prosperity. In
1858, when the matter of the tremendous appreciation of land values in
Canada in the years since the first Wades immigrated was introduced in
one of his letters, Ralph invited his nieces and nephews to go back and
read the old letters written by their parents' generation that he knew
were in their possession, and study the matter for themselves.[25]

With their reverence for documents as sources of information for the
formal reconstruction of History, historians are likely to be especially
well-disposed to Ralph Wade's understanding of the documentary purposes of the family's correspondence and to the Wade family network's
willingness to use family correspondence as a basis for intergenerational
family memory. We do not know if the Wades self-consciously retained
the letters for either of these purposes, or, as is more likely, retained them

out of affection for the memory of a generation that had pioneered in the settlement of a new world but had now largely passed from the scene.

It must be understood, however, that this situation was actually rare. There is little evidence that letters, the first generation's communication bridge, were seen, so soon after the fact of their production, as precious personal artifacts of an epic in family history, let alone as documents to be studied. Nor, relatedly, is there much evidence of what eventually occurred in the Wade family correspondence: the involvement of the children of the immigrants or of the homeland correspondents in continuing the cycle of exchange created by their parents. What seems more often to have been true of the archived collections consulted for this study is that someone in the second generation who found these letters in his or her possession did not throw them in the trash, but left them in a box or a drawer. Maybe they were reread from time to time, or perhaps they were simply left to gather dust. Maybe they were eventually forgotten, to be rediscovered years later when the correspondents had become little more than a faint impression in family memory.

For now, we can separate these issues, and begin the discussion of the fate of the immigrant letter by attempting to understand the second generation's limited involvement in correspondence. There are two aspects of the problem that need to be understood: the nature of the epistolary relationship between first- and second-generation correspondents, and of that among second-generation correspondents. We have already witnessed two of the principal circumstances under which the immigrants' children took over the burden of correspondence: when the older folk were ailing, disabled, or dispirited, as in the cases of the McCoys, Robert Wade, and John Bishop, or after they had died, as in the case of the Barkers. A third, less common circumstance was one in which, as in the case of the Birket family, the children's generation became involved in correspondence for instrumental purposes. John C. Birket, a son of immigrants, carried on a correspondence with his father's brother in Preston, England, about opportunities for investment in real estate in Peoria, Illinois. Since at the time John's father was alive and vigorous at fifty-eight, it is more likely that he was handling the burden of business correspondence for his father than that he had taken over the larger burden of representing the American Birkets in the family epistolary network.[26]

Such an instrumental purpose gives us some insight into the circumstances under which the immigrants' children became involved in writing to their parents' cohort. If, as the example of Emily Tongate suggests, her generation only reluctantly took over the burden of writing, it was conceivable that what induced some of those who did so, in addition to feelings like Emily's of an obligation to family, were a variety of instrumental purposes. It was, in other words, deemed necessary to write in order to accomplish some end beyond communication itself and the expression of loyalty and affection. After John Barker's death, his children separately wrote to their aunts and uncles, no doubt out of affection, but their letters, too, are filled with bitterness against one another, and they thus appear simultaneously to be seeking allies in their own intrafamilial quarrels.

Picking up the burden of writing may have instrumental purposes as well under circumstances of family tragedy. When Hanna Wright died following a long and painful illness, the letter that announced her death was written not by her husband Joseph, but by his son, Joseph Jr. Perhaps Joseph Sr. was too dispirited by his grief to write, but the letter his son authored established other purposes beyond conveying the sad news of Hanna's death. Joseph Jr. may have been assigned the task of recruiting his Aunt Martha's services as a housekeeper and cook. Stating that he had always thought of his aunt as like "a tender mother" to him, he wrote what perhaps Joseph Sr. felt it impossible to ask directly of his sister—to give up her secure life in Ireland and migrate to the Ohio frontier to serve her male kinfolk in a moment of need. Perhaps, too, Joseph Jr. was deemed more fit for the task as a stylist, for he certainly proved skillful in evoking the pathos of a frontier family of men and young children attempting to live without their wife and mother:

> We are at present very lonesome separated from our friends and has not yet got any one to keep house for us—it's a hard matter in this Country to get one Suitable so that for some time we will have to live without a female. I think thy heart would pity us if thee was to See us sitting down to our Solitary meals.

Without skipping a beat, Joseph Jr. then went on to invite his Aunt Martha to come and join them. It does not appear that the invitation was accepted.[27]

Reluctance to write, and the willingness to write only for instrumental purposes and out of obligation to their parents, suggest the resistance that the immigrants' children displayed toward assuming, as a routine matter, the duties of writing in their parents' behalf, or in their place. It is not difficult to understand what was at the core of these difficulties. The children had become habituated to having the epistolary network held together by parents, who, after all, knew members of their own cohort much better, even at an epistolary distance, than did their children. The difficulty of asserting a second-generation presence in epistolary exchange might especially be true of particularly intimate correspondence such as that between Mary Ann Archbald and Margaret Wodrow. Archbald and Wodrow were lifelong soulmates whose letters evoked shared memories of people, events, and landscapes that no one else, of whatever age, had shared with the two of them. It was perhaps not that the immigrants' children wished, as in Marcus Lee Hansen's famous formulation, to forget the immigrant past, and particularly the dislocations, alienation, and embarrassments associated with migration and resettlement.[28] It was instead that they did not know that past, at least as memories of a lived history that could be shared with others. Theirs was a different history. It did not span continents, and it did not encompass a rending of relationships that henceforth must be maintained by letters.

Similar circumstances inhibited the sharing of correspondence among the immigrants' children and members of their own cohort in Britain, of which there are even fewer examples in the archived collections. Even when the former had been born in Britain, they had usually lived there as only as infants or young children, and had few, if any, memories of the world from which they had been taken. Under such circumstances, creating relationships with cousins through the post was likely to be difficult.

Kate Bond's son Bob, who was born in England but came to the United States as an infant, provides an example of just how far the immigrants' children could travel experientially from the world of their European cousins. Peter, Kate's nephew in England, had a chronic illness which would ultimately claim his life when he was a youth. To raise the boy's spirits and perhaps at his mother's urging, Bob wrote him a letter, which was enclosed in one of her letters to Bob's aunt and uncle. We shall look more deeply into the meanings of this letter in a later chapter on Kate Bond, but for now we need to note that Bob's formative years had been spent in Kansas, and that he had come to fancy himself, in personal style, a cowboy, which is what he emphasized in his letter to his English cousin. What he could not, or did not know how, to say was that he had a rebellious streak that had recently led him to reject the settled agrarian world of Great Plains wheat farming, small-town respectability, and the trappings of ethnic communalism that were integral to his parents' American dream. He hardly seemed comfortable thinking of himself as anything approaching "English American." He had recently wandered further west to Colorado to work in a lumber camp. Bob would eventually come home to help his father farm and would take over the farm upon his father's death, but his world was complex, and his identity subject to its own multiple negotiations which were different than the negotiations of his immigrant parents. So vast was the gulf in experience and mentality between them that the cousins would have needed a great deal of motivation, time, patience, and commitment to forge a relationship. But, in fact, all four were lacking. This letter appears be the only one Bob sent Peter, who would die within the year.[29]

Yet long-term correspondence, though rare, could be sustained, even in the midst of these vast differences in lives. Sarah J. Porter, the daughter of Robert Porter, had left Ireland as a child and settled with her parents on the Illinois prairie. She wrote her Irish cousin episodically for three decades. She was inspired in the desire to keep in contact by a nostalgic longing for, as she said, "the scenes of my early days and pictures [of] the old places so well remembered by me." She showed little interest in the activities of her Irish family, the large majority of whom she had never known. But the idealized life of the Irish village served as a counterpoint in her imagination to the fast-paced, materialistic and, perhaps, ultimately, loveless, world around her. In the United States, she complained, giving vent to her disenchantment, some of the family were doing well, but others were merely "dragging out an existence." Her letters served imaginatively to propel her back in space and time to an idealized world rooted in faith and community. "I know it is hard to get along in Ireland," she wrote in 1887, "but think of the associations. Why it thrills me yet when I think of the happy times I had and witnessed in Mullaglass. Nothing on earth is so beautiful as true piety lived." Her last letter, written five months before her death in October 1916, lamented that she had never been able to return to "Dear Old Ireland," and that life had been "very hard" for her in the years since she had left Ireland—which encompassed, of course, almost all her life. She seems to have been speaking less of her material situation, for in that letter she noted significant holdings in mortgages and two farms and the possession of a teacher's pension, than difficulties caused by a broken engagement in her youth, and, much later, a marriage to a younger man, who had once been her student, that had failed. Through all her personal disappointments, romantic dreams of the Ireland of her youth, as she continually reimagined it, helped to sustain her. Porter's romantic attachment to a fantasy Ireland comes close to David Lowenthal's characterization of the nostalgist as someone who is pleased "not so much by the past itself as its supposed aspirations, [and by] less the memory of what actually was than of what was once thought possible."[30]

This romantic embrace of the past was not common among the immigrants' children—or perhaps if it were, it must have been expressed not in letters but in daydreams, to which we do not have access. More common, in all likelihood, was what one imagines to have been the case with Bob Bond: when he sought to recover the past, it was more likely that it lay in North America—in Bob's case, in white American myths of frontiers and cowboys, and, for better or worse, memories of the family farm in Kansas—than in Britain. For the immigrants' children, even more perhaps than for children generally, the price of excessive devotion to their parents' experience was to deny their own experience and thwart their own identity projects.

The absence of nostalgic engagement with their parents' past no doubt influenced the attitudes of these children toward the immigrant generation's correspondence. The research for this book has yielded only one comment, and that a casual but also most revealing one by a member of the second generation, touching on the fate of the parents' letters. While it is not possible to generalize from one example, the comment nonetheless may at some level be representative of second-generation attitudes. In a letter to a cousin in England, Frank Reid wrote:

> If you have any of the old letters which mother and father sent you from this country or if anyone else in the family have any, please take the stamps off and send them to me as a stamp collector. If you have any old letters of England please [send] me some of them also, but queer as it may seem the stamp of this country, that is of course the old ones, are rarer here than foreign ones, as those of higher denomination were not used much in this country, but were all used [to] carry letters across the ocean, the postage being more than in the country. So I trust there are some good ones on the old letters of mothers.[31]

Frank states his interests and priorities quite clearly: he cares not for the letters themselves, only for the stamps, and in this regard his parents' letters rank alongside, if just a bit above, "any old letters of England" as potential sources for strengthening his collection. Frank Reid's preferences here, it should be noted, could in part be said to have been directed by his own family history. Knowing that his mother's letters in all likelihood may have contained references to his father's binge drinking and violent behavior toward members of the family, he may have had special reasons to want to avoid the letters themselves—as opposed to the envelopes. Why save your parents' letters when they only evoke painful, bitter memories? But might it not be just as likely that Frank would have wanted the letters back in order to have control of a written record of the events that had led to his father's arrest and his mother's changing residences in the hope she would escape further contact with him? What is clear, under any circumstance, is what Frank actually says: his interest is not in the texts. Whatever the choices before Frank Reid, his apparent lack of concern for the fate of the letters is not at odds with a consensus in his second-generation cohort, which manifested little interest in their parents' letters. Rather than being sacred relics of the past, those letters were mostly regarded with indifference.

In explaining the patterns of retention of letters, however, we need first to note an essential point in beginning to make sense of the history of the archived collections that are the evidentiary basis of this book: in the case of the large majority of archived collections, the decision to save these letters and ultimately the decision to regard them as a part of History worthy of being archived, was made in Britain by the descendants—and especially the more distant descendants—of the homeland correspondent. There are few cases of collections which are a two-way conversation, because letters sent from Britain to North America were archived only in a very few instances.

The immigrants' children, like Frank Reid, might have had reasons to wish to remember or not to remember their parents and their parents' worlds. They may have conceived of their letters as potentially enlightening or emotionally sustaining, or not thought about them at all. They may have been fascinated by the old stories of epic migrations on sailing ships across the Atlantic that were told in letters, or, having heard the oral versions of them frequently, they may eventually have become bored by them. Under any circumstance, they did not possess their parents' letters. It was the British family that saved letters sent from North America, if they were saved at all, and it was the British family whose, in most cases twentieth-century, members later gave them over to an archive in North America, Britain, or elsewhere for preservation and use by researchers. It was, in contrast, the North American family that lost letters sent from Britain, or threw them away. Of course, for all we know, at least some North American families may continue to possess them privately down to this day, as Charlotte Erickson believed at the time in the late 1960s when she wrote the "Introduction" to her collection of the immigrants' letters sent home to Britain.[32] There is, of course, no accounting for what might still exist in private hands, though it remains true that Erickson herself leaves no record that, in her own decades of inquiries among private families, she had actually located any letters sent from Britain to America. We may note only what does seem clear: the great imbalance in interest in preservation and archiving letters between North America and Britain.

It is difficult to make sense of this pattern, which if confronted directly as an analytical problem is a vast parallel project, equal in demands to the one undertaken in this study to find meanings in the letters as texts. The few efforts at formulating an explanation are, in truth, a leap through a void, tentative and guesswork, because no one has yet undertaken such a systematic exploration of family custodianship, historical consciousness, and the development of an institutional infrastructure for gathering together these documents for historical research.

But the question might be opened briefly by considering some general hypotheses, which Erickson, after years of efforts at tracking down immigrant correspondence, offered tentatively to explain how we may account for any group of letters—on either side of the Atlantic—surviving and becoming archived. Consider Erickson's three suggestions. The first is that letters stood a better chance of being saved when "a family did not move too frequently."[33] Mobility here is associated with losing or throwing away possessions that are deemed cumbersome and inessential. However much relevance such mobility might have to understanding the situation of the entire universe of immigrant families of all nationalities that saved letters relative to all those who did not, if we were to apply this formulation to understanding the differences between the British and North American families, it is not clear that we would get very far. At least since the 1893 statement of Frederick Jackson

Turner's "Frontier Thesis," the considerable geographical mobility of
North Americans has been noted by many historians, but as the historical geographers Colin Pooley and Jean Turnbull noted in a study of
internal migration within Britain since the eighteenth century, changes
of residence have also been a most common feature of modern British
life.[34] Yet such mobility does not appear to have impeded saving letters
among the British.

The second of Erickson's suggestions is that letters were more likely
to be saved when they "had some bearing on the settlement of an estate."[35] A paper record of intrafamilial discussions and negotiations as
well as correspondence about estate matters with lawyers, in the cases
in which they needed to be employed by survivors, obviously would
have been helpful to the parties in numerous ways. But the fact is that
estates are mentioned in only a few collections. To be sure, when they
arise, estate matters do at times make a dramatic appearance in some
letter-series, because they have caused bitter, ultimately divisive problems, or because, at the least, they lead to a good deal of complicated
negotiations, emotional and financial alike, among siblings. But in other
families, including ones in which the deaths of the immigrant generation's parents are discussed in letters, there was either too little heritable
property to be the subject of a probate process, or the disposition of
what heritable property there might eventually be had been worked out,
privately and informally, long before among the parties, perhaps before
emigration took place.[36]

The third explanation advanced by Erickson is that letters survived
because "someone happened to be interested in family or local history,"
which at first seems tautological but raises far more significant issues
than appears to be true on the face of it.[37] Letters may well only have
survived because for many years they were forgotten about and lay in
the dusty recesses of a closet, but ultimately it was the recognition of
their value to both family memory and History that led to their availability in archived collections. They had to be donated for the inspection of members of an anonymous public that took interest in the formal reconstruction of the past. In this connection, we note again the
imbalance in the record of the parties on both sides of the ocean. It was
on the British side of the correspondence that the historical importance
of the correspondence for research was recognized. Perhaps it was the
realization of the opening of a new epoch in family history with the migration of family and kinfolk to new and exotic worlds that initially led

to the interest in these letters and made them worth saving. The link at the other end of the chain, the European connection, might not in the minds of the North American family, preoccupied for some time with setting down new roots in a foreign land, have been conceived as emotionally compelling, especially in families in which the parents only spoke bitterly of their homeland as a place of poverty, unrelenting toil, and lack of opportunity for advancement.

Yet neither in Britain nor in the fewer examples we have of the donation of letters in North America did the realization of the value of these letters for family memory or History take place either simultaneously with correspondence or soon after the passing of the generation involved in generating the letters. The instance provided by the Wade family, late in Ralph Wade's life, is an exception. In the case of Erickson's collection of letters, for example, sixteen of twenty-five, almost two-thirds, of the letter-series still required the permission of, or an expression of thanks (or other acknowledgment) to, living individuals who had presumably donated the originals or copies to archives in the recent past.[38] Erickson herself stimulated some of these donations through her patient pursuit of letters in private hands in Britain, but ultimately, of course, it was up to the descendants of the correspondents to understand the claims of History to the letters in their possession and make the donation.[39]

Since Erickson did her research in the mid-twentieth century, from the late 1940s on into the 1960s, and the collections she analyzed were largely of mid-nineteenth century letters, the donations were made by the third and later generations after the corresponding generation—in other words, by grandchildren and great-grandchildren.[40] The same pattern may be noted in the North American cases and the one Australian case we have: the third and later generations made the donations of the letters to archives.

A certain distance in time is evidently needed before the private possessions of families may be conceived as documents, by which one's ancestors' place in History may be understood, and by which History itself may be illuminated through specific case studies or examples of those living within it. As Lowenthal has observed, distance in time may indeed "purge the past of personal attachments and make it an object of universal veneration." As memory fades of specific individuals, with all of their ordinariness and abiding imperfections and moral ambiguities, so does the personal investment fade in resisting the past. What is left,

Lowenthal observes, is the "majesty and dignity" of the larger human story of perseverance from which we might seek to draw solace, wisdom, and inspiration.[41]

There were probably many paths by which this conceptual evolution came about, and produced an interest in forming archivable collections. It seems likely that many of these paths were circuitous. Until relatively recently there was little room in Western scholarly historical narratives for relating the stories of ordinary people and daily life, and hence for finding the inspiration to place one's kin in scholarly written History. The social history of immigration was, as we have seen, an exception, for under the leadership of some ethnic historians in the early twentieth century, there was an effort to widen that narrative to include immigrants. But that work was a minor current in the historical literature, at least to the extent it rarely more than superficially penetrated the school curriculum, which remained focused on the great deeds of great men. Under any circumstance, none of those involved in making donations of these collections to archives appears to have been an academic historian who might have been inclined to see the value of these materials by virtue of a career in scholarship. It was probably chance encounters and serendipitous conjunctures, therefore, more than formal personal study or even significant immersion in the scholarly literature, that defined these paths.

In 1942, for example, Howard Finley of Berwyn, Illinois, the great-grandson of William and Elizabeth Peters, privately published and personally distributed the individual diaries kept by both William and Elizabeth during their 1830 voyage to Canada with their five children. The diaries are interesting reading, if only because of the contrast between husband and wife. William, a Methodist minister, makes pious but mundane observations about the sea, weather, and seasickness, and the opportunity he had to preach on shipboard. Elizabeth was much more engaged with people, beginning with the difficulties she and other women experienced caring for children aboard ship.

In an "Introduction" to the diaries, Finley explained what had stirred him to take an interest in this editorial work. He had met an elderly man who had addressed letters to England for Finley's grandmother, a daughter of William and Elizabeth, early in the twentieth century. Finley did not say what the circumstances of this encounter were, but he came away from it with the energy to delve further into the family past and study these diaries, which were apparently already in his possession.

Finley also had in his possession a solitary letter which William Peters had sent, the year after he left Britain, to his brother Richard that, Finley explained, his father had been given in 1904 by an English relative.

Both a copy of the diaries and of the letter were given to the National Archives of Canada. The North American and English branches of the family had corresponded for approximately eighty years before the exchange of letters apparently ceased. (The fate of all these letters is unknown.) Finley's generation was almost certainly out of touch with the English family. Absent what may have been a chance encounter, Finley would not have been inspired to draw these slim resources together, contextualize them within the larger narratives of History, and present them to the world as illuminating to those narratives.[42] It is not difficult to imagine similar chance encounters inspiring similar activities. The actual correspondence between branches of family had declined some years before, waning with the passage of individuals in now distant generations. The network had dissolved or, with random and infrequent contacts among its surviving members, nearly done so; and for those like Howard Finley the melding of family memory and oral tradition and History had commenced.

One may be tempted to lament what appears to be a sad recitation of efforts to regain hold of a moment in time that had passed too long ago to be repossessed. But to conclude that such efforts to construct a historical narrative in which to place one's ancestors and ultimately oneself creates a disembodied and inferior product compared to the vitalizing epistolary contacts of the first generation is to fail to understand its importance for the identity narratives of those who might crave continuity with the distant past while living in their own present.

That efforts were made to retrieve the past in order to serve the needs of their own personal identities under even more unpromising circumstances, without letters or other writings as a guide, by those experiencing the same urgency suggests as much. Without a documentary record, no matter how fragmentary, and with only a thin slice of oral tradition from family stories, the past was likely to be lost or retrieved only with even more extraordinary difficulty. Such was the case, for example, for Alexander McGraw, whose father, Thomas, and one of Thomas's brothers had left Bally Lane, a small Irish village near Newry in County Armagh, for the United States as youths, in 1800. More than seventy years later and long after his father had died, Alexander embarked on a pilgrimage to Ireland to rediscover the family's Irish connection. An affluent gentleman, then well into middle age, he lacked any documentary record from which to reconstruct his father's preemigration past. If Thomas had written any letters to his widowed mother and his siblings in Ireland, he had made no copies of them. If he had received letters from them, none had survived.

Alexander knew only the year his father had emigrated, the name of his village, and some incidental details of his resettlement. Thus informed, he walked into Bally Lane on a day in July 1871. Enquiring after the location of any "old person," he was led to an eighty-two-year-old woman, who in the manner of traditional village narrators, related what she knew of the emigration of Joseph and Thomas McGraw from Bally Lane. "I had a sad feeling that day and the next in Belfast," Alexander wrote his brother, "I seemed to be in communion in spirit with our dear father who bid adieu to home and country seventy years ago, for a better home and government far away."[43] The source of Alexander's melancholy is not clear. Was it a consequence of his realization that his father had been forced to emigrate because of poverty, or his own feeling of having been cut off from a source of his own identity for so long?

Whether McGraw's sadness was a passing mood or an abiding grief for his dead father, his quest for a connection to the past had been successful. But without a documentary record that might be provided by a cache of letters, and lacking the resources to travel back to the homeland and locate "an old person," other descendants of immigrants would be largely bereft of the consolations, however filled with mixed emotions, of such communion. Their narratives of identity would be characterized by a foreshortened time line, as if the New World were somehow all that was relevant for knowing their stories.

PART II

Four Lives in Letters

Introduction

The concluding four chapters are case studies in the epistolary construction of selves that as much as possible let letters between
immigrants and their families provide direction for the story. Letters
cannot speak for themselves. But the effort is made to understand the
narrative of the individual in relationship to his or her correspondents
over time, and let that narrative guide the analysis. In effect, the exposition returns to the central themes established in Part I, but takes another path to discover them. Thomas Spencer Niblock, Catherine Bond,
Mary Ann Archbald, and Thomas Steel have already been briefly and
episodically introduced.

Social historians write about ordinary people and daily life. There
have been billions of ordinary people, and there have been many, many
days in which they lived. There were in the nineteenth century two million British immigrants to North America. How then might we see these
four lives as typical?

On the surface, in terms, for example, of social characteristics, there
are indeed commonalities shared among these four individuals and the
general body of British immigrants and many other people, immigrant
and nonimmigrant alike, in the nineteenth century. But such social characteristics are not central to this analysis. For example, each of the four
shared to one extent or another the libertarian and physiocratic ideals
of self-sufficiency and social independence through agriculture that were
common to many British immigrants. While certainly not irrelevant, the
practice of North American agriculture is not necessarily a significant
aspect of the way these individuals explain their lives through their
letters. The material world is here, of course, but it is only one context
for the relationships embodied in letters. There seems, too, an effort in
these case studies to balance the genders. Yet while men and women
may be, during most of historical time, almost evenly distributed among
humanity, they were not evenly divided in the British immigrant popula-

tion, which during the period of this study was skewed, as immigrant populations often are, toward male numerical dominance. Balancing off male and female *correspondents* is not convincingly representative, for the overwhelming majority of the collections of immigrant letters that form the evidentiary base of this study, like the large majority of immigrant letters, is based on the writings of men. Even when letters are signed by married couples, the male voice often predominates.

None of these four correspondents can be realistically offered to the reader, therefore, as typical of women or men as population cohorts, or farmers. They were not chosen with that in mind. By way of a more systematic response to the problem of representativeness, we return to claims made throughout this book. Immigrants (and hence immigration) cannot be understood exclusively through the study of nation-states, regions, and population cohorts. If we are to have a realistic psychology of immigration, immigrants must also be regarded as individuals involved in families and small networks of friends and kin. Taking the latter perspective, we find a dense thicket of personal relations and intense emotions that inevitably elude us at the macrolevel. Depending on how the analysis is framed, they might even elude us at the mesolevel, in which we may be tempted to see the family, both nuclear and extended, as an interdependent and functional social and economic unit, and lose sight of the individuals within it and the complicated human relationships they share. Personal relations, abiding attachments, and intense emotions are, in fact, inevitably a part of the baggage that all immigrants, and all human beings, whether sedentary or mobile, carry with them throughout their lives. They are an inevitable part of personal identity, because they form the continuities by which individuals know themselves over the course of their lives. In the specific instance of immigration, the salience of the personal dimensions of continuity seems even more intense and problematic for the individual, because separation serves to create an acute consciousness of relationships that otherwise may become so habitual as to be taken for granted.

All letter-writers reformulated personal relationships through correspondence, because these relationships were vital to the individual personal identity narratives of the letter-writers. Archbald, Bond, Niblock, and Steel each gave evidence of a felt need to correspond, not merely of a habit of corresponding, and with varying degrees of self-consciousness, to work at a type of writing that sought to appraise the extent of loss and gain in the experience of immigration and resettlement. In presenting these lives a claim is being asserted that unless we understand how immigration and resettlement—even materially successful immigration and resettlement, as was the case for all but Niblock—involve losses that consciously engage the individual, we cannot understand either. The principal source of loss in each case is a loss of continuity with the past.

Neither loss nor a closely related yearning for aspects of an older self engaged in a fondly remembered past is unique to these four lives. Both characterize all lives, even the most successful ones. But immigration historians only infrequently ask questions about the quality of immigrant lives at this level of inquiry, so it has been difficult to understand just how representative the experiences of these four immigrants might be. For this type of understanding of immigrants to be possible, we must continue to read the immigrants' letters and try to know them through their efforts to compose their lives.

These essays are not *biography* in a conventional sense. They do not proceed systematically to analyze a life from one point in time to a subsequent point, as if origins logically explain what comes after them. Instead, the time line is frequently fractured in laying out the narrative, and there is a gradual unfolding of the character of the individual that fluctuates back and forth among a number of positions—textual, chronological, and relational. The method is a response to two perceptions. The first is that lives do not advance evenly. Individuals are not destined necessarily to be at a later point in time what they were formerly. They must strive to grow as the circumstances of life change, and also strive for the continuity by which they may know themselves in order to remain the selves they believe themselves to be. The second is closely related, rooted, too, in how immigrant letters tell readers what may be learned from them. These letters speak to their readers tentatively, proceeding in a number of directions simultaneously. But these directions do not necessarily become parallel lines. They may veer off toward different directions from the course on which they embarked, but they may also intersect, which is fortunate for those who want to tie the seemingly disparate elements of personal correspondence together. Or they may double back on themselves, giving the appearance of contradiction. In the end, there is still, irreducibly, the challenging puzzle of the individual.

7

Thomas Spencer Niblock
A Dialogue of Respectability and Failure

I left England for Sydney in 1838, a child in experience, in knowledge of the world—and I remained a child for years—sufficiently
long to mis-apply my efforts and my little property, which was
consequently lost. In all, however, I trace the hand of God.
—Thomas Spencer Niblock to Edward Thomas Spencer,
his brother-in-law and benefactor, July 20, 1849

Early in the morning of Sunday, May 15, 1853, an American
steamship plying the seas off Cape Howe on the coast of northern Victoria, and bound for Sydney from Melbourne, entered waters known to
Australian navigators as particularly perilous. The captain of the *Monumental City* made what was later revealed before a board of inquiry to
be an especially thoughtless navigational error that led him off course.
The ship became wedged on rocks not far off the shore of Tullaberga
Island. Testimony is confused about what happened next, as the ship,
which was badly damaged, buffeted by increasingly powerful winds
and by rain, and rocked by heavy surf, began to list. Its decks were
swamped again and again by massive waves. Depending on whose testimony one believes, the captain allowed his sailors, all of whom survived, to escape without offering aid to the vulnerable families aboard,
and eventually he himself abandoned them to their deaths. Or, in another telling, he did all he could to save his passengers, but was unable
to overcome the panic of many passengers, who would not enter the
lifeboats for fear of the breakers, or take the hawser line that had been
extended over the boiling sea from ship to shore. Not all of the eighty-
eight passengers perished, but of those thirty-three who did and whose
bodies were found, twenty-six lie buried in the shallow soil of the rock
bluffs of Tullaberga Island.[1]

Among the dead whose bodies appear never to have been recovered were the English-born Thomas Spencer Niblock, a thirty-three-year-old recent immigrant to Australia, and his wife, Matilda, an Australian, whom Niblock had married in 1843, during a previous, unsuccessful immigration to Australia. With Thomas and Matilda were their son Joseph, whose age at the time of his death is not precisely known, but who was born in Australia during his father's first residence there. According to later family testimony, there was also an infant, whose name we never learn from his father's correspondence, who would have been born shortly after his parents returned to Australia.[2]

In the weeks prior to the catastrophe which destroyed the Niblock family, Thomas had failed to find gold at the diggings in Victoria, had then failed to find any sort of work, from outdoor labor to clerking, in Melbourne, and had sold the remaining volumes of his library, which he had carried with him around the world, to get the money to feed his family. Matilda, only recently having given birth to her second child, had also sought and failed to find work. As Niblock told his brother-in-law, Edward Thomas Spencer, a prosperous importer of sugar, in what was probably his last letter to his family in England, from all these recent failures he drew the conclusion that he was meant to be a farmer, and that he was certain he was unfit for and uninterested in commerce. We do not know why he drew this particular conclusion about his lack of aptitude for business. For years, he had been proving himself unfit for a number of lines of work, including agriculture. Moreover, he himself had recently proposed that his brother-in-law give him money to open a small store.

What we do know, however, is that he had informed Edward of the very same lack of interest in commerce in a letter in July of 1849.[3] After his first failed migration to Australia in 1845, he had returned to live in Britain for four years, and had failed to find suitable work, probably in commerce and perhaps in his brother-in-law's employ, that would support the respectability to which he aspired. He proposed in his July 1849 letter that Edward provide him with a loan that would allow him to leave England and migrate to Canada to buy a farm. After less than two years, it was clear that he had failed at farming, whereupon he decided, with Edward's help, to return to Australia.[4] From Australia now, he stated he was ready to return to Canada to farm.[5]

In the span of eight years, between 1844 and 1852, the Niblocks had lived in Australia, England, Canada, and then again Australia. They had also spent a great deal of time at sea, much of it as steerage passengers, because they lacked the money to travel cabin class. For Thomas Niblock, movement itself seems to have become as good a solution, if an increasingly desperate one, as he could conceive of to the problem that dogged him for most of his brief adult life: finding a place in the world that would support his view of himself as a pious, respectable Christian who was self-supporting, prosperous, and a more than adequate provider for his small family.

What vision of the future led to his final journey from Melbourne to Sydney? We are not privileged to know. If he wrote Edward to explain his final migration within Australia, the letter did not survive. But had he done so, the explanation probably would not have convinced Edward, who by then had been supporting his brother-in-law for at least four years. Nor would it probably convince readers in the twenty-first century who read Niblock's letters up to that point in his correspondence with his family in England.

Thomas Spencer Niblock expresses himself well in his letters, and, while travel does not especially broaden his mental world, he is not without admirable strengths of character, especially strong and generous emotions toward his wife and children, his sisters, and his benefactor brother-in-law. But he lacks the capacity for introspection, let alone realistic self-evaluation. If the capacity for interrogating one's actions in the world and evaluating their efficacy is a significant test of the transformation of the child into the adult to which Niblock alluded in his letter to Edward Spencer in 1849, it is not clear that he had come quite as far as he was willing to credit himself. In short, there is every likelihood that beyond the fact that he was bound for Sydney, Thomas Spencer Niblock did not know where he was going.

Niblock presents himself as a good man in his letters, with plausible, indeed worthy, aspirations; and yet he fails at everything he sets out to do and continually exercises bad, ultimately fatal, judgment in the service of those aspirations. We know much less about individual failure than individual success in history, and in that context alone Niblock is interesting, for he fails across a broader geographical landscape than we are accustomed to considering when we think about the lives of people in the mid-nineteenth century. His is transnational and international failure, involving activities on three continents and a transoceanic network of family connections and subsidies and strained relationships.

There may be a temptation for the twenty-first-century reader to see Niblock as a precursor of a number of contemporary immigrants who migrate and remigrate to numerous destinations, and whose transnational activities have been celebrated for defying distances, national boundaries, and the oppressions of capitalist labor markets.[6] But Niblock is no cosmopolitan who artfully made the globe his stage for seizing opportunity and realizing ambitions. His career as an international migrant is explained as much by a flight from failure and from understanding his role as the author of his own pressing difficulties, as it is by practical ambition to succeed.

Historians of nineteenth- and early-twentieth-century European immigration sometimes come upon examples of individuals whose initial migration seems to liberate them for the rest of their lives from the desire, which is very much the goal of the large majority of European immigrants, to settle down again.[7] Niblock reminds us that such people sometimes have a more complicated narrative than may be conceived around the tactics of social mobility. What seems to be pushing them is not only a lack of opportunity in the social structure in which they reside, but also a refusal to confront themselves. This is a harsh judgment, to be sure, but it need not be taken to extremes and obscure an understanding of Niblock as one of us. It will not do to confine our understanding of Niblock to isolating a pathology and tracing its origins and the guises in which it manifests itself. Niblock's difficulties were not atypical. Nor were his choices, though usually poor ones, atypical. Instead, Niblock was a conventional failure, who found it impossible, as his letters attest, to accept that judgment about himself.

Before attempting to reconstruct Niblock's story, it is useful to examine the nature of the fragmentary evidence of his brief life. We know Thomas Spencer Niblock through two collections of well-crafted letters, all of them originals, written in his own hand. There are thirty-three letters (1849–1857) at the National Archives of Canada.[8] In addition, three letters, written in 1845 or 1853, are at the National Library of Australia.[9] They were placed there in 1955 by Francis M. Morris, a distant Australian relation of Matilda Niblock and a family historian who provided the archives with information that supplies some useful, if tentative, contextualization for understanding the Niblock family, not only in Australia, but also in England.[10] As collections of immigrant letters go, and within the usual constraints of the one-way conversation of collections that contain only letters from, but not to, the emigrant, thirty-six letters is a significant enough number to enable readers to get some fairly confident understandings of the writer and the qualities of the relationship to his or her correspondents. Confidence in this case is reinforced by the fact that the cast of correspondents is quite stable and the tone is consistent from letter to letter. Twenty of the letters are written to Edward Thomas Spencer, a first cousin and the husband of Niblock's sister; these are mostly "begging letters," frequently urgent in tone, that are descriptions of desperate personal circumstances and pleas for money. Of the remaining letters, fourteen are to Niblock's sister, Christiana ("Chrissie") Spencer, Edward's wife. Men often, though hardly invariably, wrote chatty, unbusinesslike letters, full of colorful descriptions and "small talk" to mothers, sisters, and wives that were at variance with the subjects (money and politics) and tone ("serious" and businesslike) of letters sent to male correspondents. Niblock's letters to Christiana attempted to sustain this carefree tone. When he could not do so, he was disinclined for a time to write to her. Early in the correspondence, as he was about to travel to Canada after disembarking in New York City, he informed Edward that he would not write to his sister, because he was too agitated and anxious about the tasks that lay before him.[11] But it is testimony to the desperation of his life that he was unable consistently to adopt this voice in corresponding with Christiana. At times, explicitly or by suggestion, he had to discuss his privations with her and his debts and need for money, and these subjects ultimately became, with increasing insistence, the center of his connection to Edward and Christiana.

The two remaining letters were written after the Niblocks' death. The earlier of the two (1854), which was written to Edward Spencer by William F. Bullen, a Canadian public official and businessman in the town of Delaware, who had advised Thomas during his brief career as Canadian farmer, expresses condolences on the death of the Niblocks. It also describes the status of the now increasingly prosperous farm, still owned by Edward who was renting it out, that Thomas abandoned when he went to Australia for the last time. The second of the two (1857) was forwarded to Edward by a third party, and appears to have been a response to the efforts of Edward and Christiana to discover more about the fate of Thomas and his wife and children, whose bodies were never recovered from the sea. In that letter, S. Charles Johnson, an Australian maritime man who had come to own the wreck of the *Monumental City* and had visited Tullaberga Island after the wreck, explained the circumstances of the disaster that took the lives of the four Niblocks.

All these letters are rich in information, descriptions, emotions, and pleas, as well as suggestions about states of mind of writers and readers and about the qualities of various relationships. Yet there is inevitably much that we cannot know that causes unease for anyone interested in transforming the suggestive, but relatively sparse information that the Niblock letters reveal about his life into a coherent narrative of that life. It is not only the always significant problems of the one-way conversation that we have come to expect in examining immigrant letters. There are also the inevitable silences of one kind or another, especially those regarding other family members, that press on our understanding, and suggest relationships about which we have little other evidence.

We expect not to find any correspondence from or to Rev. Joseph Niblock, D.D., the educator and cleric who was father to Niblock and his sisters, for he died two years before the archived collections of Niblock letters commence. But, like Joseph's wife who appears to have died some years prior to him, Rev. Dr. Niblock is mostly absent even from mention in the surviving letters. No fond family reminiscences are evoked, nor scenes of childhood recalled. The father is referred to only once, as the holder of a life insurance policy, but nothing more is said of him.[12] While Niblock's other sister, Amelia Niblock Wellesley, the wife of a Royal Navy captain, is mentioned, if infrequently, in the correspondence to Christiana, there are no letters to Amelia in the archived collections. There is internal evidence that Niblock wrote occasionally to his other sister, but it seems we can know nothing definite of this correspondence or of the relationship that sustained it. Niblock speaks of Amelia rarely, which seems peculiar in light of his effort to sustain as much as possible a chatty tone in his correspondence with Christiana. One would think that family talk and shared memories would be especially useful in sustaining that tone.

There is, however, a common factor in both silences: money, or more precisely, the lack of money. Rev. Dr. Joseph Niblock appears to have had none, and was proclaimed a failure in accumulating wealth by the family historian, Francis M. Morris. Amelia Wellesley, as a Navy wife, probably had few resources, relative to Edward and Christiana, to share with her ever-needy brother.[13] Perhaps this is a cynical conclusion. Or is it? To answer the question, we need to analyze Thomas Spencer Niblock's letters and construct his narrative.

A graduate of both Oxford and Cambridge, Rev. Dr. Joseph Niblock had a long list of educational accomplishments, culminating at age twenty-eight in his Doctorate in Divinity. For a time he was an Anglican curate in Hertfordshire and master of a free school there. He removed to London, where he opened a school, the London High School, which seems to have been dedicated to providing an education for the sons of well-to-do families, but which ultimately failed. He ended his days as an evening lecturer at a parish church school in London. When he died in 1843, his principal legacy was a life insurance policy, the only beneficiary of which was Amelia. Years later, at a time when her brother was trying without success to make a living in England, Amelia volunteered to split the proceeds of the policy with Thomas and Christiana, and in turn, Christiana offered to simply give Thomas her share.[14] These arrangements were spoken of only once and do not appear to have ever been acted upon, as if both Thomas and Christiana were reluctant to take money away from the generous but not affluent Amelia.

Growing up in Rev. Dr. Niblock's household, one might have come to love learning and value a formal education. Certainly, too, there was the expectation that one would be a practicing Christian, who was pious, well-disposed toward others, and well behaved. These were character traits that Thomas Niblock attempted to cultivate amidst the constant difficulties of his life. But one could not expect to be launched into adult life with expectations for adult prosperity on the basis of a parental financial subsidy. Thomas appears to have understood this. This knowledge may well have provided the family circumstances in which he decided to strike out on his own and go to Australia at age eighteen.

He had enough formal education to write well, and he wished to continue to cultivate his mind, as his acquisition of a personal library that he carried with him around the world suggests. But there was probably little money for him to continue his education. Perhaps his father gave him some small sum to help him go to Australia and settle there. Maybe this sum was actually Thomas's inheritance, given in advance of his father's death at a crucial turning point in the son's life. But there is another possibility, too. One wonders whether Rev. Dr. Niblock actually approved of Thomas's emigration, let alone approved of his son's emerging adult character. If he did not, considering another possible narrative of the relationship of father and son, perhaps that explains why he failed to make his son one of the beneficiaries of his insurance policy, and why Thomas almost never spoke of his father in his letters to his sister. How Thomas pulled together the resources to emigrate to Australia we cannot know. Nor can we know how it was that he came to take possession of what Morris called the "Scone Allotment," a "little property" that Niblock lost there, or how he lost it.[15]

All that is clear about these early years, before the bulk of the archived correspondence begins, is that at age twenty-five Niblock returned from Australia to England with Matilda and Joseph, embarking as steerage passengers early in May. It was during this journey, in a letter written to Christiana from Rio de Janeiro, that the part of his epistolary career that has been archived commences, though there is soon to be a significant gap of four years in the archived letters until he proposes to emigrate to Canada. It is a confessional letter that seems to have been intended to prepare her for his return, as if his reemigration was not anticipated by his English family. He explained that while he did not know what awaited him in England, he had come to believe that remaining in Australia would "only involve fresh misfortunes." The circumstances of his return he acknowledged to be "humiliating," so much so that he was embarrassed enough to have considered settling in Rio de Janeiro, but he came to understand that that would hardly be practical without a knowledge of Portuguese.[16] In this instance at least, Niblock saved himself from the potentially disastrous effects of what appears to have been a lifelong tendency to rush to conclusions in making the most momentous decisions of his life, especially decisions regarding emigration and resettlement.

Whatever Niblock's prospects were in England and whatever he was actually to do there during the next four years, his life seemed unreal to him and at a dead-end. He spent much of the time, he said, eager to "commence life again," which for Niblock meant somewhere else. Though assisted while there in some form (employment or loans, perhaps) by Edward Spencer, he came to the conclusion that he could not provide for his family in England, which he characterized bitterly as an "overgrown country where even good address, talent and good connections fail of securing success."[17] Presumably he believed he possessed these traits, so he was humiliated and frustrated by his lack of success. England would forever be his home, he wrote Christiana later, but added, with bitter finality, "though I do not desire to ever see it again."[18] He did not have the resources to finance his own emigration, so in a letter dated July 20, 1849, and sent from somewhere in England, he approached his brother-in-law, who was the only person who had helped or encouraged him during the unsatisfactory years after his return to his homeland. His tone was defensive, as if he anticipated resistance and as if he did not quite believe himself equal to the task of convincing anyone, let alone a "man of business," as he described Edward, that he could be trusted to conceive a practical plan. Well-spoken and talented as he was willing to characterize himself, his self-confidence nonetheless seemed to be reaching a low ebb. It cannot have bolstered his confidence that he was a supplicant before his cousin and brother-in-law, who represented the successful line of his extended family—in sharp contrast to his own branch.

"Emigration—bona fide emigration," by which he seemed to mean permanent resettlement based on a better plan than the one that to his mind had led him to Australia, was his goal. He proposed not to return to Australia, which he judged too long a journey for his wife and son, but rather to go to farm in Canada, where, in addition, society was "somewhat more civilized and held together by some sense of religious principle" than in Australia, and where a man like himself, who had no inclinations toward commerce and no desire to amass wealth, could achieve "a competence." With its various risks, he recognized that this plan necessarily appeared "a perilous one when viewed in a business light." He knew, too, he said, that "benefits received too often beget a fancied right to receive more," and imagined his brother-in-law feared the possibility of endless requests for money from abroad.[19]

What argument did Niblock advance to assure Edward that his plan had credibility and that he was not about to become a permanent ward-in-exile of his brother-in-law? Niblock said, first, that he had made "many enquiries" into the opportunities that farming in Canada presented. But he did not identify the sources of his information, nor did he lay out in detail what they had told him. He dismissed further elaboration, saying simply that he was constrained by "the limits of a letter." He did make confident-sounding calculations in the most general terms, which appeared based on this information, about the amount of money he would need: £200, one-half of which would be used for passage money, down payment on a piece of land, utensils, supplies, and wages for hired help, and the other half of which would assist him in surviving the first two or three years until he became self-supporting. After that

(near London Ontario)

time, he believed, he would be able to pay whatever money was due the landowner, and pay his brother-in-law back with interest. He presented as security the money that Amelia had promised him when she offered to share the proceeds of their father's life insurance policy.[20]

It is not clear whether Niblock and his brother-in-law ever had a conversation or exchange of letters that delved deeper into what Thomas had discovered in his "many enquiries" about farming in Canada that gave Thomas the opportunity to gain credibility by presenting a more elaborate accounting of the subsidy that he requested. Was the plan, if one could even call it that, really based on "many enquiries"? It is difficult to believe so. Soon after he began life in Delaware, Canada West, eight miles from London, Niblock would be proven far off the mark in his calculations of the sum of money he would need.

Moreover, what reason was there to believe that someone like Niblock, who does not seem to have had much experience as a farmer and was not then farming in England, could actually achieve a "competence" in such a brief time or ever under the conditions that then existed in postfrontier Canada? As we have seen, many British emigrants of a variety of social classes and occupational backgrounds shared this yeomen ideal with Niblock, but it is doubtful that many of them would prove as unprepared for the rigors of North American farming as he was. Niblock was able to do the physical work, but the equally essential work of anticipating needs, conceiving of priorities, and marshaling resources eluded him. By his own admission, he came eventually to understand that he lacked many of the requisite skills needed for making a farm.[21]

It is quite possible that Spencer understood that his brother-in-law was a poor candidate to succeed in Canada. Spencer had not sustained a prosperous enterprise ignoring the bottom line, or being so poor a judge of character that he failed to recognize those traits in people that signaled that they were unlikely to pay their debts. Perhaps he consented to aid his brother-in-law not because he believed Niblock would succeed, let alone pay him back with interest, but because his brother-in-law's problems had become an issue in his marriage. We may easily understand how this might be true. During his four years in England, Niblock seems to have been needy and ineffectual to the extent that the situation necessitated a conversation with Amelia about sharing their father's life insurance policy with her siblings, which Joseph Niblock apparently had not desired when he designated her the sole beneficiary.

Then, he may well have had another conversation with Christiana about her simply giving him her share of what Amelia was to give her of the proceeds.

Perhaps the sisters and especially Christiana, with whom Thomas seemed to have a particularly close relationship, worried excessively about their brother, a role that may have been easier for them to fall into, since they had spent years without a mother. Christiana's worries may have led her to insist that her husband do something for her feckless brother in the hope of alleviating his wife's anxieties. In short, it seems quite possible that Spencer helped his brother-in-law to get him as far away from England as possible, and thus restore the peace of his marriage, hoping against hope that maybe he would eventually get his money back, but never really believing the likelihood very considerable. Canada was to be the dumping ground for this family's problem child.

Niblock's possibilities for succeeding in Canada began to unravel soon after his arrival. We are hindered in efforts to discover the full extent of his difficulties with money, and particularly his growing indebtedness, by the vagueness of his own discussions of actual sums of money—whether it was money needed, earned, or owed. What is clear is that he misjudged how much money he would need, largely because he had no idea how much work was required to make a farm in North America. The task must have appeared daunting, to say the least, to those who did not really know what to anticipate when they arrived, and, it seems, "many enquiries" aside, that Niblock was at the very least unclear about what would be required of him on a number of different levels.

An instance of his lack of preparedness was the peculiar decision he made to take with him two young and very reluctant servants, Mary Ann and Alexander, about whom he began to complain bitterly almost immediately. Alexander, a city boy with no farming experience, was described as "a sad plague and load upon us" in Niblock's first letter from Canada. In the end, though helpful now and then, neither servant proved more than another mouth to feed. They were, as Niblock observed with what seems studied understatement, not "thoroughly actuated by that identification of interests which should exist." He eventually conceded that he could not afford to keep both of them, and let Mary Ann go.[22]

Less than a month after sending his letter proposing emigration to Edward, the Niblocks were crossing the Atlantic. What preparation was possible in the time between receiving Edward's agreement to assist him and leaving for North America may be imagined. Niblock himself would later characterize their leave-taking as a "sudden departure." After receiving assistance and an advance of £40 from Edward's brother, who owned a mercantile business in New York City, the Niblocks traveled to Canada.[23] They arrived in Canada in early September. As anyone with a knowledge of the situation or any guidebook might have informed him, the season of the year was not auspicious, for the coming of autumn and the inception of colder temperatures were not far away.

Upon arrival, he was advised by everyone he spoke with that all his efforts must be focused on making plans to survive the winter.[24] His first thought was to obtain employment in London and lodging there for the winter, and save as much money as he could toward the purchase of a farm at a later date. This seemed sensible, since at the time he had no more than £30. But all his efforts to secure winter employment failed. There was little in the way of an urban labor market. What was needed was seasonal farm labor, and it was hardly likely that a farmer would agree to feed the three Niblocks and their two servants all winter, when there would be little work to do.[25]

He soon found his options rapidly narrowing. It was clear that, ready or not, he would have to begin farming immediately, but his plan to buy a fifty-acre farm was judged impractical by the local people with whom he spoke. They insisted that to feed him and his family and keep all of them warm enough to survive the frigid temperatures, he would need one hundred acres of at least partially heavily wooded land from which to draw his firewood. Of course, with the heavily wooded land came the necessity for accomplishing the most arduous activity demanded of the postfrontier farmer in Canada—clearing the land of dense forest growth by felling trees, chopping them into firewood-sized parcels or preparing them for use as building material, and disposing of brush.[26] As he ran out of room to maneuver, Niblock did what numerous other farmers in postfrontier Canada found it necessary to do—he went much deeper in debt than he had originally intended in order to buy an already developed farm, with buildings, some cleared land, and a stock of already cut firewood and lumber. He placed himself thereby in the position of having to make arrangements to finance his payments in two sets of major obligations: one involved repayment to be completed in 1854 to the landowner for the acreage, and another, to be completed in a year, to the previous occupant for the improvements already made on the farm—thirty cleared acres, two log huts, and two barns. He also contracted some lesser debts for provisions and materials.[27] All these repayments were dependent on his brother-in-law's guarantees.

So common was Niblock's situation, including the tentative, risk-ridden solution he adopted for dealing with it, that John Langton, an astute observer and accomplished letter-writer who was himself an English immigrant to Canada but had arrived fifteen years earlier, believed it provided a key to the way in which "Canadian fortunes" were being made. Langton had settled in southeastern Canada when it was in its emerging postfrontier state, and his diaries and edited letters home to his family in England, which have informed this study, contain significant insights into life in postfrontier Canada in the nineteenth century.[28] He described the trap in which Niblock and others were being snared.

There were, Langton said, two types of postfrontier farmers. There were the "needy and extravagant" who took land in its virgin state and paid heavy rates of interest on their mortgages to a local attorney or banker, while taking credit from a storekeeper. Those who provided money to these settlers made it their business to know the situation of each of them and to take advantage of their many difficulties through offers of assistance—at high rates of interest. The pioneers worked hard and made improvements, and they brought in crops. But they could only subsist; they could not make any money. Transportation was undeveloped, and there was no outlet for their surplus. They could not meet their obligations, and were forced to sell out for half the value of the land they had improved.

No sooner had they left than there appeared the second type of settler, described by Langton as "some new emigrant who is frightened of the discomforts of the woods and is glad to give a handsome price for a ready built house and a few acres of cleared land." This seemed clearly to describe Niblock, but so, too, did Langton's scenario for what came next—ever deepening debt within a few years of settlement to those locally who took the measure of his timidity and need, and provided him, like the man who had preceded him, with credit and loans, big and small alike. These rural creditors, said Langton, "habitually lie in wait to prey upon the distresses of others . . . like a rattlesnake, waiting for a bird to drop into its mouth which its eye has already fascinated." Within the few years, many of these farmers, too, like the pioneers who preceded them, were forced to sell out and turned over a further im-

proved farm for a fraction of the value they had put into it.[29] In Niblock's case, of course, he was not lacking in resources that acted as a
safety net, for his brother-in-law was pledged to assist him. But what
Niblock soon came to see was that his dream of instant yeoman self-
sufficiency was impossible. It would take him years to have enough
money to be independent of Edward, and years beyond that to pay
Edward back with the interest he had promised.

These problems were exacerbated by Niblock's lack of preparedness
for farm-making and his difficulties in managing money. Because he had
badly underestimated the costs of the ocean voyage, he arrived with less
than he thought he would have, even with the advance on the money
that Edward had promised and that had been provided to him in New
York City. The forest-clearing work and the efforts to drain some of his
land, which like most of the land in the vicinity contained sections that
were perpetually marshy or prone to retain standing water seasonally,[30]
were too much for one man, especially one lacking experience, yet he
could not afford to hire labor to help him for any extended period of
time. Joseph was too young to be of any assistance, and Alexander was
not strong enough for heavy work and inexperienced, and, sullen and
rebellious, he was also uncooperative.

Niblock was sensible enough to understand his ignorance of much of
what he had to know in order to succeed, so especially lamented that he
lacked enough money to hire someone to teach him. Furthermore, Niblock had not properly estimated the supplies he would need. For example, in his calculations he failed to budget accurately for a plow, yoke,
harrow, and oxen to plant his first crop, or for a stove and exhaust
pipes. He wrote of buying beds, a table, and a cow, and then hay to feed
his animals, as if he had not fully reckoned with the need for them.[31]
(These problems with expenses would at times be worsened by bad
luck, as was the case when one of the oxen he purchased sickened and
died, and had to be replaced. A second ox would die as he was about to
begin his spring planting in 1852).[32] He did not have the tools or skills
to do any building for himself, even though he was surrounded everywhere by wood for lumber. He had believed that he would only very
gradually draw on the £200 Edward had agreed to advance him, but
by the end of September, the first month of his residence in Canada, with
but £2.10 to his name, he wrote to Edward for another advance of £40.[33]

Thus, from the beginning of his settlement in Canada, there began a
cycle of pressing practical needs and equally pressing obligations to pay

bills and interest payments that necessitated desperate-sounding letters to Edward and Christiana in which he begged for help.[34] Not long into his stay, it becomes clear, he was also getting small sums of money from an unidentified family friend ("John") and from Christiana and from Amelia, both of whom also sent the Niblocks packages containing luxuries such as sugar plums and books for Joseph, and useful items such as vegetable, flower, and fruit seeds.[35] Edward responded generously to Niblock's pleas for assistance, although not always in as timely a fashion, probably because of the slowness of the mails, as the situation required from Thomas's point of view. To his mortification, Niblock sometimes found himself missing payments on his loans, because they fell due before he received Edward's drafts. He skulked around the neighborhood hoping to avoid contact with his creditors.[36]

In late April 1852, the tone of Niblock's letters suddenly changed. In the past, he had been desperate about money and exhausted by his labors and responsibilities, but he had rarely been pessimistic about the more long-term future, about which he was largely silent. While he had assured Edward that he would pay him back in 1854, he gave few details. He was overwhelmed by his labors, but also proud that he could do much of the heavy labor required of him and retain his health and grow stronger. Now, however, prospects for the future seemed bleak. He had lost another ox just before plowing needed to begin, and thus faced the unanticipated expense of replacing it.

Clearly this was a setback and may have depressed his mood, but, as he told Edward, he had now reached the conclusion that he did not have the material resources that it took to make a real farm. He lacked a horse and wagon, and money to employ help, not to mention a decent house to live in. (The Niblocks continued to reside in a building that had served the previous occupant as a granary.) The situation, he told Edward, was not likely to change in time for him to be able to pay off the debt on the land in 1854, as he had hoped he would be able to do. He was not quite ready to declare defeat, and suggested that Edward might pay off all the debt on the land, and free him completely of this especially heavy burden.[37]

But Spencer had clearly had enough of this continual drain on his money and the cycle of crisis, begging, and draft writing that almost every letter from his brother-in-law initiated. He probably had little faith left in his brother-in-law's ability as a farmer, so no doubt wondered what good would be done by freeing him of the biggest debt

Mnch decision to go back

What a SCHISM — things would

looming on the horizon, if Thomas would eventually find other ways to become insolvent. In a July 9, 1852, letter Spencer appears to have proposed that Niblock reemigrate to Australia with Edward's assistance, perhaps in the hope that the Niblocks might thereafter become wards of Matilda's family. Typical of Niblock, he wavered only briefly before making up his mind to uproot his family. Within a week of receiving Edward's proposal, he wrote to say he was seriously considering the matter, and a week after that, before hearing again from Spencer, he wrote to accept the offer, holding out the possibility that after making money in Australia, he might return to the Canadian farm he was abandoning, if Edward decided to hold on to the property.

Though advised by at least one of his most respected local contacts not to exchange problems he understood and might well conquer for a new set of unknown ones,[38] Niblock wasted no time in leaving Canada. By late September, the Niblocks were in New York City, awaiting a ship for Australia. Niblock left Canada owing, he said, about £200 in debts beyond the approximately £400 he had already spent. Edward retained the option on the Canadian farm.[39] While we cannot know what Niblock's future would have been had he stayed in Canada, the region he left soon entered a new and promising stage of development. Within a year of Niblock's emigration from Canada, the railroad reached London, providing an outlet for farm products and the basis for a sustainable market economy. Edward's tenant was prospering in 1854 and was reported to be likely to make the improvements to the farm he had agreed to make in taking over the lease that Niblock surrendered to his brother-in-law.[40] Niblock knew the railroad was coming, and he knew, too, that it would better the prospects of local farmers. But he was too impatient at the prospect of succeeding in Australia to endure any longer the discomforts of his life in Canada.

The cruel irony of Niblock's situation began to emerge soon after he came to Canada. He had emigrated to Canada in search of independence, but the more he sought to achieve that goal the more the goal was subverted by his lack of money, his lack of preparedness for the task before him, and probably, too, ultimately, by the weakness of his own character. Rather than independence, his dependence on his family deepened after he left England for the second time, and with this increasing dependence inevitably there came a compromise, in his own eyes and that of his family, of his character. The repeated experience of failure inevitably inspired his insecurities about his character, as did the necessity of continually having to solicit assistance.

Though Niblock was quite willing in his letters to confess that he was in trouble and needed help, he did not seem capable of sustained reflection on his role in authoring the crises that punctuated his adult life. Indeed, in a sense he sought the opposite: he struggled amidst the difficulties that threatened to overwhelm him to sustain the same view of himself—a conception of his ideal self that he carried all over the world, from one unsuccessful emigration to another. The pathos of Niblock's life is precisely this effort, which became inscribed in his writing, to maintain his increasingly tenuous hold on the assurance of his own respectability, the heart of his identity narrative, amidst everything that compromised it—ill luck, personal failure, and bad judgment.

Niblock's formulation of respectability was based on his understandings of his manly duty to fulfill his obligations to his family and to act like a Christian in his dealings with his neighbors. These understandings were predictable for a man of his education, social class, and family background. They were frequently articulated on the surface of his letters, or suggested as he related his activities, hopes, and fears. Did he express himself in such matters to impress his sister and brother-in-law with his seriousness and responsibility? Was he playing the role of Christian paterfamilias, or was the role, the man? The answer to all these imposing questions is "Yes." Niblock certainly wished to cast his character in the traits that were ideal expectations for a man of his class and culture, because he needed to gain the confidence of Edward and Christiana Spencer. His writing certainly contains evidence of sly, manipulative devices that are intended to make him appear as a worthy and deserving man. But this is not to say that the values underlying these representations were not his own, and that thinking of himself as conforming to these values—or at least intending as much as possible to do so—was any less vital to his own identity narrative. We see in his writing a good measure of anxiety and even panic about the integrity of these representations, as if it were not only others' confidence in him that had to be bolstered, but also his faith in himself. His self-confidence and his commitment to his self-representation as a respectable Christian family man and provider were inevitably reinforced when others gave evidence of seeing him as he wished to be seen.

There is little evidence beneath the surface of this man of a secret Thomas Niblock, let alone of a questioning of the values by which he sought to define himself. The performance of the role of Thomas Niblock *was* Thomas Niblock. Put another way, while the literal truth of some of what Niblock wrote may be doubted, the narrative truth for Niblock—in the sense of the consistency between his writing and his understanding of himself—probably should not be.

We might look more deeply into Niblock's self-representation and observe the processes of the discursive construction of personal identity in his letters. Niblock desired to feel that he was a responsible, effective, and affectionate head of his family, and to be seen by others as successfully fulfilling the roles of spouse, father, and brother. He wrote frequently of his concern for Matilda's precarious health and her agitated state of mind amidst the continually difficult circumstances of their life together.[41] He appeared, too, in the role of doting, worried, and proud father—worried, for example, that Joseph was growing up in a wild place with little more to do than roam the woods with his dog, but proud, too, when the boy showed an interest in books and gave other evidence of moral and intellectual development.[42] In the midst of his own toil, he made sure to write to his sister near the time of her birthday and he spoke emotionally of her devotion and loyalty to him through his travails. He expressed concern about his brother-in-law's tendency toward overwork.[43]

As a Christian, Niblock was thoroughly conventional and predictable. Though he did attend a Baptist prayer meeting during his first week in Canada, there is little evidence of formal religiosity in his letters.[44] The fact that the only house of worship conveniently located near him in Delaware was of his father's faith was no inducement for him to attend the Church of England,[45] and, in fact, in the context of whatever obscure dynamic seems to have alienated father and son, may have been the reason why he stayed away. Niblock was instead more of a Christian through culture and habit. Christianity provided the standards by which he judged the conduct of others as well as his own conduct, which helps to explain his claim that while there were many churchgoers around him in Canada, there were few Christians.[46] What marked being a Christian was the capacity for thinking and acting morally.

In the environments in which we know Niblock best, aboard sailing ships surrounded by sailors, and in the rude, postfrontier environments in Australia and Canada, Niblock's expectations of moral conduct were continually frustrated, if not outraged. He commented on the foul and blasphemous language he heard from sailors aboard ship on the way to

North America.[47] In common with many English immigrants, and especially those who went to Canada to settle, he criticized the Americans he encountered in New York City and along the Erie Canal corridor, describing them as guilty of "cool hearted knavery" ("They care for nothing but the dollar."), and of being blasphemers and "ruthless ruffians."[48] He expected a much better moral atmosphere in Canada, which is one especially important reason he presented for desiring to emigrate there in 1849 rather than to return to Australia.[49] At first he believed he had entered a community of Christians. In his first weeks in Canada, everyone he met seemed eager to assist him. They claimed to understand his situation as a new settler with limited resources and experience, and were, he said, "liberal and lenient" in their financial dealings with him. They freely extended him loans and credit. Only gradually did he come to realize that his neighbors, whom he saw at first as motivated simply by good-heartedness, exacted terms for what they did for him, and that everyone around him was motivated by self-interest. Late charges, for example, on loan payments that were past due were not waived.[50] He was soon of the belief that the only true Christian in his midst was Matilda, in comparison to whom he himself felt unworthy. He described his own spiritual condition as "a lukewarm state—almost apathy," as a consequence of hard work and worry.[51]

Yet as poor as he believed the moral tone of his Canadian community to be, Niblock nonetheless fretted endlessly about how his neighbors regarded him. Debt was the source of all his anxieties about the compromise of his integrity in the minds of his neighbors. In Canada, Niblock lived under circumstances in which debt was a way of life for most farmers, but he was never able to regard it as simply a common, inconvenient part of the social order of the new world he had entered. For him, debt may have been anticipated as a necessity, but it was experienced as an embarrassment at least; and when he was unable to pay back his loans or his interest at the agreed-upon time, it was a source of mortification. This must have been a terrible burden for anyone as needy and as poor at handling money as Niblock, for he was always in debt and suffered debt as a blow to his respectability.

If Niblock could have kept his money dealings private, he might have believed it possible to avoid the intrusive scrutiny of his neighbors that caused him so much embarrassment. But inevitably gossip circulated about the financial circumstances of the settlers. It was driven both by boredom and malice, but also by self-interest, for the neediness of others was the source of wealth for those with the capital to make loans. Canadians, observed Niblock in complaining about the difficulty he experienced in maintaining his privacy, were "the most singularly inquisitive people."[52] Fears that his mail might be read or lost, if a well-meaning neighbor picked it up for him without his permission but nonetheless as a courtesy, as was the local custom, or its contents, such as drafts from Edward, might be stolen, caused him to have his family send their letters not to the convenient post office at Delaware, but to London. He believed the postal arrangements were more secure and private there, though the walk to the London post office was a twenty-mile journey, back and forth.[53]

Each time a note fell due, Niblock and Matilda, who shared this anxious state of mind with him, were thrown into panic and despair about not being able to make the payment. It was not enough, therefore, that Edward send him money; it had to be sent so that payment could be made on the exact day it was due. But all the goodwill Spencer could muster for his ever-needy brother-in-law aside, he could not control the speed of the mails, in consequence of which Niblock experienced a severe emotional crisis occasioned by having to make a late payment. He described this state variously as "nervous excitement" and "great mental mortification, vexation and anxiety." He vowed eventually that he would never borrow money again, at least from strangers, because "the anxiety I have suffered has nearly killed me."[54]

At the center of his agony was the loss of respectability in the eyes of the community. Writing desperately to Spencer on the last day of grace for the repayment of a loan owed a local man, he wrote that Edward's draft had not arrived and he now faced late fees. But it was not the fees that concerned him as much as his loss of respectability: "The eyes of the neighborhood [are] upon me, for everything is known to everybody here—the poor man is waiting for his money which he thought as sure as could be. I do not know how to meet him."[55] When he was able to meet an obligation and do so in a timely manner, his relief was deeper than the convenience of not owing money. "I am now out of debt here," he observed on one occasion after using £30 Edward had sent him to pay off a debt, "and my character improved, instead of injured among my neighbors no doubt—but I do not know how I could have met them yesterday which was the day I appointed—after so many delays—without the money."[56]

The depths of Niblock's ethical problem as a debtor and supplicant are revealed in the rhetorical devices he employed in his letters to impress Edward and Christiana with his difficulties, and to convince them to commit vastly more money to subsidizing him than they had initially been led to expect he would need. He was brought by his despair and anxiety about his integrity to subvert that integrity through self-representations that ultimately served to diminish him. This is apparent in his tendency to cover himself with pathos. The problem is not that he described the severe privations he and his family were suffering, for these were real enough and certainly were legitimately a part of any description of the life of the settler in rural west Canada at the time. It is instead that he described his situation in ways that suggested that somehow he was a victim of these circumstances rather than their author. After all, Niblock set out for Canada with little understanding of the labors or expenses that lay before him.

Christiana was particularly likely to be the target of these manipulations. His conventional understandings of femininity and the maternal role she may have played in his life over the course of many years, probably led him to understand her as more likely than his serious, manly brother-in-law to feel rather than to think her way through life. She would respond to him with sympathy because she was a woman and the sister who worried about him, especially in the absence of the mother whom they had lost many years before. It is in a letter to her that he identified the farm from which he wrote as, "The Wanderer's Home," which, he said, may seem a "romantic or foolish" way to describe himself and his new home, "but is a plain matter of fact as far as we are concerned and in a worldly sense."[57] He did not fashion himself as a "wanderer," torn from his roots and struggling to create new ones, in his letters to Edward.

Christiana, however, was not always the sentimentalist her brother imagined her to be. In response to one of his requests for money, she had apparently written to protest his continual pleas and claimed that he had already been given the means to be self-sufficient. Thomas then adopted a more aggressive form for conveying the pathos of his situation. "You will blame me," he said, "for you wish me to live in a bare farm rather than ask further assistance. The sentiment is right—but the result would be continued starvation."[58] In his next letter to her, he invoked pity explicitly, "If you knew how much and what different kind of work there is before me—all to be done at once—you would pity me. You cannot conceive the additional labor a person has who cannot afford either to buy tools or hire assistance."[59]

When Niblock addressed Edward, he did not have confidence in the efficacy of appeals that avoided the question of his own bad judgment, but he was nonetheless skillful in putting the matter in a way that preserved a view of himself as the victim of circumstances beyond his control. In one letter he described the expenses he had sustained in buying livestock and household and farm goods on one-year credit, and spoke of his need to make other purchases for which he lacked the money. He needed, he said, a fireplace, seed, and materials to improve his roof and drain his land. "What will you say to all this?" he wrote,

> Will you still help me forward? Do you think it will be any use to do so?, or shall I fall in the midst of my efforts because I could not foresee how small matters accumulate and by asking you to help me with a large amount at first, either obtain it—or be refused and continue in the stagnant state I was fast falling into?

He asked to be sent £20 immediately, but slyly added that while £50 might seem too much, he had come to see how small necessities mounted up. Then, too, he added, if his crops failed or were disappointing, he would not be able to pay his outstanding notes when they came due. "I shall await your reply," he said in closing, again casting himself in the role of victim of circumstances beyond his control, "with such an anxiety as it has never been your lot to feel."[60]

When not portraying himself as the prisoner of circumstance, Niblock sought to ingratiate himself to Edward and Christiana through flattery and to drive the point home through self-mockery and self-deprecation, both of which also served implicitly to make a point about the rigors of his new life. This appeared, for example, in the guise of fond remarks toward his sister, which nonetheless drive home the difficulties he faced. He wrote of himself as "a plain, plodding downright working Canadian farmer," whom he then contrasted to his sister—a sophisticated and discerning "city dame" who must eventually tire of his relation of the tedious details of farm life.[61] Some of the tendency toward self-deprecation may have been intended to satisfy his brother-in-law's own piety. Edward's Christian beliefs presented Niblock with a difficult task: Niblock needed to encourage his brother-in-law to believe

[handwritten margin note at top: What a contradiction he was caught in... before the eyes his brother in law]

he would succeed and was worth the investment of his money, while also ensuring him that he would not be swayed by success from understanding his true position before God. Thus, he needed simultaneously to boast and to refuse to do so. He had to appear to be making a success of his farm while acknowledging that ultimately his success was in God's hands.

> I could tell you much that would gratify you [he claimed in writing of his reputation in the area] as to what is said of my prudence in laying out money and my success in farming if it were not that I fear you would consider 1st that I take too much credit to myself instead in giving honor to God—2nd that I have an overweening opinion of my exertions and 3rd that I am too credulous and imposed upon by flattering neighbors—but none of these I trust is the case. If the Lord will still continue to bless me, I see a fair prospect of success before me & I trust & pray He will do so for the sake of those dependent upon me.[62]

[handwritten margin note: fine & clear & o) quotation]

The next year, in a letter to Christiana, he said that he was "on the right path of life" and that it is "intrinsically honorable to earn one's bread by the sweat of the brow as I now do." Yet he knew, too, he said, that he was but a "worm" in the eyes of God, who had favored him by finally giving his life direction.[63]

[handwritten margin note: But] Writing of this type is not as common in the correspondence as the ordinary description of his difficulties and pleas for assistance. Moreover, it is somewhat more formally religious than the usual character of Niblock's Christianity, which is more a matter of right conduct than of formal declarations of belief. But there is no reason for us to doubt that on some level it represented his own beliefs and his understanding of his personal identity, even though it was intended simultaneously to play a tactical role in his efforts to influence those on whom he had come to depend. His epistolary relationship to his sister and brother-in-law had increasingly become the instrument of his ambition to succeed in his faltering Canadian project. To the extent that he framed himself and his relation to Edward and Christiana in a tactical way, however, it subtly worked to subvert his character while he was at the same time attempting to build it up, and it undermined his desperate effort to hold on to his respectability.

By the time of his return to Australia, Niblock's confidence that he could continue to regard himself as a Christian family man who pos-

[handwritten note at bottom: maybe... but what if he did not realize it!]

sessed positive plans for ensuring the prosperity of his family seems riddled with doubt. We may imagine him torn between hope and despair, knowing increasingly that his options were not simply narrowing but disappearing, and that the prospects of a failure too devastating to be denied loomed immediately on the horizon. He was not able to face this terrible knowledge directly in his correspondence, which in the last two letters we possess—one from Cape Town, to Christiana on New Year's Day of 1853; the other from Melbourne, to Edward and dated April 15 of that year—reveal an increasingly dissociated state of mind. He acknowledged that he stood on the edge of a precipice and simultaneously sought to distance himself from actually assimilating the implications of his desperate situation. This was evident in his return to the sentimental pathos of his role as a victim, fated by circumstance to roam endlessly and never have a home. This representation was evoked in writing to Christiana, to whom he now offered "another epistle from the Wanderer."

But he was forced to acknowledge, too, that his resources were declining rapidly, to the extent that he allowed a Cape Town contact, Captain Pilkington, to pay for goods the family required to complete the journey to Australia. (Pilkington's aid was easier to accept, and did not embarrass Niblock, because it was extended "in the most delicate manner.") Moreover, he was apprehensive about the future, especially in anticipating the arrival of a second child at about the same time as they would be in the first weeks of their resettlement in Australia. But he was hopeful as well. The prospect of the second child seemed to inspire the understanding that he needed to have a plan, or at least to prepare himself mentally for the challenge ahead. Thus, he was encouraged when Pilkington provided him with letters of introduction, which he believed would help him find work in Melbourne.[64]

But what precisely did Niblock intend to do in Australia? As was his habit of mind, he was considering a variety of seemingly mutually exclusive options and making no effort to create priorities among them. He imagined a quick turnaround in his fortunes. He had left Canada believing that he would get "a government situation," which would pay, according to what he said he had been told by a source he did not identify, the (unlikely) sum of £20 a week. He added, however, that he might also "try the gold diggings in which case I may be able to remit you a thousand pounds very shortly." Niblock anticipated that it was doubtful that Spencer would have any faith in such a prediction, so he added hopefully, "Extravagance of statement is borne out in Australia by extravagance of fact." He related, too, that friends had told him of a Canadian neighbor who had gone to California and was making £9 a week at the gold diggings there. Why should not he be as fortunate? After all, he was now armed with the experience of hard work. His recent unsuccessful experience in Canada was no basis for predicting his future. His Canadian "sojourn," a word whose tentativeness hardly did justice to the hopes ("bona fide emigration") he had brought with him to Canada, had failed to conclude to his satisfaction because he could not make a success of farming there without greater means than he had at his disposal. But he had benefited nonetheless from the "experience of actual labor and therefore gained an ability to descend to it when requisite." Under any circumstance, he concluded, forgetting the experience of his first immigration, "there is better security in Australia." The more temperate climate, too, would be better for Matilda's sometimes precarious health.[65]

Once in Australia, Niblock put in his lot with a group that went from Melbourne to the Victoria goldfields, where after six weeks of "steady application" he had nothing to show for his efforts "but the pleasures of unsubstantiated hope . . . tempered by much hardship and discomfort." The root of the problem was not the folly of believing that he would strike it rich and make thousands, as he had predicted from Canada, but rather, he said, that he lacked the capital to stay at the diggings long enough to find gold. Yet in writing of his experience in the goldfields, Niblock described the disappointments of so many of the miners almost as if he were an outside observer. "Numbers of poor deluded beings from all parts of the globe arrive here daily—sometimes 4 or 5 ships in a day each with hundreds of passengers," he wrote Edward in his Melbourne letter, after leaving the goldfields with nothing to show for his efforts but the loss of much of what little remained of his resources. "It positively makes my heart ache to see them for they are coming to their ruin. They will soon be miserably disappointed & sorely rue the day they left their native shores." Did it occur to Niblock he might be describing himself? Apparently not, even as he related the misery in which he and his family found themselves after he left the goldfields. Unemployed, failing repeatedly to find work, and living off the sale of his library and few remaining valuables, which would soon be completely gone, they might go hungry. Moreover, he had come to feel acutely his sharply falling status, though he found an explanation for this less in his circumstances than in the insensitivity of those with whom he interacted. The working classes of Melbourne, he said, demonstrated "delight" in making people "bred above them" feel poorly because they found themselves in need. The clergymen of his own class, however, to whom he sold his books, did not belittle him. Respectable, educated Christians, they gave him fair market value for his books and did not take advantage of him or remind him of his desperate circumstances.[66]

What were the options that lay before him? Unlike many of the Melbourne working class, Niblock had no trade; nor did he possess any tools. Artisanal work, which was available in abundance in Melbourne, was closed to him. Gone too, it seems, was the prospect of government employment, about which he no longer spoke. But if Edward would send him the resources, he said, he would open a small shop (though in an addendum, dated May 2 and mailed with the April 15 letter, he acknowledged the conviction that he was "not fit for business of any sort.")

There was another vision, too, that was emerging simultaneously: the return to Canada. If he were able to make "a few hundred pounds" (it is unclear at what, but perhaps at the shop he proposed), "both I and Matilda will gladly return to the retirement we so (as it appears) unfortunately left and where hope whispers that with all of the severity of the climate we may get acreage so as to live in peace and sufficiency if not competence and this is our fixed resolve." He had come to understand, as he related on May 2, that "[my] proper calling is as an agriculturalist and that I never ought to have left it." The Canadian climate, he now said, reversing himself on this matter, too, would be better for Matilda than the cold wet Melbourne winter that they were then experiencing. Though his situation was "well-nigh desperate," he thanked God nonetheless for bringing him to his insight about his proper calling and then appealed to Edward to assist him. In arguing that he had failed at both farming in Canada and gold mining in Australia for want of capital, he was subtly reproaching his brother-in-law and laying the emotional basis for claiming another subsidy.[67] His fourth emigration in fifteen years had failed, but rather than look backward—beyond, that is, putting blame elsewhere—he was beginning to plan his fifth.

We cannot know under what influence, with what resources, and with what plan to redeem himself this driven man uprooted his family yet again and set out for Sydney. In less than two weeks, they were all dead. Niblock wrote many letters, but the one we want most from him has either disappeared or was never written. Yet is there reason to believe that this phantom final letter would have been any different in purpose or in content from those that he had written before? An articulate and gentle, yet cunning and, in the end, uncomprehending man, Thomas Niblock wrote many letters, but ultimately they resolved little for him. His letters did not serve as a site for questioning the way he lived in the world. There is little of the intense, painful routine accounting of the ways in which individual decisions had led to a variety of gains and losses that we find in the letters of some immigrants. Kate Bond, to whom we turn next, increasingly used her letters to interrogate the decisions she and her husband had made to emigrate from England, resettle in Connecticut, and then migrate to the Kansas prairie. Instead, buffeted constantly by failures which shook his personal identity to its core, Niblock struggled only to hold on even more desperately to the person he hoped to be.

8

Catherine Grayston Bond
Letter-Writing as the Practice of Existential Accounting

I wish we was nearer so that we could see each other some times. I feel lonely many a time so far from you all. We left to better ourselves, but some times I thinck we should have done as well if we stayed. We have our own home and our children are all with us; but there is a lot of care.

—Catherine [Kate] Bond to her brother, January 9, 188?

Catherine Grayston Bond's letters to her brother, Robert, and his wife, Ellen, record a deceptively simple story. A twenty-four-year-old Englishwoman and her husband, James, leave Lancashire in 1869 to work at farming and domestic service on the Connecticut estate of a wealthy American. Then, at some time between 1874 and 1879, they and four children go to Russell County in central Kansas, which had only recently opened to white settlement, and realize the dream of many English emigrants. Using their savings, they buy a partially improved farm on the prairie from one of the area's pioneers. Here they spend the rest of their lives, growing wheat and corn and raising livestock, while making a home for the six of their ten children who survived infancy.

Kate, as she often called herself, came from a family of agricultural laborers and estate gardeners, and had gone into service as a girl. James, too, was a farm laborer, who grew frustrated in England because of his inability to find a farm tenancy. They wished more than anything else to avoid working for wages and being dependent, as they had come to feel was their inevitable fate, if they remained in England. Writing from Connecticut and later from Kansas, Kate described their struggles to

257

realize their goals, but spoke even more often about her longing for her brothers, sisters, and father and for the familiar environs of rural England, and about the cycle of birth, illness and aging, and death.

As the years passed, a tone of resignation came to characterize most of her letters, as did feelings of loneliness, grief, and isolation. Reading her letters, it is clear that the Bonds were able to make a home and farm for themselves in Kansas at a time when thousands of others had failed there because of the instabilities of wheat farming on the prairies. They did not have to send any of their children out to work because they could not support them, which had been Kate's lot as a girl. She had entered service to help relieve the stresses of maintaining Peter Grayston's household of seven children. But one would be hard-pressed on the basis of the letters to conclude that the Bonds prospered there. Absent, too, from the correspondence is the relation of membership in any sort of community, whether ethnic or local, which led Charlotte Erickson, to whom we owe a debt for the discovery of Kate Bond's letters, to conclude, "The Bonds do not seem to have had much social life."[1]

On first reading, Kate's letters do suggest that she had little human contact beyond her children and a somewhat distant emotional relationship with her husband, and the transnational connection she established through her infrequent but heartfelt letters to her brother and sister-in-law. She did once visit, and she occasionally exchanged letters with, the American branches of her family—a sister in West Virginia and a brother in Missouri. But these visits and letters appear to have been few and far between. Read at this level, Kate's letters inevitably call to mind not so much the difficulties of emigration and resettlement as the dreary, toil-ridden, economically marginal world of prairie farming, the pathos and frustrations of which were captured in late-nineteenth-century fiction by writers such as Hamlin Garland, and gave birth to the Populist political insurgency on the Great Plains.

These political and fictional narratives lead us to think we know the Bonds' story, for they seem effortlessly to assimilate it. It is the story of the struggle of the isolated family farm set against the backdrop of the cruelties of nature and the conflict between the yeoman ideology of agrarian self-sufficiency and the juggernaut of profit-driven agricultural capitalism.[2] It seems easier to discount the immigrant element in the Bonds' story to the extent that they were English and thus supposedly assimilated effortlessly. In fact, Kate's letters reveal little in the way of ethnic identification or ethnic communal activity.

Conflating info

These agrarian narratives are certainly valuable in understanding the outer boundaries of the Bonds' experience of American life. But the extent and the nature of their value can only be understood if we interrogate Kate Bond's correspondence more closely, searching for gaps and silences as well as focusing on what she makes explicit, and attempting to concentrate our attention on how Kate develops her ongoing efforts to establish continuity and meaning in her experience of life in the letters she wrote. This need for further inquiry begins to become apparent as soon as we seek contextualization of the Bonds' narrative in other sources, such as their obituaries. When James died in 1897, one of the region's principal newspapers, the *Russell Record,* did two respectful articles on him, both of which provide a challenge to the picture of the Bonds' life suggested by the often sad and resigned tone of Kate's letters.[3] First, we note that far from living an isolated existence, bereft of community, James had been a member of the Odd Fellows, a popular fraternal order among British immigrant as well as American men in the United States, throughout his decades of residence in Kansas. His funeral was conducted according to the ritual of the Odd Fellows and it was said, "Quite a number of the fraternity in Russell were in attendance."[4] The crowd at the funeral might have been the result of James's popularity as well as his long and loyal membership in the order. James, the paper stated, was "a well known Englishman," and, it implied, was well liked: "He was a pleasant companion; his quaint dialect and general laugh and manner will be missed by all who knew him."[5]

The picture of Kate's life that we might draw from her letters is similarly challenged in an obituary that appeared in the *Russell Reformer* when she died eleven years after her husband. Far from being without a 1908 community, she was a churchgoer who attended religious services at a number of local churches. "The deceased was confirmed in the Church of England and never united with any other," the paper recorded, "although she has attended others quite regularly." Moreover, it was observed, Kate, who in her last years when suffering from heart disease had moved to Russell, the county seat, had not been able to socialize with others as she had done in the past. Her health, the newspaper suggested, had interfered with the desire "to become as well acquainted as she otherwise might have done" with local residents.[6] The extent of ethnic identification and ethnic group activity in the Bonds' Kansas life may be unclear, but they certainly do not appear to have lived without community.

One of the *Russell Record* death notices about James Bond also challenges another picture that emerges from Kate's correspondence—that
the Bonds had accomplished making a home and keeping their children
at home, no mean accomplishment to be sure, but little else. The newspaper recorded that James had gone out to Kansas with enough money,
or acquired enough money within a few years of migrating to Kansas,
to buy "Andrew Hill's homestead," the farm of a local white pioneer
that included house, barn and outbuildings, and land, both cultivated
and wild. Moreover, during his two decades in Kansas, he "had accu-
mulated considerable wealth in real estate and property," enough to
guarantee his family's security, and to earn a reputation for willingness
"to help those who honestly deserve help." In fact, local court records
and other local sources reveal that at the time of James's death in 1897,
the family had a 400-acre farm, approximately 140 acres of which was
then under cultivation in wheat and corn. A fair-sized creek passed
through their land, which helped to accommodate their livestock:
twelve milk cows, a herd of twenty beef cattle, and thirty-seven pigs.
The farm was valued at approximately $3,000, exclusive of the value of
five horses and farm machinery and implements, toward the end of a
deep economic depression that had devastated the Great Plains. James
had debts of approximately $500 owed on loans, which were paid back
to his creditors immediately out of the estate and through the sale of
some livestock and the proceeds of an excellent crop the next year.
Within two years of his death, Kate and her oldest son, Bob, who took
over running the farm after his father died, had bought an additional
160 acres of adjacent farmland. Kate was left sufficiently well-off that,
when her health declined and she moved into Russell (probably to be
near one of her two daughters), she occupied a large house on a substantial lot in the center of town.[7] Well beyond their own lives, James
and Kate Bond were able to lay the foundation for a number of generations to prosper on their farm, which over a century later is still in the
possession of their descendants.[8]

Our difficulties knowing the Bonds ultimately eventuate from the
interpretive problem that is axiomatic to decoding personal letters,
whether or not written by immigrants: we must be conscious as we read
them that what is not written about may nonetheless have importance
to knowing the lives of letter-writers. We have already seen the ways
in which intentional silence strategically asserted itself in immigrant
correspondence. For Kate Bond, however, there seems no strategy of in-

tentional silence. Instead, her letters seem to be vehicles for the development of some projects but not for others. The Bonds' experience of farm-making, their involvement in the community, and their achievements in building secure foundations for their family life were important to Kate Bond. These were the practical activities that preoccupied her daily life during the years in the United States that are represented in her letters. But while her letters do contain occasional, short descriptions of her daily activities, they took on another purpose as the years passed. They became the place in which she was engaged in a ruminative inventory of the choices she had made and was making in life, while in the midst of living.

In Kate Bond's letters, then, we see a recurring process of existential accounting by which she weighed what she and her husband had gained and what they had lost in emigrating, resettling, and moving still further away from England into the heartland of the United States. They had gained security and a homestead, but, looming larger as she aged, were the losses she noted briefly and matter-of-factly, for Kate does not indulge much in nostalgia: a pleasant and, it seemed to her, less worry-ridden way of life in rural England, embedded in the comforts of the large and consoling family into which she had been born, and in relation to which she continued to understand her personal identity. The perception of isolation and resignation we find in the letters does have explainable roots in the quality of some of her relationships—with her husband, with the families of her brother and her sister which were both settled in the United States, and with the memories of her five dead children and the difficulties she faced in raising those who survived. But that perception springs, too, from the intense yearning for those from whom she had been separated (increasingly, she realized, irrevocably separated) by emigration, and the Christian understanding of death she brought to interpreting her losses.

In analyzing Kate Bond's letters from this perspective, a contemporary reader is once more struck by the losses to our understanding of immigration history that have resulted from the impatience of past generations of analysts with the poor writing and the presumed trivial content of the letters of ordinary immigrants, and especially of women immigrants, who were more likely than male correspondents to write exclusively about private relations. Kate Bond is not a mature stylist, and her letters, especially the earlier ones, are riddled with grammatical and spelling errors. Over the years, her technical command of English markedly improved. But the principal subject matter, which is the relationships she formed within her nuclear and extended families, remains the same throughout her correspondence. If one is looking, as were the previous generations of analysts who found such letters at best quaint and at worst without value, for discussions of politics, public issues, the farm economy, and development of social structure on the prairie, her letters are not helpful.

But if Kate Bond's letters are read with an understanding of their purposes in her own quest for meanings, it becomes apparent that she had an active mental life that for decades worked at making sense of the choices she had made. In the flatness of her descriptions and occasional narratives of daily domestic life and the lack of an explicit, strong subjectivity to be observed in Mary Ann Archbald's letters, Kate Bond comes close to substantiating Carolyn Heilbrun's contention that the writings of nonelite woman display the lack of a well-defined sense of self. The narrow horizons imposed on them by the patriarchal social order are said to overwhelm their subjectivity, and leave them with little on which to situate their lives but familial relationships.[9] To understand Kate's letters from this perspective, however, is ultimately to fail to understand the source of their energy, and to fail to take the opportunity to understand how women like Kate Bond created the meanings that explained their lives for them. Kate's self is defined within the framework of these relationships, and her ruminative inventory of the choices that she and her husband had made is, for her, central to, not an impediment to, the work of crafting personal identity.

Kate Bond's letters were discovered in the possession of a descendent of the Bonds' English relatives during the early stages of Charlotte Erickson's research in the 1940s. Erickson had photostats of the original letters made, and in 1949 deposited them in the archives at Cornell University, where they reside in the Collection of Regional History. Erickson reprinted an edited version of the letters in *Invisible Immigrants* in 1972. Around the same time, the owner of the letters deposited the originals in the Lancashire Record Office in England. Since there are few other sources that make reference to the Bonds, we may only know Kate Bond well through this collection. So we need to pay attention before analyzing her letters to the familiar detective work by which the authorship, provenance, and various technical issues in composition may assist us in understanding the letters and the letter-writer.

There are, in effect, two sets of Kate Bond's letters: the easily accessible, edited version reprinted by Erickson and the archived originals (or the photostatic copies of them). We recall that in editing letters for publication, Erickson "omitted references to letters, to health, and messages from other immigrants and to other persons, once the network of friends and acquaintances of the immigrant had been established in the early letters" as well as "most accounts of ocean voyages, most lists of American prices and some rather shallow descriptions."[10] These deletions were a response to publishers' pressures to limit the size of the final draft of *Invisible Immigrants*.[11] But they also conformed to Erickson's project. Erickson sought to use letters to analyze immigrant social aspirations, which she understood to be best approached through the study of the emigrant's occupation and socioeconomic position in Britain and material aspirations.

Erickson understood the analytical value of some of the deleted material. For example, she was aware of the centrality of networks in facilitating migrations, finding work, and establishing communal bonds. She began to use the term *network* in her work before it became one of the principal concepts in immigration historiography. She made valuable observations about immigrant networks in *Invisible Immigrants*.[12] But network analysis, understood in terms of transnational social ties sustained by personal letters, was not a significant part of her analytical work.

I have consulted both the photostats at Cornell as well as Erickson's edition of the Bonds' letters, and found significance in some of the materials that were deleted in the latter. The unedited letters, to which all my endnotes here refer, establish further details about Kate's own family and about the formation and maintenance of the transnational and other networks sustained by the flow of letters back and forth between Kate and both her English and American extended families.[13] They certainly establish the existence of a wider network of correspondents than Robert and Ellen Grayston in England. Furthermore, Kate's anxieties about the possible meanings of not receiving mail from England; her guilt at being such an infrequent letter-writer; her relationships with her American relatives; her relationships with and the lives and deaths of her own children; the religious frameworks she ultimately employed to explain the losses she suffered; comments about her children's cognitive development and schooling; and evidence that Kate wrote other letters than those which have been archived, all are subjects of significance to this analysis, though they were not central enough to Erickson's to be included in their entirety in the edited collection of Bond's letters.

The Bonds emigrated from England in the summer of 1869, and Kate's first letter, of the total of twenty-two letters in the archived collection, is dated July 1870. Kate established the location of the first eleven letters as Milford, Connecticut, the location of the Hubbell estate, to which Kate and Jim had immigrated to work. The balance of the letters was written at the farm, the post office for which was in nearby Bunker Hill, Kansas. Though undated, the last archived letter she wrote was probably written in 1899. Photostats of the envelopes, which would provide us with postmarks and hence dates, of these letters do not exist in the Cornell collection, nor are most of the letters themselves precisely addressed. They are usually addressed simply to "brother" or "sister."

On the basis of internal evidence that allows a process of elimination, it is clear that most of these letters are written to her brother Robert (10), Robert's wife and Kate's sister-in-law Ellen (5), and Robert and Ellen as a couple (1). There is a strong likelihood that of the letters (6) whose recipient or recipients cannot be definitely identified, two are to Robert and two others to Robert and Ellen.[14] Of Kate's six siblings, Robert appears to have been the second oldest brother, though it is not clear whether he was slightly older or slightly younger than Kate. After Robert's death in 1897 and then at the time of Ellen's final illness in 1899, Kate wrote her last letter in the archived collection to a niece, who was one of the couple's surviving children.[15] (She does not appear to have continued to correspond, however, with her brother's children after 1899.) Kate wrote other family members, nuclear and extended, too, though we know of them only because they are mentioned in her archived letters. The almost exclusive representation of the relationship to Robert and Ellen in the archives, therefore, is not a product of their being "favorites," but rather an artifact of a process of collection and depositing by a descendent.

Twenty-two archived letters in twenty-nine years represents a letter sent to England once every year-and-a-half. This is hardly a significant flow of mail, and it leaves us wondering what we miss in the Bonds' life by having so little to fill these gaps. But the gaps are themselves elusive. Kate Bond did not write these letters as infrequently as she mailed them. Though her letters certainly are not long, she worked at composing them over a period of time rather than at one sitting. This was especially the case after the Bonds migrated to Kansas, when the dating of the letters becomes less and less precise, as if they were the product of a long process of composition, interrupted by the demands of motherhood and farmwork, and, at the time of finally being prepared for the post, could no longer be precisely dated. Since the exact dates of these letters cannot be reconstructed, approximations may be made from a combination of internal evidence and the relatively few events in the Bonds' lives for which there is external documentation. One of these events is an instance of what was thought to be arson that destroyed some of their wheat crop in August 1888.[16] The other events are the births and deaths of their children and extended family members for which there is external documentation.[17] Of course, part of the process of composition was thinking about what to say, even before sitting down to write. Kate's mental work, specifically, her habit of existential accounting, suggests that she spent a significant amount of time pondering what for her were the biggest questions of her life prior to writing about the matters she formulated in her correspondence.

Bond's technical command of English grew significantly over the years. Absent any evidence of adult reading, or of any effort on Kate's part deliberately to improve her writing (for example, by seeking help from others), her growing mastery of English probably had two sources. One certainly was the practice of writing and reading letters. Kate wrote more than the twenty-three archived letters, as her unedited letters particularly make clear in their references to other correspondents. She corresponded for years not only occasionally with the American families of a brother and a sister, but also with her sister, Sarah, who came from England twice, at the beginning and toward the end of the 1890s, and whose visits required planning through the post.[18] She also wrote to various aunts and uncles occasionally, and received letters from them.[19]

Kate's growing facility with written English may also have a relationship to the cognitive development and schooling of her children, which is the subject of mention in her letters. We may speculate that conscious as she was, as is evident in her letters, of the value of American public education and pleased with its widespread availability at no cost, she may have been highly motivated to offer her children assistance with their schoolwork and to read to them in order to improve their ability to learn.[20] The improvement in her style and usage begins to take place at the time of the formative cognitive development and early schooling of her oldest son, Bob.[21] The growing technical command of English enabled Kate Bond to achieve a facility in expressing the more complex, ruminative formulations of her later letters that she lacked at the beginning of her letter-writing in the United States in 1870. The practice of existential accounting itself demanded a growth in her abilities, so her command of language might well have developed, too, in proportion to the demands she came to make on herself to express more complex formulations about her own experience.

There are five other letters in the archived collection, but they were not written by Kate. One of these was written by Kate's oldest child, Bob, who was named for his uncle, and was written to Robert and Ellen's sickly son, Peter, who died in 1890 or 1891. This invaluable letter, which was not included in *Invisible Immigrants*, provides, as we shall see, some important insight into the dynamics of the Bonds' Kansas household.[22] The other four letters were written by Kate's younger brother, James Grayston, who emigrated to the United States sometime in the 1860s, with his older sister, Ann, who was older, too, than Kate. Pregnant at the time of her emigration, Ann had come to the United States to marry an Irish Catholic laborer, Pat Moran, whom she had met while she was employed in domestic service in England. James Grayston eventually married Moran's sister, Catherine, which completed the three American branches of the Bond family: James and Kate Bond; James and Catherine Moran Grayston; and Pat and Ann Grayston Moran. Three of James's letters (1877, 1878, and 1879) appear to have been written to his sister Sarah Grayston, and the last (1899) to his niece, the daughter of Ellen and Robert, following Ellen's death.[23]

While there are too few of these letters to gain much in the way of understanding of brother James's role in the Graystons' transnational family network, the letters of 1877, 1878, and particularly 1879 are helpful in two ways. Because there is a hiatus between approximately 1874 and 1881 in Kate's correspondence in the archived collection, Grayston's letters provide some factual information that helps to fill in the Bonds' narrative for those years. While they do not relate precisely the time at which the Bonds came to Kansas, or how they put the money together to buy the homestead they purchased, they give us some proximate understanding of both matters. But even more significant than facts alone, these three letters provide an understanding of Kate and James Bond's lives from perspectives that Kate herself did not choose to develop, and in doing so give us some insight into the ongoing development of Kate's consciousness of the meanings of her experience.

Kate never discussed their farm assets in much depth, and though on one occasion she would write to her brother, "I like a Western life," her letters frequently emphasize the difficulties of farming on the prairie more than the benefits. Her comments on their livestock, the numbers of which grew significantly, were more likely to be about the work required to maintain them than the money to be made.[24] When James and Catherine Grayston were living in Grafton, West Virginia, in 1878, at the residence of Pat and Ann Moran, James received a letter in which, he said, Kate related that she and James "onley just make a living now."[25] The next year the Graystons and their children went out to Kansas to live with the Bonds, while James helped Kate's husband farm. After staying in Kansas for about three years, they moved to Kansas City, Missouri.

James Grayston was deeply impressed with what his sister and brother-in-law were achieving in Kansas, where they had moved only about a year before. "Kate and Jim," he wrote his sister, "is quite the aristocrats, at least they would think themselves so if they were in England and had a hundred and sixty acers of land and a house of their own and twenty acers of wheat, two horses, and a cow and kill all our own game, plenty of hares, rabbits, prairie chickens, geese & wild duck."[26] While there are a number of possible explanations for her refusal to do so, Kate would not usually have developed such detail about their possessions. But more significant is the fact that it is very doubtful that their situation had changed so radically in one year to explain these contrasting comments, which seems to underscore that Kate was developing a more complex system of accounting for understanding the development of their lives.

Before examining the relational contexts of existential accounting as these emerge in her correspondence, it is necessary to understand how Kate mobilized language in her letters to prepare her inventory of the choices that she and Jim were making. Many immigrant letter-writers engaged in the mental work of comparing the past they had left be-hind with the present they were making for themselves, and eventually they put these thoughts on paper to share with their correspondents. What makes this inventory especially outstanding in Bond's letters is the persistence of these evaluative statements over time, the changing conclusions that they reach, and the growing complexity of the statements in which they are embedded. Existential accounting presents itself in her letters in conditional (*if* and *but*) and "I wish" statements. The point of both types of constructions, in all the variations in which they are presented, is to examine simultaneously a desirable future possibility and the requirements of the present. Both are projected implicitly or explicitly against the backdrop of a remembered past.

Kate Bond begins this evaluative work shortly after emigrating, with statements that are essentially hopeful about the future and which focus on material improvement. She believed that she and Jim were taking steps to ensure a prosperous future. She reserved the possibility of returning to England with enough money to be self-sufficient for the balance of their lives, though she also acknowledged that the world of relationships she had left was itself changing as a consequence of emigration and death:

> We don't regret leaving Old England for we are doing a great deal better than if we had stayed there. [And later that same year:] We have plenty and want for nothing. (1870)[27]
>
> You will see us [back] someday, but not yet for we shall never come back for our living. (1871)[28]
>
> If we had stayed in England, we should only have gotten a living and scarcely that and here we can get everything we want and save plenty of money. (1872)[29]
>
> We had very poor crops the last two years, but it is still better than working for another. (1884?)[30]

After a number of years toiling to make a farm on the Kansas prairie and experiencing a variety of difficulties that deeply affected the quality of their lives, these statements take a decided turn toward negative evaluations of the present. As evaluations, they seamlessly combine an understanding of their material situation and the larger problem of the quality of their lives, both in the context of relationships and of the style of daily life:

> I wish I was nearer so that we could see each other sometimes. I feel lonely many a time so far from you all. We left to better ourselves, but

some times I thinck we should have done as well if we had stayed. We have our home and our children are all with us; but there is a lot of care. (188?)[31]

If we was to sell all we should not have what we brought from Connecticut after working all these years. I often tell Jim we should have more pleasure of our life if we lived in Old England even if he only had his days labour for he got payed for it but we work many a month and don't get any pay. (1889?)[32]

Increasingly throughout the 1890s, Kate Bond's letters reveal both resignation and an understanding that she must make the best out of the choices she has made in life, while awaiting the promise of reunion with her loved ones and Christian salvation in death. The focus of these remarks narrows to her relationships with her children and to her extended family, conceived in the abstract as a single body, in England. One context, which we shall examine at greater length for these remarks, was the death of her oldest daughter and closest companion, Margaret, at eighteen in 1889,[33] the occasion for the most profound grief she expressed in her letters. In the second of these statements, in offering consolation to Robert and Ellen, she juxtaposed Margaret's death and that of their son, her nephew, Peter, who was sick most of his life and had died.

I suppose you have heard of Maggie's death. I miss her so much now. . . . But I supose we should have parted if she had lived and perhaps it is better as it is, for I know where she is now and wants for nothing. (1890)[34]

Peter is in heaven and at rest and it is those that are here that need our care now. If it had not been for my younger ones I thinck they would have laid me beside her before now. (1891?)[35]

We have our troubles and there is a time for us all if we are only ready when the time comes. We are great way apart from each other. Still I always feel the same affection for all of you though I know we shall never meet here on earth, yet I feel sure we shall in heaven. It was that thought that kept me up when I lost Maggie. Its only for a little while and theres work for me here or I should not be left here. (1892?)[36]

I would like to see you, but I shall never leave Kansas. This is my home as long as I am on this earth, so we must look forward to the meeting in a better world. This life is not for long for either of us at the longest. (1898?)[37]

You must write me often for I don't get many letters from the Old Country now. I often think of them[.] But this is my home now as long as I live. If it is Gods will to spare me until Jim [her youngest son and last child] grows up. He is 13 years old. But I thinck they have it tougher in this country than in England if they are left to do for themselves. (1899?)[38]

The course of these remarks is increasingly away from a concern with their material situation and toward a preoccupation with problems of relationships within the context of family. Though certainly not without worry and tremendous effort, the Bonds had gradually succeeded in creating security and prosperity for themselves to the extent that even in the midst of the severe depression on the 1890s, which devastated wheat farmers in the Great Plains,[39] Kate was able to stand back from family and farm economics and concentrate increasingly in her evaluation of her life on the nature and quality of her relationships. Over time these relationships emerged in her letters, in which they become expressed through the language of loss, grief, estrangement, and longing. The sense of isolation she felt is probably what impelled her toward the yearning that is increasingly evident in her letters for the consoling presence of the family into which she was born, even as she acknowledged increasingly that this reunion would occur beyond the grave. We may examine these relationships in the contexts of both her nuclear and extended families.

In Kate Bond's early letters to England, she tried unsuccessfully to convince her brothers Robert and Isaac, her sister Sarah, and her father to emigrate to the United States. When she and James were working in Connecticut, she inquired into specific employment possibilities for Isaac, whom she feared would always be poor in England because he had a particularly large family to support. These efforts were not successful in Isaac's case, to Kate's dismay, apparently because his wife, Jane, opposed emigration. Kate was ultimately destined to maintain her relationship with these siblings and to her aging father, who died in 1888 or 1889, through the international mails. We cannot know the frequency of these letters to those other than Robert and Ellen, but they are alluded to indirectly in the unedited archived letters. We do know that Kate anticipated other letters, especially from her sister Sarah. She sent small sums of money home to her father from time to time, and when they were young, to her siblings. Like many immigrants, Kate had to live with the disappointment of not being able to reunite the family she wished to have in her midst in the United States.[40]

While these initial efforts were being made to establish migration chains, however, two branches of the Bond family took root in the United States in addition to the line begun by Kate and her husband. These were not chain migrations in the technical sense, for example, that the immigration of Isaac was intended to be, for Kate sought informally to sponsor Isaac, finding him a job in the same town in which she lived and having him and his family close by her. As we have noted, her sister Ann came to the United States to join Pat Moran. With her Ann brought her brother Jim, who eventually married Moran's sister.[41] Over the years, the three families did interact and exchange letters, and for about a year Jim and Catherine Grayston and Kate and Jim Bond lived as one expanded household in Kansas.[42] But the three families also appear to have lost contact for significant periods of time, and though Jim and Catherine lived for decades only three hundred miles away in western Missouri, after their brief residence in Kansas there is little indication of frequent contact, and some indication that, if there were not exactly estrangement, the relations between them were not close.[43] This situation provides one context for understanding the loneliness and isolation that characterize Kate Bond's evaluation of her life.

At the root of the emotionally distant relationship Kate had with her brother's Missouri family and her sister's West Virginia family one senses prejudice on Kate's part toward the Irish and toward Roman Catholics, attitudes which were common among nineteenth-century British Protestant immigrants to North America, and were given a great deal of encouragement by home-grown American nativism.[44] But, if her attitudes were widely shared, Kate was nonetheless singularly challenged among the British immigrants whose letters form the evidentiary base of this study. None of them seems to have had Irish Catholics as close relations. In Bond's case, however, both these siblings married outside their Protestant, Church of England faith and outside their own national group. There is no doubt that Kate looked down on such intermarriages, and had been raised in a cultural environment that conditioned her to do so. (She also appears to have disapproved of Ann's pregnant condition at the time of her marriage, and refused to write a letter congratulating the newly married couple, though knowing, she said, this would be interpreted as hostile.)

From the beginning of her correspondence, in fact, we find evidence of beliefs that could well have negatively effected her relationship to her Irish Roman Catholic kin. Within a few years of immigrating to the United States, Kate observed that she found that "the Yankes are very distant peopel," who "don't thinck much of John Buls."[45] But she also found something in common with Americans from the start of her life in America, for in Connecticut she discovered that many of them shared her prejudices. Her first letter home in the collection contains the ironical and self-congratulatory comment, "The Yankes tell us if there would [be] more English they could send some Irish back," which was probably intended to be a witty remark.[46] Several months later, she remarked, in what was intended to be a simple declaration of fact, "We have three [churches] just over the river but no Roman Catholic. They will not have any their."[47] Wherever "over the river" was precisely, it was probably a doubtful observation, but if such a policy did exist it was not one with which she voiced any disagreement.

If such sentiments were kept private, they need not have imperiled relationships with her siblings and Catholic in-laws. Those relationships faced a stern test when, in 1878, the Graystons and their children left Grafton, West Virginia, where they had been living near the Morans, and went out to Kansas to live with the Bonds and to help them farm. Kate Bond had long anticipated this possibility, and thought it a significant opportunity for her brother to begin to improve his lot. "If we could get brother Jim along with us I thinck it would be a very good thing for us both," Kate wrote her brother Robert around 1873, "for Jim is doing nothing where he is and if we can get along together he will have a chance for himself in a few years and it will be company for us both."[48]

"If we can get along together," was a phrase full of ominous possibilities. In Kansas, Catherine Moran Grayston entered an environment that was especially culturally alien to her. Though mass was performed on occasion in private homes and public buildings by visiting priests, there was no Catholic church in the county until 1898. Center Township, where they resided, had only five residents, according to the 1880 federal census, who had been born in Ireland. On the other hand, Center Township had the largest population (100) of residents born in

England of any township in Russell County. Some of them had come together to form the Anglo-American world of Protestant congregations in which the Bonds worshiped alongside Americans, and the Odd Fellows lodge with which Jim was for many years affiliated.[49] It would certainly be no surprise to find they shared Kate's prejudices against the Irish and Catholics.

The situation was a difficult one for Catherine Grayston, who missed the company of Irish Catholics. But she may not have been completely alone in her isolation, at least in her religious alienation, for to Kate's disgust her brother and his children were now Catholics as well, a situation she attributed, as her language suggests, to her sister-in-law's manipulation: "She has Jim as good a Catholic as herself. All his children are christened at chapel." In a letter to her brother Robert, sent after the Graystons had left Kansas to live in Missouri, Kate attributed their departure from Kansas to her sister-in-law's cultural alienation: "Jims wife did not like the prarie. There was no Catholic Chapel and there is very few Irish round her, but there is plenty of English. But she has got where ther is plenty of Irish and Chapels too."[50]

Kate left no doubt about her feelings about her sister-in-law's religion and perhaps her ethnicity as well, and at the same time suggested the origins and depths of her own prejudice: "I often wonder what mother would have thought if she had been liveing and could have sen his wife as I saw here. None of you see her after marriage. Than is the time to know what they are."[51] How "often" Kate did such "wondering," while her sister-in-law was living in her household, and whether she was capable of keeping her prejudices to herself, or in some way, subtle or not, actually communicated them, must be left to the imagination. It is difficult to believe, however, that, if only in some highly nuanced way, she failed to signal her beliefs to her sister-in-law, as the two women worked alongside one another, day in and day out.

The matter never came up again in Kate's correspondence. She wrote to, and was written to by, her brother Jim, whom she saw briefly in 1890 coming back from the only visit she appears to have taken to see the Morans in West Virginia. (That journey was prompted by the first of two visits to the United States of her sister Sarah, whom she met in West Virginia. Sarah came back to Kansas with her, which also gave Kate and Sarah the occasion to stop on the way and see her brother in Missouri for what seems to have been the first time in a decade.)[52] Kate never mentioned her sister-in-law again, even when speaking of that visit and later exchanges of mail with her brother. She mentioned Pat Moran only once in her letters.[53] It is difficult to believe that social prejudices had not opened a breach in the relation of these three families. Though the possibilities thus existed for the Bonds to have close ties with the Graystons and the Morans, Kate unfortunately closed off the avenues for developing such ties, particularly in the case of the relatively nearby Graystons.

Surrounded by a large nuclear family and in the midst of a marriage that accompanied her from young womanhood to old age, Kate Bond was hardly alone during her years in America. Kate and Jim Bond were married in 1868, and spent just over three decades together. One generalizes very carefully about the quality of a marriage from the record of a relative handful of letters, but it is possible to have some impressions of a relationship that is central, if implicit in, the descriptions of daily life and the ruminative statements found in letters such as those Kate wrote home to Robert and Ellen.

The portrait that tentatively emerges of the relationship of Kate and Jim is of a fond, but distant marriage that does not seem to have had much emotional intimacy. Early in Kate's letters, when plans are beginning to emerge for their future in the United States and in particular, the migration to Kansas, Kate's letters are characterized by a curious lack of agency on her part in the most important decisions that they faced as a couple. The constructions that she uses to describe the process of these decisions suggest she is being acted upon rather than taking a part in the decisions that are determining their future:

> Jim tels me that when we have been here five years I may go back and see you all. (1871)[54]
>
> He is going out to Kansas where I hope he will buy a farm; for the next time we move I hope will be to stay for good. . . . I should very much like to see you all again. But it is hard to say weather I shall or not for we shall be two thousand miles further out if Jim buys land out at Kansas, but if we do well there I can see no reason why I cant visit you. (1873?)[55]

Kate writes here as if these significant decisions are in Jim's hands and she has little authority in the matter. In marked contrast when she writes to her siblings and tries to inspire them to emigrate and join her, while she is active at the same time in trying to find them work with her own employer, Mr. Hubbell, her language is noteworthy for the presence of agency (the *I* constructions) for she is the one doing the planning, inspiring, and hoping.

> I dare say Father will not like you to leave him, but if you come if I was in your place I would bring Sarah and him on with you. I don't know wether one woman can do all herself, but you will only have your family in the house. Please to write to us soon so we can give the master answer. But I hope you will come for you may never get such a chance again. (1872)[56]
>
> I wonder if the gentleman has written to Isaac yet. I gave Mr. Hubbell his address. I did not ask him before spring. It will be a good place for him if he can get it, and Jane is very foolish for if she stands in his light. I know it has been a good thing for us coming here. (1872)[57]

Once Kate and Jim had settled in Kansas, the tone of her letters did reveal a feeling of common endeavor, seen in the repetition of *we* constructions, as if, as for other farm couples, their farm was a cooperative enterprise rather than a project exclusively of her husband.

> We had one sow had six little ones and she killed every one. But we have two more come in. Yet we have to many, if the corn crop fails more than we can seed. . . . We killed severl last winter and we have most of the met yet to sell. (1881?)[58]
>
> We have 22 head of cattle, but we only milk six of them, and sell the cream. Butter is 2 cent a pound. Thats a penny your money. Cream is 10 cents a inch, so it pays better and not near the work. . . . We have had very poor crops the last two years, but still it was Better than working for another. (1884?)[59]

If the farm brought Kate a greater sense of common purpose to her marriage, it did not necessarily produce a sense of common priorities. Jim seemed to favor using what disposable income they had for purchasing machinery and livestock, while Kate longed for "more pleasure" of the sort she associated with village life in rural England, though she never went into detail about exactly what she found absent in their lives. The growth of their livestock and of the farming technology they possessed indicates Jim established their priorities, and that if

Kate did not share them completely, she nonetheless yielded to Jim's authority and the practical logic of his priorities.[60]

Nor did the cooperative enterprise of the farm create emotional intimacy between them. Kate lost four children as infants, and suffered the loss of the child closest to her, eighteen-year-old Maggie, in 1889. When she commented on these losses, her remarks were always reflections of her own profound, abiding grief. She never noted the grief of her husband, nor commented on what the losses might have meant to him.[61] Kate described at considerable length her feelings about the death of Maggie over the course of several letters,[62] but after Jim's death she recorded the brief, but heartfelt:

> You will be sorry to hear of my husband's death. He died on the 2 of Oct. He had been suffering for a long time from Brights Disease and Diabetes. He has wasted away to skin and bones. I had seen for a long time he would never get well and he knew it himself. He [had] plenty of time to prepare for the change that he knew was coming. The last words he said was its all right. He has been a good father and a kind husband and has left a good home for us."[63]

Kate did not mention Jim in the final two archived letters she wrote in the next two years. The couple's emotional distance is not unusual in the context of many nineteenth-century marriages, in which the expectations of companionate behavior were low by present understandings of the ideal relations of husband and wife, but it does help to explain Kate's loneliness.

In contrast, there appears the emotional intimacy of her relationship with her oldest daughter, which is expressed in deeply emotional ways. By the time Maggie died in 1889, Kate had already lost the four infant children. These deaths sometimes lay heavily on her mind. Knowing that she would be going to Kansas and unlikely again to visit the Connecticut grave of her second son, John, who died after a brief illness when he was not much more than a year old, Kate visited the cemetery. She wrote, "Last Saturday the children and me went over to the grave yard to look at Johnnies grave. I cant forget the little fellow though I know he is far better off and happier than I could make him, but he went from us so quick."[64] But these four children were infants, with whom in the case of the other three there seemed even less time to bond. Kate does not even record in her archived letters the death of one of the other three, and makes only the briefest mention of the other two. Nor does she relate the births of most of the others who survived, which we are able to know only through other sources.

Maggie, however, was her closest companion. As the oldest daughter, she soon began to fill the role of her mother's helper. Kate's comments that suggest the farm is a cooperative enterprise have to do with the work she does with Maggie as well as her feeling of practical, common endeavor with Jim. She wrote in July of perhaps 1884, "Maggie and me have enough to do home. We have six cows, 8 pigs, and about 2 hundred chickens; but they are no trouble for there is wheat enough round on the ground to feed them."[65] One pictures mother and daughter working together in the barnyard or in the kitchen, and Kate teaching her closest female child and constant companion the various household and farm skills that would prepare her for a life as a farmwife. Maggie was described at the time of her death as "a beautiful girl both in character and features, just budding into womanhood."[66] It was also she who kept her company when James and Bob were off for days during the harvest assisting neighbors.[67] There is no evidence in their relationship of the types of problems that created difficulties in her relationship to her son Bob, who was rebellious and for a time rejected his parents' history and aspirations and the life they were making for themselves.

Maggie's fatal illness, her failure to fight to live, and then her death weighed very heavily on Kate's mind, and she recorded the circumstances and her feelings at considerable length in a letter composed on a day when Jim and Bob were away doing cooperative harvesting. She wrote,

> I suppose you have heard of Maggies death. I miss her so much now that they are away. They don't come home at night and it is so lonely without her. But I supose we should have parted if she had lived and perhaps it is better as it is, for I know where she is now and wants for nothing. She give herself up at the begining and I thinck that made it worse, for the medcine took no efect on her. But she was ready and willing to go and missed a troblesome world.[68]

In letters in the next years, she continued to develop her feelings about Maggie's death. She consoled Ellen, after Peter died, writing, in a way that subtly implies her isolation, "I know it is a loss that none but a mother can feel." She asks Ellen to consider persevering for the sake of her other children. It is in this context that she wrote, "If it had not been for my younger ones I thinck they would have laid me beside her before now."[69] In her next letter in the collection, in lamenting the distance that separated her from her brother and sister-in-law in England, she wrote, "We are a great way apart from each other. Still I always feel the same affection for all of you though I know we shall never meet here on earth, yet I feel shure we shall in Heaven. It was that thought that kept me up when I lost Maggie."[70] She anticipated that her reunion with her daughter would not be long in coming relative to the eternity to which she looked forward, "Its only for a little while and theres work for me here or I should not be left here."[71] But her experience of grief remained profound, and she seemed to spend time looking at pictures of her daughter, and thus intensifying it. In sending a picture of Maggie home to England after her death, Kate said, "I am sending you one of Maggie's picture it is all I have left of her. . . . They are good pictures of her. I miss her so much."[72] The tone of lonely resignation that is so much a part of the last decade of Kate's letters is greatly rooted in the grief of this loss.

This was not the only crisis the couple experienced with their children during the same years, for the difficulties they had with their son Bob doubtless deepened the gloom that settled over Kate's life. In 1888, a year before Maggie died, and perhaps during her terminal illness, Bob left home, and went to work in Colorado at a lumber camp. Kate commented that she thought the break was irrevocable: "I don't thinck he will come home to stay anymore."[73] There seem to be two mutually reinforcing sources, one material and the other cultural, of Bob's disaffection, which was ultimately an alienation from his parents' history and way of life and from his father's lifetime goals.

Kate attributed the fact that he was "discontented" to his conclusion that "there is nothing made farming," a view she frequently seemed to share, even as they added the acreage in wheat and the number of livestock to their farm.[74] Bob certainly had significant enough exposure to prairie wheat farming to make up his own mind. He had been assisting his father with the heavier farmwork since his early teenage years. In a letter Kate had sent, probably in 1884, when Bob was on the eve of his fifteenth birthday, she noted that Bob was away doing harvesting with his father, who didn't believe the boy was strong enough for such heavy work and had made some accommodation to his youth by buying additional farm machinery.[75] Perhaps Bob saw looming before him the future of unrelenting toil that seemed to characterize his parents' lives, and decided that the efforts involved were not worth it. In doing so, though Kate makes no reference to Jim's feelings in the matter, the boy was walking away from being his father's workmate and assistant, and from the life that his father had dedicated himself to making.

Bob had also begun to fashion a different identity for himself that put him at odds with the Russell County wheat farmers and his parents in a more profound way. As a boy, he had spoken of his desire to return to England when he grew up, probably for a visit rather than to stay, and seemed to share Kate's dreams of visiting their extended family.[76] But within a few years, he underwent a rapid change in his conception of himself that allowed him to be more comfortable, if not with farming, with another part of the Western environment. By this time, the once frail Bob had grown into an athletic young man, who was 6'9". He bragged in a friendly letter to his sickly English cousin of his prowess as a hunter, rider, and ice skater. He had given himself the nickname "the Cow Puncher," and in a photograph, reprinted in *Invisible Immigrants*, that he sent his cousin, he appeared dressed in what he described as "regular western cowboy style," complete with a broad brimmed hat and a thick cowboy belt with a fancy wide buckle that featured a prominent Texas lonestar in the center. Bob's picture showed him, as Kate in a letter sent not long after described it, faintly apologetically, in "just his everyday clothes." His cowboy dress was indeed far different than the sort of formal "dress" clothes immigrants usually posed in when they had their "likenesses" taken to send home to the Old Country. The photograph was nothing less than an aggressive assertion of difference.[77] Not long after his letter to Peter, Bob left home for Colorado. He would return to farm with his father, and then leave again, to return once and for all only after his father's death, when his mother needed him to run the farm.[78]

Bob Bond's rapid transformation appears proof of the confident generalizations that have long been made about the easy assimilation of the English immigrant, though it is true that Bob, a newborn when his parents left England, could hardly be described as first generation. He is more an example of a member of the "1.5 generation" of children, born of immigrants, who are raised in the place of resettlement. But on second glance, what captures the attention in Bob's transformation is that the generational tensions he represents are cultural ones as well as differences about whether a son would follow his father's occupation. We

have not associated those tensions with the presumably easily assimilated English. One wonders what Jim Bond, with the "quaint dialect"
that obviously marked him as "a well known Englishman,"[79] or Kate,
with her longing for her English family and English village life, felt
about this transformation in Bob's personal identity, which cut him
off from his parents. Under any circumstance, when, the day before he
died, Jim Bond, obviously weak and desperately ill, was threshing wheat
in his fields, he was there without his oldest son.[80] Both Bond parents
had lost those whom they had been preparing most to succeed them.

In three decades in the United States, Kate and Jim Bond were successful in realizing significant aspects of their immigrant dream, a dream
not unlike that held by many English immigrants. They had escaped
working for wages, bought themselves a working farm, and achieved
the foundations of a secure family life. But if this is all we were to know
of their story, we would be able to understand much less of their lives
than is necessary to begin to know their experience, as they lived it and
understood it. This knowledge, by itself, may reduce them to an ideological projection or to membership in a socioeconomic cohort. At best,
however, through it we might see immigrants like the Bonds as socioeconomic agents in the improvement of their material lives, an insight we
should never undervalue, because it provides a key to understanding the
quest of ordinary people for self-determination and for dignity and respectability in their community. But the same knowledge may not necessarily allow us to see immigrants as reflexive agents in efforts to achieve
conscious understanding of their own experience.

Few and far between as they might be, Bond's surviving letters give
us access to a number of dimensions that clarify that material dream—
the immigrant's first project—and suggest its limitations as an exclusive guide to our understanding. They encourage us to ask other questions, which seek to know the immigrants' ongoing work constructing
their narratives of personal identity. Thus, they invite us to probe more
deeply into the quality of lives led as well as the quantity of things obtained. The letters do so particularly effectively because Kate Bond,
through her own habits of mind, explicitly provides her readers with
the tools that enable them to penetrate the ordinary surfaces of daily
life. Her existential accounting alerts readers to the fact that there were
losses as well as gains in the experience of immigrants, and that some
gains made some losses inevitable.

she is most interesting see p23!

Mary Ann Wodrow Archbald

Longing for Her "Little Isle" from a Farm in Central New York

In the future it must be the pen alone that will waft the soft intercourse from soul to soul.
 —Mary Ann Archbald to Margaret Wodrow, February 1807

Once more I am permitted to end the year with you and fain
would I for a little while lose the present in the past.
 —Mary Ann Archbald to Margaret Wodrow, December 31, 1824

Your letters are now so necessary to me that I cannot live comfortably without them and would wish to die with one of them in my
hand, or at least under my pillow but at any rate if recollection is
granted you will be in my mind at that awful moment.
 —Mary Ann Archbald to Margaret Wodrow, April 1840

In the Firth of Clyde, not far off the coast of Ayrshire in
western Scotland, lie two islands—Great Cumbrae and Little Cumbrae. Though only three-quarters of a mile off the coast of Millport,
Great Cumbrae's principal town, Little Cumbrae has been the much
less thickly settled of the two. Most of the 723-acre island was then,
according to a 1934 travel guide, depopulated, and "except for a few
patches of grass . . . a moorland of bracken and heather, burrowed
by rabbits and grazed by sheep."[1] Small as it is, the island nonetheless
long remained partly wild, with caves whose unexplored, subterranean
depths were a part of local lore for many centuries. Fierce and constant
winds caused the sea around Little Cumbrae to boil. The rough passage
over dangerously shallow waters, which was made more perilous by frequent, dense fog, probably discouraged anyone from going there to view

the sunset, which was said to be particularly beautiful from the island's beaches.

There was no regularly scheduled passage to Little Cumbrae until steamboats appeared on the firth in the early nineteenth century. This isolation guaranteed the integrity of the island's small cemetery and its principal ruins—the burial ground and ruined chapel of St. Bey and the remains of an ancient tower, or perhaps a castle, said to be erected for defense against Vikings, but brought to ruin by Cromwell's forces during the Civil War.[2] Isolation also provided security for its often outcaste population, said in 1599 to be composed mostly of "rebels, fugitives, and ex-communicates."[3]

In 1515, Little Cumbrae was assigned by the Register of the Privy Seal to Hugh, Earl of Eglinton, whose family held on to it for centuries. The Eglintons, who merged over time with the Archbalds and other local families, were known as enlightened landlords who stimulated the regional economy in order to grow wealthier alongside it. Over the centuries, they undertook to encourage trade by facilitating navigation. Beginning in 1757, this project led them to erect a series of ever more technologically advanced lighthouses on Little Cumbrae. Now slightly less remote, the island experienced a rise in population and modest economic development. By 1764, there were seventy people living and working there, most of whom were the Eglintons' tenants and employees, who raised sheep and tended the lighthouse. Also residing here at least part of the year were branches of the Wodrow family, which was long associated with Church of Scotland clerics, theologians, and church historians.[4]

Infrastructural improvements did not benefit the Eglintons as rapidly as they had hoped, and led them into substantial debt. By the last years of the eighteenth century, Hugh, the twelfth Earl of Eglinton, was in enough debt that he opened the ancient tombs of Little Cumbrae and made off with their valuable relics and armor. This did not take him very far, so he sold off a number of small properties and raised the rents of others throughout his regional holdings.[5] Among the tenants who was informed, in 1803, that his rent would be raised was Eglinton's distant kinsman, James Archbald III. Then forty years of age, James was living on Little Cumbrae with his wife, Mary Ann Wodrow Archbald, then forty-one, and their four young children, James IV (Jamie), Margaret Ann, Patrick Peter (Peter), and Helen Louisa (Louisa), each of them under ten years of age. James raised sheep, and Mary Ann made yarn and knitted clothing.

The prospect of much higher rents threw the Archbald family into crisis. James and Mary Ann feared that accepting these high rents would lead them into ruinous debt, and destroy their ability to educate and to provide foundations for the adult respectability for their children. James was not able to find a more suitable tenancy, perhaps because rents were rising throughout the region, and the other offers he received were just as likely to mortgage the future.[6] There seemed no choice but emigration. Already well into midlife and settled in their ways, the Archbalds were also deeply attached to their homeland, and faced this prospect, Mary Ann more than James, most reluctantly. She understood the dilemma they faced, but vowed she would do nothing to encourage or discourage James in the proposal to emigrate.

As this resolve reveals, like Kate Bond at the time her husband decided to go to Kansas, Mary Ann understood that, as wife and mother, she was not an equal partner in the making of this momentous decision. It was ultimately James's decision, based on his appraisal of their situation.[7] In the future, Mary Ann's protofeminist defense of women, stated from time to time in personal and public letters criticizing men for their refusal to allow women a voice in public life, or to take women's voice in literature seriously, makes it clear that she continued to resent such powerlessness.[8] But her relative powerlessness as a woman does not completely account for her resolve to leave the decision to James. Mary Ann did not appear equal to the task of contesting the largely material logic on which James had to approach the decision. What she would lose in emigrating was not measurable in material terms.

Various branches of Mary Ann's family and some friends already lived in the United States. Her much older half-brother, Andrew, had resided in western Virginia since 1768 and wished to unite the two families in the same place. Both the Archbalds rejected Virginia, however, believing the climate unhealthful and his location difficult to reach.[9] Her uncle James Ruthven, an affluent craftsman and cousin John Ruthven, close and generous friends, resided in New York City, and probably encouraged her and James to emigrate with promises of assistance.[10] A generous Scottish friend, Mr. Fisher, who resided in Albany, offered to escort them across the ocean and help them resettle on a farm in central New York State. His offer took on special significance because he had recently proposed marriage to Mary Ann's beloved friend, her first cousin Margaret Wodrow, who might then come to New York with the Archbalds.[11]

r one of the main insights of the book.

Next to the difficulties she faced leaving her nearly ninety-year-old mother,[12] and the graves of her first four children, Mary Ann found most difficult the thought of leaving Margaret. Wodrow had been her closest companion since early childhood, and was to remain, through correspondence, her closest companion until Archbald's death finally separated them. She had named her oldest daughter after Margaret, and took pride that her other daughter, Louisa, closely resembled her. They had grown up near one another, and spent much fondly remembered time in their paternal grandparents' houses, one of them at Little Cumbrae. They shared the almost instinctual mutual understanding and hence, near-effortless conversation of those who, friends from childhood, do not need to explain themselves to each other in adulthood. They had the same adult tastes in literature (affection for Walter Scott, in particular) and a dislike of orthodox Calvinism in religion.[13] Yet this was insufficient to convince Margaret to accept Fisher's proposal. She told him she did not know him well enough and would not abandon her own aging father.[14]

Nonetheless, the Archbalds had run out of options. Late in 1805 James terminated negotiations over his lease, and in April 1807 they left for the United States, with the intention of buying a farm in central New York State. They were certainly not poor when they emigrated, and possessed the resources to buy an excellent homestead. Sales of personal belongings and of their sheep herd, and perhaps gifts from relatives and kin, yielded, even after they had paid for their passage, the relatively large sum of £600 on which to start a new life.[15]

The Archbalds would do well farming and raising sheep in the United States. Within a few years of resettling, they lived comfortably in a roomy, well-decorated house on a 169-acre farm along the Mohawk River, near the village of Auriesville. They took on manageable debt and only then to improve their circumstances. Though frequently cash poor in the way that American farmers often were, they never experienced want. They did ensure the foundations of respectability for their children, though on American terms, which were not ones that Mary Ann herself ever found it possible to value, for she found them materialistic and mundane, and lacking respect for intellectual and artistic endeavor. This should come as no surprise for, as we have seen in the case of Kate Bond, many immigrants brought more complex measures than material comfort and security to evaluating their experience.

It was the same for the Archbalds, and particularly for Mary Ann.

When they finally decided to leave Scotland, the Archbalds regarded their emigration realistically but bitterly, as a reluctant step undertaken for the sake of their children, and forced on them by avaricious kinsmen. At the time of their departure, James felt this acutely enough that he instructed Mary Ann to inform Margaret Wodrow in her last letter to her friend before they sailed, that if there were a disaster at sea and the Archbalds should perish, none of their £600, then in a Scottish bank, was to go to any of his kin.[16] For her part, Mary Ann was equally bitter. If she were ever to return to Scotland, she wrote Margaret a few months before she departed for America, "it will be entirely on your account and from no attachment to any particular spot on earth." She grew more bitter still when, shortly after arrival, she thought of Little Cumbrae and imagined others living in the house she continued to regard as her own, and using the writing desk she had left behind.[17] This mood would pass, however, and soon she would be writing of Little Cumbrae in intensely nostalgic ways.

Over the next sixteen years until his death in 1824, James gave himself over completely to the work of farming. He may well have come to take pride in his success, and to feel confident that he had not only made the necessary decision in emigrating, but also had made a positive choice. Yet, for years and more insistently as he grew older, he voiced the hope that someday he might return to Scotland.[18] We cannot precisely know James's feelings in the matter. We do not have access to his thoughts, for he left no personal letters behind when he died of what seems to have been a heart attack while working. He was too busy to write letters and not a confident writer, to the extent that Mary Ann wrote the business correspondence that arose from the operation of their farm. His thoughts on the matter, however, may ultimately have been suggested by words on his tombstone, though we do not know if he or Mary Ann chose them: "Far from his native land that he loved so well, here lie the remains of James Archbald."[19]

In contrast, we have access to the ample testimony of Mary Ann's thoughts on emigration, dating from before the couple left Scotland. It remained a significant project for the rest of Mary Ann's life to evaluate that decision and its consequences, and particularly to develop ways of formulating her thoughts about their Scottish home, emigration and resettlement, and the life they had made for themselves in the United States. Her letters to Margaret Wodrow between 1807 and 1840 were the principal site for the development of this project. Her views were highly nuanced—bitter and critical at times, balanced at other times, and ironical at still other points, and frequently all of these at once. She often criticized herself not only for her conclusions, especially when they were negative, but for the self-absorption that led her back continually over the same ground, even as she traversed a variety of paths across it.

In this activity, Mary Ann Archbald's evaluative efforts seem to resemble Kate Bond's existential accounting. Up to a point this is certainly true, for Archbald does indeed work constantly at assessing the positives and negatives of the experience of emigration and resettlement. Yet the contrasts are more telling than the similarities. It was not only that the Bonds left England enthusiastically, while the Archbalds were reluctant migrants who came near to seeing themselves as going into exile. An evaluative process yielding a conclusion is much less the point of Archbald's writing than it appears to be of Bond's. Though not expressed in especially complex terms, Bond's views churned in her mind; they grew and changed over time as she struggled to find meaning in the changing circumstances of her life. She may well have needed the opportunity to state her views to assist her in coming to a judgment. Kate Bond's interim conclusions were sensitive to her experience of family life, both nuclear and extended, and of the difficulties of prairie farming. In her understanding of their emigration, Archbald's views did not grow; they became relatively fixed within a few years of resettling; different letters expressed different aspects of her evaluation, but her thinking never changed. She experienced her life in terms of loss, and that is more or less the way she expressed it throughout her decades in the United States.

What developed over time in Archbald's case was the practice of stating what she had lost, which became central to her letters to Wodrow. A dramatic example is the manner in which through the performance of writing, Archbald ritualized commemorations of the past, and in so doing sought imaginatively to relive it. This was especially the case for some years in her annual New Year's letter, ideally begun at 11:00 P.M. on December 31, so that she could spend the turn of the year anticipating the stroke of midnight in Margaret's symbolic presence. She aspired to a spiritual communion with her friend that mystically seemed for the moment to break down the barriers of time and space. She sometimes expressed the same feelings of being impelled toward a different dimension of being when opening a letter from Margaret—it was as if, she wrote Margaret, time was suspended and space conquered, and she was back in Scotland decades ago.

It is not difficult to understand why Mary Ann Archbald came to view her experience in terms of loss. Even before emigrating, Archbald was on the path to evaluate her life in such terms. Neither she nor her husband had brought much money into their marriage, and neither had personal resources sufficient to make it possible to remain in Scotland. What property they had they sold to help finance their emigration. Both were the poor relations of more affluent extended families. When she met James, he and his brothers were renting farmland on Little Cumbrae. They were hardworking young men, with little, if any, parental support or savings of their own. James's few and usually relatively minor business reversals before emigrating had already thrown the couple into crisis.[20]

Mary Ann claimed that she herself had labored under "many privations . . . from infancy."[21] Her father, Robert Jr. (1711–1784), had had to retire from the ministry at age forty-six because of ill-health, and, family oral tradition had it, a problem with alcohol, and spent the last three decades in the isolation of Little Cumbrae. It is not clear how the family supported itself in those years after his retirement. Robert may not have been a supportive parent either, for Mary Ann, who never discussed her own father in her archived letters, wrote years later of her gratitude to Margaret's father for his "parental conduct" toward her.[22]

Margaret, who never married, inherited enough when her father, a successful minister with a large church at Stevenston, about fifteen miles from Little Cumbrae, died in 1810, to live independently for the remainder of her long life. She certainly had more personal resources than Mary Ann, to whom she eventually sent money (though it is not clear that Archbald asked for it, or needed it). Margaret willed her own money to Mary Ann's children.[23] The Archbalds' lack of resources equal to their ties to prominent lineages underscored their humiliation and powerlessness in confronting the demands of their landlord-kinsmen for higher rents.

While the couple seemed equally without wealth, Mary Ann nonetheless appears through her marriage to have lost social status, and with that loss, just as with their lack of resources, she further lost the feeling of continuity with a distinguished family past associated with her country's national narrative, with which she intensely identified. Mary Ann was well aware that she had married beneath her. James was not only relatively poorer at the time of their marriage, but also, while he enjoyed reading, had little formal education. His manners were somewhat rustic, though better than those of his two brothers, whom Mary Ann described as "clownish" on first encounter. To find his courage, James had been drinking before coming to sit and chat with Mary Ann and her aunt in an early formal encounter while courting. While alcohol loosened his tongue and he was certainly not drunk, Mary Ann, who had a strong aversion to alcohol, noted his need to imbibe to break down his natural shyness and to prepare himself for the rigors of the parlor. Strikingly handsome, James was nonetheless one of several eligible bachelors with whom she had had the opportunity to interact. She warned herself in her diary against involvement with him, but lamented the snobbery that prompted the warning. She yielded to her strong attraction, and perhaps to the feeling that it was time for her to marry.[24]

The contrast to her own extended family could not have been greater. Descended through the Wodrows from a long line of prominent Church of Scotland intellectuals, her lineage had value for her that could not be measured by wealth, but rather by a connection to Scottish tradition, history, and letters. Her great grandfather, Rev. Dr. James Wodrow (1637–1707), was a prominent Protestant dissenter and rebel who was hounded by the authorities for organizing unauthorized religious meetings in efforts to uphold the independence of Scottish Presbyterianism. He would end his long career in the Church of Scotland triumphantly as a Professor of Divinity at Glasgow University.[25] Robert Wodrow (1679–1734), his son, studied under him at Glasgow. Robert declined the offer of large and prestigious parishes and served for many years at a small parish at Eastwood, where the lighter duties allowed him to pursue his research interests in Scottish church and natural history. Though he took an active part in the governance of the Church of Scotland and was involved in the central controversies within the church in his day, historical scholarship was his principal activity. An eminent historian, he authored a significant two-volume history of the Church of Scotland between the Restoration and the Revolution.

Robert Wodrow's importance for Scottish letters grew after his death. His published history went through a second edition (1828) during Mary Ann's lifetime. It was the subject of discussion in Margaret and Mary Ann's correspondence, and Margaret sent all four republished volumes to the United States to be added to the library that Mary Ann had brought from Scotland. Also in the nineteenth century, posthumous collections of Robert Wodrow's letters and three posthumous collections of church documents and biographical materials on the clergy, amassed for his uncompleted, comprehensive synthesis of the history of the Church of Scotland, were published, though only one of them in Mary Ann's lifetime.[26]

Rev. James Wodrow, the uncle of Mary Ann and father of Margaret, assumed his father's duties at Eastwood until his death in 1784 at Little Cumbrae, where he was buried in the small cemetery that was the location for the remains of a number of Wodrows and Archbalds. In her archived American letters, Mary Ann never wrote of her father, and spoke of her mother only to lament having to leave her. She never recalled scenes from the life of her own birth family. Instead, her memories of childhood went back to the parsonage at Eastwood, and especially to New Year's Eve celebrations, the central holiday of Scottish tradition—known as an occasion for reunion with family and friends—which she recalled having spent with Margaret and her grandparents. It was through that relationship, rather than through her birth family, that her claims to respectability were made during her years in Scotland. Though poor as a youth, she wrote Margaret, displaying an acute sensitivity to status, she had been "treated often with kindness and attention by those in a rank above me, but this was owing entirely to my connection with your family."[27]

The intense identification with family lineage and such places associated with it as the old manse at Eastwood and Little Cumbrae provide insight into those aspects of Mary Ann Archbald's personal identity that followed her throughout her life in Scotland and in America. The sites of her childhood were permeated by romantic legends, stories of heroic national epics, and the comforts and consolation of family, all of which melded together to make them sacred ground for her. Like Mary Cumming's writing from Virginia of "castles" and "castle building," when describing her dreams of returning to the north of Ireland to reoccupy the houses and other sites of her youth, Archbald developed her own expressive symbol for her experience of emigration.[28] She frequently evoked "the little isle," in efforts to express her longing not so much for Little Cumbrae, as such, but for continuity with the world of her past. It was a place of both pleasure and pain, for the graves of her first four children were there.[29] Even in the simplest and shortest of sentences, the term came to express a myriad of complex feelings. But at the most

290 | *Mary Ann Wodrow Archbald*

basic, emotional level it was the place where she had felt the most intense sense of belonging that she would feel in the course of her life. Certainly nothing about life in Auriesville, New York, over three decades ever gave rise to a similar feeling.

If ethnicity is thought of in terms of formal identification with fellow ethnics and formal group affiliations in the land of resettlement, Archbald manifested little ethnicity in the United States. Her letters from the United States do not suggest that she went to significant lengths to seek out the company of Scots, nor do they consistently voice a strong preference for it. One of the most vividly and fondly recalled social encounters in her letters to Margaret was the first visit she and James made to an elderly Scots Irish couple who were old settlers in her area and lived nine miles from her home. But this came fully thirteen years after she had settled in Auriesville, and she did not write of them again.[30] She spent more time, especially in her early years in America when one would most have expected her to seek out Scottish company, with her Dutch American neighbors, about whom she frequently complained because of what she took to be their coarseness and lack of interest in anything but farming, family, and church.[31] Nor did she belong to any Scottish churches or organizations in America. The Archbalds worshiped alongside these same Dutch and Americans of New England ancestry, whom she also frequently criticized for cunning self-interested behavior, at a nearby Reformed Church, which had been founded by Dutch settlers of the Mohawk Valley after the American Revolution. Though probably not dissimilar in creed to the Calvinism of her youth, it was not Presbyterian, which was the faith of her ancestors. (The local Presbyterian church, across the river, might have been inconvenient to attend.) Her affiliation with the Reformed Church could hardly be said to have served ethnic purposes in her life.[32]

Archbald's Scottishness was instead a deeply personal attachment to a past that was as mythic as it was historical, and that provided the context for her personal identity. It might be expressed in personal and localized terms, as memory, or in more abstract national terms, such as the suggestion of an idealized national character. It was less contemporary Scotland that interested her than historical Scottish intellectual and literary culture of the sort associated with her eminent ancestors or with the works of Robert Burns and Walter Scott, or the scenes and local island society of her youth. Hers was a bourgeois cultural, ethnic feeling. She took little interest in the folk traditions of the Scottish peasantry. Nor did she comment on contemporary Scottish society and politics. These were not matters that she developed in her letters, and perhaps as much to the point, they were not matters on which she sought information in her letters to Margaret.

There are more comments about American than British or Scottish affairs, perhaps because such commentary gave her an excellent opportunity to vent her trenchant and well-practiced critical faculties. She took limited interest, mostly to disapprove and then on only one occasion in the archived letters, in the modernization of western Scotland, which after her emigration underwent rapid economic development. Just as often it was not Scotland, but rather Little Cumbrae, that "abode of peace, of comfort, and friendly intercourse," for which she longed. Her referent for her past and for Scottishness varied depending on the grip that nostalgia, pride, or defensiveness against American habits and values, with which she would never be at peace, had at the moment.[33]

At other times, however, the more abstract *Scotland* did serve her. Thus, when a return to Scotland was a goal early in her years in the United States, she found a precedent in Scottish history for metaphorizing her return. Not without a trace of self-mockery, she compared herself to Flora McDonald, the Jacobite patriot who voluntarily went into North American exile in the 1770s. But MacDonald refused to side with the American Revolutionaries against the British Crown, though the Crown had once kept her in prison for a year. Tenuously, perhaps, in Archbald's mind, their situation was similar to McDonald's, for James's wealthy titled kinsmen had spurned and persecuted the Archbalds. During Mary Ann's youth, McDonald had returned to Scotland, an elderly, popular heroine, and her funeral was the occasion for a massive demonstration of public adulation. It pained Archbald greatly that the west coast of Scotland was changing, because she wished Scotland to live forever in such heroic legends, and in rustic simplicity and romantic isolation.[34]

Unfortunately, her illustrious family history and its diverse associations with the Scottish nation and landscape brought no money with it, so Mary Ann was forced to accept emigration as a solution to their difficulties, alongside humbler Scots who were without close connections to great families and great events in the national narrative. Born into a family of unrenowned intellectuals and clerics, educated through schooling and her own persistent autodidactic efforts, and possessed of a keen, inquiring, and cultivated mind and artistic and musical talent, Archbald believed herself intended for better things than the life to which her marriage and emigration had destined her. This was the life of a farmwife in postfrontier central New York, where, she would often complain, she was surrounded by crude neighbors and reduced to unending, though loving, servitude to her husband, children, grandchildren, and visitors. Much of her mental life on the New York farm was a struggle to seize from the coercions of daily routines and obligations an identity which was in keeping with this elevated self-understanding, and which provided continuity for this understanding amidst the discontinuities of what she experienced as multiple losses—of place, status, and relationships. It is a fitting emblem of this quest that, whether by her request or the wishes of her surviving children, the title of one of her grandfather's histories of the Church of Scotland is inscribed on her own tombstone.[35]

In a variety of ways, as Mary Ann Archbald passed through stages in the life cycle (farmwife and mother of young children; widow; grandmother; aged and dependent shut-in), in her postemigration years she attempted to free her body and mind of daily obligations in order to pursue activities that allowed for continuous renewal of this abiding conception of herself. Among these activities were keeping a diary, copybooks, and a commonplace book, and painting and playing the guitar, but the most important was letter-writing, especially to Margaret Wodrow. For three decades, the reconfiguration and vitalization of this friendship though personal correspondence served a source of continuity and renewal for her self-making identity narrative.

We know Mary Ann Archbald almost exclusively through her own writing. She did a great deal of writing throughout her lifetime. Long before she left for America, she had developed the habits of keeping a diary, which by the time she emigrated totaled seven volumes, and of writing letters regularly to friends and family. These literary activities doubtless obtained greater practical significance for her because of residence off and on throughout her life in the relative isolation of Little Cumbrae. As she explained in a letter to one of the Ruthven family, "Placed at infancy at a distance from all my friends their letters have ever formed my principle enjoyment so that whatever cause obstructed these letters was sure to give a very sensible blow to my happiness, one of my chief sources of which was and is to think often upon and hear frequently from my friends."[36] As she and Margaret Wodrow had been exchanging letters with regularity for years during periods between visits, their separation promised further opportunities to resume being, as she wrote, "together in mind" through correspondence. "Will we not," Mary Ann said of the future of their friendship in her last letter before leaving for America, "write more fully and more punctually than ever?"[37]

She was also a frequent reader of fiction and history, especially Scottish, both before and after emigration. She was exposed to a wide variety of literature and the artists and intellectuals involved in its production from early in life, and read intensely and deliberately. She read with an eye toward cultivating her mind and improving her own writing skills.[38] She declared near the end of her life that "the reading mania" had been responsible for the fact that she had never been lonely.[39] She emigrated with as large a library as it was practical to carry, and had Margaret send her books. The two women exchanged views on books. Mary Ann did not keep a diary in the United States until the last year of her life, but she produced two volumes of a commonplace book of quotations, and transcriptions of passages from literature that was doubtless intended to provide her lasting instruction in her efforts at self-cultivation, and she transcribed into copybooks some of her letters, especially those of which she was most proud, because of their literary qualities.[40]

While diary-writing declined after 1808, letter-writing may well have increased in importance for her after resettlement in the United States, if not necessarily in the frequency of correspondence instead in the number of individuals with whom she exchanged letters and the length of her letters. But, even more importantly, the letters, especially to Margaret Wodrow, came less than a decade into her life in America to assume an overwhelming emotional significance, for the consciousness increasingly dawned in Archbald that she would never see either Scotland or her loved ones there again. She and James regularly discussed return. But while they lived well in America, they had not enough money to return home and live the respectable Scottish rural life to which they aspired, so increasingly these conversations about reemigration took on the character of pleasant, if insistent, fantasizing.[41] Furthermore, their children, all of whom were informally, but with a good deal of seriousness, instructed in their Scottish heritage, nonetheless grew up in the United States and came to have American spouses and careers. For them, Scotland was an idea, an especially noble one, but not their future. James and Mary Ann had always aspired to attain a closely knit family, and never would have been willing to agree to permanent separation from their children. Everything conspired to keep the couple in the United States.

These letters written from the United States between her arrival in 1807 and approximately June 13, 1840, seven months before her death, and Archbald's other manuscript writings are to be found in the History of Women Collection at Smith College, to which they were given by Archbald's great-granddaughter in 1964. (Her personal library of books brought with her from Scotland had been donated to the college two years earlier.) Some of her letters were conveniently transcribed in 1951, in their entirety or nearly so, into a typescript by Archbald's great-grandson, Hugh Archbald, who provided occasional editorial commentary to guide the reader on the physical condition or unusual features of some of Mary Ann's letters.[42] Ninety-four letters appear in this transcription, which has been used because of the convenience of its form, and the fact that it was microfilmed, in the research for this book.

These transcribed letters were not the only ones Archbald wrote in the United States. The last of her copybooks, which ended in 1825, establishes more American correspondence, at least up to that time, than Hugh Archbald transcribed. Some correspondents, moreover, do not appear in either the copybooks or in Hugh Archbald's transcriptions. It is almost certain that Mary Ann wrote to her mother until her death in 1814. There is no record, however, of this correspondence in Mary Ann's copybooks, and the letters themselves have not been archived. This correspondence was probably freighted with painful emotions because of Mary Ann's guilt for having, as she said in an 1812 letter to Margaret, "deserted the path of duty" and left her aged mother behind. Perhaps it was too painful for Mary Ann to retain copies of these letters, or perhaps being of a practical rather than a literary nature, they had less to recommend them as exemplars of style and were deemed less worthy of copying.

It does seem apparent that in spite of such gaps, these transcriptions contain the bulk, though probably not the entire list of the most personally significant correspondence in which Archbald engaged—her forty-six letters to Margaret Wodrow. What may be missing from this particular group of letters, because destroyed by Margaret—perhaps by mutual agreement—are letters dealing with matters, such as a family scandal, that neither woman desired to see retained in family memory. An example is provided by the absence of documentation of the fact that Louisa Archbald appears certain to have had a child out of wedlock. In all likelihood Archbald would have written Wodrow about the consequences of this pregnancy for the family, but no archived letter supports this surmise. A brief reference in a letter some years before suggests how the friends dealt with such matters. Margaret had apparently written Mary Ann that she was destroying some personal letters she had received, though whose letters and why she did so are not stated. Mary Ann replied, "Burning letters is a work I should be at, too, but I am very bad at it—Your's in particular must I fear be left for them who come after me."[43] Since there is no trace of Margaret's letters to Mary Ann, perhaps Archbald eventually changed her mind.

It is unclear if Hugh Archbald transcribed these American letters from drafts or from the originals. Mary Ann did make drafts of at least some of her letters before writing out the final copies; there are drafts in her own copybooks up to 1825. There is reason to believe, however, that Hugh Archbald had access at least to the surviving originals of the letters to Margaret. He notes regarding the last letter in the collection, a letter from Mary Ann to Margaret, "On the back of this letter is written in a round, old style, old woman's uncertain handwriting, 'This is the last letter I ever received.'"[44] Presumably, Hugh Archbald would not have had such information unless he had seen an original. At some point, therefore, Mary Ann Archbald's original letters were returned to her family in the United States by her friend Margaret, or by a descendant or friend of Margaret's. While Archbald's other correspondence in this collection might have been reconstructed from Mary Ann's copybooks, the letters to Margaret were transcribed from the posted originals. Though true to much of the original content, Hugh Archbald did make some editorial decisions effecting content. According to Alison Scot, who has examined a number of the originals and their transcriptions, he regularized Mary Ann's punctuation, and omitted here and there "passages that were devotional, meditative, or purely descriptive," as well as some in which Mary Ann wrote about her current reading activity. Yet there are many such passages that remain in these transcriptions, so while the letters are not verbatim transcriptions, they certainly appear to have retained most of the significant content of the originals.[45]

The remaining forty-eight letters, those not sent to Margaret Wodrow, served a variety of purposes and were sent to a number of different correspondents in Scotland, and, more often, in the United States; as such, the latter are not *immigrant letters* in the sense that term has been used in this book. Seven of the letters are, in effect, business letters from the Archbalds' first years in the United States, a time during which they were discontented with their place of settlement, because, she said on one occasion, of "the cold climate and the cold countenances of our Dutch neighbors." In light of James's apparent lack of fluency as a writer and his preoccupation with the farm, it fell on Mary Ann to write these letters.[46] They sought to find alternative sites in other states, especially conditions right for raising sheep, which James preferred to growing crops, and at the same time tried to find buyers for their first farm on the Mohawk. Mary Ann wrote to several prominent individuals, including Thomas Jefferson, seeking information about opportunities in Virginia and the Ohio River Valley, but apparently received little encouragement. This quest ended in April 1810, when they sold their farm, Creekvale, in Montgomery County and bought another not far away near Auriesville, which they would call "Riverbank." It was larger, and it also had a better house, which enjoyed an excellent view of the Mohawk. Here they grew wheat and raised Merino sheep, and enjoyed excellent harvests for a number of years. As she had on Little Cumbrae, Mary Ann spun yarn and knitted clothing to supplement their income.[47]

No additional business correspondence appears. The remaining correspondence is comprised of personal letters sent to friends and relatives. There are four to her older son James, who became a railroad engineer and moved to northern Pennsylvania; four to Mr. Fisher, who had helped the Archbalds to emigrate and remained a friend and visitor to their farm for many years; and here and there a few to several other correspondents. Especially prominent among these letters to friends and relatives, however, are the twenty-three letters sent to members of the Ruthven family, and in particular to her cousin John Ruthven in New York City, a correspondence that continued until his death in 1833, after which his wife returned to Scotland. Much of this correspondence concerns family, common acquaintances, and the exchange of visits. The Ruthvens enjoyed the countryside and visited frequently, but not nearly as much as Mary Ann liked visiting them in New York City. When her children were very young, she rarely ventured much beyond the local area, but when they were older she went to New York City on perhaps two or three occasions. A visit to the affluent, refined New York City cousins, which she undertook without her husband, who remained to do the necessary farmwork and attend to the children's needs, allowed her to partake of their bourgeois respectability and interact with their affluent, cosmopolitan friends.[48]

Interaction with the Ruthvens served another vital and in this instance epistolary purpose for Archbald. Until 1832 or 1833, when the well-regarded former husband of her daughter Margaret, who had died in 1829 shortly after childbirth, became a local postmaster, Archbald lacked confidence in the local Auriesville post office and tried as much as possible to find alternatives to using it. No incident of theft, loss, or violation of privacy appears to have taken place to prompt this lack of trust, which seems instead a product of widely shared and familiar anxieties about what *might* happen to her letters, on the part of one whose dependence on getting and sending letters for the maintenance of emotional well-being was especially insistent. She also was impatient with the infrequent nature of the postal service, which as late as 1840 occurred but once a week, and perhaps less frequently in the winter and early spring. While she posted letters when necessary, she also sought alternatives, even occasionally after 1833. The Ruthvens often acted as personal couriers, especially for letters sent from Scotland, bringing letters sent to her at their New York City address, or finding someone to take them to Auriesville. At other times they placed on ships bound for Scotland letters she wished to post. She had visitors in her neighborhood whose destination was New York City take her letters to the Ruthvens. When the Ruthvens visited her, they no doubt came away with letters from Archbald to be posted from New York City.[49] She was never completely free, however, of the local post office, even as she sought alternatives to it.

Archbald thus wrote many letters and had an active correspondence with a number of individuals, but the most significant for her was certainly Margaret Wodrow. Their distribution in time and among her correspondents in the transcribed collection suggests their developing importance in Mary Ann Archbald's identity narrative. In her first decade in the United States (1807–1816), she wrote only nine letters to Margaret. To some extent, this may be explained by the disruption of moving from Creekvale, their first farm, to Riverbank, around April 1810, and by the fact that Mary Ann was seriously ill for some time after the move. For eighteen months following the sale of their first farm, Mary wrote very few letters. There is no letter from Mary Ann to Margaret again until October 1811.

It is certainly explained, too, by the interruption in the flow of mail between the United States and Scotland as a consequence of international tensions that gave rise to the American embargo of trade with Britain and then to the War of 1812; there were no letters sent to Margaret at all in 1813 or 1814, two years in which the bulk of her correspondence in the transcribed collection is to the Ruthvens. Mary Ann felt this interruption acutely—to the extent that the first activity, she said, in which she engaged shortly after hearing a cannon sound at Johnstown, eight miles away and across the Mohawk River, announcing peace in March of 1815, was to sit down to write to her friend.[50]

In the next decade (1817–1826), there are seventeen letters, and there are fifteen in the following decade (1827–1836). The last four letters to Margaret are in 1838 (2) and 1840 (2), a time when Archbald was increasingly feeble and infirm. Gradually, too, Margaret appears to have become Archbald's only correspondent, and thus the last remaining link with Archbald's abiding sense of herself as the heir to her own past. Death removed her other friends from the scene, most prominently among them John Ruthven, who died in 1833, and her letters allude increasingly to the deaths of other friends with whom she might have corresponded, but whose letters are not archived.[51] Eventually perhaps there was no one left to write to but her most cherished friend; seventeen of Archbald's last twenty letters (1828–1840) in the transcribed collection were written to Margaret Wodrow. Of the previous twenty letters (1821–1828), ten had been written to Margaret.

Archbald produced approximately forty-six letters in thirty-three years to her oldest friend. It was certainly not the volume of letters that the two friends seem to have agreed upon—a letter every few weeks or perhaps once a month—before they parted in Scotland.[52] The difficulties of exchanging mail regularly in the winter and early spring months and Mary Ann's very heavy daily responsibilities to young children and to the farm would have made writing and posting letters so frequently very difficult. Under such circumstances, like many other letter-writers, Archbald did not compose her letters at one sitting. She sometimes took months to complete a single letter. The length of time it took to post her letters was especially noteworthy in the case of the highly ritualized New Year's letter. This letter was begun not so much because there was an urgent practical message or bit of news to convey, or because Mary Ann owed Margaret a letter, but instead because the production of the letter at that particular symbolic moment of reunion and celebration in Scottish tradition was intended to provide a context for singular spiritual communion. Her New Year's letters were usually not posted for between four to six months. The infrequency of winter postal service and the relative absence during that time of year of travelers who might be recruited as personal couriers also probably account for this lag in time between inception and posting.[53]

The ritualized New Year's Eve letter highlights the significance of the epistolary relationship shared by the two women, not only for Mary Ann's emotional health but also for her larger identity narrative. Although Archbald wrote letters to Wodrow at other times during the year, she endeavored each year to start a letter to her friend on New Year's Eve in order to conjure up past images, moods of friendship, and celebrations within the bosom of the family circle they had shared. In the early years of her residence in the United States, this meant waiting until she and her family had returned from a supper or a party and her children and husband had retired. Then, before the fire, in the shadows cast by a solitary candle and in the quiet of the farmhouse, with the depths of winter just beyond the door, Archbald sat down to write. The physical setting prompted a contemplative mood, which Archbald sought to flood with thoughts of the shared past.

Mary Ann created mental pictures that placed her imagination back in a setting in which she and Wodrow had enjoyed their most intimate conversations, or celebrated the New Year. "Once more I am permitted to end the year with you and fain would I for a little while lose the present in the past," she wrote in 1824. She was returning in her mind, she continued, four decades to the "happy group seated round the parlor table in the Manse and waiting till 12 would strike and still further back to . . . the old manse." Archbald took a palpably sensual delight in describing to Wodrow the physical setting in which she wrote, the isolation from her sleeping family, and the feelings she was conjuring up for the task of writing, leaving the impression that the space was being prepared for the two women to begin an intimate conversation.[54]

This longing to attain through letters a continuity of bodily sensations, the hunger for a feeling of intimacy and coziness we have come to associate with intimate female friendship in the nineteenth century, was not restricted to the setting in which a letter might be written.[55] As material objects, letters inscribe the physical body of their writers and hence evoke physical sensations. She expressed "longing" for the sight of Margaret's handwriting, and at the moment of first receiving one of her letters and seeing the familiar script, she professed feeling a "thrill." When she wore garments without pockets, she carried Margaret's letters, which she frequently reread, in her bosom where, she explained on one occasion, "it has been an inmate ever since[it arrived;] its friendly rustling as I moved was music to my ears."[56]

While writing to Margaret, Mary Ann often spoke of trying to imagine what her friend was then thinking as she began her day, or finished supper, or anticipated the New Year. Mary Ann expressed the hope that she was in Margaret's thoughts. These fond thoughts could, however, take a decidedly melancholy, even accusatory tone, if she felt neglected, because she had not heard from Margaret for what she regarded as too long a time. In her 1821 New Year's letter, after complaining that it was months since she had received a letter, she wrote pleadingly, "If only I could make you understand the heart of a stranger in a strange land forgotten by that friend whose place can never be supplied."[57] More often than not, Wodrow was a generous correspondent, so the effort to conjure up an intimate conversation need not be interrupted by complaint or fear that their friendship was in jeopardy because of neglect.

The dreamlike state in which these New Year's letters were composed suggests a larger pattern in Archbald's epistolary practice, for subconscious and semiconscious mental processes that served to guide her in thinking about and reconciling herself to loss and separation inspired her letter-writing on a number of occasions. At times she was simply conscious of having daydreamed for a prolonged period of time about Scotland, before sitting down to write.[58] But at other times, troubling dreams suggested to her the finality of her separation from Little Cumbrae and from Margaret, and helped to inspire the mood she brought to writing. In one dream, she returned to her friend and to the island, but found Little Cumbrae so changed and confusing that she left the dream remembering the thought that she must be "content to end my days on the banks of the Mohawk."[59] Far more disturbing was a dream experienced when ill and feverish. The relation of the dream began the text of what passed for the New Year's letter in 1822, which was written on January 13 because she had been so ill on New Year's Eve. In her dream she was in Scotland, in a house with transparent walls, and alongside others who were looking for people who had been dear to them in life, she was searching for Margaret. In this setting, in which vision was facilitated by transparency, but vulnerability heightened by the inability to hide from disappointment and rejection, everyone shared Mary Ann's fear they would not be recognized, and indeed in the dream Margaret failed to recognize her. Archbald did not draw an obvious meaning from the dream—that separation would eventually cause the death of their friendship. She offered instead a sort of mock-apology for writing about this fantastical episode, and excused herself by adding that her life in America "seems now more like a dream than anything else," so there was, in effect, no real difference between writing of actual daily events and of the disturbing fantasies she experienced while asleep. Her dreams were as good a guide for evaluating her situation as what passed for her waking life.[60]

Yet it is important to understand that in spite of these occasional, emotional, and subjective states of mind that inspired her letter-writing, and for all the commentary on these sources of inspiration, Archbald's letters ultimately were mostly recitations about the quality of her daily life, about her husband and children and her neighbors, and about the declining cohort of mutual acquaintances whom she and Margaret shared. These letters were *evaluations,* however, not merely relations or descriptions. Early in her correspondence from the United States, she proved unable or unwilling to satisfy Margaret's desire, shared especially with the more educated recipients of immigrant letters, for vicarious tourism. Margaret desired anecdotes about American life—the activities of daily experience; the contemplation of the American landscape; the practices of public manners; the rituals of interpersonal relations; and the like. Margaret complained, it seems in a good-natured way, and demanded stories out of daily life. Mary Ann confessed in response in November 1816 that she was indeed "miserably poor at narrative."[61] Thereafter, no doubt reinforced by Margaret's continuing efforts to elicit different content, she heard her friend's voice attempting to guide her pen. Her letters record anticipations of Margaret's criticisms of her writing for its usual lack of strong descriptions of people and of landscapes. Such frequent double-voicing enriches Archbald's writing by helping the reader to understand its aspirations to intimate conversation.[62] Kate Bond probably aspired to no less in her letters, but though she had an active mental life she lacked the technical abilities to achieve such complex thoughts in prose.

In spite of self-criticisms that ran through her mind while writing, Archbald's letters did not change much over the years. She did discipline herself to write economically in order to save postal costs, which Margaret usually assumed,[63] but this seemed the limit of her ability to tailor the content of her letters to meet demands external to her own desires, even when such constraints were suggested by her favorite correspondent. In fact, relatively early in their exchange of letters between the United States and Scotland, her letters adopted a tone from which, thereafter, they did not often diverge. As she said in typifying one of them in 1830, they were usually "of the croaking order."[64] By this she meant, as she confessed, that they often consisted in significant part of complaints about her life. Such complaints were balanced with mention of all the things about which she had to be thankful—food, clothing, nature, family, interesting visitors, and so on.

But when Mary Ann did engage in, or at least acknowledged the need for, a more balanced evaluation, she explicitly wrote of the need to do so as if she had to remind herself, or as if she heard Margaret's voice reminding her to question her assumptions. In her 1826 New Year's letter, for example, when she wrote at length of Jamie's success as an engineer, but spoke relatively little of her other children (and then without enthusiasm), it was Margaret's voice that she heard calling her to account:

> You will be thinking that I am giving too much paper to him [Jamie] in exclusion of the rest—the truth is it is at present the brightest spot in my horizon and I thought it my duty to fix my eye upon it as I am but too apt to dwell upon the clouds and overlook the sunshine.[65]

As her language suggests, Archbald here acknowledges this imbalance, but she does not change the course of her exposition. She is, in effect, arguing with Margaret, but the argument is not resolved and she does not change the direction of her thought. This was typical of her. Archbald's letters are rich in subject positionings: she wrote articulately, with sharp observations, from the perspectives of wife, mother, daughter, grandmother, mother-in-law, cousin, friend, outsider and foreigner, Scot, Briton, Christian, citizen, and woman,[66] but no matter what her position, a persistently critical or negative tone characterizes much of her writing. The tone was self-critical at times: while she wrote, she recorded her own admonitions to herself to seek balance, particularly to be grateful for the comfort and security of her life and her children's lives. But even then she sometimes failed to heed her own advice, arguing with herself and with Margaret and sometimes other correspondents simultaneously.[67]

Archbald complained about many things. We would expect, of course, to find the more mundane complaints out of daily life about the physical limitations and infirmities associated with aging, or the tumult caused by a house full of visitors and children. But other complaints frequently exercised concerned the limitations of American society, culture, and politics. She was critical of the boorishness of her Dutch American neighbors as well as the materialism, cunning, and greed of Americans. She bemoaned the destruction of the landscape by various development projects and farmers' activities. She charged that the American ministry was corrupt and taught false doctrine. She lamented the absence of "genius" in American cultural life, the corruption, ideological pretenses, and banality of American politics, and the condescension with which women's voices were received in the public sphere. She addressed the inadequacy of her children's intellectual development in the circumstances of mind-numbing, incessant work and household chores they did on the farm and then in their efforts to support themselves and their own families. She had sharp words about the moral, cultural, or aesthetic shortcomings of American youth and at times of her children's American spouses.[68] Eventually she found it necessary to address the poor state of dental hygiene among Americans.[69]

When she did not explicitly complain, she nonetheless tended to evaluate the world and her relationships from frankly subjective, opinionated perspectives that moved in the same negative or critical directions. As her list of complaints suggests, much of Mary Ann's writing was ultimately founded on the need to work through the problem of having to live with the many consequences of the bargain she and James had struck when they left Scotland. They had traded a familiar landscape, rich historical associations, and well-established personal relationships for material comfort and security and their children's future prospects in what Mary Ann referred to more than once as "a land of strangers."[70]

It was a mark of the intense friendship shared between the two women that Archbald allowed herself to appear persistently in this stance, precisely because it was so easily criticized for its lack of balance. She was willing to leave herself vulnerable to this response, because Margaret was the one friend from whom she was not only willing *with Margaret*

to accept criticism for being opinionated, but also before whom she was willing repeatedly to risk a willful assertion of ego few people persistently allow themselves in their dealings with others.

Archbald was well aware of this interpersonal dynamic in her letters. She referred mockingly to the self-absorption and negativity in her letters in remarks in 1832, but simultaneously she drew some serious implications for the quality of the friendship. "If egotism be a mark of friendship as has been said," she stated, after noting the extent to which her letter had been filled with complaints and criticisms, all largely unrestrained by balance, "I am sure this is one of the most friendly letters that ever was written[;] with such an example before you, I hope you will in the future say more about yourself."[71]

This revealing statement gives us additional insight into the dynamics of this remarkable friendship. We do not have Margaret Wodrow's letters, of course, so we do not know precisely the language with which Margaret responded to the stance Mary Ann repeatedly assumed in her letters. But in combination with the instances of double-voicing, in which Mary Ann heard Margaret criticizing her for the tone and content of her letters, the suggestion of Margaret's own self-restraint in *her* letters (she needs to be *invited* to say more about herself and to be willful and opinionated) tells us that it was habitual for the two women to play a certain role in relation to one another. Margaret was mostly objective, restrained in self-revelation, balanced in her evaluations, and rarely willful in her assertions, while Mary Ann was often knowingly the opposite.

The delight in such a friendship comes in the appreciation, indeed valorization, of these differences and the ways in which they could be played against one another, and in the anticipation of the other's accustomed response to one's own accustomed way of presenting oneself. When describing in 1811 a portrait of Margaret that hung at the new house at Riverbank, Mary Ann suggested these roles in their relation to one another, saying, "Your picture occupies a favorite corner of the dining room and looks at me as I enter with its smirking smile."[72] Margaret's gaze seems to have offered Mary Ann this reassuring—because unchanging—message, "I know who you are and what you are up to; and you know that I know; and this is the secret we shall always share!"

Our understanding of this pleasure Wodrow and Archbald drew in the roles they played in relation to one another should not be allowed to obscure the seriousness of purpose that frequently characterized their epistolary relationship. Their letters were the place where Archbald, playing her accustomed egocentric role, developed the theme of loss and was from time to time forced by her friend, playing her part as the less opinionated, more objective and matter-of-fact party, to evaluate the validity of those claims. We are able only to detect the echo of Margaret's writing, but the reader may occasionally hear a subtextual dialogue evaluating the ways in which Scotland and the comparisons of Scotland and the Scots and America and the Americans weave their way throughout the three decades of Mary Ann's correspondence. Mary Ann labored for years to fix her homeland in her imagination as an idealized place of warmth, intimacy, and community, and in so doing to take the measure of what she had lost in her American exile. How did these efforts stand up to Margaret's responses to these claims about Scotland?

Mary Ann and James hoped to return to Scotland from the moment they made the decision to emigrate. Their fondest dream was to resettle on Little Cumbrae, though that was recognized soon after their resettlement as impractical in light of the fact that the costs of living there were unlikely to become any less prohibitive. Archbald was not without bitterness about the humiliating treatment that had forced them to leave, and to some extent this bitterness carried over to the island itself, but it was a superficial feeling compared with the much more powerful emotions her former home conjured up. These associations sometimes caught her unawares, as if reminding her that she could never forget her former home. After a storm, the noise of rushing water in the creek near her farmhouse one day called to mind the sound of the rush of the surf on the beach at Little Cumbrae; and standing on the banks of the Mohawk evoked memories of standing at the sea on a sandbank on the island, watching the play of water and wind on the firth.[73]

After nearly a decade in the United States, Mary Ann moved beyond this nostalgia for the landscape to a stronger assertion of Scottishness and aversion to her American circumstances. In 1816, she professed suddenly, and without further explanation, that in the United States "the general character of the people and other untoward circumstances have worn me out." In consequence, she had come to the conclusion "that my country people [are] a set of superior beings, and the land they inhabit is the spot most highly favored by providence."[74] She began to comment favorably within a few years on the children's pride in Scottishness, and especially the affection of the two oldest, Jaime and

Margaret, for speaking "their mother tongue."[75] Peter was too young when they emigrated to have any comfort later with dialect, but he shared his mother's feeling "that nothing bad can come out of Scotland."[76] She claimed that James spoke a more authentic Scottish around the house than when they lived on Little Cumbrae.[77]

Her feelings increasingly raw, Mary Ann grew sensitive to casual comments that appeared insensitive to her suffering. She answered sharply when Margaret referred to the United States as "your country," for, she said, Scotland would always be her country.[78] When Margaret wrote that the island was as beautiful as ever, she begged that this not be spoken of, because she was so discontent with the prospect of remaining in the United States. She recalled her bitter comments that she had no loyalty to any particular place that would bring her back to Scotland, and that it was their friendship alone that would do so. Correcting these former assertions, she confessed, "I did not think it possible that local attachment could be carried to such an irrational length after all my brags about the world being my country and such like nonsense."[79]

While it may never be clear what Margaret made of this mood that settled over Archbald's letters for about five years, was it merely coincidence that in its midst, on two occasions, she introduced, apparently at some length, news of scandals then taking place in Scotland that hardly put the Scots in their best light? It may be that Margaret was just indulging in gossip or being an honest reporter, but it may be as well that she did not feel comfortable with either Mary Ann's emotionalism or her sacralization of Scotland and its people, and chose to play her accustomed role in the relationship by restoring balance. In 1821 she wrote of a local scandal prompted by a corrupt lawyer, to which Mary Ann responded that while there were certainly instances of this sort among lawyers in every country, she particularly hated to think this could be the case in Scotland.[80] The next year brought news, related apparently at some length, from Margaret of another scandal—this one perhaps sexual in nature, because the only one of her four children to whom she showed the letter was her own Margaret, the oldest daughter and closest confidante. (It was so disturbing that Margaret Wodrow or some later descendent appears to have excised a section of Mary Ann's letter that commented on the details of the scandal.)[81]

The news was sufficiently troubling to prompt a long statement, acknowledging error in vaulting the Scots above the rest of humanity, and restoring balance to Mary Ann's judgment not only about Scots but about Americans as well:

> Amidst all my cares and regrets about my native land still I could indulge in the fond dream of its being superior to every other country upon earth and when I meet here with instances of avarice and chicanery I say with James, "it is just like the Yankees—how different the people at home." I did not think these same people at home perfect whilst I was among them but absence was like death[;] their faults were buried or softened and their good qualities only remembered.[82]

Another source of disillusionment had recently arrived, and she referred to it in this same letter. One of the Ruthvens had written from Scotland that the advance of shipping and trade on the western coast had turned people toward moneymaking, including some of her more idealized former neighbors.[83] Seen in this light, how different were the Scots from those cunning, self-interested Yankees who were so frequently anathematized in the Archbald household?

Mary Ann's testimony here is as close as we come in any of her letters to an explicit declaration of the necessity of reevaluating her thinking on any subject. Throughout the remaining archived correspondence, Archbald does not indulge in romanticizing her homeland and its people. Longing for the "little island" remains throughout the correspondence, including one of her last letters in 1840 to her friend, but it is a longing for one's original home, not idealization of a people or its culture.[84] It is the self's memory, and not ideology or idealized collective memory, asserting itself through Archbald. Perhaps we may attribute this transition to the passing of a mood and to changes in external circumstances that functioned to divert Archbald from thoughts of her imminent return. The death of James in 1824 increased her emotional and practical dependence on her children, for Jamie took control of her finances and Louisa cared for many of her daily needs. The marriages of all four of her children fixed them to American lives and American spouses, and in so doing fixed the now-widowed Mary Ann to those lives.

It was around this time that she had her two dreams of separation, which apparently had helped her to gather up her thoughts about the point she had reached in life. Perhaps, too, the alienation and isolation of advancing age (Mary Ann was sixty-two when James died) increasingly began to replace the alienation and isolation of being an outsider. As she turned inward toward family and her epistolary relationship to Margaret, she may well have moved away from preoccupation with the relative claims of Scots and Others. She certainly never stopped being critical of the United States, but after this period in the early 1820s, she never again expressed claims for the superiority of Scotland and its people that had helped to make her American daily life seem tedious and unreal. To this extent, like her dreams, her intimate, transnational conversation with her friend may well have helped to smooth her path, assisting her to accommodate herself to the finality of separation, both from Margaret and from Little Cumbrae, while preserving the larger continuity of the narrative of her life. In this, her extraordinary articulateness aside, her letters played a role for her that letters played for more mundane stylists.

10

Dr. Thomas Steel
The Difficulties of Achieving the Reunited Family

> I cannot help wishing sometimes that you and Lilly were out here with your means of living all properly secured.
>
> —Thomas Steel to James Steel, March 18, 1854

In 1853, Thomas Steel, a forty-four-year-old Scottish medical doctor and farmer, had been living in rural Waukesha County, Wisconsin, for a decade.[1] The first year on the prairie had been hard, filled with privation, loneliness, and disappointment. He had left England as a member of a community of two hundred Utopian socialists who had banded together out of a number of smaller associations, and had decided to call the cooperative commune they wished to establish "Equality." They quickly fell to arguing among themselves, and began to disband within months of their arrival.[2] Steel left the commune in December 1843, just as winter arrived. He spent the cold months in the cramped cabin of a family of settlers. He tried to make a living practicing medicine, but soon realized that in an economy without cash, he was destined to be paid for his services—and his interrupted meals, sleepless nights, and wanderings around the thinly settled countryside in the middle of the night to the cabins of sick and injured farmers—in eggs, bread, chickens, and unfilled promises.[3]

But with substantial assistance from his affluent father, James, a senior civil servant in London, he had bought a partially improved farm, soon got some land under cultivation, and enjoyed a bountiful first harvest in 1845. He had improved the house he bought with his land into a comfortable residence.[4] Early that same year, he had taken a wife, Catherine Freeman, the daughter of British emigrants, and by 1853 they had four bright and healthy children. His father-in-law and brother-in-law helped him plant and harvest his crops, and the elder Freeman loaned him money to add to his acreage.[5] He had connected with others among the substantial British (and particularly the Scottish) communities in his neighborhood to socialize, begin a curling club, and celebrate Robert Burns's birthday and other British holidays.[6]

Though not without criticisms of his American neighbors, whose self-interested materialism and religious zealotry he disliked, he conceded that they had their virtues. His medical practice had taken him into their log cabins, and he encountered them as neighbors, and had come to value the frankness and neighborliness they sometimes manifested. Though he remained rather distrustful of most of them, it hardly effected his pleasure in his new home.

Though reluctant to forsake his allegiance to the British monarchy, he obtained American citizenship papers in order to secure his property.[7] But there was more to this decision than expedience, for the longer Steel experienced American political institutions, the more value he saw in a politics that ultimately depended on free discussion and that encouraged organization at the local level. He served as a Justice of the Peace and a clerk of the township School Board, and took part both in the organization of the first school in his neighborhood and in the affairs of the county medical society.[8]

He eventually also made his peace with the frustrations of his medical practice, which, even when he added pulling teeth to his repertory of skills, he knew would never increase his wealth and would make frequent and inconvenient demands on his time, but did bring the rewards of respectability and service.[9] By 1853 he was now out of debt for the first time in years, and possessed a small surplus of cash. His farm yielded enough to feed his family, and his father's subsidies allowed them to buy necessities beyond what they themselves produced.[10] By the time he experienced several years of bad crops in the late 1840s and early 1850s, Steel had a sufficient enough surplus to prevail. In addition to these parental subsidies, his unmarried sister Lilias (Lilly) and father, who lived together in London, frequently sent boxes of books and clothing and the medical equipment and medicines Steel needed to sustain his doctoring. Prescribing the quinine his father bought for him in London enabled Steel to gain a reputation for effectiveness in treating the malarial fevers that plagued settlers in marshy prairie regions.[11]

In the winter of 1853, life for the immigrant country doctor appeared to be going well. Perhaps in the context of this growing success and security, he seemed to be developing more confidence in the assertion of his political, social, and religious views. He was, by character, education, and training a rationalist and an empiricist, and he described himself as a "radical" in politics and religion, as the socialist commitment that inspired his 1843 emigration suggests.[12] He was the sworn enemy of moldy orthodoxies, ossified traditions, and all superstition. He found inspiration in the 1848 revolutions in Europe, and took pleasure in imagining a transformation of Britain along democratic lines.[13] He espoused feminism, and in a rather sharply worded letter criticized his more conservative sister for resisting the ideas of the second women's rights convention at Seneca Falls, about which he had sent Lilly a clipping from the American press.[14] He had embraced Universalism, because, guided by a humanistic reliance on science and reason, it opposed superstition, espoused universal salvation, and dispensed with the dreary business of sin, devils, and damnation. In helping to pay for the $50 subscription that had brought the Universalist minister to Waukesha County to preach, Steel was pleased to have offended the local American evangelicals, whom he believed narrow-minded and obsessed with evil.[15] He had opposed the Mexican War as a war of aggression by his adopted country.[16] He opposed slavery as a blot on its honor, and voted for antislavery parties when he had the opportunity.[17] He was outspoken in his support of the American practice of separation of church and state.[18]

By every apparent indication, Steel seems representative of a successful immigration, at home and reasonably comfortable in his adopted country. There were, however, disturbing currents beneath the surface of this material prosperity and self-confident assertiveness that Steel himself was finding it difficult to confront. There would seem little room for Steel, a rationalist with a scientific education, to become a spiritualist. Certainly even more than his neighbors he had an understanding of the physical processes of death that would have made him an unlikely candidate to seek communion with spirits. So his participation in seances in which tables moved and rapping was heard, as spirits were invoked by those seated in the darkened parlors of his home and the homes of his friends, seemed peculiar, no less to him than to those who knew him.

Spiritualism had become a fashionable form of popular recreation at the time, as well as a way of continuing to be engaged by metaphysical mysteries in an age in which science and technology seemed increasingly to be able to provide convincing answers, though not always emotionally satisfying ones, to all problems.[19] Moreover, seances proved a diversion from the tedium of the long Wisconsin winter, about which Steel complained in his letters.[20]

But Steel went beyond disengaged participation to make the winter evenings pass amusingly in the company of British and American friends and neighbors. In letters to his sister, he wrote in detail of his sojourns in the spirit world during seances. At one seance, about which he wrote at length in a letter, he had invoked the spirit of his mother, Elizabeth, who had died in 1841, and asked her to verify her identity by answering questions about his sister, Eliza, who had died an agonizing death in childhood when he was a boy. "What was the name of the little sister that we lost when I was a child[?]," the doctor asked; and, as he called out the letters of the alphabet, "the table rose at the letters E, L, I, Z, A." In similar fashion, the name of Eliza's attending physician and of the Steels' landlord at the time of his sister's death were spelled out by his mother's spirit, who also identified, at least through a plausible phonetic spelling, Eliza's fatal disease, by tapping out "H, O, O, P," indicating whopping cough. Elizabeth Steel's spirit also indicated its pleasure in watching the lives of James and Lilly in England, and keeping track of Eliza and other kin at various levels of the spirit world. But particularly gratifying to Steel was his mother's confirmation of the Universalist creed Thomas had embraced several years before. His mother indicated that while, upon death, spirits entered the next dimension at a level defined by "their moral and intellectual advancement in this world," they could proceed to other levels as their characters evolved. The doctor concluded that his mother's message was that, beyond the grave, "There is no place of punishment."[21]

Steel was skeptical when he began his experiments with spiritualism, and indeed occasionally engaged in sarcasm and dismissal in describing the phenomenon in his initial letters that touched on the subject.[22] But his interactions on this and subsequent occasions with his mother's spirit and his growing knowledge of the career and teachings of the American Swedenborgian clairvoyant and healer, Andrew Jackson Davis, lessened his resistance to believing that there was a spirit world.[23] Having denied sin and embraced human perfectability through Universalism and social reform, in spiritualism Steel was able to dispense with the reality of death, which had been his constant companion during his twenty years of medical practice, and which had apparently left him continuing to grieve for his mother and sister for many years. To Lilly, he wrote in considerable detail about his experiments with spiritualism and the enlightenment it was affording him. He did not completely accept the reality of the spirit world, though he had come to believe, against the ethos of his medical education, that there was much in the world that he lacked the tools to understand. As he wrote to her, paraphrasing Shakespeare, "There [are] more things in heaven and earth than is dreamed in our Philosophy."[24]

But he was reluctant to spell this out in his letters to his father. James Steel was much more generous with money than with his emotions, especially, it seems, when it came to Thomas. Under the best of circumstances, his children knew from experience, he was a scold and likely to be somewhat negative or, at best, wary, in dealing with others. Lilly's letters to her brother suggest that she sometimes had to step carefully around her father's moods, and that she felt it necessary to struggle to represent what were likely to be his views in her mind in preparing herself and in preparing others to deal with him.[25]

James Steel probably felt justified in looking at his son somewhat critically. He had seen Thomas make a number of bad decisions over the years. He had become accustomed to adopting a contrary position to those advanced by his son, as if Thomas could be depended on to require correction in order to reach proper conclusions. Even as Thomas himself aged, directed his own growing family, superintended a prospering farm, and, as the son continually took pains repeatedly in his letters to let the father know, healed and saved lives and grew in public stature in his adopted American community,[26] his father continued to resist the son's decisions and plans, and to warn that they were likely to have unforeseen, negative consequences. James's resistance was never spiteful or mean-spirited, and he was more likely to simply suggest that he should have been listened to in the first place, than explicitly to review a catalog of past errors in humiliating detail.[27] He certainly never sought to hurt his son's feelings, and showed much concern in his letters, and in his generous and frequent gifts of money, about the difficulties he experienced in his medical practice and farm-making effort. But James resisted his son on the big matters—his marriage, his land-buying plans, his desire at times to give up medicine, and above all else, in importance to his son, his own migration with his daughter to join Thomas in Wisconsin.

When Thomas broached the subject of spiritualism with his father, he was cautious and defended inquiry into the phenomenon in a more abstract and emotionally distant way.[28] Whether because he did not want to injure his father by conjuring up painful memories, or he did not want to risk his father's censure for indulging in faddish nonsense that mocked his expensive education and his profession, Thomas certainly did not speak of communicating with his mother and sister. Even if Lilly did not completely accept the reality of the spirit world, she was a loving, supportive sister who was inclined not to be critical of her brother, and she was quite willing to be his confidante, sharing secrets he wished to keep from his father, and his strategic ally, continually helping him find ways to bring his father around to his views.

Thomas Steel was devoted to the ideal of a cooperative, united, and happy family, whether based in a biological connection, or in its fictive, ideologically conceived form, as in a self-constituted community of Utopian socialists. Perhaps this longing was overdetermined by the experiences of his childhood. There seems no doubt that the death of his mother had created a gnawing void in his life, and that his sister's death remained a painful memory, and perhaps even an inspiration for him later in life to take an interest in being a healer. (Though they were never spoken of, there were also two older brothers, both of whom died when Thomas was young—John, who died in 1826, and Andrew, also a doctor, who died in 1832.)[29]

Whatever its precise origin, the longing for family as the center of a perfectible domestic life was certainly apparent in his letters. His correspondence with his sister and father is filled with touching portraits of his domestic life and of his children's emotional and intellectual development, and gives frequent evidence of his affection for and dependence on his wife.[30] He was certainly devoted to his father and sister. He hoped to compensate his father for the years of subsidies that had helped him to succeed in America, and compensate his sister, too, for her own indirect generosity, for the money that James gave his son, the son saw as that much less money the father could leave the then still unmarried Lilly in his will.[31] Though he never refused money from his father, his continuing dependence on him, after a decade in Wisconsin, to provide the difference between marginality and prosperity did disturb him. It was a source of guilt, embarrassment, and ambivalence.

In Steel's letters, there is a persistent, if low-keyed, note of feelings of personal inadequacy and powerlessness that recurs from time to time over the course of many years. Steel fought these feelings, mostly successfully, but his occasional trumpeting of his achievements as a physician, farmer, and community activist in his letters to his father suggests a need to convince himself as well as his father that he was indeed the effective man he wished to be. His continuing dependence on his father did not help him to gain a confident sense of himself, so it is understandable that he would seek ways to assert his agency in this relationship.

How did he seek to do so? Steel shared with others one of the commonest immigrant social aspirations. He wished Lilly and his father to join him in America, and thus form one large, united family. But obtaining agreement on this goal from a father used to resisting his son's ideas and plans was a frustrating, and at times painful, project. He worked at it off and on for almost a decade before finally succeeding. It probably seemed easier at the point in time of his experiment with spiritualism, which was also the point of an especially frustrating impasse in his protracted discussion with his father about emigrating to Wisconsin, to be united with the spirit of the dead than it was to bring together the destinies of his living family members under one roof.

Thomas Steel's second migration to North America was much more successful than his first, a fruitless three-month journey that had taken place shortly after he graduated from medical school at Glasgow University in 1834, and which he freely conceded at the time, in the seven letters he wrote back to England, was folly. The difference between the two was not the enormous parental subsidy that sustained the second emigration, for the first also required the use of parental resources. Its failure was a product of very bad planning, inexperience, and bad luck. It certainly did little to increase James Steel's confidence in his son's judgment, which does not appear to have been high to begin with.

Against the advice of his father, who warned him he was ill-equipped to succeed at finding a situation for himself and then making a new life in North America, and of Dr. Sheridan, a senior medical school professor, he had gone first to Canada and then to the United States in search of a place to establish himself.[32] Then twenty-five years old, he knew no one, and had no idea of how medicine was practiced in the rough, postfrontier circumstances of rural Upper Canada and the Ohio and Mississippi valleys. Burdened by too much luggage and uncomfortable in heavy clothing that was inappropriate for the sultry summer weather, the young doctor pursued one unavailing situation after another, in Canada and then Louisville and finally New Orleans, all the while exhausting his funds, and increasingly more ashamed of his incompetence.

He daydreamed, he wrote his father, about making a quick fortune, and returning to buy a small estate in Scotland, where he would hold a salon on winter evenings and regale young ladies with tales of his North American adventures.[33] But gullible and inexperienced as he was, he allowed himself to be talked out of a potentially promising situation in Canada by an older practitioner who did not want any local competition. He only realized how easily he had been manipulated when he was hundreds of miles away.[34]

Steel was certain that he could practice medicine in New Orleans, which had a reputation as an unhealthy place. But because he knew no one in the city, he could not get anyone to testify that he was indeed the same individual named on his university degree, and therefore could not get a medical licence.[35] He thought of offering himself as a clerk, but had arrived at the season when all the commercial men and their families were beginning their annual exodus from the city to avoid yellow fever—proof at least that doctors would not go begging, if they could get licensed. Lonely and disheartened, he longed to get a letter from his family, but they could not write to him because he had left no itinerary. He daydreamed, as he journeyed down the Ohio Canal, about how pleasant it would be if his family were united on a farm in the lush Ohio countryside.[36]

As failure appeared inevitable, his letters grew increasingly confessional. He felt it necessary to admit that he possessed a multitude of personal inadequacies. One certainly, to his mind, was self-involvement, for which he would reproach himself, and his sister, too, would criticize him years later in exchanges of letters during his second migration. His heightened consciousness of his heedlessness to others led to the realization, he wrote to his father in his last letter before he left Canada for the United States, that he "did not know I loved you all so much as I now find I do."[37] In his loneliness, he grew increasingly anxious imagining that there was sickness in his family.[38]

Another inadequacy was his failure to follow the advice of both his father and Dr. Sheridan regarding emigrating and starting a medical career. He was not completely willing to make his peace with Dr. Sheridan, who had refused to extend him any help, probably in the form of letters of introduction to medical colleagues in North America.[39] But

Thomas was quite willing to concede the advice he had received from his father was sound: "I confess that I was headstrong and foolish in coming out to this country without some concerted scheme. I now perceive too truly that your advices on the subject were all good . . . and my ideas were foolish."[40]

After three disastrous months in North America, Steel wrote that he had booked passage to England, buying his ticket with the last £20 he possessed of the considerable sum his father had given him to finance his trip. He was returning as a failure, or as he said, "like the prodigal son after having spent my substance." He feared he had become an embarrassment to his family, and that his father was anxious over the thought of having to support him. Anticipating that James would want nothing to do with him, Thomas stated that he would write from Liverpool to see if his father would welcome or reject him.[41]

There is no evidence that James failed to welcome him back. Yet it was probably not coincidental that within six months of his return, he felt pressured to choose a relatively low-paying situation that would take him far away for many months at a time. He signed on as a doctor aboard ships going back and forth to India. He also spent six months practicing medicine in China.[42] The experiences of the next decade, until Steel's second migration to America, are a mystery. What seems certain is that, while the quality of his relationship with his father changed greatly for the better as he matured, a pattern to their interactions seen in this failed emigration project was set in the years before Steel shipped out to Asia. The tensions evident in this pattern survive the transition that Steel made from a callow and ineffectual young man in 1834 to an experienced and more self-sufficient emigrant in 1843. Thomas had particularly strong needs for the warmth and support of family, and often blamed himself for being too selfish to do more to provide a basis for receiving that warmth and support. He often reached out to his father to find that the older man maintained an emotional distance and resisted his son's overtures.

Thomas Steel's second emigration produced the imposing circulation of letters between Wisconsin and England. Between his emigration with the members of "Equality" in 1843 and the decision of James and Lilly Steel in 1854, after years of negotiation and argument that formed the center of much communication among family members, to join Thomas and his family in Wisconsin, approximately 482 letters were exchanged between Thomas Steel and his father and his sister. In the context of research on immigrant personal correspondence, this correspondence is unique, for it is rare to have access to letters generated on both sides of the ocean, though unfortunately this is the case only for the years 1845–1846.

It seems clear that in the Steel family's case James and Lilly not only saved Thomas's letters, but then brought them to Wisconsin, where they were joined into a unified collection of family letters, all of them originals, which was eventually to be donated in 1959 by a granddaughter of Thomas Steel to the Wisconsin Historical Society.[43] The archived collection is not precisely a two-way conversation, however, for while James and Lilly seem to have saved all of Thomas's letters, Thomas was not quite as diligent or successful in saving all the letters written by his father and sister. For every letter from London that bears the signature of Lilly or Thomas, there are nine that he sent to London from Wisconsin. This is not an artifact of a lack of diligence in correspondence on the part of his sister and father, for we know from the surviving letters that this was a cycle of correspondence governed by the strictest reciprocity.

This two-way conversation is no less useful for not being in perfect balance. What there is of true correspondence, of the one-for-one exchange of letters in the archived collection, is enhanced by the diversity of voices and perspectives among the parties represented within the collection. James wrote letters to his son and Lilly to her brother, but sometimes a letter by James would end with an addendum written by Lilly. James, it seems clear, allowed Lilly to use the balance of the paper he had begun when he had nothing left to write. Thomas wrote separate letters to his father and to his sister, but, though rarely, to both in the same letter. He did not address his father and sister in the same way, whether in terms of tone or content, though content was a matter of ongoing negotiations among Thomas and his father and sister.

The diversity of voices in the archived collection allows us greater access to the internal dynamic of the relationships shared among the three principal participants in this epistolary exchange. These dynamics become particularly evident, for example, when Thomas recruited Lilly in his efforts to influence his father to take some course of action that Thomas regarded as necessary for his welfare or for that of his family, both nuclear and extended, but that he knew his father would resist. All the while, he wrote to his father touching obliquely, or not at all, on the same matters. The epistolary "conspiracy" of siblings against parents is by no means unique to the Steel family. We have seen it develop, for example, in the Mickle family correspondence, in which the brothers in their own private correspondence question the emotional state of their sensitive and overworked father, and hence his ability to make wise decisions about emigration and purchasing land in Canada.[44] What makes the conspiracy of siblings especially interesting in the case of the Steel family is that Thomas depends on the influence of a sister, whose authority in family affairs must be mobilized through the restrictive prisms of gender conventions. As a young woman and a daughter, Lilly was constrained in her dealings with her father, who appears to have been a rather difficult man to begin with, but she was an effective advocate for her brother (more than for herself), at least in certain contexts in which James was inclined to assume a relatively flexible stance.

A striking example of Lilly's positive influence on her brother's behalf, and of the epistolary conspiracy of siblings to which the two-way conversation and multiple voices in this collection gives access, is the assistance Lilly provided to her brother in preparing James for Thomas's marriage. By his telling in letters to his father and particularly his sister, whose sympathies he often seemed skilled at soliciting by tugging at her heartstrings, Steel was leading a miserable, lonely existence in his first year after breaking with his socialist comrades. He ate poorly; the clothes he brought from England became ragged; the house he bought with his land purchase was then inadequate; and his sleep was continually interrupted by people requiring medical attention in the middle of the night, but rarely able to pay him. He needed someone to look after him and provide him with company. He let Lilly know first, and his father know only gradually, that he was courting Catherine Freeman.[45]

For practical reasons, James advised against marriage. Not unlike the correspondence of Thomas Spencer Niblock, every letter from Thomas Steel spoke of expenses he must make to improve his house and land, and hence of money his father, like Niblock's sister and brother-in-law, must provide him. A difference between the two men was that Steel had a profession that should have enabled him to become self-supporting. But he quickly learned, as he wrote his father on a number of occasions, that he could not make nearly enough money practicing medicine. James believed that his son hardly had the resources to provide for a family, and he was doubtless anxious about being put in the position of having to provide even more in the way of subsidies to his son, whose needs, he believed, would only escalate if married. What James seems to have had in mind, however, were the expenses of keeping an English country house, with servants, frequent visitors, and well-appointed rooms.[46]

This was not what Thomas planned. Thomas reasoned that he could not succeed at building a self-sufficient life on the American prairie, and hence in using his father's subsidies effectively, without a "partner in business," the practical metaphor he used for marriage, perhaps in the hope it would assist in selling the idea to his practical-minded father.[47] He recruited Lilly to make his point in her own, perhaps softer, way with James. In July 1844 he presented her with arguments to make in his behalf, and sought to toughen her resolve:

> Now my dear Lilly knowing my father's prudent and no doubt correct views on these matters I trust you will be my advocate[;] put him in mind that what might be a very foolish step in England may be a wise one here—living so cheap[.] I will have no house rent—no taxes worth mentioning and in a very short time our food will be raised by ourselves[—]a cow poultry a few pigs and etc.[;] and how the [deuce?] am I to manage all that by myself—In case you should have any scruples I must put you in mind how dreary a thing it is to return home after a hard days work no eye to bright at your approach to be made happy by your fortune or sympathize in your misfortunes.[48]

When, where, and how Lilly presented the arguments to her father, we cannot know. Nor unfortunately is there a reply from Lilly that says, in effect, "Mission accomplished!" Meanwhile, Thomas continued to make his own case. In letters written after these instructions were given, his remarks to his sister were often upbeat, as befits a man in love and making plans for marriage, while to his father, they struck a depressed tone and strained to evoke sympathy.[49] James's resistance to his son's desire to marry relaxed considerably in subsequent letters. He certainly cannot be said to have been willing to express himself enthusiastically about the prospect, but enthusiasm may well have been beyond James Steel under the best of circumstances.

With knowledge that the marriage was impending obtained eventually from Lilly, he cautioned Thomas about going into debt, and told him that his goal ultimately must be to live "solely" by his own resources. While, in a joint letter, Lilly offered congratulations, James stated that he could "only hope that you have made a judicious choice" in Catherine.[50] But he did not oppose the marriage, which took place early in 1845. Catherine, a well-educated and gracious woman whose father had been a cabinetmaker at Buckingham Palace prior to emigrating, continued the public relations campaign in the couple's behalf by beginning her own sisterly correspondence with Lilly soon after the wedding.[51]

One result of reading the two years of mutual exchanges of letters is that the reader comes to have intuitions about the roles and positions assumed in their letters by James and Lilly for the years in which we do not have their replies to Thomas. Of course, whether these intuitions are accurate or inaccurate guesswork, we cannot know. What helps the reader in the case of the Steel family correspondence is that Thomas often explicitly summarizes the arguments or questions of Lilly and James to which he responds prior to responding to them, so that a type of dialogue is maintained through paraphrase, even in the absence of James's and Lilly's actual letters. But then, too, we must assume that Thomas's paraphrases are correct.

Lilly's probable role in facilitating Thomas's marriage should not imply that all worked smoothly in this massive exchange of letters over the course of the twelve years it was maintained. Before we confront the ultimate problem—Thomas's strong desire to reunite his family in Wisconsin and James's strong reluctance to leaving England—the correspondence functioned to confront, it is profitable to look at the technical problems and personal issues that Thomas, James, and Lilly had to sort out for the participants to maintain an epistolary relationship.

Within a few years of Thomas's second emigration, by mutual agreement the Steels were attempting to sustain a correspondence of approximately two letters a month, depending on seasonal shipping schedules on the Atlantic. There are few, if any, examples in archived collections of such a volume of letters produced by immigrants and those to whom they wrote. Lilly and James had the advantages of time for writing and convenient postal arrangements to facilitate their production of letters. They lived in London, the commercial, financial, and postal center of a great empire; Lilly did not work or spend time in housekeeping; and James was sufficiently senior in his career that he had occasion relatively frequently to sit down and write to his son.

But there were many of the impediments typical to immigrant correspondents that challenged Thomas's ability to produce the volume of letters he exchanged with his father and sister. Not the least of them, as we might expect, was that the time and mental energy taken up by farm-making, medicine, and his growing family left little space in his life for letter-writing. His production of letters is also especially noteworthy when one considers that not only did he attempt to maintain a one-for-one ratio of letters sent to letters received, but also that his letters are generally articulate and, though he certainly does not appear to have worried much over his often irregular punctuation, they are technically well-composed.[52] They are written in neat and readable script, with no evidence of corrections, and at four sides of a good-sized sheet of paper, they are relatively substantial in length.[53]

Either his finished letters were second drafts, or he knew exactly what he wanted to say and had the powers of concentration and the skill to do so effectively, whatever the conditions around him (for example, temperature; a poor writing surface; noisy children) about which he complained, when he sat down to write.[54] Additional evidence of Steel's care in producing letters was that from time to time they contained elaborate illustrations—maps of his region and neighborhood, of his property and of new acquisitions of land carefully done to scale, and diagrams of improvements to his house. There were even two well-executed line drawings (reproduced in this book): in 1844, of the cabin in which he was then living, and, in 1847, a touching, but now sadly faded, rendering of Catherine standing in the yard at the front of their house and holding her first-born, the one-year-old James.[55]

Steel also faced difficulties with the contemporary postal system. During these twelve years, neighborhood post offices opened and closed. They also became, by his reckoning, less "respectable" and hence less secure, with the shifting of population toward classes of people he deemed less trustworthy (though he never specified exactly who these might be). These changes required him, he believed, to change the post office he patronized.[56] Wherever the precise location, during these years Thomas Steel never lived closer than six to eight miles to a post office.[57] This was inconvenient, even for one who traveled on horseback around his neighborhood frequently because of his profession. Yet there is no mention in his correspondence of dependence on personal couriers to post or collect his mail.[58] The Steels had come to depend on such a brief turnaround time for the exchange of letters that, weather and everything else being equal, a personal courier, following a private travel schedule, might actually have broken the rhythm of the exchange.

In part, too, Thomas's desire to visit the post office himself was the result of the fact that letters from his father so often contained gifts of money (usually a £5 note, but sometimes a larger bill) that Thomas felt obligated to collect his letters himself. James Steel sent his son money with such regularity that only in the case of especially large amounts, as on the occasion when Thomas received money in order to buy land adjoining his for his father and sister, did he depend on arrangements with banks or commercial agents in distant Milwaukee, nearly twenty miles away, to facilitate these transfers.[59] Prompted by the need to acknowledge the receipt of these bank notes and hence reassure his father that his gifts had arrived safely, Steel developed an elaborate system of accounting for received mail. He would not seal the letters he brought to the post office to be mailed until he had found out if there were a letter there for him to collect. He acknowledged the letter awaiting him by marking a "+" symbol on his own letter, and then sealing it.[60] James was hardly content with the amount of assistance that his son's new life required, but at least he lived with the knowledge that his money had reached its destination. The correspondence records no lost money through the twelve-year period.[61]

Surmounting these technical challenges, however, was not nearly as significant for the Steel family's exchange of letters as overcoming the problems caused by the differing expectations of the three parties involved. Lilly, James, and Thomas engaged in explicit negotiations for several years in the hope of developing a shared understanding of purposes of their transnational conversation. A skillful and articulate letter-writer, Thomas Steel was nonetheless by inclination not an especially disciplined one in the sense of finding a practical theme that he knew to be of interest to his reader, and then sticking to it. He was instead at his best as a writer relating anecdotes and gossip out of the life of the local British community in which he socialized. Or, just as often, he took his stories out of his medical practice, which afforded an unlimited number of instances of travel to the remote cabins of humble settlers in the middle of the night to deliver a baby or relieve the distress of a badly dislocated shoulder, and then of the solitary return home at dawn through the lonely woods. For Steel, encounters with the extremes of American nature, with the solitude of the forest or of the prairie as the sun rose at dawn, were intense experiences that empowered his imagination. He delighted in recalling them, all the more when there was an element of danger or discomfort in the experience. Returning home on horseback, with the temperature at 15 degrees below zero, in the early morning in January from the public celebration of Robert Burns's birthday in Waterville, at which, he proudly noted, he had been chosen chairman of the long evening's festivities, he related in a letter to his father his exhilaration in the experience of the winter sublime. It was the sort of pleasure he learned to appreciate as singular to American life, however different from those benefits of life in more cosmopolitan and cultured environments:

> I made the mare exert all her speed—but though her color is black she looked white enough all the way home[,] the perspiration freezing on her so as to resemble a white sheet. Such things to us are an oasis in the desert living as we do in the backwoods of civilization—you who are living at the very center of civilization can scarcely appreciate your advantages. One year here would give you a zest to your pleasures.[62]

Unfortunately for Thomas, such dramatic and colorful word pictures were not what either James or Lilly desired in his correspondence. In the fall of 1845, their various objections to his letters became especially insistent and explicit. In a letter of November 1, addressed to Lilly, Thomas had related at length the story of a trip to Milwaukee, across very poor roads, with a neighborhood friend to shop for supplies. The journey took a somewhat dangerous turn on the way back when they were lost in a rainstorm at night. The relation of this adventure, which obviously turned out well, took up almost all of his letter. The balance of what room was left on the final page was devoted, in increasingly smaller script on ever more crowded lines, to acknowledgment of a letter from James, inquiries about James's recently poor health, relation of the activities of various local people known to his father, and description of the growth of his medical practice. He neither asked questions about nor made any comments on Lilly's life. Though it is obvious to the reader that Thomas enjoyed writing at length about the adventure of his journey, he himself acknowledged, in remarks for Lilly, toward the crowded end of this letter, "I know I am a very bad letter writer—and many of my letters must disappoint you much—but never attribute such to any want of affection towards you[;] you are [surely?] in my mind."[63]

In response, it was James, not Lilly, whose voice often was crowded out by her father's, who replied to Thomas's letter, which, in its own self-critical remarks, had given him an opening to be critical of his son's letter. He bluntly pointed out the inadequacy of this narration:

> Your letter although a long one does not satisfy us, as it leaves so many things untold[;] if you could by any means put yourself, or rather fancy yourself placed in our position you would give us information on many things that perhaps you don't think worth communicating—you can fancy us following the same routine as when you left, but we have very little idea of your locality, its advantages and disadvantages, its scenery and production, your employment and [enjoyment?], as well as your hopes and fears.[64]

In using the first person plural, James made it seem as if he spoke for Lilly as well in his criticism of his son's letters, though Lilly is actually nowhere to be seen in these remarks. In fact, Lilly had already spoken, in fewer words but just as bluntly, earlier that autumn about the inadequacy of her brother's letters, and her criticisms were quite different. Her father was away on business, perhaps affording her the psychological opportunity she needed to address her brother directly. She found his letters self-absorbed, and characterized by few signs of interest in her and few expressions of affection. He had been married just six months before, and perhaps she sensed a shift in his affections away from her and toward Catherine. She wrote accusingly, "I feel that you are so much taken up with your own concerns that you do not care much about this part of the world—is it not so?"[65] It seems clear that the implication to be drawn was that he did not care either for his old home or for the people who lived there, including his sister.

While not without concern for his son's happiness or interest in vicarious tourism, what James wanted was to know what Thomas was making of the opportunities before him and how he was planning to take advantage of them, and perhaps, above all, in both contexts, how the money sent from London was being used. Lilly, on the other hand, desired intimate conversation, friendship, and the appearance of concern for her, partly, it seems, as we shall see when we analyze the protracted correspondence about resettlement in America, because of her discontent with the quality of her life in England.

Thomas Steel did not quite master the challenges posed by these complaints. He never completely surrendered the opportunity to gossip about his Wisconsin friends, or to write the adventure narrative he particularly enjoyed composing. He sometimes gave evidence of feeling the pressure of having to respond to letters that he received, when he had nothing to say, largely because his life at times seemed to him monotonous. He confessed toward the end of some of his letters that they were "poor"—meandering, shallow, and superficial—performances. He was sorry that his letters often seemed so self-involved. "My letters are all so selfish," he wrote to Lilly in 1846 in a brief letter that did not reveal a great deal of effort on his part, "I do not sorrow much about anybody else."[66]

But he also made many concessions to his father's demands for a different type of writing. His letters to his father increasingly developed discussions of farming, improvements to his land and home, property acquisitions, purchases of equipment and supplies, and other themes that ultimately touched on how James's subsidies were being used, and on whether there were likely to be a need for them in the future. In turn, these discussions, which comprised the heart of most of Thomas's letters, provided James with ample opportunity to give his son advice on numerous matters, but most especially on his medical practice and farming. He did not hesitate to advance views on how Thomas should cultivate his prairie acreage or care for his livestock on the basis of scientific treatises about soil chemistry or British newspaper articles about scientific farming. James also drew lessons from his own Scottish boyhood experience on farmland that probably had been under cultivation for more than a millennium.[67]

He was quick to react to Thomas's growing distress over the lack of money to be made in medicine and the desire expressed to leave medical practice entirely and concentrate on farming. Medicine might eventually provide enough income to make Thomas independent and it gave him great claims to respectability, so James urged him to continue his practice, but limit it to office visits at his home. He also suggested that Thomas open a dispensing pharmacy at home, and was willing to assist him by sending him, as he had been doing throughout these years, British pharmaceuticals.[68] These were topics that could be sustained by father and son over the course of many letters.

Thomas was less successful in addressing Lilly's problems with his letters, and increasingly depended just as much on Catherine's sisterly correspondence as on his own epistolary efforts to please her.[69] He wrote to Lilly as an individual much less frequently than he wrote to his father, whose questions about his activities seemed to require—because

James regularly gave him money—respectful, direct, and rapid answers.
Moreover, the two men shared masculine concerns. With Lilly, however,
Steel displayed awkwardness of the sort we have seen in a number of
other male correspondents writing to women. At times it bordered on
neglect. Often he appended a brief section for his sister in letters to
his father, or at least inquired about her, but this could hardly address
Lilly's feelings of being neglected, feelings that were probably heightened by the fact that it was she who assumed much of the responsibility
for acquiring and packing up the clothing, books, and other items that
comprised the elaborate gift boxes sent to Thomas from England.

When he did write to her as an individual, he did not succeed very
well in evoking strong affections, let alone a tone of intimate conversation, though he did discuss matters, such as politics and eventually spiritualism, that were close to his own heart. The tone might be fond, but
it was more likely to be didactic, and it is not at all clear that Lilly was
interested. Nor, as her unenthusiastic response to his feminism suggests,
did she necessarily agree with opinions that he held, which put her in a
difficult position. If her private sentiments were to resent his attempting
to be her tutor, she does not seem to have wished to use her letters to
argue with him. Her idea of the transnational communion of souls did
not include ideological or philosophical debate.

In time, Thomas Steel did find a theme, the reunification of his family in
Wisconsin, that he believed both his father and his sister would find
appropriate to their separate sets of interests. He developed this theme
with growing insistence as the years passed. In this at least, his letters
offered his sister a great deal—an alternative, which she seemed to desire, to the life she was leading. For his part, however, James Steel came
to wonder whether he had expressed himself too strongly on his desire
for practical content about prairie farming and the local economy.

James was deeply ambivalent about coming to America, and tried for
years to avoid relocating there without alienating his son. Perhaps he
had fears about traveling, or about the effects of the journey on his
health. Perhaps he could not bring himself to trust his son's judgments
about the ease of the journey, the beauties of the American landscape,
or the extent to which civilization had come to the American prairie.
But now, James's demand for practical content gave Thomas the opportunity to combine descriptions with increasingly aggressive advertise-
ments for his life in Wisconsin. Moreover, when James asked Thomas

about how his subsidies were being used, Thomas was able to argue that James should come to visit or resettle, and to see for himself and experience the fruits of his own generosity.

Gratitude does help to explain Thomas's conscious understanding of his passion to merge what was left of his birth family with the family he had formed in Wisconsin. Whatever the underlying psychological tensions and drives working at him might have been, and his experiments with spiritualism suggest they were profound enough, he acknowledged gnawing feelings of debt to his father for material help and emotional support. This debt was mixed perhaps with a degree of guilt for his past errors, which he could well imagine had exacted psychological as well as material hardships for his father. He also felt a sense of debt to his sister, for the money that Thomas received was that much less money that Lilly, James's principal legatee, would inherit.[70] He could never repay all this generosity and concern for his welfare, but if he could persuade his father to make a material as well as a moral commitment to coming to settle in America, he might buy James and Lilly land, bring it under cultivation, and have a new life awaiting them when they arrived in Wisconsin. This investment would provide a secure foundation for their resettlement in America—a basis for James's peace of mind in retirement and especially for Lilly's security and respectability after James's death, whether she remained single or eventually married. In a November 1845 letter addressed to Lilly in which he confessed to being "a very bad letter writer" whose correspondence failed to meet her expectations, he stated that not only was she frequently on his mind, but also that "every improvement I make I think how you will like it when you come out here along with my father."[71]

James Steel was not always as reluctant to come to the United States as he would prove to be during the years his son worked to induce him to do so.[72] He certainly had been unenthusiastic about his son's decision to cast his lot with the Utopians, and, according to Lilly, had predicted the consequences of doing so would be negative.[73] But while Thomas's decision to emigrate with the Utopians and his rapid disillusion with them probably did little to increase his credibility in James's estimation, there was no sign at first that James read his son's decision as an indictment of emigration as such.

From the offhanded way in which Thomas began to bring up the matter of emigration in his letters, it seems that there had been an informal understanding that once he was settled, a discussion of the possibility would begin. Less than a year after his arrival in Wisconsin, Thomas began to express the hope that his father and sister would join him.[74] At first, Thomas's goal was to have James and Lilly come for a seasonal visit, but soon these hopes escalated into more ambitious schemes: a visit of one or two years; a prolonged visit that was a test of whether they might wish to settle permanently; dividing their residence over the medium term between Wisconsin and London; and permanent emigration itself.

While James would shift his ground frequently on these proposals, and frustrate the realization of any of them for years, Lilly wanted to emigrate, though she did not have the authority to see her desires realized. Her life with her father in Britain does not seem to have been promising or emotionally fulfilling, and she wished for a change in her circumstances. In February 1845, she wrote of feeling "very solitary—and almost melancholy," even in the midst of the opportunities provided by a number of friendships, and in August of 1845 she wrote in an addendum to one of her father's letters that "she could not help wishing that my father and I were with you." Not long after her brother's apology later that year for his poor letter-writing, and his statement that everything he was doing to improve his property was being done with her future in mind, she went to hear a lecture about America by the travel writer James Buckingham, that impressed her greatly. America, she wrote Thomas, was destined to be a very great country, and added simply, with what seems evident longing, "I wonder if I shall ever see it?"[75] What made her statement especially telling were her complaints about her health in her letter six weeks previously, which was composed while her father was away and not, with his symbolic presence, looking over her shoulder. In a dark and distracted tone, quite different than in her other letters, she spoke of the decline of her health, but of her mental rather than her physical health. She complained of being nervous and excitable, and of being bothered by the London weather. She lamented the rapid march of time.[76]

A young woman in the throes of unhappiness about her characteristically female lack of options and the invariability of her routines, Lilly wrote that some male acquaintances were considering immigrating to America, so she was conscious that her peers (and perhaps potential suitors) were changing their lives.[77] Meanwhile, she was involved increasingly in an epistolary relationship with Catherine which promised that, if she were to go to America, she might gain a close friendship. Yet she gave no evidence of being able or willing to leave her father and come to America by herself. In short, she appeared to be without much control over her own future. In the decade-long discussion of whether James and Lilly would come to America, it would always be James, never Lilly, who took exception to plans advanced by Thomas to come to America.

From Thomas's perspective the most frustrating aspect of these discussions must have been the contradictory signals his father sent him about his desires. Within the year of his arrival in Wisconsin, Thomas proposed that James consider a visit, but only after the roads improved sufficiently to make travel from Milwaukee and around his neighborhood feasible.[78] The next year, 1845, he proposed a visit for "a year or two if not altogether."[79] He must have been encouraged when his father consented that same year, not long after this proposal, to provide the funds for the purchase of farmland, ultimately totaling 176 acres, adjacent to Thomas's own farm, which then totaled about forty acres. The idea was to secure Lilly's financial independence if and when she were "to come out and reside in this country." But Thomas also would soon argue that the two farms together would secure a foundation for the security of the larger, combined family, "making us independent."[80] The land purchase was eventually negotiated, and while those negotiations were underway, James himself spoke of the prospect of a visit, which Thomas then began to plan, a year in advance, for 1847. Late summer, he told his father, would be ideal, for he and Lilly could avoid the worst of the heat and the mosquitoes.[81] As this scheduling suggests, Thomas now began a cycle of making assumptions about the future and planning elaborately for it on the strength of his father's somewhat tentative promises.

Late summer 1847 came, and no travel plans were announced. But James now promised that he and Lilly would come to Wisconsin in two years. Though disappointed, Thomas at least had a commitment and a date for their arrival. He grew anxious nonetheless, as political instability spread across Europe. He was certain that revolution was in the offing in Britain and urged his father to consider leaving England earlier, in late 1848 or early 1849.[82] He began to project plans for their arrival, whether in anticipation that revolution would soon force them into exile, or that the original date of September 1849 would continue to be their time for leaving England. He would either enlarge his house to accommodate them, or build a larger one on the shore of Spring Lake, which bordered his property.[83]

Fretting that they might find local society somewhat thin, he encouraged them to bring out some of their English friends, and perhaps start a little community of their own.[84] For Lilly, he described at considerable length attractive aspects of the life that she would have: a large garden, the growing availability of books, and plans to go to Milwaukee and purchase a piano that she would play.[85] When his father worked out pension arrangements with his employer, he wrote James, he could have his money placed in a British bank, and then travel to Canada in the summer, thus simultaneously getting his money, enjoying a pleasant vacation on the Great Lakes, and escaping the heat.[86] As if these inducements would not be enough, his young son was recruited, via the lad's quoted invitations, to tell his grandfather and his aunt in one of his father's letters that he wished them to come visit him.[87]

The year 1849 began promisingly, with James writing in January that he had been reading about travel on the Mississippi River, as if perhaps he were getting ready to take the journey himself.[88] But ominous signs soon appeared. Lilly had unexpectedly become silent on their plans, and James was ill over the winter. For Thomas, James's health was proof that he needed to retire and come to a healthier climate, so again he wrote of plans to enlarge the house and of the need to buy a piano for Lilly.[89] But in May, James announced that they could not travel that year. The principal reason given was that James had failed to secure the proper retirement arrangements, but other arguments, too, now made their appearance in his letters: he had been sick and the American climate was unhealthy, he had heard that travel in the United States was very primitive, and his overall impression was that the United States was still a very rough sort of place. He began to make more detailed inquiries about Thomas's region and its commercial potential, as if looking for impediments to resettlement. Soon he would begin criticizing the American government.[90]

Thomas responded to all these questions and contentions, though not always entirely convincingly. Travel from the East Coast to Wisconsin was easy, efficient, and inexpensive.[91] His community was civilized in ways that even Londoners would appreciate. He wrote to Lilly that he had recently been to an event in which the table had been adorned with fine china and silver, and such good things to eat as oranges, almonds, and raisins.[92] A number of retail stores were about to open, and there was unlimited potential for the development of water power.[93] He defended the American government, and spoke of the superiority of republican institutions.[94] Forgetting that he had written in February that he was covered with boils and that the whole family was sick with one malady or another he claimed that the climate was healthier than England's.[95] But it soon became clear that James and Lilly were not coming to Wisconsin, and the subject declined in the family correspondence.

In the fall of 1851 discussion recommenced, only to reach yet another impasse just a few months later. James recently had retired, so he could no longer plead that he still had to negotiate his pension and complete his work. He now wrote that he was thinking of living in Milwaukee rather than with Thomas, who responded enthusiastically, stating that with their ample funds James and Lilly could purchase a large house and live very well in the city.[96] Thomas began to plan for their arrival in 1852. He wrote to Lilly in December that they should think of coming out for a two-year trial period, and reach a conclusion at the end of that time about the permanency of their removal to Wisconsin.[97] As the time for Lilly and James to announce their travel plans approached, however, ominous signs again began to appear. James again raised questions about the difficulties of traveling within the United States and about the general quality of American life.[98] Thomas nonetheless continued to make plans for their arrival and began to improve his house in the anticipation that Lilly and James would be living, perhaps at least at the start of their stay, with him. In May, his hopes were again dashed. Lilly explained in a letter received early in the month that James now argued that Thomas had never really urged him to come for a visit or to emigrate, and he was thus not conscious of any commitment he had made to do so. Under these circumstances, he felt justified announcing that he and Lilly had no intention of coming to America, though whether in the short term or in the long term is unclear.[99]

Thomas might be forgiven had he shown some impatience with this disingenuous argument, for in letter after letter for years they had discussed uniting the family in Wisconsin. Yet he now showed admirable restraint on hearing this news. He acknowledged the evidence that the process of making a decision about coming to Wisconsin had caused his father considerable anxiety, and said he was pleased that at least this source of pain had been removed from the lives of his father and sister.[100] He subsequently said almost nothing again on the subject, at least insofar as the archived correspondence reveals, other than to note rather plaintively, but tactfully in a March 1854 letter to his father, "I cannot help wishing sometimes you and Lilly were out here with your means of living secured."[101]

It was during that winter of shattered hopes that he engaged in his most intense experiments with spiritualism, conjuring up the spirit of his mother. Prior to this time, he had mentioned his long-dead mother only once in his correspondence with Lilly and James, and the circumstances were telling ones. When, in February of 1845, he had moved into his new house and was preparing for marriage to Catherine, one of the first things he asked his father to send him was a portrait of his mother.[102]

Now he attempted to move beyond this symbolic reconstitution of family. Of course, it is overly simplistic to suggest that because Thomas Steel could not be united at this time with the living members of his family, he worked instead at being united with those who were dead. Spiritualism, it has been observed, did have a place in the ongoing development of Thomas Steel's formal political and religious thinking. His embrace of spiritualism was certainly reflective of and further stimulation for the millennial mood, which overtook him in the late 1840s and early 1850s, and which was expressed in his growing support for secular reform, European revolution, and Universalism.

That mood, too, probably influenced his feelings about family reunification, even though we must also be aware of the deeper psychological underpinnings of those feelings. If, as Christopher Lasch and others have observed, the nuclear family ideal of unity, affection, companionship, and mutual understanding under one roof has been a type of privatized bourgeois utopia throughout modern Western history, Steel's often frustrated desire to unite his family may well be seen as a sort of privatized correlative of his public embrace of other ideas about the salvation of humanity.[103]

Yet there seems little doubt that his investigations of the spirit world also expressed unresolved longings about his own family. There are not only the "conversations" with his mother that revealed his concern for and anxieties about her welfare and that of his sister Eliza, but there was another conversation that spoke directly to his concerns about living members of his family. In May of 1853, he wrote Lilly of a recent seance in which he and Catherine were the only participants, and in which his mother had "purported to be with us." He inquired of his

mother's spirit about Lilly's welfare, even though he was in routine letter contact with his father and sister. Through vigorous movement of
the table in response to his questions, the spirit indicated that Lilly was
at that moment sick and without medical care—a problem, of course,
that Thomas, as a physician, could well have addressed if only his father had consented to allow him to realize his sense of obligation to his
sister. We recall that almost twenty years before, during his failed first
emigration Steel had experienced the same anxiety about his powerlessness to treat illness in the family from which he was then absent. He
seemed destined, by personal history and by profession, to fill the vacuum created by separation with anxieties about the health of loved ones
for whom he felt responsibility.[104]

Thomas Steel's prolonged experience of longing, frustration, and distress finally ended, along with his prodigious letter-writing to England
in behalf of the unified family he so profoundly desired, in 1854 when
James Steel finally consented to come out to America with Lilly. While
the precise circumstances are not clear, because the exchange of letters ends abruptly, James and Lilly immigrated to Wisconsin that year,
with very different consequences for each of them. James died shortly
after arriving in the United States. In what proved to be his last con-
test of wills with his son James had proven himself right, for either
America or the journey there did not agree with him.[105] Whether it was
their original intention to remain permanently in the United States or
not, Lilly, who now had no reason to return to England, stayed in Wisconsin, where in 1861 she married Catherine's brother, James Alfred
Freeman.[106] Especially after the loss of his father, the marriage must
have greatly pleased Thomas Steel, for it further deepened the existing community of family that surrounded him and assisted in securing
the future of his sister, about whom he had been anxious for so many
years. There is no evidence that Steel ever involved himself again with
spiritualism.

What can we make of Thomas Steel's narrative, as I have constructed
it out of this correspondence, and what might it more generally tell us
about immigrants? Obviously Steel strains our conception of the typical
immigrant population. Certainly, if we take the conventional socioeconomic criteria, there cannot be any doubt that Steel is in a minority.
He was highly educated, cultivated, well-read, and articulate. He was a
professional and well-respected, if less than frequently well-paid, in the

community in which he was regarded as a reliable and humane healer. He enjoyed substantial, though hardly unproblematic, resources in the form of subsidies from his father that aided in his achievement of stability and success in Wisconsin.

Yet in his preoccupation with the work of the immigrant's second project, Steel had much in common with many other immigrants, whether we think of the equally articulate Niblock and Archbald, or the humbler, less educated and less conventionally articulate population of artisans, industrial workers, and farmers such as Kate and Jim Bond. Steel had greater resources to achieve his goals than did the Bonds, but, as it turns out, his narrative reveals the limits of those resources to achieve the results Steel and other immigrants so often desired.

In Steel's individual case, family reunification negotiated through the post turned out to be at least as fraught with emotional stresses, longstanding tensions, and situational misunderstandings as were the actual face-to-face relations of people who were family to one another. The achievement of that goal was not as simple a matter as we might be led to believe by the alluring metaphor of chain migration, through which we visualize strong links added to one another in steady, methodical fashion. Analysis of the ways in which the chains were forged and the consequences of forging them requires us to penetrate the surfaces of immigrant life.

But so, too, does the analysis of any aspect of the problem of personal identity, which was at the emotional core of the quest for family reunification, that immigrant personal correspondence provides keys for unlocking. Everywhere we turn the immigrants' letters cause us anxiety about the confident generalizations derived from such familiar conceptual models as assimilation and ethnicity, which prove not quite adequate for explaining the complexity of individual lives. Whether we are thinking about Thomas Spencer Niblock, or Kate Bond, or Mary Ann Archbald, or finally Thomas Steel, by way of conclusion we may find it necessary to acknowledge that to study the ethnic group or any other large cohort is not always to find a way to know the individual. Indeed, held up to the example of the individual, we may well come to understand that we do not know the cohort nearly as confidently as we thought we did.

Abbreviations for Archives and Repositories Consulted

CCCC	Cape Cod Community College
CU	Cornell University
IHS	Indiana Historical Society
ISHS	Illinois State Historical Society
NAC	National Archives of Canada
NLA	National Library of Australia
NLI	National Library of Ireland
NYPL	New York Public Library
OHS	Ohio Historical Society
PRONI	Public Record Office of Northern Ireland
PSU	Pennsylvania State University
RSFI	Religious Society of Friends in Ireland
SLKE	Sevenoaks Library, Kent, England
SmC	Smith College
TMRL	Toronto Metropolitan Research Library
WHS	Wisconsin Historical Society

Notes ⁴⁸ ᵖ⁻ᵃᵍᵉˢ ⁴⁹ ⁿᵒᵗᵉˢ

NOTES TO THE INTRODUCTION

1. My interest in this book is in immigrant letters to family and friends in the homeland. The reader should be aware, however, that, though discussed in this book only occasionally, immigrants wrote business letters and other types of personal letters, principally to other immigrants, coethnics, and non-coethnic, native-born settlers in the host societies. Whether because of the vagaries of the processes of saving and collection, or the fact that fewer of these were written, they appear to be much fewer in number. See H. Arnold Barton, "Neglected Types of Correspondence as Sources for Swedish-American History," *Swedish-American Historical Quarterly* 33 n. 2 (1982): 76–8.

On the psychological and material purposes of personal correspondence for the ordinary letter-writing immigrant in the historical past, see Eric Richards, "A Voice from Below: Benjamin Boyce in South Australia, 1839–1846," *Labour History* (Australia) 27 (November 1974): 65; Charlotte Erickson, *Invisible Immigrants: The Adaptation of English and Scottish Immigrants in Nineteenth-Century America* (Coral Gables: University of Miami Press, 1972), 5–7; H. Arnold Barton, "Two Versions of the Immigrant Experience," *Swedish Pioneer Historical Quarterly* 30 n. 3 (1979): 159–61; Niels Peter Stilling, "The Significance of the Private Letter in Immigration History," *The Bridge* 15 n. 1 (1992): 35–50.

2. The special qualities of handwritten, personal letters were made clear to the Pakistani immigrant cabdriver, Hamid Ali, when he took advantage of the availability of a video teleconferencing facility in Brooklyn, at $5 a minute, to call-see his family in his homeland. For four minutes his sister "harangued him for not writing. He protested that he phoned weekly; his sister told him letters were better; they could be fingered and re-read and kept under pillows." Deborah Sontag and Celia W. Duggar, "The New Immigrant Tide: A Shuttle between Worlds," *New York Times* (July 19, 1998). Also see Sarah J. Mahler, "Theoretical and Empirical Contributions toward a Research Agenda for Transnationalism," *Transnationalism from Below*, Michael Peter Smith and Luis Eduardo Guarnico, *Comparative Urban and Community Research*, v. 6 (New Brunswick: Transaction Publishers, 1998), 76–81.

3. A. Langton, *Early Days in Upper Canada: Letters of John Langton from the Backwoods of Upper Canada and the Audit Office of the Province of Canada* (Toronto: Macmillan, 1926); John Langton to father, Fenelon, Upper Canada, February 28, 1834, NAC; George Flower, *Diary, v. II [1816–]*, Chicago Historical Society; George Flower Letterbook, 1816–1817, George Flower Letters, ISHS.

4. Thomas Mallon, *A Book of One's Own: People and Their Diaries* (New York: Ticknor and Fields, 1984); Janet Gurkin Altman, *Epistolarity: Approaches to a Form* (Columbus: Ohio State University Press, 1982); William Merrill Decker, *Epistolary Practices: Letter Writing in America before Telecommunications* (Chapel Hill: University of North Carolina Press, 1998); Bruce Redford, *The Converse of the Pen: Acts of Intimacy in the*

Eighteenth-Century Familiar Letter (Chicago: University of Chicago Press, 1986); Martine Reid, "Ecriture Intime et Destinaire," and Bernard Beugnot, "De l'Invention Epistolaire: A la Maniere de Soi," in *L'Epistolarité à Travers les Siècles: Geste de Communication et/ou d'Écriture*, ed. Mirelle Bossis and Charles D. Parker (Stuttgart: Franz Steiner Verlag, 1990), 20–6, 29–38.

5. Sydney Shoemaker, *Self-Knowledge and Self-Identity* (Ithaca: Cornell University Press, 1963); Jerome Bruner, *Actual Minds, Possible Worlds* (Cambridge: Harvard University Press, 1986), and *idem, Acts of Meanings* (Cambridge: Harvard University Press, 1990), and *idem*, "Life as Narrative," *Social Research* 54 (Spring 1987): 11–32; Joseph B. Jahasz, "Social Identity in the Context of Human and Personal Identity," in *Studies in Social Identity*, ed. Theodore R. Sarbin and Carl E. Scheibe (New York: Praeger, 1983): 289–318.

6. Redford, *The Converse of the Pen*, 9, 16.

7. A list of titles of outstanding, representative works on European immigrants would be very difficult to create without major omissions, but I have in mind such works on immigrant social bonds as, for example, these studies, each of them distinctive in conceptualization or methodology, and in some cases, pioneering: Micaela di Leonardo, *The Varieties of Ethnic Experience: Kinship, Class, and Gender among California Italian-Americans* (Ithaca: Cornell University Press, 1984); Bruce Elliott, *Irish Migrants in the Canadas: A New Approach* (Kingston and Montreal: McGill-Queen's University Press, 1988); Victor Greene, *For God and Country: The Rise of Polish and Lithuanian Ethnic Consciousness in America, 1860–1910* (Madison: Wisconsin Historical Society, 1975); Jon Gjerde, *From Peasants to Farmers: The Migration from Balestrand, Norway to the Upper Middle West* (New York: Cambridge University Press, 1985), and *idem, The Minds of The West: Ethnocultural Evolution in the Rural Middle West, 1830–1917* (Chapel Hill: University of North Carolina Press, 1997); Walter D. Kamphoefner, *The Westfalians: From Germany to Missouri* (Princeton: Princeton University Press, 1987); Virginia Yans McLaughlin, *Family and Community: Italian Immigrants in Buffalo, 1880–1930* (Ithaca: Cornell University Press, 1971); Timothy J. Meagher, *Inventing Irish America: Generation, Class, and Ethnic Identity in a New England City, 1880–1928* (Notre Dame: University of Notre Dame Press, 2001); Deborah Dash Moore, *At Home in America: Second Generation New York Jews* (New York: Columbia University Press, 1981); Robert Orsi, *The Madonna of 115th Street: Faith and Community in Italian Harlem, 1880–1950* (New Haven: Yale University Press, 1985).

8. David A. Gerber, "Ethnic Identification and the Project of Individual Identity: The Life of Mary Ann Wodrow Archbald (1768–1840) of Little Cumbrae Island, Scotland, and Auriesville, New York," *Immigrants and Minorities* 17 (July 1998): 1–22; Philip Gleason, "Identifying Identity: A Semantic History," in Gleason, *Speaking of Diversity: Language and Ethnicity in Twentieth-Century America* (Baltimore: Johns Hopkins University Press, 1992), 123–49.

9. The word "correspondence" seems to have long been associated with the special relationship of parties engaged in an epistolary exchange. In English, according to *The Compact Edition of the Oxford English Dictionary*, 1971 ed., s.v. "correspondence," it has evolved in the direction of expressing "mutual response, the answering of things to each other; but before its adoption in English, it had been extended so as to express the action or relation of one side only without however abandoning the mutual notion, which is distinctive in the modern sense of epistolary correspondent." On the personal letter as a form of relationship, see Reid, "Ecriture Intime et Destinaire"; Beugnot, "De l'Invention Epistolaire"; Decker, *Epistolary Practices*; Redford, *Converse of the Pen*.

10. A perspective advanced with intelligence and energy in Kathleen Anne DeHaan, "'He Looks Like a Yankee in His New Suit.' Immigrant Rhetoric: Dutch Immigrant Letters as Forums for Shifting Immigrant Identities" (Ph.D. diss., Northwestern University, 1998).

11. Elizabeth J. MacArthur, *Extravagant Narratives: Closure and Dynamics in the Epistolary Form* (Princeton: Princeton University Press, 1990).

12. Suggestions toward the conceptualization of the problem of the letter as artifact are found in Stephen Fender, *Sea Changes: British Emigration and American Literature* (Cambridge: Cambridge University Press, 1992), 18–19; David Fitzpatrick, *Oceans of Consolation: Personal Accounts of Irish Migration to Australia* (Ithaca: Cornell University Press, 1994), 28; Wendy Cameron, Sheila Haines, Mary McDougall Maude, eds., *English Immigrant Voices: Labourers' Letters from Upper Canada in the 1830s* (Montreal-Kingston: McGill-Queen's University Press, 2000), xxi, xxvi; and in the general remarks in David Lowenthal, *The Past Is a Foreign Country* (Cambridge: Cambridge University Press, 1985), 43–4, 365–7; Wolfgang Helbich and Walter D. Kamphoefner, "How Representative Are Emigrant Letters? An Exploration of the German Case," in *Letters across Borders: The Epistolary Practices of International Migrants,* ed. Bruce Elliott, David A. Gerber, and Suzanne Sinke (New York: Palgrave, 2006).

13. Fender, *Sea Changes,* 17–20, uses the suggestive term "vernacular publication" to conceptualize the process by which the letters of British emigrants in North America were written, saved, and ultimately archived, thus to be transformed into documents. One might usefully appropriate the term, as has Orm Øverland, "Learning to Read Immigrant Letters: Reflections towards a Textual Theory," in *Norwegian-American Essays,* ed. Øyvind T. Gulliksen et al. (Oslo: Norwegian American Historical Association, Norway, 1996): 211–5, to refer to acts of sharing personal letters through oral communications, which not only served to make public a private letter, but also elevated it within its own lifetime from a private writing to a social document that satisfied the hunger for information about people who had emigrated and about the destinations in the new worlds where they had resettled.

On the history of political discourse through correspondence among eighteenth-century European intellectuals, see Dina Goodman, *The Republic of Letters: A Cultural History of the French Enlightenment* (Ithaca: Cornell University Press, 1994).

14. William Cobbett, *The Emigrant's Guide; in Ten Letters Addressed to the Tax-Payers of England; Containing Information of Every Kind, Necessary to Persons Who Are About to Emigrate; Including Several Authentic and Most Interesting Letters from English Emigrants, Now in America to Their Relations in England* (London: William Cobbett, 1829).

15. Anon ["An Immigrant Farmer . . ."], *The Emigrant to North America from Memoranda of a Settler in Canada* (Montreal: N.p., 1843). For more on such editorial manipulations in the Canadian context, see Terry McDonald, "Come to Canada While You Have a Chance: A Cautionary Tale of English Emigrant Letters in Upper Canada," *Ontario History* 91 (Autumn 1999): 111–30.

16. Erickson, *Invisible Immigrants;* Ronald Wells, ed., *Ulster Migration to America: Letters of Three Families* (New York: Peter Lang, 1991).

17. In addition to the Grayston-Bond Letters, similar efforts to use both the edited and original versions of collections that have been of interest to both Professor Erickson and me were made in the case of the Hails, Laing, and Roberts letter-series. All four of these collections are archived at the Collection of Regional History at Cornell University.

18. Oscar Handlin, *The Uprooted: The Epic Story of the Great Migrations That Made the American People* (New York: Grosset and Dunlap, 1951); John Bodnar, *The*

Transplanted: A History of Immigrants in Urban America (Bloomington: Indiana University Press, 1985).

19. Rowland Berthoff, *British Immigrants in Industrial America, 1790–1950* (Cambridge: Harvard University Press, 1953); Erickson, *Invisible Immigrants*, and *idem, Leaving England: Essays on British Emigration in the Nineteenth Century* (Ithaca: Cornell University Press, 1994); William Van Vugt, *Britain to America: Mid-Nineteenth-Century Immigrants in the United States* (Urbana: University of Illinois Press, 1999).

20. Van Vugt, *Britain to America,* 50–9; Erickson, "Agrarian Myths of English Immigrants," in *idem, Leaving England,* 34–59.

21. Erickson, "British Immigrants in the Old Northwest, 1815–1860," in *idem, Leaving England,* 60–86. This view of British migration to the United States in the nineteenth century is confirmed in an expert recent synthesis of the history of *worldwide* British emigration; Eric Richards, *Britannia's Children: Emigration from England, Scotland, Wales, and Ireland since 1600* (London and New York: Hambledon and London, 2004), 172–3.

22. Van Vugt, *Britain to America,* 50–9; Erickson, "Agrarian Myths of English Immigrants," 34–59; for Greenlee's letters, see Wells, ed., *Ulster Migration to America,* 28–71.

23. Berthoff, *British Immigrants in Industrial America,* 143–208; Van Vugt, *Britain to America,* 148–52; Erickson, *Invisible Immigrants, passim.*

24. Bruce S. Elliott, "English," in *An Encyclopedia of Canada's People,* ed. Robert Paul Magosi (Toronto: University of Toronto Press, 1999), 462–88, and in *ibid., idem,* "Irish Protestants," 763–83, and J. M. Bumstead, "Scots," 1115–42; Elliott, *Irish Migrants in the Canadas*; James White McAuly, "Under the Orange Banner: Reflection on the Northern Protestant Experience of Emigration," in *The Irish World Wide: History, Heritage, Identity,* vol. 5, *Religion and Identity,* ed. Patrick O'Sullivan (Leicester: Leicester University Press, 1996), 48–50. J. R. Miller, "Anti-Catholicism in Canada: From the British Conquest to the Great War," in *Creed and Culture: The Place of English-Speaking Catholics in Canadian Society, 1750–1930,* ed. Terence Murphy and Gerald Stortz (Montreal and Kingston: McGill-Queen's University Press, 1993), 25–48; William Jenkins, "Between the Lodge and the Meeting-House: Mapping Irish Protestant Identities and Social Worlds in Late Victorian Toronto," *Social and Cultural Geography* 4, n. 1 (2003): 75–97. Robert J. Grace, "From Ireland to Canada: An Historiographical Overview of the Major Issues," *The Immigration and Ethnic History Newsletter* XXXVI (November 2004): 1, 8.

25. Bumstead, "Scots," 1139–40; Elliott, "English," 483–4; Ralph Wade to William Wade, Hope Township, Canada West, February 14, 1851, December 26, 1854, Ralph Wade to Friends, Hope Township, Canada West, November 12, 1856 (quote), December 19, 1857 (quote), May 14, 1858, October 4, 1866, Robert Wade Letters and Family Papers, MG 24I127, NAC.

26. Erickson, *Invisible Immigrants,* 3; Wilbur S. Shepperson, *Emigration and Disenchantment: Portraits of Englishmen Repatriated from the United States* (Norman: University of Oklahoma Press, 1965), 49–50, 182–3, 194. Cf. Richards, *Britannia's Children,* 173, which maintains that the British felt "little sense of alienation" in the United States, but doesn't analyze ordinary social encounters or attitudes among the British in the United States.

27. Linda Colley, *Britons: Forging the Nation, 1707–1837* (New Haven: Yale University Press, 1992), 17–54, 327–36, and *idem, The Significance of the Frontier in British History* (Austin: British Studies, University of Texas, 1995), 13–15. See also Keith Robbins, *Great Britain: Identities, Institutions, and the Idea of Britishness* (New York: Addison, Wesley, Longman, 1998), 237–59; Krishan Kumar, *The Making of English National Identity* (Cambridge: Cambridge University Press, 2003), 158–65; Berthoff, *British Immi-*

grants in Industrial America, 185–208; E. R. Norman, *Anti-Catholicism in Victorian England* (London: George Allen and Unwin, 1968); Donald Harman Akenson, *God's People: Covenant and Land in South Africa, Israel, and Ulster* (Ithaca: Cornell University Press, 1992), 97–150, *passim*; Desmond Bowen, *History and the Shaping of Irish Protestantism* (New York: Peter Lang, 1995).

Some historians of Ireland would argue that such an interpretation of the anti-Catholic foundations of Britishness, however much it may work for the English or Scots, will not necessarily work for the Irish Protestants, whose Britishness, they would argue, cannot be assumed but must be proven. This is the view presented by Kerby Miller, Arnold Schrier, Bruce Boling, and David N. Doyle in their compendious edition of the writings of Irish immigrants to North America, *Irish Immigrants in the Land of Canaan: Letters and Memoirs from Colonial and Revolutionary America, 1675–1815* (New York: Oxford University Press, 2003). Miller and his associates argue that in the eighteenth century, and especially in the revolutionary era from 1770 to 1815, Irish Protestants and Catholics shared common political views and aspirations and a sense of common destiny that was larger than their sectarian differences. Whether or not this is actually the case, we may leave it up to historians of Ireland to decide. What is significant for the present study, which concerns the nineteenth century, is that Miller and his associates also argue that the sense of common identity they find in the era represented in the documents they have collected declines rapidly after 1815, in consequence of which Irish Protestants can be found adopting strongly anti-Catholic ideological, political, and social orientations. See *ibid.*, 8–10. In contrast, Donald Harman Akenson, *Small Differences: Irish Catholics and Irish Protestants, 1815–1822—An International Perspective* (Montreal and Kingston: McGill-Queen's University Press, 1988), argues that the two peoples had much in common in the nineteenth century as far as the social patterns of daily life. Akenson is much less successful arguing that either group recognized this, or cared to attempt to do so.

28. Colley, *Britons*, 329–32; Robbins, *Great Britain*, 277–81; Norman, *Anti-Catholicism in Victorian Britain*, 16–17; Akenson, *Small Differences*, 108–26.

29. L. Perry Curtis, *Anglo-Saxons and Celts: A Study of Anti-Irish Prejudice in Victorian England* (Bridgeport: University of Bridgeport Press, 1968); Colley, *Britons*, 35.

30. John Fisher to Lydia Fisher, Brothers and Sisters, Palmyra, NY, June 20, 1830, in Erickson, *Invisible Immigrants*, 113.

31. Henry Johnson to Jane Johnson, Hamilton, Canada West, September 18, 1848, McConnell-Johnson Letters, TMRL; Louise Wyatt, ed., "The Johnson Letters," *Ontario History* 40, n. 1 (1948): 27–9.

32. John Kerr to John Graham, Napoleon, AK, May 25, 1851, in Wells, ed., *Ulster Migration to America*, 159–60, and 115, 123, 126, 157–61 for more on Kerr's ambivalent views on Ireland's Catholics.

33. Mary Ann Archbald, to Governor [Dewitt] Clinton, Riverbank, October 1821, History of Women Collection, SmC.

34. Van Vugt, *Britain to America*, 139–48.

35. Catherine Bond to Brother, Milford, CT, July 5, 1870, Catherine Bond to Ellen, Milford, CT, December 1, 1870, CU, Van Vugt, *Britain to America*, 139–48.

36. John Wade to Ralph Wade, Hamilton, Smith Creek, Upper Canada, September 9, 1835, NAC.

37. Henry Johnson to Jane Johnson, Hamilton, Canada West, September 18, 1848, TMRL.

38. Shepperson, *Emigration and Disenchantment*, 16–17, 70, 84, 194–5; Erickson, *Invisible Immigrants*, *passim*.

39. Robin Cohen, "The Fuzzy Frontiers of Identity: The British Case," *Social Identities*

1, n. 1 (1995): 42; T. C. Smout, "Problems of Nationalism, Identity and Improvement in Later Eighteenth-Century Scotland," in *Improvement and Enlightenment,* ed. Tom Devine, *Proceedings of the Scottish Historical Studies Seminar,* University of Strathclyde, 1987–8 (Edinburgh: John Donald, 1987), 11.

40. Henry Johnson to Jane Johnson, Hamilton, Canada West, September 18, 1848, TMRL.

41. Bruno Ramirez, *Crossing the 49th Parallel: Migration from Canada to the United States, 1900–1930* (Ithaca: Cornell University Press, 2001), 1–14; Ninette Kelley and Michael Trebilcock, *The Making of the Mosaic: A History of Canadian Immigration Policy* (Toronto: University of Toronto Press, 2000), 50, 53.

42. Mary Ann Archbald to Margaret Wodrow, Riverbank, August 10, 1822, SmC.

43. Thomas Steel to James Steel, Milwaukee County, May 29, 1846, February 9, 1848, June 3, 1849, Thomas Steel (1809–1896) Papers, 1660–1909, Wis Mss 51PB, WHS.

44. John Kerr to John Graham, Pittsburgh, PA, June 16, 1843, January 23, 1844, in Wells, ed., *Ulster Migration to America,* 118, 121.

NOTES TO PART I

1. Two recent and very significant works that make use of immigrant letters extensively in this way, as opposed to in occasional references, are Kerby Miller, *Emigrants and Exiles: Ireland and the Irish Exodus to North America* (New York: Oxford University Press, 1985); and Stephen Fender, *Sea Changes: British Emigration and American Literature* (Cambridge: Cambridge University Press, 1992). Miller uses some five thousand Irish immigrant letters to advance one argument: many Irish emigrants felt themselves less voluntary immigrants in search of opportunity and freedom than exiles, who were pushed out of their homeland as a consequence of British oppression. Fender also uses letters to advance a single argument: immigrants felt it necessary to advance the virtues of the lands in which they settled in direct proportion to their continuing emotional attachment to the homelands from which they knew themselves to be permanently separated. Both authors advance important ideas, but of necessity their reading of immigrant letters must be limited to the thesis they wish to prove, a thesis which stands quite apart from the purposes in writing of the immigrant letter-writers.

2. Among these recent collections, and including a few outstanding ones that are concerned with immigrants to other destinations than North America, are Charlotte Erickson, *Invisible Immigrants: The Adaptation of English and Scottish Immigrants in Nineteenth-Century America* (Coral Gables: University of Miami Press, 1972); Samuel L. Bailey and Franco Ramella, eds., *One Family, Two Worlds: An Italian Family's Correspondence Across the Atlantic, 1901–1922* (New Brunswick: Rutgers University Press, 1988); H. Arnold Barton, ed., *Letters from the Promised Land: Swedes in America, 1840–1914* (Minneapolis: University of Minnesota Press, 1975); Herbert Brinks, ed., *Dutch American Voices: Letters from the United States, 1850–1930* (Ithaca: Cornell University Press, 1995); Frederick Hale, ed., *Danes in America* (Seattle: University of Washington Press, 1984); and *idem,* ed., *Their Own Saga: Letters from the Norwegian Global Migration* (Minneapolis: University of Minnesota Press, 1986); Walter D. Kamphoefner, Wolfgang Helbich, and Ulrike Sommer, eds., *News from the Land of Freedom: German Immigrants Write Home* (Ithaca: Cornell University Press, 1991); Wendy Cameron, Sheila Haines, and Mary McDougall Maude, eds., *English Immigrant Voices: Labourers' Letters from Upper Canada in the 1830s* (Montreal and Kingston: McGill-Queen's University Press, 2000); Patrick O'Farrell, ed., *Letters from Irish Australia, 1825–1925* (Sydney and Belfast: New

South Wales University Press and Ulster Historical Foundation, 1984); Leo Schelbert and Hedwig Rapport, *Alles Ist Ganz Anders Hier: Auswandererschicksale in Briefen aus Zwei Jahrhunderten* (Freiburg: Walter-Verlag, 1977); Josephine Wtulich, ed. and trans., *Writing Home: Immigrants in Brazil and in the United States, 1890–1891* (Boulder: Eastern European Monographs, 1986); Adolph E. Schroeder and Carla Schultz-Geisberg, eds., *Hold Dear as Always: Jette, A German Immigrant Life in Letters* (Columbia: University of Missouri Press, 1988); Selveig Zempel, ed., *In Their Own Words: Letters from Norwegian Immigrants* (Minneapolis: University of Minnesota Press, 1991); Kerby A. Miller, Arnold Schrier, Bruce D. Boling, and David N. Doyle, *Irish Immigrants in the Land of Canaan: Letters and Memoirs from Colonial and Revolutionary America, 1675–1815* (New York: Oxford University Press, 2003).

3. Among the collections of the past, see Theodore Blegen, ed., *Land of Their Choice: The Immigrants Write Home* (Minneapolis: University of Minnesota Press, 1955); Alan Conway, ed., *The Welsh in America: The Immigrants Write Home* (Minneapolis: University of Minnesota Press, 1961); Henry S. Lucas, ed., *Dutch Immigrant Memoirs and Other Writings*, 2 vols. (Assen: Van Gorcum, 1955); George Stephenson, ed., "Typical 'America Letters,'" *Yearbook of the Swedish Historical Society of America* 7 (1921): 52–93.

4. These points are made with considerable skill by Paula S. Fass, "Cultural History/Social History: Some Reflections on a Continuing Dialogue," *Journal of Social History* 37 (Fall 2003): 39–46.

NOTES TO CHAPTER 1

1. William I. Thomas and Florian Znaniecki, *The Polish Peasant in Europe and America,* 5 volumes, vols. 1 and 2 (Chicago: University of Chicago Press, 1918), vols. 3, 4, and 5 (Boston: Badger, 1919–1920). (The notes will follow the 1928 two-volume reprint edition, which used the original plates of the first printings, published at New York City by Alfred Knopf.) Three statements of the decisive general contribution of the work are Dorothy Ross, *The Origins of American Social Science* (New York: Cambridge University Press, 1991); Lester R. Kurtz, *Evaluating Chicago Sociology: A Guide to the Literature with an Annotated Bibliography* (Chicago: University of Chicago Press, 1984); Norbert Wiley, "Early American Sociology and *The Polish Peasant*," *Sociological Theory* 4 (Spring 1986): 20–34.

2. Eli Zaretsky, ed., "Editor's Introduction," in *The Polish Peasant in Europe and America* (Urbana: University of Illinois Press, 1984), 3; Ross, *The Origins of American Social Science,* 435; and see also Herbert Blumer, *Critiques of Research in the Social Sciences, I: An Appraisal of Thomas and Znaniecki's "The Polish Peasant in Europe and America,"* (New York: Social Science Research Council, 1939), for the proceedings of a conference called by the Social Science Research Council to appraise the book, which was held as a consequence of the vote that named it the most influential work of the last two decades in sociology.

3. Marcus Lee Hansen, "The History of American Immigration as a Field for Research," *American Historical Review* 32 (April 1927): 500–18; George Stephenson, ed., "Typical 'America Letters,'" *Swedish Historical Society Yearbook* 7 (1921): 52, and *idem,* "The Background of the Beginnings of Swedish Immigration," *American Historical Review* 31 (July 1926): 708–31; "When America Was the Land of Canaan," *Minnesota History* 10 (September 1929): 237–60; Theodore Blegen, "Early 'America Letters,'" in *Norwegian Migration to America, 1825–1860,* ed. *idem* (Northfield, MN: Norwegian

American History Association, 1931), and *idem,* "The 'America Letters,'" *Avhandlinger utgitt av Det Norske Videnskaps-Akademi i Oslo, II. Historisk-Filosofisk Klasse* 5 (1928): 1–25.

4. Blegen, "The 'America Letters,'" and *idem,* ed., *Land of Their Choice: The Immigrants Write Home* (Minneapolis: University of Minnesota Press, 1955), vi.

5. Blumer, *Critiques of Research in the Social Sciences;* Kurtz, *Evaluating Chicago Sociology,* 84–7; Robert E. L. Faris, *Chicago Sociology, 1920–1932* (Chicago: University of Chicago Press, 1970), 8; Wiley, "Early American Sociology and *The Polish Peasant,*" 35–6. This criticism was largely the point of Blumer's analysis of the work, *supra,* which was written for, and served as the central point of discussion at, the 1938 conference convened by the Social Science Research Council to discuss *The Polish Peasant.* In rather sharp contrast, immigration historians, who have not been concerned with the same theoretical dilemmas that have preoccupied sociologists, have been less critical of the study and more positive about its intellectual legacy, largely because of the value they see in the themes Thomas and Znaniecki opened for discussion; see the special issue symposium on *The Polish Peasant* in the *Journal of American Ethnic History,* v. 16 (Fall 1996), and especially in that issue, John Bukowczyk's "Introduction," and the essays by Kathleen Neils Conzen, "Thomas and Znaniecki and the Historiography of American Immigration"; and Dirk Hoerder, "Immigration History and Migration Studies since *The Polish Peasant.*"

6. Thomas and Znaniecki, quoted in Faris, *Chicago Sociology, 1920–1932,* 17.

7. Ross, *The Origins of American Social Science,* 351, 356; Faris, *Chicago Sociology, 1920–1932,* 13–18; Wiley, "Early American Sociology and *The Polish Peasant,*" 22–3, 29–30.

8. Thomas and Znaniecki, *The Polish Peasant in Europe and America,* I, 307; Wiley, "Early American Sociology and *The Polish Peasant,*" 35; Ross, *The Origins of American Social Science,* 352; Helena Znaniecka Lopata, *Polish Americans: Status Competition in an Ethnic Community* (Englewood Cliffs, NJ: Prentice Hall, 1976), 71.

9. Thomas and Znaniecki, *The Polish Peasant in Europe and America,* I, 13, 42–5, 62, and II, 1832–4; Ross, *The Origins of American Social Science,* 347–53; Wiley, "Early American Sociology and *The Polish Peasant,*" 29–31; Faris, *Chicago Sociology, 1920–1932,* 13–19; Kurtz, *Evaluating Chicago Sociology,* 31–4; Donald Fleming, "Attitude: History of a Concept," *Perspectives in American History* 1 (1967): 287–365; Kenneth J. Gergen, "Theory of the Self: Impasse and Evolution," in *Advances in Experimental Psychology,* vol. 17, ed. Leonard Berkowitz (New York: Academic Press, 1984): 55–9.

10. Thomas and Znaniecki, *The Polish Peasant in Europe and America,* I, 31–95, 85–6, and II, 1469, 1476; Stow Persons, *Ethnic Studies at Chicago, 1905–1945* (Urbana: University Chicago Press, 1987), 46–9; Kurtz, *Evaluating Chicago Sociology,* 58–9; Ross, *The Origins of American Social Science,* 35–47.

11. Thomas and Znaniecki, *The Polish Peasant in Europe and America,* I, 303–7, and II, 1202–3, 1134–70, 1483–1503, 1647–53, 1703–7, 1748–52.

12. Thomas and Znaniecki, *The Polish Peasant in Europe and America,* I, 303–7 (303, quote).

13. Persons, *Ethnic Studies at Chicago, 1905–1945,* 36.

14. Ross, *The Origins of American Social Science,* 355–67; Blumer, *Critiques of Research in the Social Sciences;* Faris, *Chicago Sociology, 1920–1932,* 18.

15. Thomas and Znaniecki, *The Polish Peasant in Europe and America,* II, 1511–1644, 1649–50, 1825–7, 1776–8; Zaretsky, ed., *The Polish Peasant in Europe and America,* 6, 20–2, 44, 46–7; Ross, *The Origins of American Social Science,* 355–6, 435. Dominic Pacyga systematically contests the relevance of the disorganization model in an analysis of Chicago's Polonia during the same period in which Thomas and Znaniecki did

their research; *Polish Immigrants and Industrial Chicago: Workers on the South Side, 1880–1920* (Columbus: Ohio State University Press, 1991).

16. David J. Rothman, "'The Uprooted': Thirty Years Later," *Reviews in American History* 10 (September 1982): 311–9; Zaretsky, ed., *The Polish Peasant in Europe and America*, 31–3; and the 1996 symposium on the work in the *Journal of American Ethnic History* 16 (Fall 1996). Handlin reduced Thomas and Znaniecki's modernization cycle to a one-dimensional depiction of *uprooting* in order to accommodate the alienation and disorganization he took to be the immediate, experiential world of the European peasant immigrant.

17. Charlotte Erickson, *Invisible Immigrants: The Adaptation of English and Scottish Immigrants in Nineteenth-Century America* (Coral Gables: University of Miami Press, 1972), 2, 7–8.

18. "Comment by W. I. Thomas," in Read Bain et al., "Part Two: Proceedings of the Conference on Blumer's Analysis," Herbert Blumer, *Critiques of Research in the Social Sciences,* 82–7. See also Evan A. Thomas, "Herbert Blumer's Critique of 'The Polish Peasant': A Post-Mortem on the Life History Approach in Sociology," *Journal of the History of the Behavioral Sciences* 14 (April 1978): 124–31; and Stephen O. Murray, "W. I. Thomas: Behaviorist Ethnologist," *Journal of the History of the Behavioral Sciences* 24 (October 1988): 381–91.

19. Wolfgang Helbich has utilized a modified version of content analysis, in which the incidence of certain broad themes in immigrant letters is the basis for generating some arithmetical calculations documenting patterns of assimilation and of cultural values; "Letters from America: Documents of the Adjustment Process of German Immigrants in the United States," *Anglistik und Englischunterricht* 26, n. 2 (1985): 201–15, and *idem,* "The Letters They Sent Home: The Subjective Perspective of German Immigrants in the Nineteenth Century," *Yearbook of German-American Studies* 22 (1987): 1–20. For the use of content analysis in examination of the personal correspondents of internal migrants within the United States, see John Mark Faragher, *Women and Men on the Overland Trail* (New Haven: Yale University Press, 1979).

20. Donald H. Akenson, "Reading the Texts of Rural Immigrants: Letters from the Irish in Australia, New Zealand, and North America," *Canadian Papers in Rural History* VII (1990): 387.

21. O. Fritiof Ander, "Four Historians of Immigration," in *In the Trek of the Immigrants: Essays Presented to Carl Wittke,* ed. *idem* (Rock Island, IL: Augustana College Library, 1964), 17–32; Moses Rischin, "Marcus Lee Hansen: America's First Transethnic Historian," in *Uprooted Americans: Essays to Honor Oscar Handlin,* ed. Richard Bushman et al. (Boston: Little, Brown and Co., 1979), 319–47. Hansen's father was Danish and his mother Norwegian.

22. Frederick Jackson Turner, *The Frontier in American History* (New York: Macmillan, 1920), 277–8, 280, 320–1; Edward N. Saveth, *American Historians and the European Immigrants* (New York: Russell and Russell, 1948), 122–37; Ander, "Four Historians of Immigration," 20 and *passim*; Blegen, ed., *Land of Their Choice,* ix–x, 61; Marcus Lee Hansen, *The Atlantic Migration, 1607–1860* (Cambridge: Harvard University Press, 1940), 13–17, 63–5, 165–6, and *idem,* "Immigration and Expansion," in *The Immigrants in American History,* ed. Arthur M. Schlesinger (Cambridge: Harvard University Press, 1940), 66–9; Thomas Archdeacon, "Immigrant Assimilation and Hansen's Hypothesis," in *American Immigrants and Their Generations: Studies and Commentaries on The Hansen Thesis after Fifty Years,* ed. Peter Kivisto and Dag Blanck (Urbana: University of Illinois Press, 1990), 46–7.

23. April Schultz, "'The Pride of Race Has Been Touched': The Norse American Immi-

gration Centennial and Ethnic Identity," *Journal of American History* 77 (March 1991): 1265–95; Lloyd Hustvedt, "The NAHA and Its Antecedents," *American Norvegica* 3 (1971): 294–306; Blegen, ed., *Land of Their Choice*, vi; H. Arnold Barton, "Marcus Lee Hansen and Swedish Americans," in *American Immigrants and Their Generations*, ed. Kivisto and Blanck, 113–25, and *idem*, "Where Have the Scandinavian Americans Been?" *Journal of American Ethnic History* 15 (Fall 1995): 46–7.

24. Erickson, *Invisible Immigrants*, 1; Barton, ed., *Letters from the Promised Land*, 4, 6, and *idem*, "As They Tell It Themselves: The Testimony of Immigrant Letters," in *Nordics in America*, ed. Odd S. Lovell (Northfield, MN: Norwegian-American Historical Association), 143; Alan Conway, ed., *The Welsh in America: Letters from the Immigrants* (Minneapolis: University of Minnesota Press, 1961), 13; Lloyd Husvedt, "Immigrant Letters and Diaries," in *The Prairie Frontier*, ed. Sandra Looney et al. (Sioux Falls, SD: Nordland Heritage Foundation, 1984), 38–51; William Mulder, "Through Immigrant Eyes: Utah History at the Grass Roots," *Utah Historical Quarterly* 22 (January 1954): 41–55; Selveig Zempel, ed., *In Their Own Words: Letters from Norwegian Immigrants* (Minneapolis: University of Minnesota Press, 1991), xii–xiv and *passim*; Adolph E. Schroeder and Carla Schulz-Geisberg, eds., *Hold Dear as Always: Jette, a German Immigrant Life in Letters* (Columbia: University of Missouri Press, 1988), 16; Walter Kamphoefner, Wolfgang Helbich, and Ulrike Sommers, eds., *News from the Land of Freedom: German Immigrants Write Home* (Ithaca: Cornell University Press, 1991), viii, 30.

25. By *populist* I do not mean to suggest a political movement, program, or ideology, but instead a sensibility that has fashioned a language for expressing support for recognition of various types of claims of ordinary people against elites. As such, populism may be found at all points of the political spectrum. There is no intention here, therefore, to attach a particular politics to any of the historians I refer to under the broad label of "populist." For a discussion of the concept of populism in the American context, see Michael Kazin, *The Populist Persuasion: An American History* (New York: Basic Books, 1995).

26. Theodore Blegen, *Grass Roots History* (Minneapolis: University Minnesota Press, 1947), 14; and note 2, *supra*.

27. Blegen, *Land of Their Choice*, v–vii, 3; Conway, ed., *The Welsh in America*, v, 4; Hansen, *The Atlantic Migration, 1607–1860*, 81–2, 151–4, 156–8, and *passim*; Arnold Schrier, *Ireland and the Irish Emigration* (Minneapolis: University of Minnesota Press, 1958), 40, 134, 149–51; Ingrid Semmingsen, "Emigration and the Image of America in Europe," in *Immigration in American History: Essays in Honor of Theodore Blegen*, ed. Henry Steele Commanger (Minneapolis: University of Minnesota Press, 1961), 26–37, 47–8; Merle Curti and Kendall Birr, "The Immigrant and the American Image in Europe," *Mississippi Valley Historical Review* 37 (September 1950): 212–4, 216–8. In more recently published work, see also Erickson, *Invisible Immigrants*, 3; Niels Peter Stilling, "The Significance of the Private Letter in Immigration History," *The Bridge* 15, n. 1 (1992): 35–50.

28. Blegen, *Grass Roots History*, 9–13.

29. *Ibid.*, 18–20, 65–7, 144, and *idem*, ed., *Land of Their Choice*, ix–x; Marcus Lee Hansen, "Migrations Old and New," in *The Immigrant in American History*, ed. Schlesinger, 12–13. On the ambiguity of Turner's historiographical legacy, including his views on race, slavery, and immigration, see Richard Hofstadter, *The Progressive Historians: Turner, Beard, and Parrington* (New York: Vintage, 1968), 118–64; Staughton Lynd, *Class Conflict, Slavery, and the United States Constitution* (Indianapolis: Bobbs-Merrill, 1967).

30. Conway, ed., *The Welsh in America*, vii.

31. Blegen, *Land of Their Choice*, 7; Mulder, "Through Immigrant Eyes," 52; Zempel, *In Their Own Words*, x.

32. Hansen, *The Atlantic Migration, 1607–1860,* 6, 11, and *idem,* "Migrations Old and New," 3–29, and "The Odyssey of the Emigrants," 30–52, in *The Immigrants in American History,* ed. Schlesinger; Blegen, *Land of Their Choice,* 7, 61; and for a recent iteration, Stilling, "The Significance of the Private Letter in Immigration History," 36.

33. Conway, ed., *The Welsh in America,* vii, 7, 13. Alternately voicing the claims of the individual and those of the masses, Blegen used both rhetorics; see *Grass Roots History,* 18–20. For a recent example, see Schroeder and Schulz-Geisberg, eds., *Hold Dear as Always,* 16.

34. Hansen, "Migrations Old and New," 4.

35. Stephenson, "When America Was the Land of Canaan," 237; Hansen, "Migrations Old and New," 4.

36. Stephenson, "When America Was the Land of Canaan," 245; Kamphoefner, Helbich, and Sommer, eds., *News from the Land of Freedom,* 30.

37. Blegen, ed., *Land of Their Choice*; Mulder, "Through Immigrant Eyes," 42–52; Zempel, ed., *In Their Own Words,* xii.

38. Husvedt, "Immigrant Letters and Diaries," 38, 51. See also Barton, "As They Tell It Themselves," 143, 144–5; Rudolph Jensen, "The Story Told in Denmark Letters: Correspondence from the Old Country," in *Nordics in America,* ed. Lovell, 199.

39. Blegen, *Grass Roots History,* 7–14, and *idem, Land of Their Choice,* xii; Stephenson, "When America Was the Land of Canaan," 237. These contemporary critiques, however, come from a variety of intellectual and political directions; cf. Gertrude Himmelfarb, *The New History and the Old: Critical Essays and Reappraisals* (Cambridge: Harvard University Press, 1987); Bryan D. Palmer, *Descent into Discourse: The Reification of Language and the Writing of Social History* (Philadelphia: Temple University Press, 1990); Casey Blake and Christopher Phelps, "History as Social Criticism: Conversations with Christopher Lasch," *Journal of American History* 80 (March 1994): 1310–32.

40. Elizabeth H. Cook, *Epistolary Bodies: Gender and Genre in the Eighteenth-Century Republic of Letters* (Stanford: Stanford University Press, 1996), vii; Joan W. Scott, "The Evidence of Experience," *Critical Inquiry* 17 (Summer 1991): 773–97; Jerome Bruner, *Actual Minds, Possible Worlds* (Cambridge: Harvard University Press, 1986), 64; Edward M. Bruner, "Experience and Its Expressions," in *The Anthropology of Experience,* ed. Victor W. Turner and Edward M. Bruner (Urbana: University of Illinois Press, 1988), 3–30.

41. Stephen Fender, *Sea Changes: British Emigration and American Literature* (Cambridge: Cambridge University Press, 1992); Orm Øverland, "Learning to Read Immigrant Letters: Reflections towards a Textual Theory," in *Norwegian-American Essays,* ed. Øyvind Gulliken et al. (Oslo: Norwegian American Historical Association, 1996), 207–25, and *idem, The Western Home: A Literary History of Norwegian America* (Urbana: University of Illinois Press, 1996).

42. Fender, *Sea Changes,* 43–44. Fisher's letters to his family from Michigan may be found in Erickson, *Invisible Immigrants,* 112–28. The letter in question is John Fisher to Brothers, Franklin, MI, June 11, 1832, in *ibid.,* 117–8.

43. John Fisher to Mother and Brothers, Franklin, MI, September 5, 1837, in Erickson, *Invisible Immigrants,* 124–5.

44. E.g., John Fisher to Mother and Brothers, Franklin, MI, November 30, 1836, March, 1838, and John Fisher to Brothers, May 29, 1838, in Erickson, *Invisible Immigrants,* 121–4, 125–7, 127–8.

45. Erickson, *Invisible Immigrants,* 1–10, 13–78, 229–62, 393–407, and *passim* (for

introductions to each of the individual letter-series in Erickson's collection); Kamphoefner, Helbich, and Sommers, *News from the Land of Freedom*, vii–ix, 1–50, 51–61, 287–98, 523–31, 605–8, and *passim* (for introductions to and afterward remarks about the individual letter-series); Wendy Cameron, Sheila Haines, and Mary McDougall Maude, *English Immigrant Voices: Labourers' Letters from Upper Canada in the 1830s* (Montreal and Kingston: McGill-Queen's University Press, 2000), xv–li, liii–lvi, 419–23, and *passim* (for introductions to the letters for the individual years, by which the collections are organized); Kerby A. Miller, Arnold Schrier, Bruce D. Boling, and David N. Doyle, eds., *Irish Immigrants in the Land of Canaan: Letters and Memories from Colonial and Revolutionary America, 1675–1815* (Oxford: Oxford University Press, 2003), 3–10, 649–83; David Fitzpatrick, ed., *Oceans of Consolation: Personal Accounts of Irish Migration to Australia* (Ithaca: Cornell University Press, 1994), 3–36, 467–641, and *passim* (for introduction to individual letter-series).

46. Erickson, *Invisible Immigrants*, 1.

47. Mulder, "Through Immigrant Eyes," 45, 46.

48. Barton, ed., *Letters from the Promised Land*, 4–5. Barton himself, however, later made effective use of just such seemingly trivial matters, which routinely arise in personal correspondence, in his own multigenerational history of his family, in which they serve as the basis for some astute formulations about personal relationships and individual motivations; see *The Search for Ancestors: A Swedish-American Family Saga* (Carbondale: Southern Illinois University Press, 1979), e.g., 105–9.

49. Edward R. R. Green, "Ulster Emigrant Letters," in *Essays in Scotch-Irish History*, ed. *idem* (New York: Humanities Press, 1969), 93–9, 101.

50. David Fitzpatrick, "Oceans of Consolation: Letters and Irish Immigration to Australia," in *Visible Sources for the History of Australian Immigration*, ed. Eric Richards, Richard Reid, and David Fitzpatrick (Canberra: Australian National University, 1989), 52; Jean Hébard, "La Correspondence au XIXe Siècle," in *L'Epistolarité à Travers les Siècles*, ed. Mirelle Bossis (Stuttgart: Franz Steiner Verlag, 1990), 167. Two unusual examples of praise for the artful qualities of self-expression in immigrant letters are Schrier, *Ireland and the Irish Emigration*, 23–4; and Marsha Penti-Vidutis, "The America Letter: Immigrant Accounts of Life Overseas," *Finnish Americana* 1, 1 (1978), but neither author goes beyond a brief observation.

51. Michael Normile to Father, West Maitland, New South Wales, Australia, November 11, 1855, in Fitzpatrick, ed., *Oceans of Consolation*, 74.

52. Nathan Haley to Parents and Relations, Liverpool, England, July 3, 1820, in Erickson, *Invisible Immigrants*, 412. Susan Kissel speaks articulately to this point in "Writer Anxiety versus the Need for Community in the Botts Family Letters," in *Women's Personal Narratives: Essays in Criticism and Pedagogy*, ed. Leonore Hoffman and Margo Culley (New York: Modern Languages Association, 1985), 53.

53. Ann Whittaker to Brother, [Monroe County,] IL, Jan[uar]y, 1849, in Erickson, *Invisible Immigrants*, 182.

54. Conway, ed., *The Welsh in America*, v–vi. In the preface to his collection, Conway justified his choice of published letters, writing that not only had they had a great influence in stimulating immigration, but they had been purged of "the personal enquiries, condolences, salutations, and endearments which the editors very judiciously cut out and which form a prominent part of manuscript letters." He went further and himself deleted "material which has no bearing on the United States, such as theological arguments, reminiscences about the old days in Wales, and flowery passages of those who seem unable to refrain from demonstrating their bardic potentialities."

55. Fitzpatrick, "Oceans of Consolation: Letters and Irish Immigration to Australia," 48–9.

56. Erickson, *Invisible Immigrants,* 9.

57. Barton, ed., *Letters from the Promised Land,* 5.

58. E.g., Cameron, Haines, and Maude, who begin an Editorial Note, which explains their interventions in the name of readability, with the statement, "We have tried to let the writers of these letters tell their own stories"; Cameron, Haines, and Maude, eds., *English Immigrant Voices,* liii. Whether the writers can indeed, across the centuries and without an interpreter's intervention, tell us their own stories or not is debatable, whether in this collection or any other. The goals of letting them do so while changing their writing so that it might be more readily understood may not be incompatible, but the tensions involved in this sort of editing are not sufficiently addressed.

Most editors of collections of non-English-language immigrant letters deal briefly (in a paragraph or two) and matter-of-factly with translation issues and discuss just as briefly, if at all, the tone they wish to achieve, as if there were nothing problematic about such a project. In sharp contrast is the work of Kamphoefner, Helbich, and Sommer, eds., *News from the Land of Freedom,* who go to great lengths to explain their decisions regarding not only translation but also usage and grammar, and even have discussions of the problems presented by individual handwriting. Every letter-series begins with a short, precise discussion of these issues as they pertain to individual correspondents. These discussions also feature analysis of the English language and American cultural influences on the writer's prose style. While the collection format does not allow the authors the opportunity for a general and extended analysis of these matters, the result is nonetheless a significant contribution to the neglected problem of immigrant acculturation as it is reflected in written language.

59. Charlotte Erickson reminded me of the intensity of this largely underappreciated struggle, describing the multiple difficulties, centering around demands to delete text and standardize writing, she experienced in dealing with the original British publisher of *Invisible Immigrants*; Charlotte Erickson to author, personal communication, October 8, 2000, March 10, 2001.

60. Thomas and Znaniecki, *The Polish Peasant in Europe and America,* I, 303–7.

NOTES TO CHAPTER 2

1. David Laing to Sister, Logansport, IN, February 19, 1873, 812m, Kroch Library, CU. It is not clear that all seven letters in the Laing collection were written to the same one of Laing's two sisters; the letter of June 8, 1873, may not have been written to the same person as the other six letters in the series.

2. David Laing to Sister, Logansport, IN, February 19, 1873, CU.

3. David Laing to Sister, Logansport, IN, February 19, 1873, CU.

4. David Laing to Sister, Logansport, IN, February 19, 1873, CU.

5. David Laing to Sister, Logansport, IN, June 8, 1873, February 8, July 12, 1874, May 16, July 11, 1875, July 13, 1876 (quote), CU.

6. David Laing to Sister, Logansport, IN, February 19, 1873, February 8, 1874, July 13, 1876, CU.

7. David Laing to Sister, Logansport, IN, June 8, 1873, July 11, 1875, July 13, 1876, CU.

8. David Laing to Sister, Logansport, IN, May 16, 1875, CU.

9. David Laing to Sister, Logansport, IN, July 12, 1874, July 11, 1875, July 13, 1876, CU.

10. Peter Burke, *The Art of Conversation* (Ithaca: Cornell University Press, 1993), 9–20, 92, and *passim*.

11. Janet Gurkin Altman, *Epistolarity: Approaches to a Form* (Columbus: Ohio State University Press, 1982), 111, 117–90.

12. Philip Gleason, "Identifying Identity: A Semantic History," in Gleason, *Speaking of Diversity: Language and Ethnicity in Twentieth-Century America* (Baltimore: Johns Hopkins University Press), 123–49. Also see *ibid.*, vii–xiii.

The conceptual supremacy of *assimilation* has been premised from the start in the anxious projections about political unity and cultural hegemony that international migration inspires. While in popular discourse *ethnicity* has often been made to appear founded on dangerous separatist impulses, immigration analysts have long understood it as a blending of old and new habits and thinking that functions as a way station on the path to assimilation. On assimilation, see Dorothy Ross, *The Origins of American Social Science* (New York: Cambridge University Press, 1991); Stow Persons, *Ethnic Studies at Chicago, 1905–1945* (Urbana: University of Illinois Press, 1987); Milton M. Gordon, *Assimilation in American Life: The Role of Race, Religion, and National Origins* (New York: Oxford University Press, 1964); Linda Basch, Nina Glick Schiller, Christina Szanton Blanc, *Nations Unbound: Transnational Projects, Postcolonial Predicaments and Deterritorialized Nation-States* (Amsterdam: Gordon and Breach Publishers, 1994), 21–41.

13. Gleason, "Identifying Identity," 128–30, traces identification from Sigmund Freud and Gordon Allport, in its psychoanalytical and psychological formulations, through to Ralph Linton, Nelson N. Foote, Robert Morton, and Alice Rossi, in its sociological and social psychological formulations.

14. Erik H. Erikson, *Childhood and Society* (New York: Norton, 1963, second edition), and *idem*, *Identity and the Life Cycle: Selected Papers* (New York: International Universities Press, 1959), *Identity, Youth and Crisis* (New York: Norton, 1969), and *Life History and the Historical Moment* (New York: Norton, 1975), 46 (for the statement of the three levels on which identity is constituted). Also see Gleason, *Identifying Identity*, 127–8, 131–43; Sydney Shoemaker, *Self-Knowledge and Self-Identity* (Ithaca: Cornell University Press, 1963); Joseph B. Juhasz, "Social Identity in the Context of Human and Personal Identity," in *Studies in Social Identity*, ed. Theodore R. Sarbin and Karl E. Schieb (New York: Praeger, 1983); Rom Harré, *The Singular Self: An Introduction to the Psychology of Personhood* (London: Sage, 1998).

15. Benedict Anderson, *Imagined Communities: Reflections on the Origin and Spread of Nationalism* (London: Verso, 1983); Also see Harold R. Isaacs, *Idols of the Tribe: Group Identity and Political Change* (New York: Harper and Row, 1977); Mary Waters, *Ethnic Options: Choosing Identities in America* (Berkeley: University of California Press, 1990).

16. Victor R. Greene, *American Immigrant Leaders, 1800–1910: Marginality and Identity* (Baltimore: Johns Hopkins University Press, 1987); John Higham, ed., *Ethnic Leadership in America* (Baltimore: Johns Hopkins University Press, 1978).

17. For an excellent and most convincing analysis of this central question and a survey of positions held by significant interpreters, see Melford E. Spiro, "Is the Western Conception of Self 'Peculiar' within the Context of World Cultures?" *Ethos* 21, n. 2 (1993): 107–53.

18. Anthony Giddens, *Modernity and Self-Identity: Self and Society in the Late Modern Age* (Stanford: Stanford University Press, 1991), 54 (the italics in the quote are Giddens's own, as it appears in his text); Mark Freeman, *Rewriting the Self: History, Memory,*

Narrative (New York: Routledge, 1993); Jerome Bruner, "Life as Narrative," *Social Research* 54 (Spring 1987): 31.

19. Kenneth S. Gergen, "Theory of the Self: Impasse and Evolution," in *Advances in Experimental Psychology*, vol. 17, ed. Leonard Berkowitz (New York: Academic Press, 1984): 49–115; John Shotter, *Social Accountability and Selfhood* (Oxford: Basil Blackwood, 1985); Rom Harré, *The Singular Self: An Introduction to the Psychology of Personhood* (London: Sage, 1998); Andrea Deciu Ritivoi, *Yesterday's Self: Nostalgia and The Immigrant Identity* (Lanham: Rowan and Littlefield, 2002), 6–8, 45. Summarizing a vast literature, Harré (*ibid.*, 178) states succinctly, "We create our minds ad hoc in the course of carrying on our lives. Stabilities and unities in these creations create the illusion of inner selves, but they have no more independent existence than the selves we produce ad hoc for others, which they may or may not confirm, and so bring more concretely into existence. At most this array of selves has the status of a vortex in the flow of a river."

20. A. Irving Hallowell, *Culture and Experience* (Prospect Heights, IL: Waveland Press, 1988 ed.), 80; Gergen, "Theory of the Self," 78–88; Giddens, *Modernity and Self-Identity*, 20, 53–5; Anthony Cohen, *Self-Consciousness: An Alternative Anthropology of Identity* (London: Routledge, 1994), esp. 20–1; Regina Gagnier, *Subjectivities: A History of Self-Representation in Britain, 1832–1920* (New York: Oxford University Press, 1991), 235–9.

21. Gergen, "Theory of the Self," 8–85; Lewis Lurcher, *The Mutable Self: A Self-Concept for Social Change* (Beverly Hills: Sage, 1977); Hubert J. M. Hermans, Harry J. G. Kempen, and Herbert J. M. Hermans, *The Dialogical Self: Meaning as Movement* (San Diego: Academic Press, 1993), Jerome Bruner, *Acts of Meaning* (Cambridge: Harvard University Press, 1990).

22. Denis-Constant Martin, "The Choices of Identity," *Social Identities* 1, 1 (1995): 5–20; Bruner, *Acts of Meaning*, esp. 107; Cohen, *Self-Consciousness*, 23–35, 55–79, 80–114; Gagnier, *Subjectivities*, 3–29.

23. Anthony Storr, *Solitude: A Return to the Self* (New York: Ballantine, 1989), 79–80.

24. R. F. Baumeister, *Identity: Cultural Change and the Struggle for Self* (New York: Oxford University Press, 1986); Stephen Greenblatt, *Renaissance Self-Fashioning from More to Shakespeare* (Chicago: University of Chicago Press, 1980); Yi-Fu Tan, *Segmented Worlds Self: Group Life and Individual Consciousness* (Minneapolis: University of Minnesota, 1982), 9–10; John Martin, "Inventing Sincerity, Refashioning Prudence: The Discovery of the Individual in Renaissance Europe," *American Historical Review* 102 (December 1997): 1309–42.

25. Peter Mühlhäusler and Rom Harré, *Pronouns and People: The Linguistic Construction of Social and Personal Identity* (Oxford: Basil Blackwell, 1990), 100, 132–66; also see Rom Harré and Grant Gillett, *The Discursive Mind* (Thousand Oaks: Sage, 1994), 99–110.

26. Harré and Gillett, *The Discursive Mind*, 1–21; Hermans and Kempen, *The Dialogical Self*, 102–21; Kenneth Gergen, "The Social Constructionist Movement in Modern Psychology," *American Psychologist* 40, 2 (1985): 266–75.

27. Paul Ricoeur, *Oneself as Another*, trans. Kathleen Blamey (Chicago: University of Chicago Press, 1992), esp. 27–55; Kenneth Gergen, "The Healthy, Happy Human Being Wears Many Masks," in *De-Confusing and Re-Constructing The Post Modern World*, ed. Walter Truscott Anderson (New York: Putnam, 1995), 136–44; Bruner, *Acts of Meaning*; Hermans and Kempen, *The Dialogical Self*.

28. On Bakhtin, see, in general, Katerina Clark and Michael Holquist, *Mikhail Bakhtin* (Cambridge: Cambridge University Press, 1984); Ken Hirschkop and David

Shepard, *Bakhtin and Cultural Theory* (New York: St. Martin's, 1989); and specifically to his relevance here, John Shotter, "Bakhtin and Billig," *American Behavioral Scientist* 36 (September 1992): 8–21; Marc W. Steinberg, "Fence Sitting for a Better View: Finding a Middle Ground between Materialism and the Linguistic Turn in the Epistemology of History," *Qualitative Inquiry* 3 (March 1997): 26–52.

29. Michael Holquist, ed., *The Dialogical Imagination: Four Essays by M. M. Bakhtin,* trans. Caryl Emerson and Michael Holquist (Austin: University of Texas Press, 1981), xvi (quote), 28, 332, and *passim*; Mikhail Bakhtin, *Problems of Dostoevsky's Poetics,* ed. and trans. Caryl Emerson (Minneapolis: University of Minnesota Press, 1984), 204–37; Hubert J. M. Hermans et al., "The Dialogical Self: Beyond Individualism and Rationalism," *American Psychologist* 47 (January 1992): 23–33.

30. Bruce Redford, *The Converse of the Pen: Acts of Intimacy in the Eighteenth-Century Familiar Letter* (Chicago: University of Chicago Press, 1986).

31. Jack Goody, *The Logic of Writing and the Organization of Society* (Cambridge: Cambridge University Press, 1986), and *idem, The Interface of the Oral and the Written* (Cambridge: Cambridge University Press, 1987); A. R. Luria, *Cognitive Development: Its Cultural and Social Foundations* (Cambridge: Cambridge University Press, 1976); Marshall McLuhan, *The Gutenberg Galaxy* (Toronto: University of Toronto Press, 1962); David R. Olson, *The World on Paper: The Conceptual and Cognitive Implications of Reading and Writing* (Cambridge: Cambridge University Press, 1994); Walter Ong, *The Presence of the Word* (New Haven: Yale University Press, 1976), and *idem, Orality and Literacy: The Technologizing of the Word* (London: Metheun, 1982).

32. Olson, *The World on Paper,* 1–19, 65–159.

33. Ong, *Orality and Literacy,* 43–4, 49–50, 104–5; Luria, *Cognitive Development, passim.* For acute observations on the paradox of the social and the private in personal correspondence, see Christina Marsden Gillis, *The Paradox of Privacy: Epistolary Form in "Clarissa,"* University of Florida Humanities Monograph n. 54 (Gainesville: University Press of Florida, 1984).

34. For the case of England, for example, see David Vincent, *Literacy and Popular Culture, England, 1750–1914,* 259–75; Jonathan Berry, "Literacy and Literature in Popular Culture: Reading and Writing in Historical Perspective," in *Popular Culture in England, 1500–1850,* ed. Tim Harris (New York: St. Martin's, 1995), 69–94.

35. Michael A. Forrester, *Psychology of Language: A Critical Introduction* (London: Sage, 1996), 161.

36. George Stephenson, ed., "Typical 'America Letters,'" *Swedish Historical Society Yearbook* 7 (1921): 52 ff., and *idem,* "When America Was the Land of Canaan," *Minnesota History* 10 (September 1929): 237–60; Theodore Blegen, "Early 'America Letters,'" in *Norwegian Migration to America, 1825–1860,* ed. *idem* (Northfield, MN: Norwegian-American Historical Association, 1931), 196–213.

37. Wendy Cameron, Sheila Haines, and Mary McDougall Maude, *English Immigrant Voices from Upper Canada in the 1830s* (Montreal and Kingston: McGill-Queen's University Press, 2000), lv; George Simons et al., to Friends, North Royalton, OH, September 20, 1840, 684M, CU.

38. Joseph and Rebecca Hartley to Brother and Sister, Lockport, NY, June 30, 1873–5?, in Michael Drake, ed., "'We Are All Yankeys Now': Joseph Hartley's Transplanting from Brighouse Wood, Yorkshire, Old England, to Lockport, New York, Told by Himself and His Wife in Letters Home," *New York History* 45 (July 1964): 256.

39. Karen Lystra, *Searching the Heart: Women, Men, and Romantic Love in Nineteenth-Century America* (New York: Oxford University Press, 1989), 27.

40. Vincent, *Literacy and Popular Culture*; Thomas Laqueur, *Religion and Respect-*

ability: Sunday Schools and Working-Class Culture, 1780–1850 (New Haven: Yale University, 1976); David Cressy, "Levels of Literacy in England, 1530–1730," *Historical Journal* 20, 1 (1977): 1–23; R. S. Schofield, "The Measurement of Literacy in Pre-Industrial England," in *Literacy in Traditional Societies*, ed. Jack Goody (Cambridge: Cambridge University Press, 1968), 311–25; Rob Houston, "The Literacy Campaign in Scotland, 1560–1803," in *National Literacy Campaigns: Historical and Comparative Perspectives*, ed. Harvey Graff and R. Arnove (New York: Plenum, 1987), 49–64.

41. Vincent, *Literacy and Popular Culture*, 95–127; David Mitch, *The Rise of Popular Literacy in Victorian England: The Influence of Private Choice and Public Policy* (Philadelphia: University of Pennsylvania Press, 1992), 11–42.

42. Vincent, *Literacy and Popular Culture*, 156–226 (226, quote); Mitch, *The Rise of Popular Literacy in Victorian England*, 59, 106–7.

43. John Fisher to Mother, Tecumseh, MI, July 12, 1831, in Charlotte Erickson, *Invisible Immigrants: The Adaptation of English and Scottish Immigrants in Nineteenth-Century America* (Coral Gables: University of Miami Press, 1972), 115; and Titus Crawshaw to Father, n.p., n.d., in *ibid.*, 335.

44. Vincent, *Literacy and Popular Culture*, 262–75; Berry, "Literacy and Literature in Popular Culture," 79–82; Barry Reay, "The Context and Meaning of Popular Literacy: Some Evidence from Nineteenth-Century England," *Past and Present* 131 (May 1991): 117.

45. R. S. Schofield, "Dimensions of Illiteracy in England, 1750–1850," in *Literacy and Social Development in the West: Reader*, ed. Harvey Graff (Cambridge: Cambridge University Press, 1981), 206–9; W. B. Stephens, "Literacy in England, Scotland, and Wales, 1500–1900," *History of Education Quarterly* 30 (Winter 1990): 545–72; Houston, "The Literacy Campaign in Scotland," 49–64; Meg Gomersall, *Working-Class Girls in Nineteenth-Century England: Life, Work, and Schooling* (New York: St. Martin's Press, 1997).

46. On the use of signatures to determine levels of literacy and the problems associated with this methodology, see Reay, "The Context and Meaning of Popular Literacy," 111–5, 127; Vincent, *Literacy and Popular Culture*, 16–7; Stephens, "Literacy in England, Scotland, and Wales," 554–5, 571; Cressy, "Levels of Literacy in England, 1530–1730," 1.

47. Harvey Graff, *The Literacy Myth: Literacy and Social Structure in the Nineteenth-Century City* (New York: Academic Press, 1979), 60–9.

48. Vincent, *Literacy and Popular Culture in Victorian England*, 24, 101–4; Laqueur, *Religion and Respectability*, 153–60; Reay, "The Context and Meaning of Popular Literacy," 115; Gomersall, *Working-Class Girls in Nineteenth-Century England*.

49. Manfred Görlach, *English in Nineteenth-Century England: An Introduction* (Cambridge: Cambridge University, 1999), 9, 12–4, 21–58; Richard W. Bailey, *Images of English: A Cultural History of the Language* (Ann Arbor: University of Michigan Press, 1991), 2–16 and *passim*.

50. Ann Whittaker to Brother, State of Illinois, January 1849, in Erickson, *Invisible Immigrants*, 182.

51. J. R. Hays and L. S. Flowers, "Writing Research and the Writer," *American Psychologist* 41, 4 (1986): 1106–13. Also see Forrester, *Psychology of Language*, 171–6, 182–3.

52. Alison M. Scott, "These Notions I Imbibed from Writers": The Reading Life of Mary Ann Wodrow Archbald (1762–1841) (Ph.D. diss., Boston University, 1995); chapter 9, *infra*; Carolyn Heilbrun, "Women's Autobiographical Writings: New Forms," in *Modern Selves: Essays on Modern British and American Autobiography*, ed. Philip Dodd (London: Methuen, 1984), 14–27 (16, quote).

53. E.g., John Barker to ?, Connorsville, IN, December 21, 1856, Barker Family Letters, SC2385, IHS.

54. The letters of Jane Johnson, an Irish Protestant immigrant, to her husband Henry show such usage. Jane Johnson writes sound formal English, but frequently interjects "Dear Henry" at or near the start of her sentences, as if she fears she cannot make her point without *speaking* directly to Henry. The result is awkward, but the frequent repetition ultimately has a certain poetic effectiveness. Jane Johnson to Henry Johnson, Antrim, May 26, 1848, January 9, 1949, in Louise Wyatt, ed., "The Johnson Letters," *Ontario History* 40, 1 (1948): 37–8, 41–2.

55. Olson, *The World on Paper*; Burke, *The Art of Conversation,* 20. Jane E. Harrison, *Until Next Year: Letter Writing and the Mails in the Canadas, 1640–1830* (Hull: Canadian Museum of Civilization and Wilfred Laurier University, 1997), 25, identifies this gap as the root of the problem in the letters of those she identifies as semiliterates, a term I reject, because it suggests that we may confidently define the measure of full literacy. For the concept of "a plurality of literacies," see John Szwed, "The Ethnography of Literacy," in *Variation in Writing: Functional and Linguistic Cultural Differences,* ed. Marcia Farr Whitman (Hillsdale, NJ: Lawrence Erlbaum, 1981), 15–9.

56. John Barker to ?, Connersville, IN, December 21, 1856, IHS.

57. John Barker to ?, Connorsville, IN, June ?, 1857, IHS.

58. Mary Ann Archbald to Margaret Wodrow, Riverbank, November 30, 1816, History of Women Collection, SmC. (Since Creekvale and Riverbank seem, in both cases, to have been the names not of villages, but of Archbald's farms, I have not attached New York to them in writing of the location from which Archbald wrote her letters.)

59. James Steel to Thomas Steel, London, England, November 30, 1845, Thomas Steel Papers, Wis Mss 51PB, WHS.

60. John Kerr to John Graham, August 12, 1844, November 24, 1845, in Ronald Wells, ed., *Ulster Migration to America: Letters of Three Families* (New York: Peter Lang, 1991), 124–6, 128–30. Graham was the maternal uncle of the four brothers, and was formally responsible for their upbringing. He supplied them with the money to emigrate. John Kerr addressed him more or less as an equal, and shared perspectives with him on raising the younger brothers, including views on how Graham might encourage them to improve their letters. Kerr probably wrote in the same vein to his brothers themselves, but there is no trace of these letters.

61. James Horner Letters, T.1592, PRONI. The collection consists of eighteen letters written during 1801–1810 to his parents (15), uncle (2), and maternal grandparents (1).

62. Janet Gurkin Altman, "Political Ideology in the Letter Manual (France, England, New England)," ed. John W. Yolton and Leslie Ellen Brown, *Studies in Eighteenth-Century Culture* 18 (1989): 114–8; Roger Chartier, "Introduction: An Ordinary Kind of Writing," in *Correspondence: Models of Letter-Writing from the Middle Ages to the Nineteenth Century,* ed. Roger Chartier, Alain Boureau, and Cécile Dauphin (Princeton: Princeton University Press, 1997), 5.

63. Ruth Perry, *Women, Letters, and the Novel* (New York: AMS Press, 1980), 9; Chartier, "Introduction: An Ordinary Kind of Writing," 5.

64. Cécile Dauphin, "Letter Writing Manuals in the Nineteenth Century," in *Correspondence,* ed. Chartier, Boureau, and Dauphin, 136–42; Chartier, "Introduction: An Ordinary Kind of Writing," *ibid.,* 5.

65. Dauphin, "Letter Writing Manuals in the Nineteenth Century," 132–3.

66. An excellent and accessible example is the correspondence of the Isle of Man artisan Radcliffe Quine, who led an itinerant life for many years in the Canadian and American Pacific coast region, and wrote to his siblings infrequently over the course of many years. Suffering from epilepsy and arthritis, and about to express anger because he believed he was being denied his share of his parents' estate by his family, he nonetheless

began a letter to his brother with this formal introduction, "I tak this opertunety of writing a few lines unto you, hoping this same will find you in good health as I have bene miserable"; Radcliffe Quine to Brother and Wife, Seattle, WA, March 26, 1882, in Erickson, *Invisible Immigrants,* 476–7. See Benedetta Craveri, "TALK!" *New York Review of Books,* January 20, 2000, 65, for a discussion of the lasting influence of these instructional books on beliefs about the style of personal letters.

67. Robert Smyth to Parents, Brothers and Sisters, Philadelphia, PA, April 18, 1839, Robert and William Smyth Letters, D1828, PRONI. (Smyth eventually spelled his name "Smith.")

68. Robert Smyth to Parents, Brothers and Sisters, Philadelphia, PA, November 18, 1839, to James Smyth, January 18, 1840, PRONI.

69. Robert Smyth to Parents, Philadelphia, PA, August 14, 1844, PRONI.

70. Robert Smyth to Parents, Philadelphia, PA, June 17, 1839, PRONI.

71. Roland Barthes, "From Work to Text," *Image Music Text,* trans. Stephen Heath (New York: Hill and Wang, 1977), 155–64; Michel Foucault, "What Is an Author?" in *The Foucault Reader,* ed. Paul Rabinow (New York: Pantheon, 1984), 101–20.

72. Louise Wetherbee Phelps, "Audience and Authorship: The Disappearing Boundary," in *A Sense of Audience in Written Communication,* vol. 5, *Written Communication Annual,* ed. Gesa Kirsh and Duane H. Rosen (Newbury Park: Sage, 1990): 164–7.

NOTES TO CHAPTER 3

1. My understanding of culture is guided by the work of Clifford Geertz: *Interpretation of Cultures* (New York: Basic Books, 1973), and *Local Knowledge: Further Essays in Interpretive Anthropology* (New York: Basic Books, 1983).

2. The discussion of return migration from the standpoint of individual experience and calculation is only touched upon here and there in the major works on the subject; see Mark Wyman, *Round-Trip to America: The Immigrants Return to Europe, 1880–1930* (Ithaca: Cornell University Press, 1993). See also Frank Thistlethwaite, "Migration from Europe Overseas in the Nineteenth Century," Xle Congrès International des Sciences Historiques, *Rapports* (Uppsala: Almqvist and Wiksell, 1960); Wilbur Shepperson, *Emigration and Disenchantment: Portraits of Englishmen Repatriated from the United States* (Norman: University of Oklahoma Press, 1965); Betty Boyd Caroli, *Italian Repatriation from the United States, 1900–1914* (New York: Center for Migration Studies, 1973); Theodore Saloutos, *They Remember America: The Story of Repatriated Greek-Americans* (Berkeley: University of California Press, 1956).

3. Janet Gurkin Altman, *Epistolarity: Approaches to a Form* (Columbus: Ohio State University Press, 1982), 88 (quote), 117, 138–9.

4. Michael Forrester, *Psychology of Language: A Critical Introduction* (London: Sage, 1996), 182–3; Louise Weatherbee Phelps, "Audience and Authorship: The Disappearing Boundary," in *A Sense of Audience in Written Communications,* vol. 5, *Written Communication Annual,* ed. Gesa Kirsch and Duane H. Roen (Newbury Park: Sage, 1990): 159–76; Susan Kissell, "Writer Anxiety vs. the Need for Community in the Botts Family Letters," in *Women's Personal Narratives: Essays in Criticism and Pedagogy,* ed. Leonore Hoffman and Margo Culley (New York: Modern Languages Association, 1985), 48–53.

5. Elizabeth MacArthur, *Extravagant Narratives: Closure and Dynamics in the Epistolary Form* (Princeton: Princeton University Press, 1990).

6. Steven Ozment, *Ancestors: The Loving Family in Old Europe* (Cambridge: Harvard University Press, 2000), 105–6.

7. Jerome Bruner, *Acts of Meaning* (Cambridge: Harvard University Press, 1990), 111–5.

8. Robert Bowles, *Extracts of Letters from America, 1823, Book the Third, Written by Robert Bowles to His Brothers John and Richard,* vol. 538, OHS, contains five letters, each of them written to both brothers.

9. Darnley Family Letters, 1843–1884, NYPL, of which thirty-two of the thirty-four letters from the years 1857–1863 are from William Darnley to his wife and children, and concern the protracted difficulties of his sending for them. See especially William Darnley to Wife and Children, New York, NY, November 11, 1858 (quote), April 24, 1860, July 4, 1863. On long-distance moral and social control through personal letters before electronic communications and jet transportation, see R. A. Schermerhorn, *These Our People: Minorities in American Culture* (Boston: D. C. Heath, 1949), 369–70; Mark Wyman, *Round-Trip to America: The Immigrants Return to Europe, 1880–1930* (Ithaca: Cornell University Press, 1993), 51; Ewa Morawska, "Labor Migration of Poles in the Atlantic World Economy, 1880–1914," *Comparative Studies in Society and History* 31 (December 1989): 237–70.

10. Blake Poland and Ann Pederson, "Reading between the Lines: Interpreting Silences," *Qualitative Research, Qualitative Inquiry* 4 (June 1998): 293–312; Altman, *Epistolarity,* 207.

11. Titus Crawshaw to Father, Fort Worth, VA, November 10, 1861, Philadelphia, PA, December 9, 1862, Hespeler, Canada West, July 31, 1863, Germantown, PA, July 19, 1863, September 19, 1864, in Charlotte Erickson, *Invisible Immigrants: The Adaptation of English and Scottish Immigrants in Nineteenth-Century America* (Coral Gables: University of Miami Press, 1972), 348–57.

12. H. Reid to Sister, New York, NY, July 1, 1879, date ?, March 28, 1882, July 5, 1882 (quote), in Erickson, *Invisible Immigrants,* 479–82.

13. David Laing to Sister, Logansport, IN, May 16, 1875, CU.

14. Titus Crawshaw to Father, Hespeler, Canada West, July 31, 1863, Germantown, PA, September 19, 1864, in Erickson, *Invisible Immigrants,* 355, 357.

15. *Infra,* chapter 10.

16. John Birket to Brother, Mount Pleasant, IL, May 19, 1843, in Erickson, *Invisible Immigrants,* 98.

17. Matthew Brooks to James and Rebecca Clark, Philadelphia, PA, February ?, 1849, Matthew Brooks Letters, T2700, PRONI.

18. Thomas and Elizabeth Barker to Uncle and Aunt, Independence, IN, March 26, 1861, Barker Family Letters, #SC2385, IHS.

19. Samuel Buchanan to Mother, London, England, 1865?, 1865?, July 5, 1865?, July 6, 1866, Cincinnati, OH, February 12, 1870, Boligee Station, AL, August 27, 1879; to Sister, Haysville, AL, n.d., Nashville, TN, June 7, 1881, Branchville, SC, February 17, 1884; to Sisters, Silver, SC, August 16, 1905. Between 1884 and the final letter in 1905 to the two remaining sisters, there are twenty-five letters, which are reports of his activities and complaints about the fact that he is being neglected. He appears to have written to the sisters considerably more than he was written to by them. Samuel Buchanan Papers, PC247, NLI.

20. William Merrill Decker, *Epistolary Practices: Letter Writing in America before Telecommunications* (Chapel Hill: University of North Carolina Press, 1998), 58, 60.

21. *Ibid.,* 59.

22. Prudence Birkbeck to Uncle, Wanborough, IL, 1818?, in Gladys Scott Thomson, *A Pioneer Family: The Birkbecks in Illinois, 1818–1827* (London: Jonathan Cape, 1953), 49.

23. Mary Ann Archbald to Margaret Wodrow, Creekvale, September 1807, September

3, 1808, Riverbank, June 12, August 17, 1818, December 31, 1819, April 28, 1821, December 31, 1823, September, 1826, July 22, 1829, May 7, 1830, November 13, 1838; Mary Ann Archbald to Rev. Dr. Wodrow, Creekvale, April 19, 1808?; Mary Ann Archbald to James Ruthven, Creekvale, April, 1809; Mary Ann Archbald Collection, History of Women Collection, SmC.

24. Alain Boureau, "The Letter-Writing Norm, a Mediaeval Invention," in Roger Chartier, Alain Boureau, and Cécile Dauphin, *Correspondence: Models of Letter-Writing from the Middle Ages to the Nineteenth Century*, trans. Christopher Woodall (Princeton: Princeton University Press, 1997), 26–32; Dena Goodman, *Republic of Letters: A Cultural History of the French Enlightenment* (Ithaca: Cornell University Press, 1994), 136–82; Orm Øverland, *The Western Home: A Literary History of Norwegian America* (Urbana: University of Illinois Press, 1996), 19–25.

25. Robert Porter ? to Friends, Chabanse, IL, December 20, 1873, Charles Porter and Family Letters, D1152/2, PRONI.

26. Andrew Greenlees to Parents, Troy, NY, August 8, 1854, in Ronald Wells, ed., *Ulster Migration to America: Letters of Three Families* (New York: Peter Lang, 1991), 3.

27. R.[ichard] and A. Hails to George Hails, Lincoln, MA, July 31, 1849, in Erickson, *Invisible Immigrants*, 318.

28. John Dixon to Parents, Uncle and All, Earlham, IA, June 17, 1871, in Charlotte Erickson, ed., "An Emigrant's Letter from Iowa, 1871," *Bulletin of the British Association of American Studies*, new series, 12 (December 13, 1966): 5–8, 35 (quote).

29. Henry Johnson to Jane Johnson, Hamilton, Canada West, September 18, 1848, McConnell Family Letters, TMRL.

30. Joseph Wright to Wife and Children, Baltimore, MD, September 17, 18, December 10, 1801, Wright Family Letters, 1801–1842, RSFI.

31. William Darnley to Wife, New York, NY, September 6, 1857, NYPL.

32. Evidence for the birth out of wedlock comes not only from reading between the lines of Archbald's letters and reconstructing a chronology from the letters, but also from the baptismal record of the church in which Louisa's son George was baptized. It lists "no father named" in place of the father's name. It was not the church at which the Archbalds regularly worshiped, but one five miles away and across the Mohawk River, suggesting a desire to avoid embarrassment in their own local community; n.a., *Baptism Record of Caughnawaga Reformed Church*, Fonda, New York, 1758–1899 (Fonda, NY, n.d.), entry of March 19, 1830, under "Helen Louisa Archbald." Alison Scott, another student of Archbald's life and letters, confirms the likelihood of these events on the basis of her reading of the letters; e-mail communication to author, July 15, 2002. On Margaret Wodrow's burning letters, see Mary Ann Archbald to Margaret Wodrow, Riverbank, April 28, 1820, SmC.

33. David Whyte to Brother, Watertown, WI, February 15, 1855, Wis Mss Aw, WHS.

34. William Darnley to Wife and Children, New York, NY, November 12, 1857, NYPL.

35. Robert Smyth to William, Philadelphia, PA, May 1, August 22, 1842, Robert and William Smyth Letters, 1832–1848, D1828, PRONI; Stephen Fender, *Sea Changes: British Emigration and American Literature* (Cambridge: Cambridge University Press, 1992), 17–20.

36. John and Leatrice MacDonald, "Chain Migration, Ethnic Neighborhood Formation and Social Networks," *Milbank Memorial Fund Quarterly* 42, 1 (1964): 84–7; Charles Tilly, "Transplanted Networks," in *Immigration Reconsidered: History, Sociology, and Politics,* ed. Virginia Yans-McLaughlin (New York: Oxford University Press, 1990); Leslie Page Moch, *Moving Europeans: Migration in Western Europe since 1650*

(Bloomington: Indiana University Press, 1992); Thomas Faist, *The Volume and Dynamics of International Migration and Transnational Social Spaces* (Oxford: Clarendon Press, 2000), 15, 119, 127.

37. The increasing narrowing of content in Archbald's letters can be traced in the last decade of her correspondence with Margaret Wodrow; see Mary Ann Archbald to Margaret Wodrow, Riverbank, May 7, 1830, April 20, December 31, 1832, November 16, 1833, September 12, November 15, 1834, August 8, November 16, 1835, April 19, September, 1836, September 21, November 13, 1838, April, June 13, 1840, SmC.

38. Robert Wade Letters and Family Papers (1819–1868), MG 24 I127, NAC; Ralph Wade to Friends, Hope Township, Canada West, October 4, 1866, NAC; *Dictionary of Canadian Biography,* 1988 ed., s.v. "Wade, Robert"; Roger G. Woodhouse, "Wade Family Correspondence," confirms that these letters are transcriptions of originals, personal e-mail (August 29, 2003); Kenneth Kelly, "The Transfer of British Ideas on Improved Farming to Ontario during the First Half of the Nineteenth Century," *Ontario History* 63, 1 (1971): 103–11.

39. Sarah J. Porter to Cousin, Chabanse, IL, July 5, 1887, "Christmas 1887," August 26, 1908, August 15, 1911, June 14, 1916, and written as "S. J. Wildman," Irwin, IL, April 10, 1889, March 14, 1895, D1152/2, PRONI.

40. Mary A. Favret, *Romantic Correspondence: Women, Politics, and the Fiction of Letters* (Cambridge: Cambridge University Press, 1993), 8–40.

41. George Martin to Alfred Martin, Rochester, NY, January 18, 1852, in Erickson, *Invisible Immigrants,* 297–300.

42. Jonathan Miller, "The Nature of Emotion: Dialogue with George Mandler," in *States of Mind,* ed. Miller (New York: Pantheon, 1983), 151.

43. Theodore R. Sarbin, "Emotions as Narrative Emplotment," in *Entering the Circle: Hermeneutic Investigations of Psychology,* ed. Martin J. Packer and Richard B. Addison (Albany: SUNY Press, 1989), 185–201.

44. Fred Davis, *Yearning for Yesterday: A Sociology of Nostalgia* (New York: Free Press, 1979), 31–6, 43–4; David Lowenthal, *The Past Is a Foreign Country* (Cambridge: Cambridge University Press, 1985), 13; Andrea Deciu Ritivoi, *Yesterday's Self: Nostalgia and the Immigrant Identity* (New York: Rowan and Littlefield, 2002), 9, 10, 30 (quote), 37, 170 (quote); Young Yun Kim, "Intercultural Adaptation," in *Handbook of International and Intercultural Communication,* ed. Molefi Kete Asanti and William B. Gudykunst (London: Sage, 1989), 275–94.

45. Joseph and Rebecca Hartley to Brother, Lockport, NY, December 12, 1868? (unsigned), to Brother and Sister, December 12, 1870, in Michael Drake, ed., "'We Are All Yankeys Now': Joseph Hartley's Transplanting from Brighouse Wood, Yorkshire, Old England to Lockport, New York, Told by Himself and His Wife in Letters Home," *New York State History* 45 (July 1964): 245–6, 248.

46. Robert Smyth to William, Philadelphia, PA, August 22, 1842, PRONI.

47. John Ronaldson to Wife, Schaghticoke, NY, October 30, 1852, April 9, December 4 (quote), 1853, East Braintree, MA, February 5, March 27, May?, 1854, in Erickson, *Invisible Immigrants,* 371–9.

48. John B. Thomas to Wife, Schuylkill County, PA, 1871, John B. Thomas Letters, 1871–1873, PSU.

49. Decker, *Epistolary Practices,* 70–1.

50. Catherine Bond to Brother and Sister, Bunker Hill, KS, Spring 1892?, CU.

51. Karen Cherewatuk and Ulrike Wiethaus, eds., *Dear Sister: Medieval Women and the Epistolary Genre* (Philadelphia: University of Pennsylvania Press, 1993), 1–5 and *passim*; Elizabeth Goldsmith, "Authority, Authenticity, and the Publication of Letters by

Women," in *idem, Writing in the Female Voice: Essays on Epistolary Literature* (Boston: Northeastern University Press, 1989), vii–x; 46–59; Ruth Perry, *Women, Letters, and the Novel* (New York: AMS Press, 1980), 69–70, and *passim*; Elizabeth Heckendorn Cook, *Epistolary Bodies: Gender and Genre in the Eighteenth-Century Republic of Letters* (Stanford: Stanford University Press, 1996), 22–5.

52. The Locke Family Papers, PC174, NLI, contain thirty-four letters written principally to Jeanette and a few to other family members between 1885–1889. Ten of the letters are composite letters, containing separate notes from Leila and from Richard, and one is signed by both of them, though it is clearly written by Leila, who uses "I," and speaks of her household duties.

53. Robert and Mary Ann Porter to Friends, Chabanse, IL, n.d., PRONI; Joseph and Rebecca Hartley to Brother and Sister, Lockport, NY, December 12, December ?, 1870, April 18, 1871?, December 8, 1872, June 30, 1873?, in Drake, ed., "We Are All Yankeys Now," 248–9, 249–50, 251–2, 254–5, 255–7.

54. David Laing to Sister, Logansport, IN, February 19, 1873, CU.

55. Joseph Wright to Hannah, Baltimore, MD, December 10, 1801, Wright Family Letters, 1801–1842, RSFI; Kerby A. Miller et al., eds., *Irish Immigrants in The land of Canaan: Letters and Memoirs from Colonial and Revolutionary America, 1675–1815* (Oxford: Oxford University Press, 2003), 200–24.

56. James W. McGarrett to "My Dear Heart," Bellvaile, MA, August 28, 1835, CCCC.

57. John B. Thomas to Wife, Schuylkill County, PA, 1871, PSU.

58. Thomas and Elizabeth Barker to Uncle and Aunt Morris, Ewing, IN, March 9, 1865, IHS.

59. Catherine Bond to Sister and Brother, Bunker Hill, KS, July 4, 1884?, CU; Ann Whittaker to Brother and Sisters, Monroe County, IL, June 24, 1851, May 1856, in Erickson, *Invisible Immigrants*, 186, 189.

60. Charles Zwingmann, "The Nostalgic Phenomenon and Its Exploitation," in *Uprooting and After*, ed. Charles Zwingmann and Maria Pfister-Ammende (New York: Springer-Verlag, 1973), 29; Davis, *Yearning for Yesterday*, 55–64.

61. Catherine Bond to Elen, Milford, CT, December 1, 1870, December 22, 1872, to Brother, Bunker Hill, KS, June 26, 1881?, January 9, 1881?, 1889, to Sister and Brother, Bunker Hill, KS, July 4, 1884?, CU.

62. Mary Cumming to Margaret, Lynchburg, VA, February 24, 1812, March 19, June 4, 1814, Mary Cumming Letters, T 1475/2, PRONI. These are not original letters, but like the other items in the Cumming collection, handwritten and typescript copies, which are also reprinted in Jimmy Irvine, ed., *Mary Cumming's Letters Home to Lisburn from America, 1811–1815* (Coleraine, Northern Ireland: Impact-Amerign, 1982). Cumming's brief life in Petersburg, Virginia, where she died after less than four years' residence (1811–1815) is described in Suzanne Lebstock, *The Free Women of Petersburg: Status and Culture in a Southern Town, 1784–1860* (New York: Norton, 1984), 11, 28–30, 150–1, 207, 209–10; Miller et al., eds., *Irish Immigrants in the Land of Canaan*, 362–78. On Archbald's "little isle," see *infra*, chapter 9.

63. Titus Crawshaw to Father, Germantown, PA (1863?), in Erickson, *Invisible Immigrants*, 354; Richard Hails to Brother George, Wayland, MA, July 24, 1848, in *ibid.*, 310.

64. Andrew Greenlees to Parents, Troy, NY, August 8 (quote), September 2, 1854, in Wells, ed., *Ulster Migration to America*, 32–3, 34–5.

65. For examples, see the easily accessible letters in Erickson, *Invisible Immigrants*; Andrew Morris to John Birchall, Bristol, PA, October 19, 1829 (146); George Martin to Parents, Coburg, Upper Canada, September 30, 1834 (277); Titus Crawshaw to Father, Mother, Sisters, Brothers, and Relatives, Philadelphia, PA, December 18, 1853 (333); John

Ronaldson to Eliza, Schaghticoke, NY, October 30, 1852 (371); Ernest Lister to Brother, Sisters, and Baby, Jersey City, NJ, August 20, 1883 (382).

66. Thomas Steel to James Steel, Milwaukee County, WI, January 12, 1844, June 14, 1845, Waukesha County, WI, November 26, 1846, WHS; Charles Julius Mickle to William Julius Mickle, Hackney, England, September 13, 1831, NAC; John Langton to ?, Coburg, Upper Canada, August 23, 1833, in W. A. Langton, *Early Days in Upper Canada: Letters from the Backwoods of Upper Canada and the Audit Office of the Province of Canada* (Toronto: MacMillan, 1926), 20, and John Langton to William Langton, Fenelon, Upper Canada, November ?, 1838, John Langton Fonds, MG 24, I 59, NAC.

67. For Christmas, see, e.g., the writing of Joseph and Rebecca Hartley, *supra*; and Catherine Bond to Brother, Milford, CT, December 1, 1870, November 28, 1874?, Bunker Hill, KS, January 9, 188?; to Elen, Milford, CT, December 22, 1872, CU. For fairs, feasts, and rent days, see, in Erickson, *Invisible Immigrants*, John Birket to Parents, Peoria, IL, May 7, 1835 (88); Thomas Wozencraft to John, GA, October 10, 1843 (132); Titus Crawshaw to Father, Mother, Sisters, Brothers, Crescentville Way, PA, 1859?, (346); Nathan Haley to Father, Cincinnati, OH, December 9, 1823 (418), and Nathan Haley to Father, Mother, Sisters, Brothers . . . Relations and Friends, Wheeling, VA, September 10, 1825 (420), John Barker to ?, Connorsville, IA, December 21, 1856, IHS.

68. Mary and Kenneth Gergen, "The Self in Temporal Perspective," in *Life Span Psychology*, ed. R. Abeles (Hillsdale, NJ: Lawrence Erlbaum, 1987), 121–37; Robert Kastenbaum, "The Structure and Function of Time Perspective," *Journal of Psychological Researches* 8, 1 (1964): 100–4; Christopher Gosden, *Social Being and Time* (Blackwell: Oxford, 1994), 5–7, 16–7, and *passim*; Michael Flaherty, *A Watched Pot: How We Experience Time* (New York: New York University Press, 1999), 2–4; Kathleen Kirby, *Indifferent Boundaries: Spatial Concepts of Human Subjectivity* (New York: Guilford Press, 1996), 19–20.

69. Karl Marx, *Grundrisse* (New York: Vintage, 1973), 539; Wolfgang Schivelbusch, "Railroad Space and Railroad Time," *New German Critique* 14 (Spring 1978): 31–40, and *idem, The Railway Journey* (New York: Urizen, 1979), 41–50. Also see Stephen Korn, *The Culture of Time and Space, 1880–1918* (Cambridge: Harvard University Press, 1983).

70. Catherine Bond to Brother and Sister, Bunker Hill, KS, February 3, 1891, August 21, 1891?, Spring 1992, CU, on the six-month visit of her sister Sarah to the United States; and perhaps much more surprisingly, years before the age of regular steamship travel for transoceanic travelers, Robert Wade to Ralph Wade, Smith Creek, Upper Canada, October 3, 1829; Kate Wade to William Wade, Smith Creek, Canada West, July 26, 1846; Ralph Wade to William Wade, Hope Township, Canada West, February 14, 1851, and to Friends, Hope Township, Canada West, November 12, 1856; Dr. R. H. Clark to Cousin, Seaton Crew, England, July 17, 1856, and to William Wade, Coburg, Canada West, July 27, 1857.

71. Thomas Steel to Lilly Steel, Milwaukee County, WI, May 10, 1844; Thomas Steel to James Steel, Waukesha County, WI, June 13, 1851, WHS. The two letters record a passage taking six weeks and sixteen days respectively.

72. For Steel's epistolary practices and perceptions, see *infra,* chapter 10.

73. Linda Kauffman, *Special Delivery: Epistolary Modes in Modern Fiction* (Chicago: University of Chicago Press, 1992), xx; Altman, *Epistolarity*, 30.

74. William and Fanney Barker Ridge to (Uncle and Aunt?), Connersville, IN, December 1, 1857, IHS.

75. John Kerr to John Graham, St. Clair, PA, August 12, 1844, Perrysville, PA, November 24, 1845, in Wells, ed., *Ulster Migration to America*, 124–6, 128–30.

76. Titus Crawshaw to Father, Mother, Sisters and Brothers, Norristown, PA, August 30, December 4, 1857, in Erickson, *Invisible Immigrants*, 342, 343.

77. Thomas Steel to Lilly Steel, Milwaukee County, WI, July 20, 1844, Waukesha County, WI, September 29, 1845, June 25, 1850; Thomas Steel to Lilly Steel, Milwaukee County, WI, November 1, 1845, May 15, 1846, WHS.

78. Titus Crawshaw to Father, Germantown, PA, September 19, 1864, in Erickson, *Invisible Immigrants*, 357.

79. Erickson notes that this dilemma was one of the constant features she finds in all British emigrant correspondence in the nineteenth century; Erickson, *Invisible Immigrants*, 5.

80. George Martin to Brother (Alfred), Rochester, NY, August 6, 1844, May 14, 1849, May 25, 1850, January 18, 1852 and to Brother (Peter), Rochester, NY, February 9, 1851, in Erickson, *Invisible Immigrants*, 287–8, 292–3, 293–4, 296, 299; John McBride to Father, Patterson, NJ, August 8, 1819, Watertown, NY, January 9, 1820, February 24, 1822, and to Brother, Watertown, NY, April 29, 1821, April 5, 1824, June 26, 1825, August 8, 1827, John McBride Letters, 1819–1848, T2613, PRONI.

81. James Steel to Thomas Steel, London, England, November 30, 1845, WHS; Mary Ann Archbald to Margaret Wodrow, Riverbank, November 30, 1816, SmC; Charles Julius and Charles Mickle to William Julius Mickle, Hackney, England, January 15, 1831, William Julius Mickle Letters, 1830–1831, MG 24 I53, NAC.

82. On Quine's conflict with his siblings over an inheritance, see Radcliffe Quine to Brother and Sister, Seattle, WA, October 3, 1876, March 22, June 2?, August 12, 1878, December 1, 1879 (quote), September 29, 1881, March 26, 1882, July 1, 1882?, March 23, 1885, in Erickson, *Invisible Immigrants*, 471–8; and for George Martin, see George Martin to Brother (Alfred), Rochester, NY, January 18, 1852, in *ibid.*, 297–300.

83. Samuel Buchanan to Sisters, Silver, SC, September 14, 1894, St. Paul, SC, June 21, 1897, Davis Station, SC, January 3, 1902, to Martin Haggard, Attorney, Davis Station, SC, January 19, 1905. It is not clear how or when the Buchanan estate was left in the hands of Dr. George Buchanan, but in 1890 George moved to formalize disinheriting Sam, who was defined in the legal documents as "not being of good character." *In Re: Buchanan Trusts Instructions on behalf of George Buchanan*, February 14, 1890; and Indenture, February 17, 1890. After the deaths of his last two sisters, as sole survivor Buchanan finally got his share of the family money, which seems to have shrunk greatly by that time; Samuel Buchanan to Martin and Haggard, Silver, SC, January 19, [1906?]; Haggard and Brennan to Samuel Buchanan, Dublin, Ireland, January 3, April 9, 1906, NLI.

84. John Ronaldson to Eliza, East Braintree, MA, May ?, 1854, in Erickson, *Invisible Immigrants*, 376.

85. Robert McElderry to Sister, Lynchburg, VA, August 15, 1850, January 22, 1851, June 10, October, 1852, September 24, 1853, Robert and William McElderry Letters, T2414, PRONI.

86. *Infra*, chapter 10.

87. Joseph Willcocks to Richard, New York, NY, December 2, 1799, York, Upper Canada, April 23, July 1, August 31, November 26, 1800, January 18, 27, 1801, April ?, 1802, Niagara, Upper Canada, August 20, 1802, York, Upper Canada, March 27, June 20, October 24, 1803, September 21, 1804, January 16, 1805, May 1, 1806, Joseph Willcocks Letters, TMRL; *Dictionary of Canadian Biography*, 1983 ed., s.v. "Willcocks (Wilcox), Joseph."

88. Dirk Hoerder and Charlotte Erickson are among the few historians who have identified the difficulties of trying to understand migrations solely within the context of massive cohorts impacted by socioeconomic change, and have briefly introduced the question

of the interpersonal and familial roots of emigration decisions. See Dirk Hoerder, "From Migrants to Ethnics: Acculturation in a Societal Framework," in *European Migrants: Global and Local Perspectives,* ed. Dirk Hoerder and Leslie Page Moch (Bloomington: Indiana University Press, 1992), 217–8, 253, n. 18. Erickson has briefly discussed the extent of troubled family backgrounds in the letters of international migrants; Erickson, "Leaving England," in *idem, Leaving England: Essays on British Emigration in the Nineteenth Century* (Ithaca: Cornell University Press, 1994), 25.

89. George Martin to Parents, Coburg, Upper Canada, September 30, 1834, and William Petingale to Father, [Bawburgh?] Mills, England, January 14, 1834, in Erickson, *Invisible Immigrants,* 277, 436.

90. *Supra,* note 11, and Titus Crawshaw to Father, Philadelphia, PA, June 18, 1866, in Erickson, *Invisible Immigrants,* 358–9.

91. Matthew Brooks to Sister, Philadelphia, PA, November 6, 1872, PRONI.

NOTES TO CHAPTER 4

1. Thomas W. Leavitt, ed., *The Hollingsworth Letters: Technical Change in the Textile Industry, 1826–1837* (Cambridge: MIT Press, 1969).

2. Leavitt, ed., *The Hollingsworth Letters: Technical Change in The Textile Industry,* 3–107.

3. Joseph Hollingsworth to William Rawcliff, Woodstock, CT, April 18, 1830, in Leavitt, ed., *The Hollingsworth Letters: Technical Change in the Textile Industry,* 71–7.

4. George Hollingsworth to William Rawcliff, Woodstock, CT, January 24, 1830, in Leavitt, ed., *The Hollingsworth Letters: Technical Change in the Textile Industry,* 60–1.

5. Janet Gurkin Altman, *Epistolarity: Approaches to a Form* (Columbus: Ohio State University Press, 1972), 13.

6. R. W. Chapman, "The Course of the Post in the Eighteenth Century," *Notes and Queries,* 183 (1942): 67–9; J. C. Hemmeon, *The History of the British Post Office* (Cambridge: Harvard University Press, 1912); M. J. Daunton, *Royal Mail: The Post Office since 1840* (London: Athlone Press, 1985); Howard Robinson, *The British Post Office: A History* (Princeton: Princeton University Press, 1948), and *idem, Carrying British Mail Overseas* (New York: New York University Press, 1984); Alvin F. Harlow, *Old Post Bags: The Story of the Sending of a Letter in Ancient and Modern Times* (New York: D. Appleton and Company, 1928); F. George Kay, *Royal Mail: The Story of the Posts in England from the Time of Edward IVth to the Present Day* (London: Rockliff, 1951); Richard R. John, *Spreading the News: The American Postal System from Franklin to Morse* (Cambridge: Harvard University Press, 1995); Wayne E. Fuller, *The American Mail: Enlarger of the Common Life* (Chicago: University of Chicago Press, 1972); William Smith, *The History of the Post Office in British North America, 1939–1870* (Cambridge: Cambridge University Press, 1931); Jane E. Harrison, *Until Next Year: Letter Writing and the Mails in the Canadas, 1640–1830* (Hull Quebec: Canadian Museum of Civilization and Wilfred Laurier University Press, 1997).

7. An excellent point made by Harrison, *Until Next Year: Letter Writing and the Mails in the Canadas,* 85, for the years before 1830, after which she believed that the processes of writing, getting, and sending letters became much more like the relatively effortless situation of the twentieth century. Certainly relative to the difficulties presented in the eighteenth century in the Canadian colonies, sending mail in the period after 1830 was easier. However, those using the post-1830 international mails and unfamiliar with the process experienced state postal systems as presenting them with puzzles and difficulties, and also

faced some circumstances similar to those confronted in the older world of less efficient postal service, such as the absence of home delivery and of neighborhood mailboxes.

8. Harrison, *Until Next Year: Letter Writing and the Mails in the Canadas,* 8–40; Philip Gaskell, *New Introduction to Bibliography* (Oxford: Clarendon Press, 1972), 214; Henry Petroski, *The Pencil: A History of Design and Circumstance* (New York: Knopf, 1992, reprint ed.), Thomas Steel to James Steel, Waukesha County, WI, April 17, May 3, 1851, Wis Mss 51PB, WHS; F. George Kay, *Royal Mail: The Story of The Posts in England from The Time of Edward IVth to The Present Day,* 426–34; Bianca Gendreau, "Putting Pen to Paper," in *Special Delivery: Canada's Postal Heritage,* ed. Francine Brousseau (Fredericton and Ottawa: Goose Lane Editions and the Canadian Museum of Civilization, 2000), 25, 29–30.

9. The immigrant-as-modernizer conceptualization failed to take hold when it was advanced years ago by Timothy L. Smith, whose understanding depended on viewing immigrants as possessing self-consciously modern values and aspirations. Smith, whose work reflected the shallow and one-dimensional modernization theory of the post–World War II decades, might have profited from the more subtle understandings of modernity advanced years later by recent theorists, such as Anthony Giddens. Giddens suggests the problem-solving conception of life in modernity that I have advanced. See Timothy L. Smith, "New Approaches to the History of Immigration in Twentieth-Century America," *American Historical Review* 71 (July 1966): 265–79; and idem, "Immigrant Social Aspirations and American Education, 1880–1930," *American Quarterly* 21, 2 (1969): 524–43.

10. Thomas Walter Laqueur, *Religion and Respectability: Sunday Schools and Working-Class Culture, 1780–1850* (New Haven: Yale University Press, 1976); David Vincent, *Literacy and Popular Culture, England, 1750–1914* (Cambridge: Cambridge University Press, 1989), 54–75, 95–127, 156–80, 226, 270–80; David Mitch, *The Rise of Popular Literacy in Victorian England: The Influence of Private Choice and Public Policy* (Philadelphia: University of Pennsylvania Press, 1992).

11. Colin Pooley and Jean Turnbull, *Migration and Mobility in Britain since the Eighteenth Century* (London: UCL Press Limited, 1998). On internal to international step migration, see *ibid.,* 275–98; Leslie Page Moch, *Moving Europeans: Migrations in Western Europe since 1650* (Bloomington: Indiana University Press, 1992), 158; and Dudley Baines, *Emigration from Europe, 1815–1930* (Cambridge: Cambridge University Press, 1995), 49–53. Moch's examples come primarily from Scandinavian experience, while Baines's general European analysis draws mostly on late-nineteenth-century research. Pooley and Turnbull present impressionistic evidence based on individual migration histories, and are tentative in their conclusions about the incidence of this type of step migration.

12. Jean Young Farrugia, *The Letter Box: A History of Post Office Pillar and Wall Boxes* (Fontwell: Centaur Press, 1969); Mitch, *The Rise of Popular Literacy in Britain,* 227.

13. Mitch, *The Rise of Popular Literacy in Britain,* 43.

14. Mitch, *The Rise of Popular Literacy in Britain,* 43; Vincent, *Literacy and Popular Culture,* 44–5, 49.

15. Joseph Hollingsworth to William Rawcliff, Woodstock, CT, April 18, 1830, in Leavitt, ed., *The Hollingsworth Letters: Technical Change in the Textile Industry,* 71–7.

16. Dinah Bish to Daughter, Belleville, Canada West, January 7, 1851, and William Peckham to Uncle, Belleville, Canada West, September 22, 1854, Hemsley Family Letters, MG 24 I 19, NAC.

17. Merle Curti and Kendall Birr, "The Immigrant and the American Image in Europe, 1860–1914," *Mississippi Valley Historical Review* 27 (June 1950): 212–3; Robinson, *The British Post Office: A History,* 159–75; Wendy Cameron, Sheila Hines, and Mary

McDougall Maude, eds., *English Immigrant Voices: Labourers' Letters from Upper Canada in the 1830s* (Montreal and Kingston: McGill-Queen's University Press, 2000), xxxv; Fuller, *The American Mail: Enlarger of the Common Life*, 209–10.

18. Charlotte Erickson, *Invisible Immigrants: The Adaptation of English and Scottish Immigrants in Nineteenth-Century America* (Coral Gables: University of Miami Press, 1972), 210.

19. Elizabeth Heckendorn Cook, *Epistolary Bodies: Gender and Genre in the Eighteenth-Century Republic of Letters* (Stanford: Stanford University Press, 1996), 5–29, 173–9; Mary A. Favret, *Romantic Correspondence: Women, Politics and the Fiction of Letters* (Cambridge: Cambridge University Press, 1993), 15–16.

20. Bianca Gendreau, "Moving the Mail," in *Special Delivery: Canada's Postal Heritage*, ed. Brousseau, 130; Robinson, *Carrying British Mail Overseas*, 135 (quote), 138. Steamship mail service was extended to New York City from Britain in 1848. In 1852, weekly mail packet service began out of Liverpool, England, for North America.

21. In 1844 letters were reaching Steel from London, England, in about six weeks in good weather; by 1849 they were reaching him in sixteen days at the same season of the year; Thomas Steel to Lilly Steel, Milwaukee County, WI, May 10, 1844, Thomas Steel to James Steel, Waukesha County, WI, June 13, 1851, WHS.

22. Konstantin Dirks, review of *Until Next Year: Letter Writing and the Mails in the Canadas, 1640–1830* by Jane E. Harrison, *Journal of Social History* 33 (Winter 1999): 467–8.

23. Chapman, "The Course of the Post in the Eighteenth Century," 67–9; Paul Johnson, *The Birth of the Modern World Society, 1815–1830* (New York: Harper Collins, 1991), 166–9; Vincent, *The Rise of Popular Literacy in Victorian England*, 34; Robinson, *The British Post Office: A History*, 244–5; Farrugia, *The Letter Box: A History of Post Office Pillar and Wall Boxes*, xvii–xviii, 117–9; William Merrill Decker, *Epistolary Practices: Letter Writing in America before Telecommunications* (Chapel Hill: University of North Carolina Press, 1998), 59.

24 Fuller, *The American Mail: Enlarger of the Common Life*, 66–7; Smith, *The History of the Post Office in British North America*, 275–6. In Britain, postal authorities claimed that prepayment was rejected by much of the public because of the desire not to pay at all: letters, it was said, were rejected when delivered by the addressee. Addressees gained knowledge that the sender had reached a destination simply by the appearance of the letter, and had no real reason thereafter to read it. Indeed there may well have been no content at all, only the address needed to convey the coded message that the letter's appearance represented. Such arrangements between sender and recipient were said to be prearranged. Robinson, *The British Post Office: A History*, 283–4, 305.

25. Fuller, *The American Mail: Enlarger of the Common Life*, 66–7, 190.

26. Thomas Steel to James Steel, Waukesha County, WI, April 29, 1849, WHS, for the first mention that Thomas was now paying for the cost of postage to London, England.

27. Fuller, *The American Mail: Enlarger of the Common Life*, 66–7, 190.

28. For Archbald's postal practices, see *infra*, chapter 9.

29. Robinson, *Carrying British Mail Overseas*, 108–24; Hemmeon, *The History of the British Post Office*, 124–31; John Willis, "The Colonial Era: Bringing the Post to North America," in *Special Delivery: Canada's Postal Heritage*, ed. Brousseau, 41–5.

30. Robinson, *The British Post Office: A History*, 244–83; Vincent, *The Rise of Popular Literacy in Victorian England*, 37, 41; Wayne Fuller, *Morality and the Mails in Nineteenth-Century America* (Urbana: University of Illinois Press, 2003), 40, 51; Willis, "The Colonial Era: Bringing the Post to North America," 45.

31. Hemmeon, *The History of the British Post Office*, 63–71, 132–75; Daunton,

Royal Mail: The Post Office since 1840, 119–43, 146–68; Robinson, *The British Post Office: A History*, 305–89, and *idem, Carrying British Mail Overseas*, 123–8, 141, 246; Farrugia, *The Letter Box: A History of Post Office Pillar and Wall Boxes*, 3–56, 74–178 (Britain), 212–3 (Canada), 217–29 (United States); Fuller: *The American Mail: Enlarger of the Common Life*, 42–70, 190–213, and *idem, Morality and the Mails in Nineteenth-Century America*, 79; John, *Spreading the News: The American Postal System from Franklin to Morse*, 52, 150–1, 159–61; Smith, *The History of the Post Office in British North America*, 114–283; Harrison, *Until Next Year: Letter Writing and the Mails in the Canadas*, 114, 144; Peter Goheen, "Canadian Communications circa 1845," *The Geographical Review* 77 (January 1987): 35–51; Brian Osborne and Robert Pike, "Lowering 'the Walls of Oblivion': The Revolution in Postal Communications in Central Canada, 1851–1911," in *Canadian Papers in Rural History*, vol. 4, ed. Donald H. Akenson (Gananoque, Ontario: Langdale Press, 1984): 200–25.

Prior to the 1848 British-American postal convention, the only postal agreement between the two nations, dating from 1792, had allowed for the exchange of Canadian, American, and British mail at Burlington, Vermont, and had enabled the British to send closed mailbags to Canada through the United States, with charges to be determined by the number of letters sent.

32. A point argued in the Canadian context by the postal historian John Willis, who sees the habits and expectations of postal system users changing more slowly than the evolving postal system itself; see Willis, "The Canadian Colonial Posts: Epistolary Continuity, Postal Transformation," in *Canada, 1849: Selection of Papers Given at the University of Edinburgh, Scotland, Center for Canadian Studies Annual Conference, May 1999* (Edinburgh: University of Edinburgh, 2001), 224–54.

33. Titus Crawshaw to Father, Mother, Sisters, and Brothers, Norristown, PA, December 4, 1857, in Erickson, *Invisible Immigrants*, 343.

34. Samuel Buchanan to Sisters, Summerton, SC, August 24, 1893, Samuel Buchanan Letters, PC 247 and PC 431, NLI.

35. Titus Crawshaw to Father, Blockley (Philadelphia), PA, May 6, 1865, in Erickson, *Invisible Immigrants*, 358.

36. Andrew Greenlees to Brother and Sister, Grand Rapids, MI, April 3, 1860, in Ronald A. Wells, ed., *Ulster Migration to America: Letters of Three Families* (New York: Peter Lang, 1991), 42.

37. Thomas Petingale to Sister, Albany, NY, December 10, 1840, in Erickson, *Invisible Immigrants*, 441. For Steel's experience with sending money, see *infra*, chapter 10.

38. Central works in the transnational paradigm are Nina Glick Schiller, Linda Basch, and Christina Szanton Blanc, eds., *Towards a Transnational Perspective on Migration: Race, Class, Ethnicity, and Nationalism Reconsidered, Annals of the New York Academy of Science,* vol. 645 (New York: New York Academy of Sciences, 1992); Linda Basch, Nina Glick Schiller, and Christina Szanton Blanc, *Nations Unbound: Transnational Projects, Postcolonial Predicaments, and Deterritorialized Nation-States* (Amsterdam: Gordon and Breach Publishers, 1994); Michael Peter Smith and Luis E. Guarnizo, eds., *Transnationalism from Below* (New Brunswick: Transaction Publishers, 1998); Alejandro Portes, Luis E. Guarnizo, and Patricia Landolt, eds., *Transnational Communities*, special issue, *Ethnic and Racial Studies* 22 (March 1999); Faist, *The Volume and Dynamics of International Migration and Transnational Social Spaces.*

39. Nicholas D. Kristof, "At This Rate, We'll Be Global in Another Hundred Years," *New York Times*, May 23, 1999, sec. 4: 5. Among the many works that substantiate this point are Karl Marx and Frederick Engels, *The Communist Manifesto: A Modern Edition* (London: Verso, 1998), 38–42; Kevin J. O'Rourke and Jeffrey G. Williamson,

Globalization and History: The Evolution of a Nineteenth-Century Atlantic Economy (Cambridge: Harvard University Press, 1999); Kenneth Pomerantz and Steven Topik, *The World That Trade Created: Society, Culture, and the World Economy, 1400 to the Present* (London: M. E. Sharpe, 1999); Tom Standage, *The Victorian Internet: The Remarkable Story of the Telegraph and the Nineteenth Century's On-Line Pioneers* (New York: Walker and Company, 1998). For a critique of the transnational canon for the failure to link the development of capitalism to international migration over long historical time, see Antonio Lauria-Perricelli, "Towards a Transnational Perspective on Migration: Closing Remarks," Glick Schiller, Basch, and Szanton Blanc, *Towards a Transnational Perspective on Migration*, 251–8.

40. Frank Thistlethwaite, "Migration from Europe Overseas in the Nineteenth and Twentieth Centuries," XIe Congrès International des Sciences Historiques, *Rapports* (Uppsala: Almqvist and Wiksell, 1960), 5, 32–60; Wilbur S. Shepperson, *Emigration and Disenchantment: Portraits of Englishmen Repatriated from the United States* (Norman: University of Oklahoma Press, 1965); Theodore Saloutos, *They Remember America: The Story of Repatriated Greek-Americans* (Berkeley: University of California Press, 1956); Keijo Virtanen, *Settlement or Return: Finnish Emigrants (1860–1930) in the International Overseas Return Migration Movement* (Turku: University of Turku-Institute for Migration Studies, 1979); Dino Cinel, *The National Integration of Italian Return Migration, 1870–1929* (Cambridge: Cambridge University Press, 1991); Mark Wyman, *Round-Trip to America: The Immigrants Return to Europe, 1880–1930* (Ithaca: Cornell University Press, 1993).

41. William Julius Mickle to Charles Mickle, New York, NY, September 17, 1830, Charles Mickle to William Julius Mickle, London, England, October 30, 1830, William Julius Mickle to Father, Ramosa Township, Upper Canada, October 30, 1830, William Julius Mickle Letters, MG 24, I53, NAC.

42. David Laing to Sister, Logansport, IN, February 19, June 8, 1873, February 8, July 12, 1874, May 16, July 11, 1875, July 13, 1876, David Laing Papers, 812m, CU; Catherine Bond to Brother, Milford, CT, September 3, 1872, to Sister, Bunker Hill, KS, undated [1890 or 1891?], to Brother and Sister, Bunker Hill, KS, July 4, 1884(?), July 5,1890, February 3, 1891, Robert Bond to Cousin, Bunker Hill, KS, January 9, 188?, Bond-Grayston Letters, 861m, CU; Thomas Steel to Lilly Steel, Milwaukee County, WI, May 11, 1844, April 13, 1845, February 12, 1847, James Steel to Thomas Steel, London, England, May 1, June 28, February 12, 1846, Thomas Steel to James Steel, Milwaukee County, WI, November 13, 1843, Waukesha County, WI, July 12, November 4, 1846, April 13, 1847, WHS.

43. Joseph Wright to Hannah, Baltimore, MD, November 12, December 31, 1801, Joseph Wright Jr. to Aunt, McMahon's Creek, OH, June 3, 1805, Wright Family Letters, RSFI.

44. Charles Mickle to William Julius Mickle, London, England, March 23, 1831, William Julius Mickle to Charles Mickle, Ramosa Township, Guelph, Upper Canada, August 2, September 13, 1831, NAC.

45. Anthony Giddens, *A Contemporary Critique of Historical Materialism*, vol. 1: *Power, Property and the State* (Berkeley: University of California Press, 1981), 26–108, and *idem, Modernity and Self-Identity: Self and Society in the Late Modern Age* (Cambridge: Polity Press, 1991), 18–36, 80–114. Also see John Tomlinson, *Globalization and Culture* (Chicago: University of Chicago Press, 1999), 128–9. Giddens has not been concerned with population movements in his conceptualization of modernity, but instead with the transformation of the local under the impact of the global. For Giddens, the local would be transformed whether or not people remained sedentary, because, for him, the issue is the changing nature of relations of power, influence, and authority between the

local and the extralocal, and not individuals sorting themselves out across space in new patterns. Mine is, therefore, a particular extension of Giddens's work, with which he himself might not be in agreement.

46. Thomas Spencer Niblock to Edward T. Spencer, Delaware, Canada West, January 27, 1850, Thomas Spencer Niblock Letters, MG24 I80, NAC; Thomas Steel to Lilly Steel, Waukesha County, WI, December 3, 1852, WHS.

47. Radcliffe Quine to Francis and Marie Quine, Seattle, WA, September 29, 1881, in Erickson, *Invisible Immigrants*, 476. The Quine correspondence that documents his efforts to claim his share of his parents' estate is found in *ibid.*, 473–8. During 1878–1885, Quine wrote to legal authorities on the Isle of Man and his siblings on the Isle of Man as well as his brother in New Zealand.

48. The Petingale correspondence, which encompasses the years 1834–1883 and contains thirty-one letters from William, who died in 1847, Henry, and Thomas to their sisters and father is found in Erickson, *Invisible Immigrants*, 436–66.

49. For the history of Archbald's correspondence, see *infra*, chapter 9.

NOTES TO CHAPTER 5

1. Dan P. McAdams, *The Stories We Live By: Personal Myths and the Making of the Self* (New York and London: Guilford Press, 1993), 51.

2. James Horner to Father and Mother, Philadelphia, PA, August 18, 1801, Horner Letters, T. 1592, PRONI; Titus Crawshaw to Father, Mother, Sisters, Brothers, Relatives, and Friends, Philadelphia, PA, December 18, 1853, Charlotte Erickson, *Invisible Immigrants: The Adaptation of English and Scottish Immigrants in Nineteenth Century America* (Coral Gables: University of Miami Press, 1972), 333. Robert Smyth to Father and Mother, Philadelphia, PA, August 3, 1837, Robert and William Smyth Letters, 10 D, 1828, PRONI; Joseph Hartley to Cousin, Lockport, NY, August 27, 1861, in Michael Drake, ed., "'We Are All Yankeys Now': Joseph Hartley's Transplanting from Brighouse Wood, Yorkshire, Old England, to Lockport, New York, Told by Himself and His Wife in Letters Home," *New York History* 45 (July 1964): 235.

3. Matthew Dinsdale to Mother, New York, NY, September 14, 1844, Wis Mss, WHS; William E. Van Vugt, *Britain to America: Mid-Nineteenth-Century Immigrants to the United States* (Urbana: University of Illinois Press, 1999), 1–2.

4. Richard Hails to George Hails, Lincoln, MA, July 31, 1849, Collection 865, Collection of Regional History, CU.

5. Joseph Hartley to Cousin, Lockport, NY, December 1, 1863, Joseph and Rebecca Hartley to Brothers and Sisters, January 5, July 22, 1868, December 12, 1870, June 30 [1873–1875?], in Michael Drake, ed., "We Are All Yankeys Now," 235, 241, 246, 248, 257.

6. Joseph Wright Jr. to Aunt Martha, McMahon's Creek, OH, September ?, 1803, Wright Family Letters, #42–70, RSFI; William Julius Mickle to Charles, New York, NY, August 13, 1830, William Julius Mickle Letters, MG24 I59, NAC; Thomas Steel to Lilly, Milwaukee County, WI, July 2, September 15, 1844, Thomas Steel Papers, Wis Mss, 51PB, WHS.

7. Erickson, *Invisible Immigrants*, 189.

8. Radcliffe Quine to Brother and Sister, Victoria, British Columbia, Canada, April 22, 1861, in Erickson, *Invisible Immigrants*, 469.

9. Edward Phillips to Phillip Phillips, Urbana, OH, February 10, 1838, in Erickson, *Invisible Immigrants*, 270.

10. David Laing to Sister, Logansport, IN, February 19, 1873, Collection 812, Collection of Regional History, CU.

11. John and Margaret Griffiths to Father and Mother, Nauvoo, IL, March 4, 1850, John Griffiths to Brother and Sister, Appamoose, IN, April 23, 1865, in Erickson, *Invisible Immigrants*, 198–200, 200–2.

12. David Laing to Sister, Logansport, IN, February 19, 1873, CU.

13. Letitia White to Jenny [Jane] Sligo, March 21, 1804, to Jane Sligo, August 24, 1804, January 1, 1805; Judith Hale to Jane, Glouster, MA, February 23, 1810, July 12, 1814, Letitia White to John and Jane Sligo, August 15, 1815, Judith Hale to Jane, Portland, ME, August 18, 1826, VFM 2323, OHS.

14. James Horner to Father and Mother, Philadelphia, PA, August 18, [1801?], T. 1592, PRONI.

15. Thomas Steel to Father, Milwaukee County, WI, September 9, 1843, Thomas Steel Papers, Wis Mss 51PB, WHS.

16. Mary Ann Archbald to Margaret, Riverbank, June 15, 1819, September ?, 1838, Mary Ann Archbald Letters, Reel 965, History of Women Collection, SmC; Thomas Steel to James Steel, Waukesha County, WI, June 16, 1847, December 20, 1850, WHS.

17. William Barker to Uncle and Aunt, Connersville, IN, March 20, 1859, John Barker Family Papers, SC #2385, IHS.

18. *Infra*, chapter 9.

19. Too widespread for it to be practical to document, the habit of rushing letters into the mail because of pressing postal deadlines may well be more complicated a phenomenon than many letters-writers suggest. The possibility exists that pleading a deadline served as a rather benign cover for the lack of desire to write any further that was prompted by weariness with the task and a lack of subject-matter. Better to plead a deadline than confess boredom or lack of imagination. Of course, there is no way to determine the validity of this claim. In light of the frequent preoccupation with postal matters, however, it is certainly plausible that postal deadlines are relevant to the rhythms of writing.

20. The pre-1840 collections are John Fisher (10 letters); Joseph Wright (22); Mary Ann Archbald (84); and Joseph Willrocks (21). The post-1840 collections are Catherine Bond (19); Titus Crawshaw (27); William Darnley (27); David Laing (7); Thomas Steel (169); Thomas Spencer Niblock (29); Ralph Wade (30); and Matthew Dinsdale (27). Changes in international postal arrangements are described in chapter 4, *supra*.

21. In percentage terms, the results for the days of the week are, where the first percentage is for the pre-1840 sample and the second for the post-1840 sample: Monday (9 percent; 12 percent); Tuesday (15 percent; 20 percent); Wednesday (7 percent; 12 percent); Thursday (7 percent; 15 percent); Friday (14 percent; 12 percent); Saturday (9 percent; 12 percent); Sunday (6 percent; 14 percent). The percentage of undated or partially dated letters is 34 percent and 3 percent. The large figure, 34 percent for the pre-1840 sample is almost wholly (93 percent) the result of Mary Ann Archbald's dating practices. Days of the week were determined through the use of a perpetual calendar.

22. The percentages for the seasonal production of letters, where the first number is for the pre-1840 sample and the second number for the post-1840 sample, are Winter (14 percent; 21 percent); Spring (22 percent; 26 percent); Summer (24 percent; 26 percent); and Fall (26 percent; 24 percent).

23. Mary Ann Archbald to Clementina Ruthven, Riverbank, November 1822, SmC.

24. E.g., Mark M. Smith, "Old South Time in Comparative Perspective," *American Historical Review* 101 (December 1996): 1453.

25. Of the undated or partially dated letters in the pre-1840 sample, 42 of 45 were

written by Archbald, fully 93 percent. This was also 50 percent of Archbald's total production of letters. The other three correspondents in the pre-1840 sample had a much smaller percentage of undated letters in their total output of letters: Fisher (10 percent); Wright (9 percent); Willcocks (0 percent).

26. John Ronaldson to Eliza, East Braintree, MA, [May?] 1854, in Erickson, *Invisible Immigrants,* 378; Wayne E. Fuller, *Morality and the Mails in Nineteenth-Century America* (Urbana: University of Illinois Press, 2003).

27. Leila Locke to Jeanette Bonavacio, Point Pinellas, FL, December 12, 1888, January 16, March 8, 13, 29, April 12, 19, 1889, PC174, Box 1, Locke Family Papers, NLI. Each letter has a concluding section written by Richard Locke.

28. Joseph and Rebecca Hartley to Brothers and Sisters, Lockport, NY, January 5, 1868, in Drake, ed., "We Are All Yankeys Now," 243.

29. Kate Bond to Ellen, Milford, CT, December 30, 1871; to Brother, Bunker Hill, KS, July 4 [1884?], July 5 [1890], CU.

30. Thomas Steel to James Steel, Waukesha County, WI, November 15, December 16, 1846, August 1, 1848; to Lilly, February 10, 1851, WHS.

31. Joseph Hartley to Aunt and Cousin, Medina, NY, September 12, 1858, in Drake, ed., "We Are All Yankeys Now," 227; Nathan Haley to Father, Mother, Sisters, Brothers, Relatives and Friends, Wheeling, VA, September 10, 1825, in Erickson, *Invisible Immigrants,* 420; John Barker to ?, Connorsville, IN, December 21, 1856, IHS.

32. Mary Cumming to Margaret, Liverpool, England, August 30, 1811 [with the same language of "second parting" nearly exactly repeated in a letter to Margaret from Liverpool, September 22, 1811]; to Margaret, New York, NY, [October or November?] 1811, Mary Cumming Letters, 47.1475/2, PRONI.

33. Thomas and Jane Morris to Father and Mother, Brothers, and Sisters, Friends, Brooks Co., VA, November 12, 1830, in Erickson, *Invisible Immigrants,* 148.

34. John Fisher to Mother, Franklin, MI, June 11, 1832 (with addenda to Brothers; and Brother and Sister), to Mother, July 18, 1833, to Brother and Sister, July 23, 1833, Thomas and Jane Morris to Father and Mother, Brothers, and Sisters, Friends, Brooks Co., VA, November 12, 1830, in Erickson, *Invisible Immigrants,* 116–20.

35. George and Elizabeth Martin to "Honoured Parents," Coburg, Upper Canada, September 30, 1834, George Martin Papers, SLKE.

36. *Infra,* chapter 9.

37. Matthew Dinsdale to Mother, Liverpool, England, August 6, 1844, WHS.

38. "Petingale Series," in Erickson, *Invisible Immigrants,* 432–5.

39. Henry Squier to Relatives, n.p., January 7, 1853, Wis Mss, WHS; Van Vugt, *Britain to America,* 26. Also see Henry Squier to Aunt and Uncle, n.p., June 27, 1851, January 7, 1853, WHS.

40. Thomas Steel to James Steel, Waukesha County, WI, February 10, 1847, July 27, 1852, WHS.

41. Henry Squier to Relatives, n.p., January 7, 1853, WHS.

42. Robert Smyth to Parents, Brothers and Sisters, Philadelphia, PA, April 18, 1839, to Father, February 2, 1844, to Brother Jonathan, June 12, 1845, PRONI; John Kerr to Uncle, "near Pittsburgh," January 23, 1844, New Orleans, LA, January 29, 1849, February 1, 1850, in Ronald Wells, ed., *Ulster Migration to America: Letters of Three Families* (New York: Peter Lang, 1991), 120, 144, 151; Joseph Willcocks to Richard, York, Upper Canada, April 23, June 9, July 1, August 31, October 1, November 3, 26, 1800, January 18, 27, 1801, April ?, August 20, 1802, June 20, October 24, 1803, September 21, 1804, January 16, 1805, May 1, 1806, TMRL.

43. Joseph Wright to Hannah, Baltimore, MD, December 10, 1801, RSFI.

44. Joseph Hartley to Cousin, Lockport, NY, December 1, 1863, in Drake, ed., "We Are All Yankeys Now," 235.

45. James Steel to Thomas Steel, London, England, November 30, 1845, WHS; Charles Julius Mickle to William Julius Mickle, London, England, December 30, 1830, NAC.

46. Joseph Hartley to Aunt and Cousin, Lockport, NY, November 28, 1859, October 21, 1860, in Drake, ed., "We Are All Yankeys Now," 232, 233–4, describe Hartley's visit to Niagara Falls to see the tightrope walker, Blondin, and the 1860 presidential campaign; James and Matilda Roberts, Thomas and Mary Bradley, Thomas and James Roberts, and the Little Yankee to Children, Waterville, CT, April 13, 1850, in Erickson, *Invisible Immigrants,* 325.

47. John Ronaldson to Eliza, East Braintree, MA, May, 1854, in Erickson, *Invisible Immigrants,* 378; Robert McElderry to Sister, Lynchburg, VA, August 15, 1850, January 22, 1851, June 10, [1851?], October, 1852, September 24, 1853, Robert and William McElderry Letters, 7T2414, PRONI; Joseph Willcocks to Richard, York, Upper Canada, April 26, 1800, April 1802, TMRL.

48. Kate Bond to Brother, Milford, CT, September 3, 1872, CU.

49. Andrew and Jane Morris to Brother, Germantown, PA, November 19, 1831, in Erickson, *Invisible Immigrants,* 152–3.

50. John McBride to Father, Patterson, NJ, August 8, 1819, Watertown, NY, January 9, 1820, John McBride Letters, T. 2613, PRONI.

51. Titus Crawshaw to Father and Mother, Norristown, PA, March 9, 1857, in Erickson, *Invisible Immigrants,* 341.

52. To "My Freands in Mullyglass," Chebanse, IL, December 20, 1873, Charles Porter and Family Letters, D1152/2, PRONI.

53. *Ibid.*

54. Robert Craig to James McBride, Birmingham, AL, December 30, 1820, John McBride Letters, T. 2613, PRONI.

55. John McBride to Brother, Watertown, NY, April 5, 1824, PRONI; David Laing to Sister, Logansport, IN, February 19, 1873, in Erickson, *Invisible Immigrants,* 362; John Fisher to Brothers, Franklin, MI, June 11, 1832, in Erickson, *Invisible Immigrants,* 118.

56. Matthew Dinsdale to Mother, English Prairie, IL, October 10, 1844, WHS.

57. Thomas and Jane Morris to Father, Aurelius Township, Washington County, OH, February 7, 1832, and Andrew Morris to Brother, Philadelphia, PA, September 24, 1832, in Erickson, *Invisible Immigrants,* 155, 156–7.

58. Kate Bond to Brother, Milford, CT, July 5, 1870, September 3, 1872, to Ellen, December 22, 1872, CU.

59. John McBride to Brother, Watertown, NY, April 29, 1821, to Father (quote), February 24, 1822, PRONI. McBride did eventually extend the same offer of assistance, in the form of a place to live, to his brother in a letter, January 8, 1827, PRONI.

60. John Wade to Ralph Wade, Hamilton, Upper Canada, September 9, 1835, Robert Wade Letters and Family Papers, MG24I127, NAC.

61. John McBride to Father, Watertown, NY, January 9, 1820, PRONI.

62. Kate Bond to Ellen, Milford, CT, December 30, 1871, CU.

63. Robert Smyth to Parents, Liverpool, England, April 18, 1841, PRONI; Matthew Dinsdale to Edward, Philadelphia, PA, June 9, 1852, WHS; Joseph Hartley to Aunt and Cousin, Lockport, NY, October 21, 1860, to Cousin, August 27, 1861, in Drake, ed., "We Are All Yankeys Now," 233, 235; Kate Bond to Elen, Milford, CT, December 22, 1872, in Erickson, *Invisible Immigrants,* 216.

64. Rebecca Butterworth to Father, "Back Woods of America" [Outland Grove, AK], July 5, 1846, in Erickson, *Invisible Immigrants,* 175–8.

65. Robert Craig to James McBride, Birmingham, AL, December 30, 1820, PRONI.

66. Joseph Wright to Hannah, Baltimore, MD, December 10, 1801, RSFI.

67. Henry Johnson to Jane, Hamilton, Upper Canada, September 18, 1848, McConnell-Johnson Family Letters, TMRL.

68. Thomas Pryterch to G. Wace, Ithaca, NY, August 8, 1870, Pryterch Letters, 2598M, Collection of Regional History, CU.

69. See, for example, the instance of the Birkets in chapter 3, "Birket Series," in Erickson, *Invisible Immigrants,* 81–4, 86–97; and John Birket to Brother, Mount Pleasant, IL, May 19, 1843, in *ibid.,* 98.

70. Emily Tongate to Aunt and Uncle, Penn Yan, NY, September 23, 1874, in Erickson, *Invisible Immigrants,* 207–8.

71. Joseph and Rebecca Hartley, Lockport, NY, June 30, [1873–75?], in Drake, ed., "We Are All Yankeys Now," 255.

72. Erickson, *Invisible Immigrants,* 179; and Ann Whittaker to Brother, State of Illinois, January 1849, January 23, [1851?], June 24, 1851, *ibid.,* 182–7.

73. Kate Bond to Ellen, Milford, CT, December 30, 1871, to Brother, Milford, CT, September 3, 1872, May 24, [1873?], November 28, [1874?], CU.

74. Andrew and Jane Morris to Brother and Sister, Bristol, PA, October 19, 1829, to Brother, Aurelius, OH, August 13, 1842, February 21, 1846; Thomas and Jane Morris to Father and Mother, Aurelius Township, Washington County, OH, February 7, 1822, in Erickson, *Invisible Immigrants,* 146–7, 153–5, 169–70, 173–4.

75. *Infra,* chapter 10.

76. Charles Mickle to William Julius, London, England, October 30, 1830, December 15, 1831; Charles and Charles Julius Mickle to William Julius, London, England, December 30, 1830, January 15, February 22, March 23, August 30, September 13, 30, December 14, 1831; Charles Julius, Sarah, John, and Charles Mickle to William Julius, London, England, July 12, 1831; Sarah Mickle to William Julius, London, England, August 31, 1831, NAC. On the problem of the group letter inhibiting candor, Yves Frenette, Gabriele Scardellato, Bianca Gendreau, and John Willis, "The Immigrant Experience and the Creation of Epistolary Space: A Case Study" (unpublished paper in the author's possession, 2003).

77. See chapter 3, Buchanan Papers, ca. 1865–1905, PC247, NLI.

78. Erickson, *Invisible Immigrants,* 411–2; Nathan Haley to Parents and Relations, Liverpool, England, July 3, 1820, to Parents, Baltimore, MD, September 20, 1820, to Parents and Friends, Cincinnati, OH, January 16, 1821 (containing addendum, St. Louis, MO, April 12, 1821), to Parents, Relations and Friends, New Diggins, MO, March 1, 1823, to Father, Herculaneum, MO, May 20, 1823, Cincinnati, OH, December 19, 1823, to Father, Mother, Sisters and Brothers . . . Relations and Friends, Wheeling, VA, September 10, 1825, *ibid.,* 413–20.

79. George and Elizabeth Martin to Honored Parents, Cobourg, Upper Canada, September 30, 1834, to Brother, Rochester, NY, May, 1844, SLKE; John McLees to Brother, New York (?), August 28, 1828, to Father and Brother, November 7, 1831, to Brother, December 12, 1832, D.904/2a, 2b, 3a, 3c, 4, PRONI.

80. William Petingale to Father, [Bawburgh?] Mills, England, January 14, 1832, in Erickson, *Invisible Immigrants,* 436.

81. Henry Petingale to Father, Newburgh, NY, March 26, 1850, in Erickson, *Invisible Immigrants,* 448–9.

82. George Martin to Brother Alfred, Rochester, NY, January 18, 1852, SLKE; Radcliffe Quine to Brother and Sister, Seattle, WA, [June 2, 1878?], August 12, 1878, to Brother John Quine, December 1, 1879, to Francis and Maria Quine, September 29, 1881, March 26, 1882, July 1, [1882?], in Erickson, *Invisible Immigrants,* 473–4, 474–5, 475–6, 476–7, 477.

83. Matthew Brooks to Sister, Philadelphia, PA, n.d. [1857?]. The date has been determined by an internal reference in the letter to being "apart nearly 30 years."

84. John Ronaldson to Eliza, Schaghticoke, NY, April 9, December 4, 1853, East Braintree, MA, March 27, 1854, in Erickson, *Invisible Immigrants,* 372, 374, 377.

85. John Thomas to Wife, Swartara, PA, August 23, 1871, Wiconisco, PA, April 27, 1872, January 19, 1873; Thomas and Mary Williams to Sarah Thomas, June 30, 1873, John B. Thomas Letters, PSU.

86. William Darnley to Wife, Liverpool, England, June 3, 1857, New York, NY, October 25, 1857, March 16, April 13, May 17, July 20, November 11, 1858, May 23, 1859, March 18, April 24, July 17, September 4, 1860, February 18, April 9, 1861, May 21, 1862, and July 4, 1863, the last of which contains a long, angry summary of all the reverses he had encountered in Canada and the United States, and a protest against the rumors that he was living with another woman; William Darnley Letters, NYPL.

NOTES TO CHAPTER 6

1. Crawshaw's archived correspondence ends suddenly after what would for him, given a usually depressive tone, have to be characterized as a genial letter, reporting that he had been married; Titus Crawshaw to Father, Philadelphia, PA, June 18, 1866; Charlotte Erickson, *Invisible Immigrants: The Adaptation of English and Scottish Immigrants in Nineteenth Century America* (Coral Gables: University of Miami Press, 1972), 358–9. Laing's, too, ends suddenly, after a long emotional letter, in which he describes the collapse of his marriage, death of his daughter, and his loneliness; David Laing to Sister, Logansport, IN, July 13, 1876; Erickson, *Invisible Immigrants,* 367.

2. The lack of finality in the Darnley letter-series is especially frustrating to interpret. While it is true that Darnley's letters end suddenly, there is another letter in the archived correspondence that may or may not be relevant to resolving the puzzle. Written in a child's hand and unsigned, dated over twenty-one years after Darnley's last, angry letter to his wife from New York, and sent from Canada to an unknown destination and individual, it is very difficult to interpret. It does speak of an "Uncle William," who has gone to Manitoba to farm for the third time. But whether this uncle is William Darnley, we cannot know; ? to Aunt, North Dumfries, Ontario, Canada, March 18, 1884; Darnley Family Letters, NYPL.

3. Rebecca Hartley to Brother and Sister, Lockport, NY, December 9 [1876?], in Michael Drake, ed., "'We Are All Yankeys Now': Joseph Hartley's Transplanting from Brighouse Wood, Yorkshire, Old England, to Lockport, NY, Told by Himself and His Wife in Letters Home," *New York History* 45 (July 1964): 262.

4. In his last archived letter to Richard, Joseph Willcocks spelled out exactly the terms of his threat to cease writing. After noting that he had not heard from Richard in three years, he warned, "My patience is nearly worn out, however, I shall wait another year before I resolve to send you no more letters." Joseph Willcocks to Richard Willcocks, York, Upper Canada, May 1, 1806, Joseph Willcocks Letters, S128, TMRL.

5. There was, however, no suggestion of bad feeling in Horner's final letter in 1810, which came fully three years after his previous archived letter to his family. Though he

said he was unlikely to return to Ireland, especially to the extent that he was then keeping a general store, he invited his brothers to join him in the United States; James Horner to Thomas Horner, Vienna, MD, November 1, 1810, James Horner Letters, T.1592, PRONI.

6. At almost fifteen years in duration, Squier's is one of the longest-running expressions of impatience and ultimately discontent about having to continue to maintain a correspondence; e.g., Henry Squier to Aunt and Uncle, Pinchbeck, England, August 20, 1856, August 19, 1859, March 5, 1862, June 22, 1869; Wis Mss DX, WHS.

7. William McElderry to Brothers, Lynchburg, VA, June 14, 1860, New Orleans, LA, January 8, 1867, Robert and William McElderry Letters, MIC 57, PRONI.

8. John McLees to Brother, New York (?), December 12, 1832, July 8, 1833, John and Catherine McLees Letters, D904/2a, 2b, 3a, 3b, 3c, 4, PRONI.

9. John Barker to ?, Connersville, IN, June, 1857; William Ridge and Fanny Barker Ridge, Connersville, IN, December 1, 1857; William Barker to Uncle and Aunt, Connersville, IN, March 20, 1859, Hamilton, IN, July 12, 1863/February 10, 1864 (the same letter, dated twice); Elizabeth Barker to Uncle and Aunt, Bensonville, IN, n.d. (ca. 1858/1859); Thomas and Elizabeth Barker to Uncle and Aunt, Independence, IN, March 26, 1861, Ewing, IN, March 9, 1865, Barker Family Letters, #SC 2385, IHS.

10. Richard Birkbeck to Uncle, Wanborough, IL, November 12, 1820, January 23, 1822, Albion, IL, May 29, 1824, Gladys Scott Thomson, *A Pioneer Family: The Birkbecks in Illinois, 1818–1828* (London: Jonathan Cape, 1953), 69, 77, 88–91.

11. W. A. Langton, ed., *Early Days in Upper Canada: Letters of John Langton from the Backwoods of Upper Canada and the Audit Office of the Province of Canada* (Toronto: Macmillan, 1926), v–vi.

12. It is known that both Lister and Ronaldson returned to Britain, but Butterworth's fate is unknown. She wrote asking her father to provide money to finance the reemigration of her and her husband, but whether this occurred is not clear. Erickson, *Invisible Immigrants*, 175, 370, 380.

13. Haggard and Brennan, Solicitors to Samuel Buchanan, Wexford, Ireland, January 3, 1906, April 9, 1906; Samuel Buchanan to Haggard and Brennan, Davis Station, SC, March 26, 1906, Buchanan Papers, PC 247 and PC 431, NLI.

14. Rebecca Hartley to Brothers and Sisters, Lockport, NY, April 30 [1876], in Drake, ed., "We Are All Yankeys Now," 259–60; Thomas and Mary Williams to Sarah Thomas, Wiconisco, PA, June 30, 1873, John B. Thomas Letters, PSU; S. Charles Johnson to C. Mapledon, Melbourne, Australia, December 14, 1857, Thomas Spencer Niblock Letters, NAC.

15. Emily Tongate to Aunt and Uncle, Penn Yan, NY, September 23, 1874, in Erickson, *Invisible Immigrants,* 207–8.

16. John Bishop to Sister Caroline and Betsy, Penn Yan, NY, September 23, 1874, in Erickson, *Invisible Immigrants,* 208.

17. Thomas McCoy to Nephew, October 10, 1842, Alexander McCoy to brother, October 10, 1842, Slippery Rock, PA, October 10, 1842, two letters sent in the same envelope—both of which shed light on Robert McCoy's predicament, A. R. and T. McCoy Letters, D.1441, PRONI.

18. There are thirty-one Archbald letters from the 1820s that are archived, and sixteen letters from the 1830s and 1840, which was the last year of her life. The principal texts are the letters to her cousin and most intimate friend: Mary Ann Archbald to Margaret Wodrow, Riverbank, May 7, 1830, April 20, December 31, 1832, November 16, 1833, September 12, November 15, 1834, August 8, November 16, 1835, April 19, September [?], 1836, September 21, November 13, 1838, February 1, April [?], 1840, June 13, 1840, History of Women Collection, SmC. See also *infra,* chapter 9.

19. Mary Ann Archbald to Margaret Wodrow, Riverbank, September 21, 1838, SmC. (As noted in chapter 2, *Riverbank* and *Creekvale* are names of Archbald's farms and are not towns, so New York has not been attached.)

20. John Wade to Ralph Wade, Hamilton Township, Upper Canada, September 9, 1835, Canada West, October 2, 1842, Robert Wade to Ralph Wade, Hamilton Township, Upper Canada, January 10, 1836, John Wade and Robert Wade to Ralph Wade, Hamilton Township, Canada West, December 17, 1842, Robert Wade Letters and Family Papers, MG 24 I127, NAC; Roger G. Woodhouse, "Wade Family Correspondence," personal e-mail (August 28, 2003). There are no more Robert Wade letters in the archived collection after the last joint letter, written with his son. (What is now the province of Ontario was called Upper Canada until 1840, Canada West from 1840–1866, and from 1867, Ontario.)

21. Ralph Wade to William Wade, Hope, Canada West, January 3, 1854, NAC. There are nine archived letters written by Ralph Wade during his first decade in Canada (1846–1856), and eighteen written during the last decade of his life (1857–1867). On the making of the Wades' culture and class in Canada, see Andrew C. Holman, *A Sense of Their Duty: Middle-Class Formation in Victorian Ontario Towns* (Montreal and Kingston: McGill and Queen's University Press, 2000).

22. Ralph Wade to Friends, Hope, Canada West, May 1, 1866, NAC. For a study of the place of personal correspondence in nineteenth-century Canadian family networks without a transnational emphasis, see François Noël, *Family Life and Sociability in Upper and Lower Canada, 1780–1870: A View from Diaries and Family Correspondence* (Montreal and Kingston: McGill and Queen's University Press, 2003).

23. Ralph Wade to Friends, Hope, Canada West, October 4, 1866, NAC.

24. Ralph Wade to Friends, Hope, Canada West, August 5, 1858, NAC.

25. Ralph Wade to Friends, Hope, Canada West, August 5, 1858, NAC.

26. John C. Birket to Charles Birket, Peoria, IL, July 31, 1856 (with a postscript by John Birket), in Erickson, *Invisible Immigrants*, 102–3; and *ibid.*, 81–4 on the Birket family.

27. Joseph Wright Jr. to Aunt, McMahan's Creek, OH, June 3, 1805, Wright Family Letters, 1801–1842, #42–70, RSFI. The family continued to write to Martha, which establishes the fact that she did not emigrate. Margaret Wright, one of Joseph Wright's daughters who had stayed behind in Ireland after her parents went to the United States, did emigrate the next year, perhaps with the understanding that she would keep house for her father and siblings.

28. Marcus Lee Hansen, "The Problem of the Third-Generation Immigrant," *Report*, Augusta Historical Society Publications (Rock Island, IL,: Augusta Historical Society, 1938): 6–7.

29. Robert Bond to Cousin, Bunker Hill, KS, January 9, 188?; Kate Bond to Brother, Bunker Hill, KS, July 5, [1890?]; Kate Bond to Brother and Sister, Bunker Hill, KS, August 21 [1891?], Bond-Grayston Letters, #861, CU.

30. S[arah] J. Porter to Cousin, Chebanse, IL, July 5, December 25, 1887, April 10, 1889, March 14, 1895, August 26, 1908, August 15, 1911, June 14, 1916. (The 1889 and 1895 letters were written using her married name, "Wildman."), Charles Porter and Family Letters, 1844–1925, D1152/2, PRONI; David Lowenthal, *The Past Is a Foreign Country* (Cambridge: Cambridge University Press, 1985), 8.

31. Frank W. Reid to Cousin, New York, NY, April 3, 1887, in Erickson, *Invisible Immigrants*, 482.

32. Erickson, *Invisible Immigrants*, 6.

33. Erickson, *Invisible Immigrants*, 6.

34. Colin Pooley and Jean Turnbull, *Migration and Mobility in Britain since the Eighteenth Century* (London: UCL Press, 1998).

35. Erickson, *Invisible Immigrants,* 6.

36. There is, in fact, only one (of twenty-five) letter-series in Erickson's own collection in which the retention of letters is attributed to the legal necessity of documenting a process of inheritance; Erickson, "Smith Series, 1851–1860," in *Invisible Immigrants,* 189. The Smith letters form a greatly truncated collection in consequence of this purpose. Edward Smith's letters do not commence in the archived collection until seventeen years after he had emigrated.

37. Erickson, *Invisible Immigrants,* 6. Also see Wolfgang Helbich and Walter D. Kamphoefner, "How Representative Are Emigrant Letters? An Exploration of the German Case," in *Letters across Borders: The Epistolary Practice of International Migrants,* ed. Bruce Elliott, David A. Gerber, and Suzanne Sinke (New York: Palgrave, 2006), in which the authors discuss briefly the relation between greater levels of education and the willingness to donate letters and, thus, suggest who would be most likely to possess this capacity for historical consciousness.

38. Most of these expressions of thanks, permission, or acknowledgment are to individuals whose relationship to the letter-writer is unspecified. The most precisely specified cases, in contrast, are: the estate of a man sharing the surname of the writer; a woman whose father, as a young boy, knew the letter-writer; the son of the letter-writer; and the grandson of the letter-writer.

39. Erickson, *Invisible Immigrants,* 9; Charlotte Erickson, *Statement of Charlotte Erickson,* 2 November 1993. Originally broadcast as part of a BBC/Open University series on the work of contemporary historians, Professor Erickson's statement describes her search for immigrant letters as well as aspects of her research. Professor Erickson was kind enough to share a transcript of her remarks with me and further contextualize them; Charlotte Erickson to David Gerber, Cambridge, England, June 14, 1998 (author's possession).

40. In only one of Erickson's letter-series is the relationship between the individual acknowledged or thanked, as the owner of the letters, stated to be a second-generation relationship—the son of an individual (Ernest Lister) whose letters, dating from the mid-1880s, represent among the most recent in time of the letters collected by Erickson.

41. In the specific context of immigration history, this formulation resembles "Hansen's Law," according to which, as the historian Marcus Lee Hansen stated, the second generation wishes to forget the immigrant past and the third generation has a great deal of curiosity about it and is impelled to attempt revitalization of aspects of it; Hansen, *The Problems of the Third Generation,* 9–20. One must remember, however, that we are speaking here much less of the behavior and consciousness of the immigrants' descendants than of the homeland correspondents' descendants. Also Lowenthal, *The Past Is a Foreign Country,* 53.

42. Howard Finley, ed., *The Diaries of William and Elizabeth Peters Recounting the Voyage to the New World on the Good Brig "Friends" in 1830* (privately published by Howard Finley, Berwyn, IL, 1942); William Peters to Richard Peters, Township of Hope, Upper Canada, September 19, 1831, William Peters and Family Fonds, 1830–1831, M-5567, NAC.

43. Alexander C. McGraw to Virgil McGraw, Belfast, Ireland, July 12, 1871, McGraw Family Papers, #2355, CU.

NOTES TO CHAPTER 7

1. W. H. Reinelt, *Wreck of the Monumental City* (Geelong, Victoria, Australia: Marine Historical Publication, n.d.); S. Charles Johnson to C. Maplestone, Melbourne, Aus-

tralia, December 14, 1857, Thomas Spencer Niblock Fonds, MG 24 I 80, NAC, Ottawa, Canada.

2. www.familysearch.org: (Thomas Spencer Niblock, b. 1820, baptized at Hitchin, Hertford, England), consulted, September 19, 2002; Niblock married Matilda Irvine at Parramatta, New South Wales, Australia, in 1843; *Church of Jesus Christ of the Latter Day Saints, Australian Vital Records Index* (CD-ROM), V1843201 27C (1843).

Confusion surrounds the birth of the second Niblock child. Matilda Niblock is known to have been pregnant as recently as approximately two months prior to the family's emigration to Australia in 1853. The child was due in April. Its birth is not mentioned, however, in Thomas Spencer Niblock's letter from Australia to his family in England, which is certainly a peculiar omission. The child is instead mentioned in the letter that accompanied the donation of Niblock's letters to the National Library of Australia; Francis M. Morris to Mr. Lynraven, January 31, 1955, Thomas Spencer Niblock letters, MS 396, Manuscripts Division, NLA, Canberra, Australia.

3. Thomas Spencer Niblock to Edward Thomas Spencer, n.p., July 2, 1849, NAC.

4. Thomas Spencer Niblock to Edward Thomas Spencer, Delaware, Canada West, July 29, August 4, 1852, NAC.

5. Thomas Spencer Niblock to Edward Thomas Spencer, Melbourne, Australia, April 15, 1853, NLA.

6. Nina Glick Schiller, Linda Basch, Cristina Szanton Blanc, eds., *Towards a Transnational Perspective on Migration: Race, Class, Ethnicity, and Nationalism Reconsidered, Annals of the New York Academy of Science*, vol. 645 (New York: New York Academy of Sciences, 1992); Linda Basch, Nina Glick Schiller, Cristina Szanton Blanc, *Nations Unbound: Transnational Projects, Postcolonial Predicaments and Deterritorialized Nation-States* (Amsterdam: Gordon and Breach Publishers, 1994).

7. E.g., Charlotte Erickson, *Invisible Immigrants: The Adaptation of English and Scottish Immigrants in Nineteenth-Century America* (Coral Gables: University of Miami Press, 1972), 394–6.

8. Thomas Spencer Niblock Fonds, MG 24 I80, NAC. Of the letters that Thomas Spencer Niblock wrote from Canada, the first three letters, all dating from September 1849, were written from London, Canada West, and all but two of the remaining letters from the farm in Delaware, Canada West, where the Niblocks resided until September 1852.

9. Thomas Spencer Niblock letters, MS 396, Manuscripts Division, NLA. These letters were written from Cape Town, South Africa, and from Melbourne, Australia, in 1853.

10. Francis M. Morris to Mr. Lynraven, n.p., January 31, 1955, NLA.

11. Thomas Spencer Niblock to Edward Thomas Spencer, New York, NY, August 27, 1849, NAC.

12. Thomas Spencer Niblock to Edward Thomas Spencer, n.p., July 20, 1849, NAC.

13. Francis M. Morris to Mr. Lynraven, n.p., January 31, 1955, NLA; "Notes on the Niblock Family," Thomas S. Niblock Fonds (NAC). (Nothing is said in the correspondence of two brothers, both born at Hitchin, Hertford, England, Edward Spencer Niblock [b. 1822] and Joseph White Niblock [b. 1819]; www.familysearch.org, consulted September 19, 2002. It may be that neither survived into adulthood, though no record has been found of the death of either of them.)

14. Reginald L. Hine, *Confessions of an Uncommon Attorney* (New York: Macmillan, 1947), 220–1; Susan M. Laithwaite (Devon Record Office, Exeter, England), "Niblock Family History," personal e-mail (November 5, 2001); Thomas Spencer Niblock to Edward Thomas Spencer, n.p., July 20, 1849, NAC.

15. Francis M. Morris to Mr. Lynraven, n.p., January 31, 1955, NLA.

16. Thomas Spencer Niblock to Christiana Niblock Spencer, Rio de Janeiro, Brazil, July 30, 1845, NLA.

17. Thomas Spencer Niblock to Edward Thomas Spencer, n.p., July 20, 1849, NAC.

18. Thomas Spencer Niblock to Christiana Niblock Spencer, Delaware, Canada West, October 29, 1849, NAC.

19. Thomas Spencer Niblock to Edward Thomas Spencer, n.p., July 20, 1849, NAC.

20. Thomas Spencer Niblock to Edward Thomas Spencer, n.p., July 20, 1849, NAC.

21. Thomas Spencer Niblock to Edward Thomas Spencer, Delaware, Canada West, March 19, 1850, NAC. Niblock stated that he needed to hire a man to instruct him in practical farm and building tasks. An example of his lack of knowledge concerned the height of his fences. He constructed them too low to keep out stray cattle, who got into his fields and ate his crops; Thomas Spencer Niblock to Edward Thomas Spencer, Delaware, Canada West, August 4, 1850, NAC.

22. Thomas Spencer Niblock to Edward Thomas Spencer, London, Canada West, September 9 (quote), September 27, Delaware, Canada West, October 29, November 13, 1849, March 19 (quote), June 9, July 7, 1850, July 10, October 21, 1851, NAC.

23. Thomas Spencer Niblock to Edward Thomas Spencer, London, Canada West, September 9, 1849, Delaware, Canada West, July 29, 1852; Thomas Spencer Niblock to Christiana Niblock Spencer, London, Canada West, September 9, 1849, NAC.

24. Thomas Spencer Niblock to Edward Thomas Spencer, London, Canada West, September 9, 1849, NAC.

25. Thomas Spencer Niblock to Edward Thomas Spencer, London, Canada West, September 9, 1849, NAC.

26. Thomas Spencer Niblock to Edward Thomas Spencer, London, Canada West, September 9, 1849, NAC. J. David Wood, *Making Ontario: Agricultural Colonization and Landscape Re-Creation before the Railway* (Montreal and Kingston: McGill-Queen's University Press, 2000), 13, 85, estimates on the basis of projections for New England farms in the United States in the same era that a settler needed to cut an acre per year of forest to draw enough firewood to survive, and that most settlers averaged clearing about one and a half acres of land per year and seldom more than two to five acres. The advice Niblock received seems to have been prudent and based on the assumption, given his acreage, that he would be in residence for many years.

27. Thomas Spencer Niblock to Edward Thomas Spencer, London, Canada West, September 9, September 27, Delaware, Canada West, November 13, 1849; Thomas Spencer Niblock to Christiana Niblock Spencer, Delaware, Canada West, October 29, 1849, NAC.

28. *Dictionary of Canadian Biography,* s.v. "Langton, John"; W. A. Langton, *Early Days in Upper Canada: Letters of John Langton from the Backwoods of Upper Canada and the Audit Office of the Province of Canada* (Toronto: Macmillan, 1926).

29. Langton, *Early Days in Upper Canada,* 53. For an intensive case study of the settlement of the Upper Canadian agricultural frontier, with an emphasis on both speculation in land and the predominance of private credit relationships between individuals, see John Clarke, *Land, Power, and Economics on the Frontier of Upper Canada* (Montreal and Kingston: McGill-Queen's University Press, 2001).

30. Thomas Spencer Niblock to Edward Thomas Spencer, London, Canada West, September 9, 27, Delaware, Canada West, November 13, 1849, January 27, July 7, 1850; Thomas Spencer Niblock to Christiana Niblock Spencer, Delaware, Canada West, February 3, 1850, April 18, 1852, NAC.

31. Thomas Spencer Niblock to Edward Thomas Spencer, London, Canada West, September 9, Delaware, Canada West, October 29, November 13, 1849, January 27,

March 19, 1850; Thomas Spencer Niblock to Christiana Niblock Spencer, Delaware, Canada West, March 19, 1850, NAC.

32. Thomas Spencer Niblock to Edward Thomas Spencer, Delaware, Canada West, April 27, 1851, April 24, 1852, NAC.

33. Thomas Spencer Niblock to Edward Thomas Spencer, London, Canada West, September 27, 1849, NAC.

34. Of the thirty-four letters Niblock wrote to Edward and Christiana from Canada, twenty-four involved money, and fifteen contained pleas for assistance. Of course, the line between discussing his needs and his expenses, on the one hand, and asking for money, on the other, is very difficult to draw to the extent that Edward Spencer had assumed responsibility for his brother-in-law's maintenance.

35. Thomas Spencer Niblock to Edward Thomas Spencer, Delaware, Canada West, January 27, February 3, July 7, 1850; Thomas Spencer Niblock to Christiana Niblock Spencer, Delaware, Canada West, April 18, 1852, NAC.

36. Thomas Spencer Niblock to Edward Thomas Spencer, Delaware, Canada West, January 27, July 26, August 22, 1850, NAC.

37. Thomas Spencer Niblock to Edward Thomas Spencer, Delaware, Canada West, April 24, July 29, August 4, 1852, NAC. For assurances, direct and implied, that the debt would be paid in 1854, Thomas Spencer Niblock to Edward Thomas Spencer, Delaware, Canada West, January 27, July 7, 1850, NAC.

38. William F. Bullen to my dear sir [Edward Thomas Spencer], Delaware, Canada West, February 17, 1854, NAC.

39. Thomas Spencer Niblock to Edward Thomas Spencer, Delaware, Canada West, July 24, September 30, 1852, NAC.

40. William F. Bullen to my dear sir [Edward Thomas Spencer], Delaware, Canada West, February 17, 1854, NAC; Wood, *Making Ontario*, 101, 137.

41. Thomas Spencer Niblock to Christiana Niblock Spencer, Delaware, Canada West, September 9, 1849, October 27, 1850, July 29, August 4, September 30, 1852, NAC.

42. Thomas Spencer Niblock to Christiana Niblock Spencer, Delaware, Canada West, October 29, 1849, July 10, 1851, April 18, 1852, July 29, 1852, NAC.

43. Thomas Spencer Niblock to Christiana Niblock Spencer, Delaware, Canada West, February 3, 1850; Thomas Spencer Niblock to Edward Thomas Spencer, Delaware, Canada West, July 7, 1850, NAC.

44. Thomas Spencer Niblock to Christiana Niblock Spencer, London, Canada West, September 9, 1849, NAC.

45. N.a., *History of the County of Middlesex Canada* (Belleville, Ontario: Mika Studio, second ed., 1972), 485.

46. Thomas Spencer Niblock to Edward Thomas Spencer, Delaware, Canada West, November 13, 1849, NAC.

47. Thomas Spencer Niblock to Christiana Niblock Spencer, London, Canada West, September 9, 1849, NAC.

48. Thomas Spencer Niblock to Christiana Niblock Spencer, London, Canada West, September 9, 1849, NAC.

49. Thomas Spencer Niblock to Edward Thomas Spencer, n.p., July 20, 1849, NAC. If Niblock had known the prior pioneer history of European settlement in the section of Middlesex County in which he chose to reside, he might have changed his mind. It is replete with thievery, counterfeiting, bastardy, bigamy, speculation, and murder; *History of the County of Middlesex County Canada*, 476–80. Wood found the London district above the mean in crime for the three years he surveyed (1838, 1842, 1846); Wood, *Making Ontario*, 73–4.

50. Thomas Spencer Niblock to Edward Thomas Spencer, London, Canada West, September 27, Delaware, Canada West, October 29, 1849, January 27, March 19, 1850, NAC.

51. Thomas Spencer Niblock to Edward Thomas Spencer, Delaware, Canada West, June 9, 1850, NAC.

52. Thomas Spencer Niblock to Edward Thomas Spencer, Delaware, Canada West, November 13, 1849, NAC.

53. Thomas Spencer Niblock to Edward Thomas Spencer, Delaware, Canada West, January 27, 1850, NAC; Stan Shantz and Don Demaray, *The Post Office and Postmarks of London, Ontario* (Toronto: Unitrade Press, 1983), 1; *History of Middlesex County Canada*, 33–4.

54. Thomas Spencer Niblock to Edward Thomas Spencer, Delaware, Canada West, July 26, August 4, August 22, October 27, 1850, January 21, 1851, NAC.

55. Thomas Spencer Niblock to Edward Thomas Spencer, Delaware, Canada West, July 26, 1850, NAC.

56. Thomas Spencer Niblock to Edward Thomas Spencer, Delaware, Canada West, January 27, 1850, NAC.

57. Thomas Spencer Niblock to Christiana Niblock Spencer, Delaware, Canada West, February 3, 1850, NAC. This was both metaphor and literal designation; he spoke of the farm as "The Wanderer's Home," as if he were speaking symbolically about himself, but he also formally named the farm by the same title. He gave no evidence of needing to explain the contradiction that is inherent in this usage. But it does seem to suggest that Niblock did not feel at home in Canada and never really believed that he would settle permanently there.

58. Thomas Spencer Niblock to Christiana Niblock Spencer, Delaware, Canada West, March 19, 1850, NAC.

59. Thomas Spencer Niblock to Christiana Niblock Spencer, Delaware, Canada West, April 3, 1850, NAC.

60. Thomas Spencer Niblock to Edward Thomas Spencer, Delaware, Canada West, March 19, 1850, NAC.

61. Thomas Spencer Niblock to Christiana Niblock Spencer, Delaware, Canada West, July 10, 1850, NAC.

62. Thomas Spencer Niblock to Edward Thomas Spencer, Delaware, Canada West, July 7, 1850, NAC.

63. Thomas Spencer Niblock to Christiana Niblock Spencer, Delaware, Canada West, July 10, 1851, NAC.

64. Thomas Spencer Niblock to Christiana Niblock Spencer, Cape Town, South Africa, January 1, 1853, NLA.

65. Thomas Spencer Niblock to Edward Thomas Spencer, Delaware, Canada West, July 29, August 4, 1852, NAC.

66. Thomas Spencer Niblock to Edward Thomas Spencer, Melbourne, Australia, April 15, 1853, NLA.

67. Thomas Spencer Niblock to Edward Thomas Spencer, Melbourne, Australia, April 15, 1853, NLA.

NOTES TO CHAPTER 8

1. Charlotte Erickson, *Invisible Immigrants: The Adaptation of English and Scottish Immigrants in Nineteenth-Century America* (Coral Gables: University of Miami Press,

1972), 211, and on the Bonds' background in rural Lancashire and their emigration, 209–
12; *Russell Journal,* April 4, 18, 1888 (on the settlement and resources of the area in
which the Bonds resided in Kansas).

2. Hamlin Garland, *Main Travelled Roads* (New York: Harper Brothers, 1930), *idem,
Prairie Folks, or Pioneer Life on the Western Prairie* (New York: AMS Press, 1969), and
idem, A Son of the Middle Border (Lincoln: University of Nebraska Press, 1979); Solon
Buck, *The Agrarian Crusade: A Chronicle of the Farmer in Politics* (New Haven: Yale
University Press, 1920); John D. Hicks, *The Populist Revolt: A History of the Farmer's
Alliance and the People's Party* (Minneapolis: University of Minnesota Press, 1931); Law-
rence Goodwyn, *Democratic Promise: The Populist Movement in America* (New York:
Oxford University Press, 1976); Craig Miner, *West of Wichita: Settling the High Plains of
Kansas, 1865–1890* (Lawrence: University of Kansas Press, 1986).

3. *Russell Record,* October 9, 23, 1897.

4. *Russell Record,* October 9, 23, 1897; Roland Tappan Berthoff, *British Immigrants
in Industrial America, 1790–1850* (Cambridge: Harvard University Press, 1953), 179.

5. *Russell Record,* October 23, 1897.

6. *Russell Reformer,* December 18, 1908.

7. *Russell Record,* October 23, 1897; William G. Cutler, "Russell County," *History of
the State of Kansas,* Kansas Collection Books, http://www.ku.edu/carrie/kancoll/books/
cutler/russell/russell-co-p2.html; "BOND," Center Township, Russell County, KS, *Kansas
Agricultural Census,* 1895 (Topeka: State of Kansas, 1895); *Russell County Atlas* (Russell,
KS, n.p., 1901); *Inventory, Appraisement and Allowance, Decedent* [James Bond], (date
of original filing October 30, 1897, Probate Court, Russell County, KS); Pauline Bender,
Russell County Historical Society, personal letter to author, April 26, 2002. I would like
to acknowledge the assistance of Pauline Bender, who helped me to turn up relevant information about the Bonds in Probate Court and state and federal census records.

8. Pauline Bender, Russell County Historical Society, telephone conversation, April 4,
2002; Family Heritage Society, *Family Heritage Album of Russell County,* Kansas (Mc-
Pherson, KS: Family Heritage Society, 1973), 48.

9. Carolyn Heilbrun, "Women's Autobiographical Writings: New Forms," in *Modern
Selves: Essays on Modern British and American Autobiography,* ed. Philip Dodd (London:
Metheun, 1984), 14–27.

10. Erickson, *Invisible Immigrants,* 8–9.

11. Charlotte Erickson to the author, personal letters, October 8, 2000, March 10, 2001.

12. Erickson, *Invisible Immigrants,* 3, 9, 32–9, 241–6, 393–7; *idem, Leaving England: Essays on British Emigration in the Nineteenth Century* (Ithaca: Cornell University
Press, 1994), 4, 25–6. The concept of network has always been important for Erickson's
understandings of family migration and chain migration, largely because of her consciousness of the centrality of letters in tying people together across vast spaces.

13. The reader is reminded, therefore, that following up on these endnote references
will require consulting the original documents, not Erickson's printed collection of Bond
and Grayston letters.

14. The first two letters from America, dated July 5, 1870, and probably sent in the
same envelope, were sent to Sarah Grayston, a sister, and to an unidentified brother, who
could not have been Robert, because there is an inquiry made about Robert, by name, in
the latter. The other four letters inquire after some siblings by name, but not Robert or his
wife Ellen (sometimes spelled "Elen"), whom Kate addressed as "sister." My supposition
is that in light of the preponderance of letters to the couple in the collection, the fact that
they were not named means that they were, in fact, the addressees.

15. Catherine Bond to niece, Bunker Hill, KS, 1899?, CU.

16. Catherine Bond to brother, Bunker Hill, KS, 1889?, CU. Efforts to discover the background to this act of arson have yielded little information. Bond never mentioned it again. The local press, which condemned the act, rejected the notion, which was apparently held by some in the area, that it grew out of partisan political rivalries; *Russell Journal,* August 15, 1888; *Bunker Hill Gazette,* August 16, 1888.

17. Erickson's method for dating the Bond correspondence, which is based on Kate Bond's references to the age of her son Bob (born July 1869) at different points in the letters (Erickson, *Invisible Immigrants,* 212), proved generally plausible when subject to confirmation by other dates (i.e., the birth dates of the two other living sons) I employed; those dates were initially provided in a letter from Jill Holt, Russell County Historical Society, Russell, KS, to author, February 26, 1996, and confirmed later in the 1900 federal decennial census. In spite of all these various date checking devices, the dates of some of the letters cannot be any more than approximated, and hence a question mark is used to indicate these approximations at the relevant citation.

18. Catherine Bond to Ellen, Milford, CT, December 30, 1871; Catherine Bond to brother, Milford, CT, May 24, 1873?, November 28, 1874?, Bunker Hill, KS, 1889?, October 14, 1897, CU.

19. Catherine Bond to brother, Milford, CT, October 11, 1870, September 3, 1872, May 29, 1873?, November 24, 1874?; Catherine Bond to brother and sister, Bunker Hill, KS, Spring, 1892?; Catherine Bond to niece, 1899?, CU. The active correspondence with the aunts and uncles declined with the death of the older generation, and Kate suffered for not having known her cousins for decades, let alone their children. In her letter to her niece around 1899, she had to admit that she had "lost track of everyone nearly."

20. Catherine Bond to El[l]en, Milford, CT, December 22, 1872; Catherine Bond to brother, November 28, 1874, Bunker Hill, KS, January 9, 188?, October 14, 1897; Catherine Bond to niece, 1899, CU.

21. These remarks are based on the difference between the letters from Connecticut (1870–1874?) and those from Kansas (188?–1899). The latter demonstrate the ability to express more complex formulations. By the time of the first letters from Kansas, Kate's two oldest children had already been of school age for at least four years. All five of the surviving children were recorded as literate by the 1900 federal census; *United States Census of 1900,* vol. 45 (Center Township, Russell County, KS), T623–498 (microfilm).

22. Robert Bond to cousin, Bunker Hill, KS, January 9, 188?, CU.

23. Erickson, *Invisible Immigrants,* 211; James Grayston to sister, Grafton, WV, July 29, 1877, June 27, 1878, January 26, 1879; James Grayston, Rich Hills, MO, June 4, 1889, CU. Two of the four letters are signed "J and C Grayston," but the content makes it clear that James Grayston was the author of each of them.

24. Catherine Bond to brother, Bunker Hill, KS, June 26, 1881? (quote), 1889?; Catherine Bond to sister and brother, Bunker Hill, KS, July 4, 1884?, CU.

25. James Grayston to sister, Grafton, WV, June 27, 1878, CU.

26. James Grayston to sister, Bunker Hill, KS, January 26, 1879, CU.

27. Catherine Bond to sister [Sarah Grayston?], Milford, CT, July 5, 1870, Catherine Bond to brother, December 1, 1870, CU.

28. Catherine Bond to Ellen, Milford, CT, December 30, 1871, CU.

29. Catherine Bond to brother, Milford, CT, September 3, 1872, CU. By this Bond meant that they would not return to England if they had to work for wages to earn their living.

30. Catherine Bond to sister and brother, Bunker Hill, KS, July 4, 1884?, CU.

31. Catherine Bond to brother, Bunker Hill, KS, January 9, 188?, CU.

32. Catherine Bond to brother, Bunker Hill, KS, 1889?, CU.

33. *Russell Record,* October 23, 1897.
34. Catherine Bond (unsigned) to brother, Bunker Hill, KS, July 5, 1890?, CU.
35. Catherine Bond to brother and sister, Bunker Hill, KS, August 21, 1891?, CU.
36. Catherine Bond to brother and sister, Bunker Hill, KS, Spring, 1892?, CU.
37. Catherine Bond to brother and sister, Bunker Hill, KS, June 7, 1898?, CU.
38. Catherine Bond to niece, Bunker Hill, KS, 1899?, CU.
39. Hicks, *The Populist Revolt.*
40. Catherine Bond to brother, Milford, CT, July 5, 1870, August 11, December 22, 1872, May 24, 1873?. Evidence of remissions sent home to family in England is found in Catherine Bond to sister, Milford, CT, July 5, 1870; Catherine Bond to brother, Milford, CT, December 1, 1870, September 3, 1872, CU.
41. Erickson, *Invisible Immigrants,* 211.
42. Catherine Bond to brother, Milford, CT, November 28, 1874?; James Grayston to sister, Grafton, WV, June 27, 1878, CU.
43. Catherine Bond to brother, Bunker Hill, KS, June 26, 1881?, indicates that she had not heard from the Graystons in the approximately one year or more since they had left Kansas, though two letters (Catherine Bond to brother and sister, Bunker Hill, KS, February 3, 1891 and Catherine Bond to sister, Bunker Hill, KS, June 7, 1898?, CU) indicate that she was now back in touch with her brother, James. There is never any mention again of Ann Moran Grayston in Kate's correspondence after the one letter to her brother, Bunker Hill, KS, June 26, 1881?, CU, in which she gave her explanation of Ann's hostility to life on the prairie. She actually depended on her sister in England for a time for second-hand news about her brother and sister-in-law in neighboring Missouri; Catherine Bond to sister and brother, Bunker Hill, KS, July 4, 1884?, CU.
44. Linda Colley, *Britons: Forging a Nation, 1707–1837* (New Haven: Yale University Press, 1992), 17–54, 321–33; Berthoff, *British Immigrants in Industrial America,* 185–208.
45. Catherine Bond to El[l]en, Milford, CT, December 1, 1870, CU.
46. Catherine Bond to brother, Milford, CT, July 5, 1870, CU.
47. Catherine Bond to El[l]en, Milford, CT, December 1, 1870, CU.
48. James Grayston to sister, Bunker Hill, KS, January 26, 1879; Catherine Bond to brother, Milford, CT, May 24, 1873?, CU.
49. Telephone conversation, pastor (unidentified), St. Mary's Roman Catholic Church, Gorham, KS, April 13, 2002; *Russell Journal,* April 14, 1888; Erickson, *Invisible Immigrants,* April 4, 1888; http://skyways.lib.kansas.us/counties/RS.
50. Catherine Bond to brother, Bunker Hill, KS, June 26, 1881?, CU.
51. Catherine Bond to brother, Bunker Hill, KS, June 26, 1881?, CU.
52. Catherine Bond to brother and sister, Bunker Hill, KS, February 3, 1891, August 21, 1891, Spring, 1892?; James Grayston to niece, Rich Hill, MO, June 4, 1899, CU.
53. Catherine Bond to brother and sister, Bunker Hill, KS, February 3, 1891, CU. Also mentioned only once in her letters was the fact that one of her Grayston nephews, Tom Grayston, did return to the farm to help with planting and harvesting, though how frequently is unclear; Catherine Bond to sister, Bunker Hill, KS, June 7, 1898?. His wages are recorded in "Payment Cash during the Year (1898)," *Inventory, Appraisement and Allowance of Personal Property Decedent* [James Bond], (date of original filing, October 30, 1897), Probate Court, Russell County, KS.
54. Catherine Bond to Ellen, Milford, CT, December 30, 1871, CU.
55. Catherine Bond to brother, Milford, CT, May 24, 1873?, CU.
56. Catherine Bond to brother, Milford, CT, September 3, 1872, CU.
57. Catherine Bond to El[l]en, Milford, CT, December 22, 1872, CU.

58. Catherine Bond to brother, Bunker Hill, KS, June 26, 1881, CU.

59. Catherine Bond to sister and brother, Bunker Hill, KS, July 4, 1884?, CU.

60. Kate records Jim's purchase of farm machinery in Catherine Bond to brother, Bunker Hill, KS, June 26, 1881?, July 5, 1890?; Catherine Bond to sister and brother, Bunker Hill, KS, July 4, 1884?, CU. In contrast are her remarks that contend that they owned less after almost twenty years in Kansas than they brought from Connecticut; Catherine Bond to brother, Bunker Hill, KS, 1889?, CU. There is no evidence that the Bonds sold off any farm assets, and we know from the Probate Court records of both James's and Kate's estates that they had acquired considerable livestock and farm machinery. It is, therefore, hardly likely they had less property, though they may well have had less cash. Her remarks do suggest different standards of wants and desires, and for measuring what they had accomplished in life, than her husband possessed.

61. These remarks need to be qualified to some extent by the fact that the statements in one of Kate's letters expressing grief about Maggie were addressed explicitly to her sister-in-law Ellen, whose son Peter had recently died, and spoke of their common experience, as women, of "a loss that none but a mother can feel"; Catherine Bond to brother and sister, Bunker Hill, KS, August 21, 1891?, CU.

62. Catherine Bond [unsigned] to brother, Bunker Hill, KS, July 5, 1890?, to sister, 1890?, to brother and sister, August 21, 1891?, Spring, 1892?, CU.

63. Catherine Bond to brother, Bunker Hill, KS, October 14, 1897, CU.

64. Catherine Bond to brother, Milford, CT, November 28, 1874?, CU.

65. Catherine Bond to brother and sister, Bunker Hill, KS, July 4, 1884?, CU.

66. *Russell Record,* October 23, 1897.

67. Catherine Bond to sister and brother, Bunker Hill, KS, July 4, 1884?, [unsigned] to brother, July 5, 1890, CU.

68. Catherine Bond [unsigned] to brother, Bunker Hill, KS, July 5, 1890?, CU.

69. Catherine Bond to brother and sister, Bunker Hill, KS, August 21, 1891?, CU.

70. Catherine Bond to brother and sister, Bunker Hill, KS, Spring, 1892?, CU.

71. Catherine Bond to brother and sister, Bunker Hill, KS, Spring, 1892?, CU.

72. Catherine Bond to sister, Bunker Hill, KS, 1890?, CU.

73. Catherine Bond to brother, Bunker Hill, KS, 1889?, CU.

74. Catherine Bond to brother, Bunker Hill, KS, 1889?, CU.

75. Catherine Bond to sister and brother, Bunker Hill, KS, July 4, 1884?, CU.

76. Catherine Bond to sister and brother, Bunker Hill, KS, July 4, 1884?, CU.

77. Robert Bond to cousin, Bunker Hill, KS, January 9, 188?; Catherine Bond to brother, Bunker Hill, KS, July 5, 1890?, CU.

78. Catherine Bond to brother, Bunker Hill, KS, July 4, 1890?, October 14, 1897, CU.

79. *Russell Record,* October 9, 23, 1897.

80. *Russell Record,* October 23, 1897.

NOTES TO CHAPTER 9

1. R. Angus Downie, *Bute and the Cumbraes* (London and Glasgow: Blackie and Sons Limited, 1934), 48.

2. Downie, *Bute and the Cumbrae*s, 49–53.

3. Downie, *Bute and the Cumbraes,* 48–9.

4. Downie, *Bute and the Cumbraes,* 48, 50–2, 95–8; John Eaton Reid, *History of the County of Bute and Families Connected Therewith* (Glasgow: Thomas Murray and Son, 1864), 76–80, 159, 216–27, 223–5.

5. *The Dictionary of National Biography,* s.v. "Montgomery, Hugh, Twelfth Earl of Eglinton (1739–1819)"; Reid, *History of the County of Bute,* 224–6.

6. Tom Devine, *The Transformation of Rural Scotland: Social Change and the Agrarian Economy, 1660–1815* (Edinburgh: Edinburgh University Press, 1994), 46–7, 50, 125–32, 148–9. Alison M. Scott, "'These Notions I Imbibed from Writers': The Reading Life of Mary Ann Wodrow Archbald (1762–1841)" (Ph.D. diss., Boston University, 1995), 43–4; Mary Ann Archbald, *Diary, 1804,* August 25, 1804, *1805,* April 6, 1806, History of Women Collection, SmC; Mary Ann Archbald to Margaret Wodrow, Little Cumbrae, Scotland, July 7, 1804, December 5, 1806, SmC.

7. Mary Ann Archbald to Margaret Wodrow, Little Cumbrae, Scotland, July 7, 1804, SmC.

8. Mary Ann Archbald to Mr. Summervil, Creekvale, 1808; Mary Ann Archbald to Margaret Wodrow, September 3, 1808, Riverbank, April 28, 1820, August 10, 1822, Auriesville, NY, November 16, 1833, November 15, 1834, September 21, 1838; Mary Ann Archbald to Editor, *Montgomery Republican,* Riverbank, 1818 (or 1820?); Mary Ann Archbald to Mrs. Hildreth, Riverbank, September, 1820; Mary Ann Archbald to Governor DeWitt Clinton, Riverbank, October, 1821; Mary Ann Archbald to James Archbald IV, Riverbank, August 6, 1828, SmC. (As noted earlier, in chapter 2, Creekvale and Riverbank are names of Archbald's farms and not towns, so New York has not been attached.)

9. Scott, "These Notions I Imbibed from Writers," 27–8; Mary Ann Archbald to Margaret Wodrow, Creekvale, December 5, 1806; Mary Ann Archbald to Mr. G, Creekvale, March, 1810; Mary Ann Archbald to Mr. Custis, Creekvale, 1810; Mary Ann Archbald to Mr. Dailey, Riverbank, September, 1814, SmC. Andrew Wodrow died in 1814, before Mary Ann had the opportunity to visit him in Virginia. They had not seen one another since Andrew's emigration, which had taken place when Mary Ann was a very young child.

10. Mary Ann Archbald to Margaret Wodrow, Creekvale, April 18, 1807, SmC. Mary Ann's mother was a Ruthven and John Ruthven's aunt. On the connection between the Archbalds and the Ruthvens, including the New York branch of that family, see Scott, "These Notions I Imbibed from Writers," 28, 49, n. 79, 49.

11. Mary Ann Archbald to Margaret Wodrow, Little Cumbrae, Scotland, July 7, 1804, SmC; Mary Ann Archbald, *Diary, 1804; 1805, passim,* esp. April 18, 1804, SmC.

12. Mary Ann's mother was living with her at the time the family faced their decision about emigration. She would eventually find a place to live with a cousin in Edinburgh; Scott, "These Notions I Imbibed from Writers," 46.

13. E.g., Mary Ann Archbald to Margaret Wodrow, Riverbank, November 30, 1816, October 11, 1817, June 12, December 31, 1818, December 31, 1819, April 28, 1820, January 1, 1821, January 13, 1822, December 31, 1832, Auriesville, NY, November 15, 1834, SmC.

14. Mary Ann Archbald, *Diary, 1804, passim;* Mary Ann Archbald to Margaret Wodrow, Riverbank, April 28, 1820, January 1, 1821, SmC.

15. Mary Ann Archbald to Margaret Wodrow, Greenock, Scotland, March 20, 1807, SmC. They left with £600 in the bank and a local debt of £160. It is not clear how much cash they brought to America nor when the debt was repaid.

16. Mary Ann Archbald to Margaret Wodrow, Greenock, Scotland, March 20, 1807, SmC.

17. Mary Ann Archbald to Margaret Wodrow, Greenock, Scotland, February 1807, SmC.

18. Mary Ann Archbald to Margaret Wodrow, Riverbank, December 31, 1818, April 28, 1820, January 13, 1822, SmC.

19. Mary Ann Archbald to Margaret Wodrow, Riverbank, September 13, 1824, SmC; n.a., *Archibald [sic] Graveyard near Auriesville, New York, Record of Cemeteries in Montgomery County* (Fonda, NY: Montgomery County Department of History and Archives, n.d.), n.p.

20. Scott, "These Notions I Imbibed from Writers," 39–40.

21. Mary Ann Archbald to John Ruthven, April, 1826, SmC.

22. Scott, These Notions I Imbibed from Writers," 25–6, and n. 2, 26; Mary Ann Archbald to Margaret Wodrow, Riverbank, November 12, 1812, SmC.

23. Scott, "These Notions I Imbibed from Writers," 31–2, and n. 18, 32; Mary Ann Archbald to Margaret Wodrow, Riverbank, June 12, 1828, May 7, 1830, SmC.

24. Scott, "These Notions I Imbibed from Writers," 32–4. Kathryn Clippinger, who has studied Archbald's preemigration life thoroughly through reading Mary Ann's diaries, has noted reference to two previous suitors, Mr. McKay and Mr. Robb; Kathryn Clippinger, "Mary Ann Archbald Suitors," personal e-mail (November 24, 2002).

25. *Dictionary of Scottish Church History and Theology,* s.v. "Wodrow, Robert"; *Fasti Ecclesiae Scoticanae,* s.v. "Wodrow, James"; Louise Yeoman, National Library of Scotland, "Woodrow Family Heritage," personal e-mail (October 3, 1997).

26. *Dictionary of Scottish Church History and Theology,* s.v. "Wodrow, Robert"; s.v. "Wodrow Society; *Fasti Ecclesiae Scoticanae,* s.v. "Wodrow, Robert"; *Dictionary of National Biography,* s.v. "Wodrow, Robert"; Robert Wodrow, *The History of the Sufferings of the Church of Scotland from the Restoration to the Revolution* (Edinburgh: James Watson, 1721–2) and second ed., ed. Robert Burns, 4 vols. (Glasgow: Blackie and Son, 1828); Mary Ann Archbald to Margaret Wodrow, Riverbank, January 13, 1822, June 12, 1828, October 10, 1828, April 20, 1832, SmC.

27. Mary Ann Archbald to Margaret Wodrow, Riverbank, April 28, 1820, SmC. December 31 is the traditional Scottish holiday of *Hogmanay,* but Archbald never referred to the day by that name, and restricted her memories of celebration to the evening hours before the turning of the year.

28. Mary Cumming Letters (1811–1815), T.1475/2, PRONI.

29. Mary Ann Archbald to Margaret Wodrow, Riverbank, August 13, 1813, March 13, 1815, January 1817, April 28, 1820, October 10, 1828, Auriesville, NY, February 1, 1840, SmC. It is quite possible that in the area of the Firth of Clyde, Little Cumbrae was vernacularly called "the little isle" to distinguish it from its larger and nearby neighbor, Great Cumbrae. My point, however, is less geographic description than the symbol that emerged in Archbald's writing. This was also, more importantly, Mary Ann Archbald's purpose in developing this usage.

30. Mary Ann Archbald to W. C. Wodrow, Riverbank, 1820, SmC. Interactions with Scots, over the course of three decades, appear from the correspondence to have been with occasional house guests and travelers and once in the context of a wedding; Mary Ann Archbald to Mr. Summervil, Creekvale, July 3, 1808; Mary Ann Archbald to Margaret Wodrow, Creekvale, September 3, 1808, and Riverbank, June 15, December 21, 1819, January 1, 1821, January 13, 1822, May 7, 1830, SmC.

31. Mary Ann Archbald to Mr. Summervil, Creekvale, 1808; Mary Ann Archbald to Mr. G., Creekvale, 1809, March, 1810; Mary Ann Archbald to John Ruthven, Creekvale, 1809; Mary Ann Archbald to Margaret Wodrow, Riverbank, November 12, 1812, November 30, 1816, October 11, 1817, December 31, 1818, January 13, 1822, Mary Ann Archbald to Mr. McFarlane, Riverbank, January 1817, Mary Ann Archbald to Mrs. Hildreth, Riverbank, September 1820, SmC.

32. Mary Ann Archbald to Margaret Wodrow, Riverbank, April 28, 1820?, SmC; Washington Frothingham, *History of Montgomery County* (Syracuse: D. Mason and Co.,

1892), 287; Rayden Woodward Vosburgh, transcriber, *Records of the First Reformed Protestant Dutch Church at Glen in the Town of Glen, Montgomery County, New York* (New York: Genealogical and Biographical Society, 1918), 2, 64.

33. Mary Ann Archbald to Mr. McFarlane, Riverbank, January, 1817 (quote); Mary Ann Archbald to Margaret Wodrow, Riverbank, August 10, 1822, SmC. ·

34. Ruairidh H. MacLeod, *Flora MacDonald: The Jacobite Heroine of Scotland and America* (London: Shepherd and Walwyn, 1995); Mary Ann Archbald to Margaret Wodrow, Creekvale, February 1807, Riverbank, August 10, 1822, Mary Ann Archbald to Dr. Wodrow, Creekvale, June 20, 1809, SmC.

35. Archbald took on additional custodial and parenting obligations that made her life yet more complicated. For a time she had living with her two of the Ruthven children who were sickly; it was thought they would profit from residence in the country. She also raised an unrelated orphan, who was without personal resources, at the request of county authorities; Scott, "These Notions I Imbibed from Writers," 53.

Archbald's tombstone reads, "Widow of James. Granddaughter of Rev. Robt. Wodrow, author, 'History of the Church of Scotland' . . . ," *Archibald [sic] Graveyard near Auriesville, New York,* n.p. (The book title on the tombstone is, in fact, incorrect.)

36. Mary Ann Archbald to Mrs. James Ruthven, Riverbank, 1816, SmC; Elizabeth S Duvall, *Archbald Collection, 1784–1814 (+1984)*, data sheet for the *National Union Catalog of Manuscript Collections* (March 15, 1966, and augmented, n.d.), SmC; Kathleen Banks Nutter, reference archivist, Smith College, "Mary Ann Archbald: History and Letters," personal e-mail (April 25, 28, 2003).

37. Mary Ann Archbald to Margaret Wodrow, Greenock, Scotland, February, 1807, SmC.

38. Scott, "These Notions I Imbibed from Writers," 17–23 and *passim.*

39. Mary Ann Archbald to Margaret Wodrow, Riverbank, November 15, 1834, SmC.

40. Mary Ann Archbald to Margaret Wodrow, Riverbank, October 11, 1817, June 12, December 31, 1818, December 31, 1819, January 21, 1821, January 13, 1822, October 10, 1828, December 31, 1832, Auriesville, NY, August 8, November 16, 1835, September 1836, September 21, 1838, April, 1839, SmC; Alison Scott, "Mary Ann Archbald History," personal e-mail (July 22, 2002).

41. Mary Ann Archbald to Margaret Wodrow, Riverbank, June 12, December 31, 1818, April 28, 1820, January 13, 1822, SmC.

42. Duvall, *Archbald Collection, 1784–1840 (+1984),* SmC; Knutter to author, April 23, 28, 2002.

43. Duvall, *Archbald Collection, 1784–1840 (+1984),* SmC; Scott, "These Notions I Imbibed Writers," 52–5, which contains footnotes that cite letters not found in the Hugh Archbald transcriptions. On Anne Ruthven Wodrow, Mary Ann's mother, and her relationship with her daughter; Scott, *ibid.,* 28, Mary Ann Archbald to Margaret Wodrow, Riverbank, November 12, 1812, SmC. On Margaret Wodrow's destruction of letters; Mary Ann Archbald to Margaret Wodrow, Riverbank, April, 28, 1820, SmC. Since there is no trace of Margaret's letters to Mary Ann, perhaps Archbald did indeed destroy them at some time.

Evidence for the illegitimacy of the birth comes not only from reading between the lines of letters and reconstructing a chronology from the letters, but also from baptismal records. Louisa's son George was baptized at a church in the village of Fonda, NY, five miles north of Auriesville, NY, and across the Mohawk. This was in itself unusual, for it was not the church where the family worshiped. The baptismal record for George contains "no father named," in place of the father's name; n.a., *Baptism Record of Caughnawaga*

Reformed Church, Fonda, New York, 1758–1899 (Fonda: n.d.), "Helen Louisa Archbald" (March 19, 1830).

44. Mary Ann Archbald to Margaret Wodrow, Auriesville, NY, June 13, 1840, SmC. Additional internal evidence, proving the transcriptions are based on the originals, is found in Mary Ann Archbald to Margaret Wodrow, Riverbank, August 10, 1822, SmC, in which Hugh Archbald notes a part of the original had been excised to remove discussion of a scandal (see *infra*, n. 80).

45. Alison Scot, "Mary Ann Archbald History," personal e-mail (July 22, 2002).

46. Mary Ann Archbald to Mr. Summervil, Creekvale, 1808; Mary Ann Archbald to Mr. G., Creekvale, May 29, 1809 (quote), March 1810, Mary Ann Archbald to Mr. McIntyre, Creekvale, 1810, Mary Ann Archbald to Mr. L, Creekvale, April, 1810, Mary Ann Archbald to Mr. Custis, Creekvale, 1810?, SmC. James's discomfort with writing may help to account for the fact that he did not write to his own father, though it is possible the father himself may have had low or no literacy. Eventually Mary Ann had to make inquiries in James's behalf to find out if his father were still alive; Mary Ann Archbald to Margaret Wodrow, Riverbank, March 13, 1813, SmC.

47. Mary Ann Archbald to Margaret Wodrow, Riverbank, October, 1811 November 12, 1812, March 13, 1815, SmC; Scott, "These Notions I Imbibed from Writers," 47–9. Mary Ann Archbald to Mr. G., Creekvale, May 29, 1809 was in actuality a letter to Thomas Jefferson; Susan Perdue (*Papers of Thomas Jefferson, Retirement Series*), "Mary Ann Archbald History," personal e-mail (September 11, 2003). Why Archbald disguised the identity of Jefferson in her copybook is unclear.

48. Mary Ann Archbald to John Ruthven, Riverbank, August 1813, July 20, 1820; Mary Ann Archbald to Margaret Wodrow, Riverbank, June 12, 1828, SmC. For the Ruthvens' visits to the Archbalds, see Mary Ann Archbald to Margaret Wodrow, Creekvale, September, 1807, September 3, 1808, Riverbank, August 10, 1822, September 13, 1824, July 22, 1829, Auriesville, NY, April 20, 1832, SmC.

49. Mary Ann Archbald to Margaret Wodrow, Creekvale, September, 1807, September 3, 1808, Riverbank, June 12, August 17, 1818, December 31, 1819, April 28, 1821, December 31, 1823, July 22, 1829, May 7, 1830, Auriesville NY, September, 1836, November 13, 1838; Mary Ann Archbald to Rev. Dr. Wodrow, Creekvale, April 19, 1808?; Mary Ann Archbald to James Ruthven, Creekvale, April 1809, SmC. Archbald's engagement with the local post office had a long history. After fifteen years in Auriesville, Archbald invited Wodrow to try sending letters to the Auriesville, New York, Post Office (Mary Ann Archbald to Margaret Wodrow, Riverbank, January 13, 1822, SmC), but this experiment appears to have been a failure, because she did not strongly urge the same course again until her former son-in-law became postmaster; Mary Ann Archbald to Margaret Wodrow, Riverbank, September 18, 1834. She was still using the Ruthvens for at least some Scottish correspondence as late as 1838 (Mary Ann Archbald to Margaret Wodrow, Auriesville, NY, November 13, 1838, SmC).

50. Mary Ann Archbald to Margaret Wodrow, Creekvale, October 10, 1807, June 20, 1809, Riverbank, October, 1811, March 13, 1815; Mary Ann Archbald to Rev. Dr. Wodrow, Creekvale, April 19, 1808?, SmC.

51. Mary Ann Archbald to Mr. Dailey, Riverbank, September 1814; Mary Ann Archbald to Margaret Wodrow, Riverbank, October 11, 1817, June 12, August 7, 1818, November 16, 1832, SmC.

52. Mary Ann Archbald to Margaret Wodrow, Little Cumbrae, Scotland, February, 1807, Creekvale, September 1807, June 20, 109, Riverbank, October, 1811, August 7, 1818, January 21, 1821, SmC.

53. Of the ten extant New Year's Eve letters, it is possible to determine in eight cases how long Archbald worked, journal-like, on them prior to mailing them: the average is 4.5 months. Mary Ann Archbald to Margaret Wodrow, Riverbank, November 30, 1816 (?); December 31, 1818 (4 months); December 31, 1819 (5 months), January 21, 1821 (6 months), December 31, 1822 (4 months), December 31, 1823 (6 months), December 31, 1824 (5 months), January 1, 1826 (4 months), January 1827 (?); December 31, 1832 (4 months), SmC.

The tradition of the New Year's Eve letter was present before emigration in the years when the two women could not share each other's company; Mary Ann Archbald to Margaret Wodrow, December 31, 1806, SmC. Why it recommenced in America when it did (1816), and why it ended when it did (1836) is not clear. It may be, of course, that there are letters missing from the archived collection but there is no internal evidence in the other archived letters that would point to such a conclusion.

54. Mary Ann Archbald to Margaret Wodrow, Riverbank, December 31, 1824, SmC. Other New Year's Eve letters that seek to evoke this intimate atmosphere are Mary Ann Archbald to Margaret Wodrow, Riverbank, November 30, 1816, December 31, 1818, December 31, 1819, December 31, 1822, December 31, 1823, December 31, 1824, SmC.

55. Carroll Smith-Rosenberg, "The Female World of Love and Ritual," *Signs* 1 (Autumn 1975): 1–29.

56. Mary Ann Archbald to Margaret Wodrow, Creekvale, June 20, 1809, Riverbank, November 12, 1812, November 30, 1816 (quote), SmC; Rebecca Earle, "Introduction," in *Epistolary Selves: Letters and Letters Writers, 1600–1945*, ed. *idem* (London: Ashgate, 2000), 8–10.

57. Mary Ann Archbald to Margaret Wodrow, Riverbank, January 1, 1821, SmC. For other complaints that she had not heard from Margaret for what seemed an unusually long time, see Mary Ann Archbald to Margaret Wodrow, Riverbank, August 7, 1818, December 31, 1819, December 31, 1823, SmC, like the one that is quoted, were probably as much prompted by loneliness and by the vagaries of the post as Margaret's lack of diligence. There were occasions when Wodrow received two letters at once or within a few days of one another, suggesting delays in postal service or in the comings and goings of the personal couriers upon whom she often depended.

58. Mary Ann Archbald to John Ruthven, Riverbank, April 1826; Mary Ann Archbald to Margaret Wodrow, Auriesville, NY, November 16, 1833, SmC.

59. Mary Ann Archbald to Margaret Wodrow, Riverbank, January 1, 1821; see also Mary Ann Archbald to George Ruthven, Riverbank, April 1826, SmC.

60. Mary Ann Archbald to Margaret Wodrow, Riverbank, January 13, 1822. For other evidence of dreams inspiring writing, see Mary Ann Archbald to George Ruthven, Riverbank, April 1826, Mary Ann Archbald to Margaret Wodrow, Riverbank, October 10, 1828, SmC.

61. Mary Ann Archbald to Margaret Wodrow, Riverbank, November 30, 1816, SmC.

62. Mary Ann Archbald to Margaret Wodrow, Little Cumbrae, Scotland, February 1807, Creekvale, June 20, 1809, Riverbank, November 30, 1816, December 31, 1820, January 21, 1821, January 13, 1822, January 1, 1826, Auriesville, NY, April 19, 1836, SmC, where double-voicing is the anticipation of Margaret's response, but not a direct reply to an explicit comment or a question from Margaret.

63. Mary Ann Archbald to Rev. Dr. Wodrow, Creekvale, April 19, 1808?; Mary Ann Archbald to Margaret Wodrow, Riverbank, October 11, 1817, June 12, December 31, 1818, September 29, 1821, January 13, 1822, July 22, 1829, Auriesville, NY, September 1836, June 13, 1840, SmC.

64. Mary Ann Archbald to Margaret Wodrow, Riverbank, May 7, 1830, SmC.

65. Mary Ann Archbald to Margaret Wodrow, Riverbank, January 1, 1826, SmC.

66. David A. Gerber, "Ethnic Identification and the Project of Individual Identity: The Life of Mary Ann Archbald (1768–1840) of Little Cumbrae Island, Scotland and Auriesville, New York," *Immigrants and Minorities* 17 (July 1998): 1–22.

67. Mary Ann Archbald to Margaret Wodrow, Creekdale, June 20, 1809, Riverbank, November 30, 1816, June 12, 1818, September 29, 1821, October 10, 1828, May 7, 1830, April 20, 1832; Mary Ann Archbald to James Ruthven, Creekvale, April 1809, Riverbank, August 1817, SmC.

68. E.g., Dutch neighbors: Mary Ann Archbald to Mr. Summervil, Creekvale, 1808, Mary Ann Archbald to Mr. G., Creekvale, 1809, March 1810, Mary Ann Archbald to Margaret Wodrow, Riverbank, November 12, 1812, Mary Ann Archbald to Mr. McFarlane, Riverbank, January 1817. American or "Yankee" materialism, greed, cunning, etc.: Mary Ann Archbald to Mr. Summervil, Creekvale, 1808, Mary Ann Archbald to Margaret Wodrow, Riverbank, March 13, 1815, November 30, 1816, December 31, 1818, January 13, August 10, 1822, October 10, 1828; Mary Ann Archbald to Mr. McFarlane, Riverbank, January 1817. Destruction of the landscape: Mary Ann Archbald to Mr. Summervil, Creekvale, 1808, Mary Ann Archbald to Margaret Wodrow, Riverbank, November 30, 1816. Absence of genius: Mary Ann Archbald to Alexander Ruthven, Riverbank, November 1817. The American ministry: Mary Ann Archbald to Margaret Wodrow, Riverbank, April 28, 1820. Women's position in society: see n. 8, *supra*. Political ideology and culture: Mary Ann Archbald to Margaret Wodrow, Riverbank, March 13, 1815, April 28, 1820, Auriesville, NY, November 15, 1834, Mary Ann Archbald to Mr. McFarlane, Riverbank, January, 1817, Mary Ann Archbald to James Archbald IV, Riverbank, August 6, 1828. Children's hard work and lack of cultural development: Mary Ann Archbald to Margaret Wodrow, Riverbank, March 13, 1815, April 28, 1820, January 1, 1826, Mary Ann Archbald to John Ruthven, Riverbank, August, 1817. American youth and her children's spouses: Mary Ann Archbald to Margaret Wodrow, Creekvale, October 10, 1807, Riverbank, November 30, 1816, December 31, 1818, January 1, 1826, May 7, 1830, December 31, 1832, SmC.

69. Mary Ann Archbald to Margaret Wodrow, Auriesville, NY, December 31, 1832, SmC.

70. Mary Ann Archbald to Margaret Wodrow, Riverbank, September 1814, March 13, 1815, Auriesville, NY, November 15, 1834, SmC.

71. Mary Ann Archbald to Margaret Wodrow, Riverbank, April 20, 1832, SmC.

72. Mary Ann Archbald to Margaret Wodrow, Creekvale, October 1811, SmC.

73. Mary Ann Archbald to Margaret Ruthven, Riverbank, 1817, SmC.

74. Mary Ann Archbald to Margaret Wodrow, Riverbank, November 30, 1816, SmC.

75. Mary Ann Archbald to Margaret Wodrow, Riverbank, January 1, 1821, SmC.

76. Mary Ann Archbald to Margaret Wodrow, Riverbank, September 29, 1821, SmC.

77. Mary Ann Archbald to Margaret Wodrow, Riverbank, January 1, 1821, SmC.

78. Mary Ann Archbald to Margaret Wodrow, Riverbank, January 13, 1822, SmC.

79. Mary Ann Archbald to Margaret Wodrow, Riverbank, April 28, 1820, SmC.

80. Mary Ann Archbald to Margaret Wodrow, Riverbank, September 29, 1821, SmC.

81. Mary Ann Archbald to Margaret Wodrow, Riverbank, August 10, 1822, SmC. Hugh Archbald noted the condition of this letter in his transcription, saying it had been cut with a knife in order to remove "a reference to a scandal which had happened in Scotland."

82. Mary Ann Archbald to Margaret Wodrow, Riverbank, August 10, 1822, SmC.

83. Mary Ann Archbald to Margaret Wodrow, Riverbank, August 10, 1822, SmC.

84. Mary Ann Archbald to Margaret Wodrow, Riverbank, October 10, 1828, Auries-

ville, NY, November 16, 1833, April 19, November 13, 1836, February 1, 1840, SmC. These letters also contain longings for "home" and for Scotland, which, without naming the "little isle" as such, strongly imply it as the place to which she refers.

NOTES TO CHAPTER 10

1. The only biographical information on Dr. Steel (1809–1896) is found in n.a., *The History of Waukesha County, Wisconsin* (Chicago: Western Historical Company, 1880), 930–1; Women's Auxiliary of the Waukesha County Medical Society, "Steel, Thomas, M.D." (Waukesha, n.p., n.d.), 119–21; WHS, Wis Mss 51PB, Thomas Steel (1809–1896) Papers, 1660–1909, 1–5. I would like to acknowledge the assistance of Michelle Mahealani Morgan, who helped me to double-check my research notes to avoid errors in the citation of individual letters in this vast collection.

2. Arthur Bestor, *Backwoods Utopias: The Sectarian Origins and the Owenite Phase of Communitarian Socialism in America, 1663–1829* (Philadelphia: University of Pennsylvania Press, 1970, second edition), 282; Milo M. Quaife, *Wisconsin: Its History and Its People, 1634–1924* (Chicago: S. J. Clarke, 1924), vol. 2, 228–9; Thomas Steel to James Steel, Milwaukee County, WI, October 23, November 13, December 2, 13, 1843, WHS. Although he changed residences only once in his years in Wisconsin that we are interested in in this essay, and then only moved a few miles, in his letters Dr. Steel frequently changed the name of the place from which he wrote, depending in part on the location of the post office he was using at the time and depending on the shifting names of the localities in which he resided. Sometimes he listed no place of residence at all in his letters. I have simplified this situation by dividing his residence between Milwaukee County, before Steel's letter of July 12, 1846, and Waukesha County, after his July 12, 1846 letter. It was around that time that Waukesha County was formed out of what had been one, much larger Milwaukee County. The constant in Dr. Steel's locating the place from which he wrote, when he did so, was to write the name of the county.

3. Thomas Steel to James Steel, Milwaukee County, WI, October 6, December 2, 1843, January 12, April 13, June 15, July 20, September 15, December 12, 1844, January 5, February 13, March 28, June 13, 1845; Thomas Steel to Lilly Steel, February 10, July 2, September 15, November 5, 1844, January 5, 1845, WHS.

4. Thomas Steel to James Steel, Milwaukee County, WI, September 13, December 2, 1843, July 20, August 11, October 4, December 12, 1844, February 13, June 13, 1845, Waukesha County, WI, April 1, September 16, 1847; Thomas Steel to Lilly Steel, Milwaukee County, WI, December 13, 1843, May 10, 1844, January 5, 1845, Waukesha County, WI, August 3, 20, 1846, September 16, 1847, May 16, 1851; Charlotte Erickson, *Invisible Immigrants: The Adaptation of English and Scottish Immigrants in Nineteenth-Century America* (Coral Gables: University of Miami Press, 1972), 19, 44.

5. Thomas Steel to Lilly Steel, Milwaukee County, WI, July 2, September 15, 1844, Waukesha County, WI, May 19, 1849, March 18, 1852; Thomas Steel to James Steel, Milwaukee County, WI, July 31, September 4, 1845, Waukesha County, WI, July 12, August 20, September 15, 1846, May 13, September 24, October 17, 1848, December 20, 1850, February 22, October 23, 1851, WHS.

6. Thomas Steel to Lilly Steel, Milwaukee County, WI, July 2, 1844, Waukesha County, WI, March 9, 1849; Thomas Steel to James Steel, Milwaukee County, WI, July 20, 1844, Waukesha County, WI, October 8, 1847, February 9, 1848, March 22, June 3, 1849, February 7, 1853, WHS.

7. Erickson, *Invisible Immigrants*, 66, 71–2; Thomas Steel to James Steel, Milwaukee

County, WI, March 28, 1845, January 8, May 29, June 28, 1846, Waukesha County, WI, August 12, 1846, October 18, 1847, February 9, 24, 1848, January 21, June 3, 1849, April 25, 1850, April 2, 1851, April 16, 1852; James Steel to Lilly Steel, Milwaukee County, WI, June 16, 1846; Catherine Steel to Lilly Steel, Waukesha County, WI, July 3, 1851, WHS.

8. Thomas Steel to James Steel, Milwaukee County, WI, April 27, May 15, 1846, Waukesha County, WI, December 15, 1846, April 1, May 29, 1847, November 24, 1848, February 12, April 9, 1849; Thomas Steel to Dear Sir, Waukesha County, WI, November 21, 1848; Thomas Steel to Lilly Steel, Waukesha County, WI, March 29, 1852, WHS.

9. Thomas Steel to James Steel, Milwaukee County, WI, September 29, October 15, 1845, February 12, May 29, 1846, Waukesha County, WI, November 4, 15, 1846, December 16, 1847, WHS.

10. Thomas Steel to James Steel, Milwaukee County, WI, September 4, October 30, November 15, 1845, Waukesha County, WI, May 13, November 2, 1848, January 22, February 10, 24, 1851, WHS.

11. Thomas Steel to James Steel, Milwaukee County, WI, September 4, October 30, November 15, 1845, Waukesha County, WI, May 13, November 2, 1848, January 22, February 10, 24, 1851, WHS.

12. Thomas Steel to James Steel, Waukesha County, WI, April 25, 1850, WHS.

13. Thomas Steel to Lilly Steel, Waukesha County, WI, March 30, May 11, August 1, 27, 1848, WHS.

14. Thomas Steel to James Steel, Waukesha County, WI, December 20, 1850, January 22, 1851, WHS.

15. Thomas Steel to Lilly Steel, Waukesha County, WI, July 25, 1849, WHS; David Robinson, *The Unitarians and the Universalists* (Westport: Greenwood Press, 1985). Dr. Steel also had recently shown an interest in affiliating with a Unitarian congregation, but at other times would identify his religious affiliation as Spiritualism.

16. Thomas Steel to James Steel, Milwaukee County, WI, May 29, 1848, Waukesha County, WI, January 16, 1848, WHS.

17. Thomas Steel to James Steel, Waukesha County, WI, June 13, 1851, October 21, 1852, WHS.

18. Thomas Steel to Lilly Steel, Waukesha County, WI, September 30, 1852, WHS.

19. Leigh Eric Schmidt, *Hearing Things: Religion, Illusion, and the American Enlightenment* (Cambridge: Harvard University Press, 2000), 199–245; Marguerite Beck Block, *The New Church in the New World: A Study of Swedenborgianism in America* (New York: Henry Holt, 1932); Earl Wesley Fornell, *The Unhappy Medium: Spiritualism and the Life of Margaret Fox* (Austin: University of Texas, 1964).

20. Thomas Steel to James Steel, Waukesha County, WI, February 24, 1851, WHS.

21. Thomas Steel to Lilly Steel, Waukesha County, WI, January 10, 1853, WHS, Wis Mss, 51PB, Thomas Steel (1809–1865) Papers, 1660–1909, 2.

22. Thomas Steel to Lilly Steel, Waukesha County, WI, March 30, 1848, February 10, 1851, WHS.

23. Schmidt, *Hearing Things,* 229, 237; Thomas Steel to Lilly Steel, Waukesha County, WI, October 22, 1852, WHS.

24. Thomas Steel to Lilly Steel, Waukesha County, WI, March 30, 1848, February 10, May 16, 1852, October 22, December 21 (quote), 1852, January 10, March 14, May 8, 20, July 12, 1853, June 28, 1854, WHS.

25. See Lilly's addenda at the close of letters to Thomas that were largely written by James; James Steel and Thomas Steel, London, England, May 1, August 3, 1845, February 25, 1846; Lilly Steel to Thomas Steel, London, England, October 2, 1845, WHS.

26. Thomas Steel to James Steel, Milwaukee County, WI, October 15, 1845, February 12, 1846, Waukesha County, WI, January 16, 1848; Thomas Steel to Lilly Steel, Milwaukee County, WI, November 1, 1845, WHS.

27. Thomas Steel to James Steel, Milwaukee County, WI, October 4, 1844; James Steel to Thomas Steel, London, England, February 2, 25, May 1, June 1, August 17, November 30, 1845, February 25, 1846; Lilly Steel to Thomas Steel, London, England, October 2, 1845, WHS.

28. Thomas Steel to James Steel, Waukesha County, WI, December 21, 1852, April 4, June 16, August 9, 1853, March 17, 1854, WHS.

29. WHS, Wis Mss 51PB, Thomas Steel (1809–1896) Papers, 1660–1909, 2, 3.

30. E.g., Thomas Steel to Lilly Steel, Milwaukee County, WI, November 5, 1844, March 13, 1845, Waukesha County, WI, October 17, 1848, January 3, 1849; Thomas Steel to James Steel, Waukesha County, WI, February 9, April 5, July 18, November 2, 1848, WHS.

31. Thomas Steel to James Steel, Milwaukee County, WI, October 4, 1844, WHS.

32. Thomas Steel to James Steel, New Orleans, LA, July 22, 29, 1834, WHS.

33. Thomas Steel to James Steel, Louisville, KY, July 7, 1834, HSW.

34. Thomas Steel to James Steel, New Orleans, LA, July 29, 1834, WHS.

35. Thomas Steel to James Steel, New Orleans, LA, July 22, 1834, WHS.

36. Thomas Steel to James Steel, Louisville, KY, July 7, 1834, WHS.

37. Thomas Steel to James Steel, Danville, Upper Canada, June 16, 1834, WHS.

38. Thomas Steel to James Steel, New Orleans, LA, July 26, 1834, WHS.

39. Thomas Steel to James Steel, New Orleans, LA, July 22, 1834, WHS.

40. Thomas Steel to James Steel, New Orleans, LA, July 29, 1834, WHS.

41. Thomas Steel to James Steel, New Orleans, LA, July 22, 26, 29, 1834, WHS.

42. N.a., "Thomas Steel," *The History of Waukesha County Wisconsin*, 930.

43. WHS, Wis Mss 51PB, Thomas Steel (1809–1896) Papers, 1660–1909, 3, 5.

44. William Julius Mickles Letters, 1830–1832, NAC.

45. Thomas Steel to Lilly Steel, Milwaukee County, WI, July 2, September 15, October 20, November 5, 1844, January 5, 1845; Thomas Steel to Lilly Steel, Milwaukee County, WI, July 20, October 4, December 12, 1844, WHS.

46. Thomas Steel to Lilly Steel, Milwaukee County, WI, July 2, 1844, February 5, 25, May 1, 1845, WHS.

47. Thomas Steel to Lilly Steel, Milwaukee County, WI, July 2, 1844, WHS.

48. Thomas Steel to Lilly Steel, Milwaukee County, WI, July 2, 1844, WHS.

49. Cf., Thomas Steel to Lilly Steel, Milwaukee County, WI, November 5, 1844, and Thomas Steel to James Steel, Milwaukee County, WI, December 12, 1844, WHS.

50. James Steel to Thomas Steel, London, England, February 5, 25, 1854, WHS.

51. Erickson, *Invisible Immigrants*, 17; Thomas Steel to Lilly Steel, Milwaukee County, WI, March 13, 1845; Lilly Steel to Thomas Steel, London, England, May 14, 1845, James Steel to Thomas Steel, London, England, August 31, 1845, WHS.

52. Thomas Steel to James Steel, Milwaukee County, WI, June 28, 1846, Waukesha County, WI, February 10, 1847, July 10, 1849, July 27, 1852; Thomas Steel to Lilly Steel, Waukesha County, WI, January 3, March 30, 1848; Lilly Steel to Thomas Steel, London, England, October 1, 1846, WHS.

53. Thomas Steel to James Steel, Waukesha County, WI, July 15, 1847, WHS, may stand out as an example of Steel's "sloppy" productions: it had a few interlinear corrections, crossed-out words, and misspellings, and it was unable to maintain any theme for more than several sentences over the course of three pages. Steel complained about the conditions under which he was writing; it was 94 degrees in the shade when he sat down to write.

54. Thomas Steel to James Steel, Milwaukee County, WI, September 13, October 6, 23, 1843, Waukesha County, WI, June 16, July 15, 1847; Thomas Steel to Lilly Steel, Milwaukee County, WI, February 10, May 11, 1844, WHS.

55. Thomas Steel to James Steel, Milwaukee County, WI, January 12, 1844 (map of Milwaukee County, within which is a diagram of his township, indicating the ranges of the township and the location of his property within one range, with topographic features noted), June 14, 1845 (map of his property and of the neighborhood surrounding it), Waukesha County, WI, November 26, 1846 (map of property and neighborhood), June 16, 1847 (drawing of Catherine and baby), August 1, 28, 1847 (diagrams of his house), WHS.

56. Thomas Steel to James Steel, Milwaukee County, WI, September 13, 1843, November 12, 1844, June 13, August 31, 1845, Waukesha County, WI, November 24, 1848, March 22, 1849, December 3, 1852; Thomas Steel to Lilly Steel, Waukesha County, WI, December 3, 1852, WHS.

57. Thomas Steel to James Steel, Milwaukee County, WI, October 23, 1843, November 12, 1849, Waukesha County, WI, April 27, 1846, February 9, 1848; Thomas Steel to Lilly Steel, Milwaukee County, WI, May 10, 1844, Waukesha County, WI, June 30, 1848, WHS.

58. Wisconsin friends, traveling to England, were at least twice asked to bring back private goods and medical equipment, which James had bought for Thomas; Thomas Steel to James Steel, Waukesha County, WI, July 12, 1846, March 22, 1849, WHS.

59. Between 1844 and 1851, there is reference in thirty-three letters in the archived correspondence to approximately £145 sent through the post in ordinary letters. This figure probably underestimates the total cash subsidy James Steel sent his son, however, because we cannot account for missing letters or money not acknowledged. In contrast, the £100 James Steel sent in payment for land purchased for him and Lilly was provided through a letter of credit payable on a banking house; Thomas Steel to James Steel, Waukesha County, WI, November 26, 1846, WHS.

60. Thomas Steel to James Steel, Waukesha County, WI, August 12, 1846, WHS.

61. According to the archived correspondence, only once was it feared that money had been lost in the mail, but the letter, in which had been placed a £20 note, was soon found; Thomas Steel to Lilly Steel, Milwaukee County, WI, March 13, 1845; Thomas Steel to James Steel, Milwaukee County, WI, March 28, 1845, WHS.

62. Thomas Steel to James Steel, Waukesha County, WI, February 7, 1853, WHS.

63. Thomas Steel to Lilly Steel, Milwaukee County, WI, November 1, 1845, WHS.

64. James Steel to Thomas Steel, London, England, November 30, 1845, WHS.

65. Lilly Steel to Thomas Steel, London, England, October 2, 1845, WHS.

66. Thomas Steel to James Steel, Milwaukee County, WI, July 20, 1844, September 29, 1845, Waukesha County, WI, June 25, 1850; Thomas Steel to Lilly Steel, Milwaukee County, WI, November 1, 1845, May 15, 1846 (quote), WHS.

67. James Steel to Thomas Steel, London, England, June 28, October 30, 1845; Thomas Steel to James Steel, Milwaukee County, WI, March 13, 1846, Waukesha County, WI, August 12, 1846, WHS; Erickson, *Invisible Immigrants*, 49–50.

68. Thomas Steel to Lilly Steel, Milwaukee County, WI, May 11, 1844, Waukesha County, WI, December 12, 1847; James Steel to Thomas Steel, London, England, August 3, October 30, December 28, 1845, February 12, 1846; Thomas Steel to James Steel, Waukesha County, WI, November 4, 1846, March 22, 1849; Catherine Steel to Lilly Steel, Waukesha County, WI, October 1, 1846, WHS.

69. Not long after he was married, Thomas began to write explicitly, in letters to his father, that rather than address a section to Lilly, he would depend on Catherine to write

to his sister; Thomas Steel to James Steel, Milwaukee County, WI, March 13, 1846, Waukesha County, WI, December 16, 1846, March 6, 1848, WHS.

70. Thomas Steel to James Steel, Milwaukee County, WI, October 4, 1844, WHS.

71. Thomas Steel to Lilly Steel, Milwaukee County, WI, November 1, 1845, WHS.

72. Thomas Steel to James Steel, Milwaukee County, WI, June 2, 1844; Lilly Steel to Thomas Steel, London, England, October 2, 1845, WHS. At one time, James Steel himself had considered going to America with the utopians, but had lost faith in the communal scheme and the individuals involved in it.

73. Lilly Steel to Thomas Steel, London, England, October 2, 1845, WHS.

74. Thomas Steel to Lilly Steel, Milwaukee County, WI, September 1, 1843, May 10, 1844, WHS.

75. James Steel to Thomas Steel, London, England, February 2, August 3, November 17, 1845, WHS.

76. Lilly Steel to Thomas Steel, London, England, October 2, 1845, WHS.

77. Lilly Steel to Thomas Steel, London, England, February 2, October 2, 1845, WHS.

78. Thomas Steel to James Steel, Milwaukee County, WI, May 10, 1844, WHS.

79. Thomas Steel to James Steel, Milwaukee County, WI, February 13, 1845, WHS.

80. Thomas Steel to James Steel, Milwaukee County, WI, September 15, 1846, February 10, 1847, WHS.

81. Thomas Steel to Lilly Steel, Milwaukee County, WI, June 16, Waukesha County, WI, August 20, 1846, WHS.

82. Thomas Steel to Lilly Steel, Waukesha County, WI, May 11,1848; Thomas Steel to James Steel, Waukesha County, WI, August 1, 1848, WHS.

83. Thomas Steel to Lilly Steel, Waukesha County, WI, May 11, 1848, WHS.

84. Thomas Steel to Lilly Steel, Waukesha County, WI, May 11, 1848, WHS.

85. Thomas Steel to Lilly Steel, Waukesha County, WI, May 11, June 30, 1848, April 11, June 20, 1849, WHS.

86. Thomas Steel to James Steel, Waukesha County, WI, June 20, 1849, WHS.

87. Thomas Steel to Lilly Steel, Waukesha County, WI, October 17, 1848, WHS.

88. Thomas Steel to James Steel, Waukesha County, WI, January 21, 1849, WHS.

89. Thomas Steel to James Steel, Waukesha County, WI, April 11, 1849, WHS.

90. Thomas Steel to James Steel, Waukesha County, WI, April 29, June 20, 1849, April 25, 1850; Thomas Steel to Lilly Steel, May 19, July 12, 1849, WHS.

91. Thomas Steel to James Steel, Waukesha County, WI, June 20, 1849, WHS.

92. Thomas Steel to James Steel, Waukesha County, WI, July 12, 1849, WHS.

93. Thomas Steel to James Steel, Waukesha County, WI, April 29, 1849, WHS.

94. Thomas Steel to James Steel, Waukesha County, WI, April 25, 1850, WHS.

95. Thomas Steel to James Steel, Waukesha County, WI, February 12, April 11, 29, 1849, WHS.

96. Thomas Steel to James Steel, Waukesha County, WI, October 23, 1851, WHS.

97. Thomas Steel to James Steel, Waukesha County, WI, October 23, 1851; Thomas Steel to Lilly Steel, Waukesha County, WI, December 2, 1851, WHS.

98. Thomas Steel to James Steel, Waukesha County, WI, April 16, 27, May 14, 1852, WHS.

99. Thomas Steel to Lilly Steel, Waukesha County, WI, May 14, 1852, WHS.

100. Thomas Steel to James Steel, Waukesha County, WI, May 29, 1852, WHS.

101. Thomas Steel to James Steel, Waukesha County, WI, March 18, 1854, WHS.

102. Thomas Steel to James Steel, Waukesha County, WI, February 13, 1845, WHS.

103. John Gillis, *A World of Their Own Making: Myth, Ritual, and the Question of Family Values* (Cambridge: Harvard University Press, 1996), 71–80, 109–29, 133–51,

and *passim*; Christopher Lasch, *Haven in a Heartless World: The Family Besieged* (New York: Basic Books, 1977); Mary Ryan, *Cradle of the Middle Class: The Family in Oneida County, New York, 1790–1865* (New York: Cambridge University Press, 1981); Stuart Blumin, *The Emergence of the Middle Class: Social Experience in the American City, 1760–1900* (New York: Cambridge University Press, 1989).

104. Thomas Steel to James Steel, New Orleans, LA, July 26, 1834; Thomas Steel to Lilly Steel, Waukesha County, WI, May 8, 1853, WHS.

105. If I have succeeded in interesting readers in Thomas Steel's life, there is probably a desire to know how Thomas dealt with this death, which seems linked irrevocably to his sincere desire to assist James and Lilly, and which was foretold in his father's fear of the possibility that sickness might accompany his emigration and resettlement. Since Thomas's correspondence ends with the emigration of Lilly and James, there are no personal documents reflecting his understanding of the circumstances. Here, at the end as at the beginning of this study, we have yet another example of the imaginative challenges, as well as the frustrations, of reading letters!

106. WHS, Wis Mss 51PB, Thomas Steel (1809–1896) Papers, 1660–1909, 2.

Collections of Letters Consulted

Mary Ann Archbald Letters and Diaries, Reel 965, History of Women Collection, Smith College, Northampton, Massachusetts.

Barker Family Letters, SC 2385, Indiana Historical Society, Indianapolis, Indiana.

Birkbeck Family Letters, in Gladys Scott Thompson, ed., *A Pioneer Family: The Birkbecks in Illinois, 1818–1827* (London: Jonathan Cape, 1953).

John Birket et al., Letter-Series, in Charlotte Erickson, *Invisible Immigrants: The Adaptation of English and Scottish Immigrants in Nineteenth-Century America* (Coral Gables: University of Miami Press, 1972).

John Bishop et al., Letter-Series, in Erickson, *Invisible Immigrants* (1972).

Robert Bowles, Extracts of Letters from America, 1823, Book The Third, Written by Robert Bowles to His Brothers John and Richard, volume 538, Ohio Historical Society, Columbus, Ohio.

Matthew Brooks Letters, T2700, Public Record Office of Northern Ireland, Belfast.

Samuel Buchanan Papers, PC247 & PC491, National Library of Ireland, Dublin.

Rebecca Butterworth Letter, in Erickson, *Invisible Immigrants* (1972).

William Corlett Letter-Series, in Erickson, *Invisible Immigrants* (1972).

Gamble Crawford Letters, T.2338, Public Record Office of Northern Ireland, Belfast.

Titus Crawshaw Letter-Series, in Erickson, *Invisible Immigrants* (1972).

Mary Cumming Papers, T/1475/2, Public Record Office of Northern Ireland, Belfast.

Darnley Family Letters, 1843–1884, New York Public Library, New York, New York.

Matthew Dinsdale Papers, Wisconsin Manuscripts DL, Wisconsin Historical Society, Madison, Wisconsin.

Mary Doherty Letters, T.2606/1–9, Public Record Office of Northern Ireland, Belfast.

John Fisher Letter-Series, in Erickson, *Invisible Immigrants* (1972).

George Flower Letters, Illinois State Historical Society, Springfield, Illinois.

Grayston-Bond Letters, Collection 861, Collection of Regional History, Kroch Library, Cornell University, Ithaca, New York.

Andrew Greenlees Letter-Series, in Ronald Wells, ed., *Ulster Migration to America: Letters from Three Irish Families* (New York: Peter Lang, 1991).

John Griffiths et al., Letter-Series, in Erickson, *Invisible Immigrants* (1972).

Richard Hails Letters, Collection 865, Collection of Regional History, Kroch Library, Cornell University, Ithaca, New York.

Nathan Haley Letter-Series, in Erickson, *Invisible Immigrants* (1972).

Harker Family Letters, VFM 2323, Ohio Historical Society, Columbus, Ohio.

Joseph Hartley et al., Letter-Series, in Michael Drake, ed., "'We Are All Yankeys Now': Joseph Hartley's Transplanting from Brighthouse Wood, Yorkshire, Old England to Lockport, New York, Told by Himself and His Wife in Letters Home," *New York History* 45 (July 1964): 222–64.

Hemsley Family Letters, MG 24 I 19, National Archives of Canada, Ottawa.

John Hesketh et al., Letter-Series, in Erickson, *Invisible Immigrants* (1972).

Joseph Hollingsworth et al., Letter-Series, in Thomas Leavitt, ed., *The Hollingsworth Letters: Technical Change in the Textile Industry, 1826–1837* (Cambridge: MIT Press, 1969).

James Horner Papers, T. 1592, Public Record Office of Northern Ireland, Belfast.

John Kerr et al., Letter-Series, in Wells, ed., *Ulster Migration to America* (1991).

Edwin O. Kimberley Papers, Wisconsin Historical Society, Madison, Wisconsin.

David Laing Papers, Collection 812, Collection of Regional History, Kroch Library, Cornell University, Ithaca, New York.

John Langton Fonds, MG 24, I 59, National Archives of Canada, Ottawa.

Ernest Lister Letter-Series, in Erickson, *Invisible Immigrants* (1972).

Locke Family Papers, PC 174, National Library of Ireland, Dublin.

George Martin Papers, Sevenoaks Library, Kent, England.

John McBride Letters, 1819–1848, T 2613, Public Record Office of Northern Ireland, Belfast.

Robert and William McElderry Letters, T 2414, MIC 57, Public Record Office of Northern Ireland, Belfast.

McConnell-Johnson Letters, Toronto Metropolitan Research Library, Toronto.

A. R. and T. McCoy Letters, D/1444, Public Record Office of Northern Ireland, Belfast.

McGarrett Family Papers, Cape Cod Community College, West Barnstable, Massachusetts.

McGraw Family Papers, Collection 2355, Collection of Regional History, Kroch Library, Cornell University, Ithaca, New York.

John and Catherine McLees Letters, D904/2a,2b,3a,3b,3c,4, Public Record Office of Northern Ireland, Belfast.

McNish Family Papers, Collection 2086, Collection of Regional History, Kroch Library, Cornell University, Ithaca, New York.

William Julius Mickle Letters, MG24 I 53, National Archives of Canada, Ottawa.

William Morris et al., Letter-Series, in Erickson, *Invisible Immigrants* (1972).

Thomas Spencer Niblock Fonds, MG24 I 80, National Archives of Canada, Ottawa.

Thomas Spencer Niblock Letters, MS 396, Manuscripts Division, National Library of Australia, Canberra.

Parsonage Family Letters, National Archives of Canada, Ottawa.

William Peters and Family Fonds, 1830–1831, M-5567, National Archives of Canada, Ottawa.

Thomas Petingale et al., Letter-Series, in Erickson, *Invisible Immigrants* (1972).

Edward Phillips et al., Letter-Series, in Erickson, *Invisible Immigrants* (1972).

Charles Porter and Family Letters, D 1152/2, Public Record Office of Northern Ireland, Belfast.

Thomas Pryterch Letters, Collection 2598M, Collection of Regional History, Kroch Library, Cornell University, Ithaca, New York.

Radcliffe Quine Letter-Series, in Erickson, *Invisible Immigrants* (1972).

H. Reid et al., Letter-Series, in Erickson, *Invisible Immigrants* (1972).

James Roberts et al., Letter-Series, in Erickson, *Invisible Immigrants* (1972).

John Ronaldson Letter-Series, in Erickson, *Invisible Immigrants* (1972).

Rose Family Letters, VFM 1903, Ohio Historical Society, Columbus, Ohio.

A. Russell Letters, Illinois State Historical Society, Springfield, Illinois.

George Simons et al., English Immigrant Letter, 1841, Collection 684M, Collection of Regional History, Kroch Library, Cornell University, Ithaca, New York.

Robert and William Smyth Letters, D/1828, Public Record Office of Northern Ireland, Belfast.

George Standings Letter, in Charlotte Erickson, ed., "An Emigrant's Letters from Iowa, 1871," *Bulletin of the British Association of American Studies,* New Series, n. 12 (1966): 5–41.

Thomas Steel (1808–1896) Papers, 1660–1909, Wisconsin Manuscripts 51PB, Wisconsin Historical Society, Madison, Wisconsin.

John B. Thomas Letters, Pattee Library, Pennsylvania State University, State College, Pennsylvania.

Robert Wade Letters and Family Papers, MG 24 I 127, National Archives of Canada, Ottawa.

White Family Letters, VFM 2323, Ohio Historical Society, Columbus, Ohio.

Ann Whittaker Letter-Series, in Erickson, *Invisible Immigrants* (1972).

David Whyte Letters, Wisconsin Manuscripts AW, Wisconsin Historical Society, Madison, Wisconsin.

Joseph Willcocks Letters, S 128, Toronto Metropolitan Research Library, Toronto.

Thomas Wozencraft Letter-Series, in Erickson, *Invisible Immigrants* (1972).

Wright Family Letters, 1801–1842, #42–70, Religious Society of Friends in Ireland, Dublin.

Index

About the Author

David A. Gerber is Professor of History at the University at Buffalo, State University of New York. He is the author and editor of, among other works, *Black Ohio and the Color Line*, *Disabled Veterans in History*, *Anti-Semitism in American History*, and *The Making of American Pluralism: Buffalo, New York, 1825–60*. His research has concentrated on the problems of personal and social identities among a wide variety of Americans, including immigrants, elites, disabled veterans of war, Catholics, and Jews.

Carolyn Heilbrun *85 —w
she cited in her note?